I0235156

BEYOND A COMMON JOY

Beyond a Common Joy

An Introduction to Shakespearean Comedy

PAUL A. OLSON

University of Nebraska Press | Lincoln and London

COVER NOTE: Correggio's *Rape of Ganymede*. In the late medieval and Early Modern period, in paintings and emblem books, Ganymede flying was used as an image of the movement of erotic and homoerotic love or of mystical love that reaches "beyond a common joy" toward the mind of God. This book argues that Rosalind/Ganymede embodies the same movements.

© 2008 by the Board of Regents of the University of Nebraska. All rights reserved. Manufactured in the United States of America. ⊖

Library of Congress Cataloging-in-Publication Data
Olson, Paul A.
Beyond a common joy: an introduction to Shakespearean comedy / Paul A. Olson.
p. cm.
Includes bibliographical references and index.
ISBN 978-0-8032-1574-0 (cloth: alk. paper)
1. Shakespeare, William, 1564–1616 —Comedies. 2. Shakespeare, William, 1564–1616—Humor. 3. Comedy. I. Title.
PR2981.O67 2008
822.3'3—dc22   2008023199

Set in Adobe Caslon Pro.
Designed by A. Shahan.

For Frances
My wife, my love, my life

Contents

Illustrations

Maps

Preface

In his comedies, Shakespeare moves comic form into "grander realms." He moves it from the TV sitcom level, where most of the comedy of his day operated, to a level where it rivaled tragedy and epic. To see this, one has to learn how to read Shakespeare with an eye for the kind of meanings and generic weights available in his time.

This book arises from my uneasiness with the many performances and readings of Shakespeare's comedies that are merely frivolous. I recall the first performance I ever saw as a teenager—a high school production of *As You Like It*, where I really could not understand the lines or the settings at all but where I could see that the lovers were silly and laughable. That was about all there was. For the most part the diet of performances I saw throughout college and during a year in London in the early 1950s fed that perception, as did my readings in that time of the romantic critics, especially Hazlitt and Coleridge. These critics offer much talk of the comedies as dreams in which the conscious powers are suspended and the nonrational takes over and writes the play. There was relatively superficial talk of magic and the empathic annihilation of the self in the displaying of characters. In more recent criticism I found talk of magic and Shakespeare's invention of love and of carnival and festival.

Lately, as producers have created a weightier comedic Shakespeare, they have fed the notion that Shakespeare was a contemporary feminist or Marxist. The message attributed to Shakespeare's comedies is serious, but it is not a message easily available in the universe of discourse of Shakespeare's time.

Of course, the playwright's content need not be easily available, but what he is saying does need to be possible to his time and audience. The discovery of what the comedies are saying may be a difficult art, but in encountering the difficulty and the puzzles, we need to be able to document how Shakespeare's language could plausibly have been interpreted by the audiences of his day.

To understand the comedies in their own universe of discourse, we ought, I believe, to take seriously the plays' frequent claims for poetry and comedy as serious philosophic and religious arts, emblematic or symbolic art, art holding the mirror to vice and virtue or showing the form of the era. This claim is made not only in the context of Shakespeare's tragedies but in the comedies and in non-comic plays when they speak of comedies. As I worked on my early essay on *A Midsummer Night's Dream* (now much vilified), as I taught my own Shakespeare courses for twenty-five years, and as I looked at the links between Shakespeare and that greatest of medieval English philosophic poets, Chaucer, I came to believe that Shakespeare deliberately designed his comedies to have a *gravitas* present in few other comedies before or during his time, save perhaps those of Ben Jonson. These appeared in the second half of his career, after Shakespeare had made the move to a higher comedy. Increasingly, I came to feel that he made his comedies to compete with epic and tragedy in weight and scope. After I finished my chapter on *The Tempest* in *The Kingdom of Science*, where I explored what Shakespeare does with the *Aeneid*, I decided to try to formulate what I believed to be the case about the comedies.

This book, then, comes out of a long period of teaching Shakespeare. It is addressed to the kinds of people who were principally my students during the last few decades, upper-level undergraduates and lower-level graduate students. It also welcomes advanced scholars to the dialogue, though it lacks some of the paraphernalia of conventional scholarship. The ends of several of the chapters include a discussion of some primary and secondary materials (also grouped in the resources section at the end of the book) that may be helpful in thinking historically about what Shakespeare is doing. Since this discussion is not exhaustive, it includes some thoughts about other places to look for Shakespeare's use of form, myth, the Bible, and the like. Of course, knowing afresh Shakespeare's plays, the Roman comedies of Terence and Plautus, the relevant scriptures and classical myths, and the map of Europe in Shakespeare's time is crucial.

The readings offered in this volume are not definitive. They are intended to set students on the path of inquiry. They are for students interested in a culture that is distant and yet our own. Further, no one should think that the resources described at the ends of the chapters provide a bead on modern interpretation. They do not. Modern criticism and scholarship appear only when they offer a plausible historical account or list sources and approaches that support the reconstruction of the historical semiology of a play. For modern criticism that does other useful things, one can go to the PMLA bibliography listing all modern essays and to the various anthologies of influential essays published to summarize recent work. My purpose is simply to provide examples of works that will help students to think independently and historically. Stephen Greenblatt's recent biography of Shakespeare, *Will in the World*, also offers many paths to pursue, not all of them ones that I would travel, and James Shapiro's account of Shakespeare in 1599, *A Year in the Life of William Shakespeare*, offers an exemplary look at how the 1599 plays mirror the "form and pressure" of the "age and body of the time."[1]

The foundation of this effort is the Early Modern sense that all things are arranged in hierarchies—kinds of governments, literary forms, forms of painting, people within the social estates that they occupy, the angels, the material universe—from the empyrean through the stars to the basest matter. The hierarchies might change. King might replace pope as head of the church, but the fact of hierarchical arrangement remained. Among governmental forms, empire was the highest in rank; among classes, kings and bishops; among literary forms, sacred scriptures and then tragedy and epic; among forms of painting, biblical and mythic painting, then heroical painting; and so forth. My argument is that Shakespeare, viewed historically (chapter 1), deliberately elevates comedy, one of the midlevel literary forms, into the higher reaches of epic and tragedy, reaching even near to the level of the sacred. He does so by changing the form of comedy (chapter 2) and by employing extended intertextual elements from classical myth and the biblical scriptures to give the comic action a numinous profundity (chapters 3 and 4). Directly or indirectly, he claims for comedy an inspired source. He uses at least some of his works to treat of the most serious philosophic themes as they bear on the fates of great empires (chapter 5). To demonstrate how this reconfiguration of the forms and tactics of comedy may come together in a single play, I offer in chapter 6 an extended analysis of *Measure for Measure.*

My means for coming to this analysis is a reconstruction of the historicized language games that are highlighted in Renaissance literary theory and echoed in Shakespeare. These games point to poetry as religious and philosophic art carrying critical overtones in a time when the critique was not so easy politically or culturally. The book attempts a reconstruction of the symbolism of Shakespeare's alteration of form, his altered and echoed biblical and classical narrative, and his horizon of imperial narrative, making use of much material from the tragedies, histories, and romances. I believe that the aesthetic assumptions of the plays written in these genres illuminate the comedies, especially in matters that do not have to do with generic conventions. It is my hope that this effort will encourage those who read these analyses to do their own analyses using the kinds of primary materials that this book uses and venturing to make their own multileveled interpretations, most of which will disagree with or modify mine.

As befits a historical reading of the plays, I accept the list of comedies in the First Folio. This assumes that Shakespeare's Folio editors understood their author's sense of genre, that Hemminges and Condell would not have invented a list based on some private classificatory scheme that the two of them made up independent of their company's and their author's sense. Their list is as follows: *The Tempest, The Two Gentlemen of Verona, The Merry Wives of Windsor, Measure for Measure, The Comedy of Errors, Much Ado about Nothing, Love's Labour's*

Lost, A Midsummer Night's Dream, The Merchant of Venice, As You Like It, The Taming of the Shrew, All's Well That Ends Well, Twelfth Night, and *The Winter's Tale.* This book could treat all of the comedies, but it would then risk excessive length and repetition. Instead I concentrate on plays putatively written from 1594 onward, when *Comedy of Errors* is now dated. I provide touchstone analyses of the major plays and incidental analyses of the others so that the reader can develop these using the resources listed at the end of each chapter. Because the book treats of plays written after Shakespeare had written in the full New Comedy mode in *Comedy of Errors*, it gives short shrift to *Two Gentlemen of Verona* and *Taming of the Shrew*, both now dated earlier than *Comedy of Errors* (though *Shrew* may still be up for grabs). *Love's Labour's Lost* is treated peripherally because it is so clearly a coterie play, though it does contain some useful observations about genre. Since the Folio editors treat *Troilus and Cressida* as a tragedy, it gets little analysis in these pages. Finally, I treat *All's Well That Ends Well* and *Winter's Tale* less than the other plays listed in the Folio, because the conclusions set forth in this book apply to them in rather obvious ways. All quotations and citations from Shakespeare, unless they are included in a quotation from another author's work or are otherwise noted, come from *The Norton Shakespeare*, ed. Stephen Greenblatt, Walter Cohen, Jean E. Howard, and Katharine Eisamen Maus (New York: Norton, 1997). The text is based on the Oxford text and is widely used in undergraduate and graduate teaching. In most cases I removed the stage directions supplied by later editors that are not found in the quarto texts published in Shakespeare's time or in the First Folio.

I am indebted to large numbers of people who have guided me as I have wrestled with this book across the years: to Robert Knoll, my near lifelong friend and first teacher in Elizabethan and Jacobean drama; to G. E. Bentley, my Princeton mentor in Shakespeare scholarship; to my patient Nebraska colleagues and friends Stephen Buhler and Robert Haller, who read sections of the book in draft; to Professor Robert Herbert, philosopher at the University of Oregon, who looked at chapter 1 from the perspective of his studies in Wittgenstein; to the Shakespeare Institute at Stratford and Professor Russell Jackson for much courtesy and help; to Clifford J. Ronan of Texas State University at San Marcos, who examined my treatment of *The Tempest* and made me go back to the drawing board in examining that play; to the readers for the University of Nebraska Press, David Brumble and Darryl Gless, who made extensive suggestions that I took very seriously in my last revision; to the Medieval/Renaissance group at the University of Nebraska, who heard the chapters in draft and gave me pointers from art history, history, and theology; to Karen Hardy, editor par excellence, who edited the book meticulously before I presented it to the University of Nebraska Press and also critiqued the consistency and coherence of my argument; to the graduate assistants at the University of Nebraska, who helped me gather research materials and check my documentation and who also read the book so carefully as to save me from foolish mistakes and stupid ideas—Sarah Croft, Joshua Dolezal, Steve Werkmeister, Stephanie Sitz, Nicole DeWall, Matt Pearson, Jennifer Overkamp, Jenni Moore, Liz Lorang, and Joe Rain; and to Margaret Goll, who read the book as an undergraduate and told me how to improve its usefulness for undergraduates. For help with manipulating the pictures for press use, I am deeply indebted to Kelly Grey Carlisle of the UNL English Department's *Prairie Schooner*. Finally, I wish to thank my wife, Frances Reinehr—to whom the book is dedicated—for reading it repeatedly, criticizing it extensively, and supporting me psychologically so that, in my old age and bodily decrepitude, I did not lose all hope of finishing this piece. The mistakes of the work are unfortunately mine.

BEYOND A COMMON JOY

I

On Historical Understandings of Shakespeare's Works

When Hamlet wishes to mock Polonius as a timeserving old fool, he asks Polonius to look up at the clouds and see things:

> HAMLET: Do you see yonder cloud that's almost in shape of a camel?
> POLONIUS: By th' mass, and 'tis like a camel, indeed.
> HAMLET: Methinks it is like a weasel.
> POLONIUS: It is backed like a weasel.
> HAMLET: Or like a whale. (*Hamlet* 3.2.345–50)

Hamlet's projections make Polonius see. Power creates perception. Hamlet knows that status, ideology, and culture create our reading and seeing. Or some part of them.

One can make many lines of Shakespeare's plays mean at least as many things as Polonius is told to notice. Yet we know that Polonius is looking so very intently at clouds—only clouds. And we, in reading or hearing him, are looking at, well, words—just words put in the mouths of actors to tell a story. As we read them we may project onto them things strange to an Elizabethan or Jacobean audience. We can interpret them in a direction that suits us or our masters through production, lighting, acting styles, gestures, and writing new or eliminating old text. And yet what we are looking at so intently are words that had many but also boundaried uses in Shakespeare's time, uses bearing family resemblances to each other.[1] Many of the words had meanings and ranges of meanings for their first audiences that they do not now have. In turn, they now have meanings and ranges of meanings that their first audiences could not have known.

But what if we could know the words as they were understood when they were first spoken, with some sense of the range of understandings given them then? What if we knew the words in their first contexts, their first uses in the job of work of Elizabethan and Jacobean language? The quest for the historical Shakespeare that counts for us is not a quest for a man but for an understanding of the words of a man. As critics and scholars of Shakespeare's plays, we seek ways in which people used language in Shakespeare's time. All we have are words and how they can be understood. This does not mean that the plays did not have many meanings in their own times, that the same word or sentence could not have had differing meanings in differing contexts—say, at the court or in the Globe among the various groups and classes. Meaning could be redirected by a gesture, an improvisation, a change of context. Hamlet is able to redirect the meaning of *The Mousetrap* that the itinerant players who come to Ellesmere already know. Through devising the dumb show and adding a few lines, Hamlet changes what the scene says. We have reason, from the two versions of *King Lear* and from other textual changes in various "good" early texts of the plays, to believe that Shakespeare—or the teams of theater people, editors, compositors, and the like who first saw his plays into print—reconstructed passages of his plays to suit varying political and cultural contexts.[2]

As if to confirm that players could change things with their acting emphases, Hamlet concerns himself with the possibility that his meaning—to hold the mirror up to Claudius—will be lost in the players' narcissism and incompetence:

HAMLET: Speak the speech, I pray you, as I pronounced it to you—trippingly on the tongue; but if you mouth it, as many

of your players do, I had as lief the town-crier spoke my lines.
... O, it offends me to the soul to hear a robustious, periwig-
pated fellow tear a passion to tatters, to very rags, to split the
ears of the groundlings, who for the most part are capable of
nothing but inexplicable dumb shows and noise. . . .

A PLAYER: I warrant your honour.

HAMLET: Be not too tame, neither; but let your own discretion
be your tutor. Suit the action to the word, the word to the
action, with this special observance: that you o'erstep not
the modesty of nature. For anything so overdone is from the
purpose of playing, whose end, both at the first and now, was
and is to hold as 'twere, the mirror up to nature, to show virtue her own feature, scorn her own image, and the very age
and body of the time his form and pressure. Now this overdone, or come tardy off, though it make the unskilful laugh,
cannot but make the judicious grieve; the censure of the
which one must in your allowance o'erweigh a whole theatre
of others. . . .

A PLAYER: I hope we have reformed that indifferently with
us, sir.

HAMLET: O, reform it altogether. And let those that play your
clowns speak no more than is set down for them; for there be
of them that will themselves laugh to set on some quantity of
barren spectators to laugh . . . . Go make you ready.
[Exeunt Players] (*Hamlet* 3.2.1–40)

Hamlet's sense of the purpose of the playing he requests is not one
that he ascribes to his intent as an author. Rather, Hamlet here speaks
of the general game of *playing* as a form of life practiced by all in the
theater: holding the mirror to nature, displaying virtue, showing the
age to itself in its very inscape, and focusing on the necessary question. It may not be accidental that he calls *The Mousetrap* a comedy
(3.2.269ff.). As we shall see in chapter 2, the theory of playing that he
sets forth derives basically from Renaissance comic theory. Of course,

one can dismiss Hamlet as the clown of the court, a creator wanting restrained and verisimilar acting so that no one will miss his satiric attack on Claudius. One may say that he does not speak for Shakespeare or for any general sense of what playing is about. However, it hardly seems likely that a Shakespearean audience would have thought the exchange about the child actors and the "little Eyases" in the same scene was simply a comment on esoteric playing in distant Denmark. Hamlet is only saying what English critics commonly said, at least about comedy.[3] There is a "nature" to be mirrored, a virtue to be shown, and an inscape of the age to be represented.

Culture, Human Nature, and Meaning

It is our business as modern readers and producers to decide whether we want a Shakespeare that *gives us his culture's vision and his vision within his culture's* or one that reflects our vision and our imprisonment in the assumptions of the present. When we read *Hamlet*, we may assume that Hamlet is talking about generic "human nature" when he says he wants the players to hold the mirror up to nature. We may similarly assume that Shakespeare mirrors some generic human nature. But what was his "nature"? And is it ours? Certainly it was not the same physical nature, with DNA and cells and genes and right-brain/left-brain concerns. It was not the same psychological nature, either, with circadian rhythms, manic-depressive syndromes, schizophrenia, and susceptibility to operant conditioning. And what was his "virtue," his "age and body of the time"? Yet when we write about Shakespeare or produce the plays, we may write or produce as if Hamlet, the character, were a local specimen with genes and chromosomes. In fact, he is only words—a text that we can make in the image of nature as we understand it *or* as his age understood it.

Let me try the example of Ernest Jones—not because he is part of contemporary critical controversy but because he is *not*. That is, his hermeneutic reflects the transitoriness of explanations of Shakespeare that purport to rest on some universal understanding of human nature, usually one discovered by twentieth- or twenty-first-century social and behavioral sciences. The Jones case reminds us of the ephemeral character of any ahistorical hermeneutic system. Jones tells us, concerning Hamlet, that "a little consideration of the genetic aspects of the matter will make it comprehensible that the trends most likely to be repressed are those belonging to what are called the sexual instincts."[4] Notice that Jones appeals to our genetic character as if he knows that his psychology somehow grows out of our genetic structures. Jones and other students of Freud believed that, of the instincts, the sexual is the most powerful. He tells us, with full assurance, that Hamlet had hated his father as a rival for his mother's sexual affection. However, Hamlet Jr. had repressed his hatred. Now, with his father dead, he hates Claudius for the same reason, and his despair over his mother's marriage to Claudius is mental unsoundness based on his uneasiness over being replaced in his mother's affection by someone else. He wishes to kill Claudius to enjoy the unrivaled sexual affection of his mother. Of course, Jones can ignore what Hamlet says about his admiration for his father because he *knows* universal human nature so well that he can tell us what is seething under Hamlet's words.

At the time, this set of assumptions influenced some of *Hamlet*'s producers. When I was a youth, I first saw *Hamlet*—Olivier's *Hamlet*—as a reflection of Freud's *Oedipus* and Ernest Jones's critique of Shakespeare.[5] There I saw the young hero, obviously erotically attached to his mother, giving her intense embraces in a scene of supposed adversarial confrontation. The actress was younger than Olivier in life but played his mother on the screen. This Hamlet wished to kill his stepfather not so much because of matters of state as of the movement of erotic desire. At first this seemed strange to me, but then I adjusted to the show because what did I know? I did not recognize that none of this was "in the lines" until put there by Freud and Jones. They had discovered "the truth" about human nature from the genes up, and they knew that Shakespeare had too.[6] The critics who saw Olivier's version of the play also knew that Freud was there because that was the way human nature was. Even those who did not know that Ernest Jones had been an advisor to the film (and that information does not matter) saw a profound exploration of "human nature." I knew it though I had read only a *Reader's Digest*–level account of Freud. We assumed, the critics at their sophisticated level and I at my naïve one, that both Freud and Shakespeare had discovered some permanent element of human nature and that both had exposed the same element. Hamlet was not troubled, as he might have been to an Elizabethan audience, because he had been denied the throne, because a possible criminal and tyrant ruled his country, because his father had been killed and his mother had not protected his right to ascend to the throne, or because he lacked the judicial tools to find out the crime, prove it, and punish it. He was troubled because he wanted his mother and hated his father and stepfather as bed rivals.

Now, we may not be so absolutely sure. With the diminution of Freud as our Decalogue on human nature and desire, we may not assume that what Shakespeare discovered through plot, metaphor, and myth was the same biopsychological reality that Freud discovered through psychoanalysis.[7] One suspects now that the psychoanalysis of the 1940s created a "seeing as" that permitted us to turn Shakespeare's Hamlet into a "truer" picture of the psychological underpinning of his actions, as elucidated by Freudian theory. Such "seeing as" is common in Shakespearean production. It has been argued that only such revisioning keeps Shakespeare alive and in production, just as Christian allegorizing kept the classics alive in the Middle Ages.

Ducks and Rabbits in Shakespeare's Duck/Rabbits

In the biological and social sciences it is, of course, well known that the same perceptual field, whether in seeing or in hearing language, can be interpreted in more than one way—the so-called duck/rabbit way of seeing "aspects," as noted by Wittgenstein (fig. 1).[8] We also may see such "aspects" of a phrase or a sentence: hence the ambiguity in the words "light house keeper," which may be understood as either "lighthouse keeper" or "light housekeeper." The syllables may be turned one way or another by the slightest change of intonation. Or consider the phrase "splendor in the grass" as it appears in Wordsworth's *Intimations of Immortality*, in the context of the desire to recover some sort of

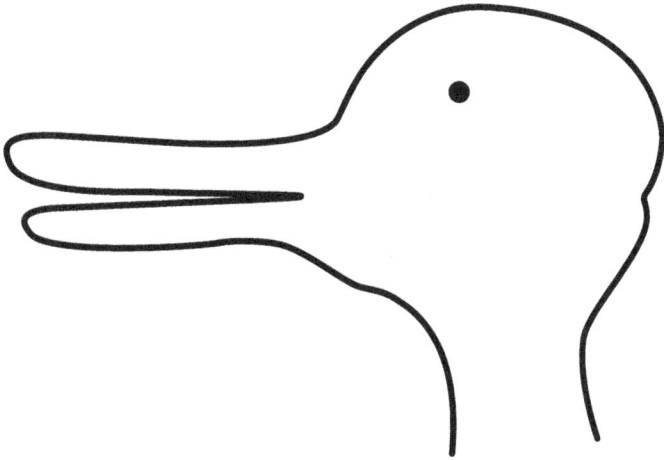

FIGURE 1. A reproduction of the Duck/Rabbit image used in Ludwig Wittgenstein's *Philosophical Investigations* and in E. H. Gombrich's *Art and Illusion*.

innocent mystical unity, versus the phrase as it appears as the title to a somewhat sexually explicit 1961 movie. The context of a phrase or word determines its meaning and also what it cannot mean.

This also happens with larger structures such as plays or stories—a new context reveals to us a new aspect of the meanings of the words. For example, *Richard II* appears to have meant "overthrow the queen" when it was played in 1601 to the Essex faction's leaders just before the Essex uprising in a performance subsidized by the Earl of Essex's friends, something far more dangerous than it was previously thought to have meant.[9] The referent of the play's king, then, appears to be Elizabeth I, with Bolingbroke as its Essex, and the possible "meaning" that occasioned the inquiry into the performance appears to have been a call to revolt.[10] This would apply whether the sometimes censored deposition scene in *Richard II* was performed on the Essex occasion or not. Few people seeing the play would have been ignorant of the fact that Richard was deposed or that Bolingbroke reigned at the end.[11] When Bacon sees the play as meaning latently—to Essex's ally, the rebel Meyrick—that Elizabeth should be deposed and Essex elevated, we know from our knowledge of the political situation, conventional political typology of the time, and the story in the play that Bacon is describing an aspect of the play that he saw as latent for Meyrick. Meyrick was hanged because the government suspected him of so seeing and using the play.

Culture, Semiology, and Interpreting a Story

One may offer a contrasting example of seeing an aspect of a play or story that seems more like projection in the encounter described by Laura Bohannon in "Shakespeare in the Bush."[12] Bohannon is doing anthropology among the Tiv in West Africa and reading Hamlet at the same time. At a meeting of the elders, she is asked to tell a story. Because of the elders' understanding of what is and is not, what things mean and what they do not, the telling is interrupted by frequent editing from the elders. For example, Bohannon tries to tell the story of the appearance of Hamlet's father's ghost. For the Tiv audience, the ghost entity cannot exist. The group suggests that the ghost is an omen, and Bohannon replies:

> "Hamlet's dead father wasn't an omen. Seeing him might have been an omen, but he was not." My audience looked as confused as I sounded. "It *was* Hamlet's dead father. It was a thing we call a 'ghost.'" I had to use the English word, for unlike many of the neighboring tribes, these people didn't believe in the survival after death of any individuating part of the personality.
>
> "What is a 'ghost'? An omen?"
>
> "No, a 'ghost' is someone who is dead but who walks around and can talk, and people can hear him and see him but not touch him."
>
> They objected, "One can touch zombies."
>
> "No, no! It was not a dead body the witches had animated to sacrifice and eat. No one else made Hamlet's dead father walk. He did it himself."
>
> "Dead men can't walk," protested my audience as one man.
>
> I was quite willing to compromise, "A 'ghost' is the dead man's shadow."
>
> But again they objected. "Dead men cast no shadows."
>
> "They do in my country," I snapped.

Of course, the elders' suggestion that the "ghost" is a supernatural presence animated by an evil force may have some legitimacy in an Elizabethan frame, but a zombie it cannot be in Shakespeare's context. Bohannon goes on to tell the rest of the story, regularly interrupted by the elders, who consistently remark on the universality of their culture's version of human nature and the impossibility of what Bohannon tells. She comes to the killing of Polonius and the events thereafter:

> "The great chief," I went on, "was not sorry that Hamlet had killed Polonius. It gave him a reason to send Hamlet away, with his two treacherous age mates, with letters to a chief of a far country, saying that Hamlet should be killed. But Hamlet changed the writing on their papers, so that the chief killed his age mates instead." I encountered a reproachful glare from one of the men whom I had told undetectable forgery was not merely immoral but beyond human skill. I looked the other way.
>
> "Before Hamlet could return, Laertes came back for his father's funeral. The great chief told him Hamlet had killed Polonius. Laertes swore to kill Hamlet because of this, and because his sister Ophelia, hearing her father had been killed by the man she loved, went mad and drowned in the river."
>
> "Have you already forgotten what we told you?" The old man was reproachful, "One cannot take vengeance on a madman; Hamlet killed Polonius in his madness. As for the girl, she not only went mad, she was drowned. Only witches can make people drown. Water itself can't hurt anything. It is merely something one drinks and bathes in."

One of the elders remarks, "People are the same everywhere; therefore, there are always witches and it is we, the elders, who know how witches work." And another says that when Bohannon brings more stories from her land, the elders will tell her *what they really mean.*

Meaning and Projected Meaning

We know there is a difference in kind between the meaning Meyrick found in *Richard II* and that which the elders of the Tiv found in

Hamlet. The first interpretation reads the words of the play in a manner that reveals an aspect of the play *conceivable* to Shakespeare's time and place, whereas the second projects on the play the assumptions of a group separated from it in time, place, and religion. Both interpretations recognize "aspects" of the stories that can be found or constructed in them, but one aspect, the Meyrick one, is found in the story in a special historical context, while the other is projected on the story from a radically different context. The projected meaning is not, as in Derrida's conception, a *différance*, or deferred reflection of something that was once there but that has passed.[13] A deferred meaning, *to be seen as deferred*, must be something *there* that one notices later—we note some meaning that we did not notice initially, a pun in a phrase when someone else in our group catches on and winks. By definition, deferred meaning cannot exist if its deferral cannot be known or glimpsed.[14] There are criteria whereby we determine whether a listener or hearer understands the meanings of words—for example, puns that slowly dawn on us as our understanding of them is deferred—nods, winks, elbow jabs, questions that properly go with what has been said, explanations to others that tell them what has been said, and so forth. Interestingly there is no speculation or playing in Bohannon's conversation with the Tiv about what the word "ghost" means (and what other religious conceptions go with it in Western religious tradition). She tells the story, and the Tiv elders remake it to fit their conceptions, appropriating the words to make a *new* rather than a deferred meaning.

We may be tempted to say that the Tiv erase common Western European meanings for *Hamlet.* One of Derrida's understandings of *différence* is that any single assignment of meaning to a text effaces or erases other possible or "surplus" meanings, meanings that can be legitimately called back to life in other contexts. However, with deferred meaning, we must establish whether what we posit as erased and called back was ever part of the usage system in the first place. It is clearly not in the Tiv case.

Again, Derrida and many contemporary critics argue that a *word* about a past event cannot mean exactly what it meant as an *event* to those who were there at the time. And in Derrida, one cannot ever be exactly "there at the time." That may suggest to us as critics that the Tiv were right. If the ghost is a zombie to the Tiv, this is all right because that is *how they can construe it*. Bohannon got it wrong in her context because *Hamlet*'s author could not know what deferred meaning would be there for the Tiv. But is that not a circular argument? Can we know that an event does not mean exactly what it meant to its first spectators without knowing exactly what it did mean to its first spectators? In Derrida's conception, that knowledge is impossible.[15] And can we then erase or eliminate a meaning that was never written, or assigned, in the first place?

The question about knowing what language means is not "Does it perfectly deliver its referent?" but "What is it doing?" "How is the language used?" For past language, if we wish to understand it historically, the question is "What *was* it doing?" We can look at how we learn past language by looking at past common usages of that language in the community using it and in its time and neighborhood or locus—in other words, what we do when we learn any language. That we can recognize usage is indicated by our recognition of misusage in, say, Dogberry's or Elbow's talk. No understanding of the word "ghost" goes with the Tiv meaning for ghost, not through any fault of the Tiv save that they are not seventeenth-century Europeans. The Tiv "meaning" is a projected one that clearly misconstrues what Bohannon is telling because the elders do not share the terms or the form of life that underlies her narrative. Shakespeare's understanding of humankind is different from theirs. This is not to say that some explanations could not have made them understand what *Hamlet*'s assumptions are. (It is equally clear that we do not share the terms or the forms of life of Elizabethan-Jacobean England.)

The Tiv example is a paradigm for how we tend to read text apart from history and culture. However, in the context described, the Tiv have little choice but to make *Hamlet* theirs since they do not know of *Hamlet*'s world. It may be argued, of course, that we are so trapped in our own time and culture as to be unable to visualize the world of others. Yet we are not so trapped as not to feel a jolt when the Tiv tell us: "People are the same everywhere; therefore, there are always witches and it is we, the elders, who know how witches work." The jolt we feel comes from our denial of the assumption that the Tiv can be interpreters of "our" stories *based on their assurance that they know human nature.* By human nature, I mean a culture's assumptions about what is possible to human beings, what customs and beliefs say about what human beings are as a species, the assumptions that a culture holds about people and assumes to be generic in all cultures. We might properly feel the same jolt when a contemporary hermeneutic is used to make sense of a past text.

A set of assumptions identical to the Tiv's, that human nature is always the same, undergirds Ernest Jones's analyses already treated and, more recently, Harold Bloom's influential analyses of Shakespeare. Bloom tells us that Shakespeare discovered human nature and that human nature as Freud knew it is what Shakespeare discovered: "My interest in Freud comes from the increasing realization that Freud is a kind of codifier or abstractor of William Shakespeare. In fact, it is Shakespeare who gives us the map of the mind. It is Shakespeare who invents Freudian Psychology. Freud finds ways of translating it into supposedly analytical vocabulary."[16] Bloom's fix on Shakespeare is essentially identical with Jones's: Shakespeare tells us what Freud tells us, and both tell us what we are. For Bloom, it is Shakespeare who is "the original psychologist" and Freud the belated rhetorician "in understanding our common bisexuality." He is the first person who "thought everything through again for himself"—the forerunner of Kierkegaard, Emerson, Nietzsche, and Freud. He also invented our species.[17]

What Language in a Particular Time and Place Cannot Say

In an effort to claim for Shakespeare the insights of Freud or Marx or Derrida or the authors of any number of other contemporary herme-neutic systems, we tend to decipher Shakespeare's language by means of terms that we regularly use today but that are unlike anything anyone said in Shakespeare's day—things that could not have been part of the conversation in Shakespeare's day because they are absent from the vocabulary or the world of discourse in the sixteenth and early seventeenth centuries. This does not mean that Shakespeare's language is restricted to what was conventional in his time. It means he cannot say what the language of his time could not say. He could not, for example, say that water is H_2O because neither the vocabulary nor the conceptions underlying the periodic table existed in his time. He could not have said that Lear suffers from bipolar disorder, though he might well have seen symptoms like those of the syndrome in the London Bedlam.

As another example of the difficulty in deciphering the meaning of words commonly used in both Shakespeare's time and ours, we find that in a standard gloss of modern English idioms, the phrase "love is blind" now means something like "people generally do not see their lovers' faults." The Internet gives examples such as "She can't see his bad habits because love is blind." Being blind in love now is not particularly a comic or unfortunate or irrational thing. It is just what goes with love: "She loves him so completely that she doesn't notice that he has faults, and that is probably good." However, if we consider the phrase "blind Love" as it was commonly used in Shakespeare's time, it connotes a personification—the figure of Cupid blinded with a kerchief or fully blinded in his eyes. This Cupid is a person who shoots arrows, sets traps, and ties up people. Though Robert Burton, in a passage in *The Anatomy of Melancholy* (3.2.3) written somewhat after Shakespeare (1621), tells us that the idea that Love (or Cupid) is blind means that lovers cannot see their mistresses' imperfections of body and mind, he does so in the context of telling us that love or lust turns us away from reason. It commonly transforms the men it infects into animals: Apuleius into a metaphoric ass, Lycaon into a wolf, Elpenor and Grillus into swine.

If we go to the dictionaries of classical mythology available in Shakespeare's time, we find that this blind Cupid is said to mean "irrational desire," "uncontrolled concupiscence," or some such thing, precisely because he cannot see the faults of the beloved and attributes false virtue to him or her. He plays a role in psychology positing faculties of the mind (e.g., reason, imagination) that we have discarded, a structure that relates the senses, concupiscible and irascible appetites, imagination, will, and reason in a hierarchy moving toward the god-like in humankind. Blind Cupid is generally the concupiscent appetite when it controls the whole person contrary to reason and leads to ir-rational action that injures others or the self. He may stand for other ideas related to ungovernable desire or, in an example cited later, in certain rather explicitly Neoplatonic contexts he may be a figure for an intuition that transcends the rational.

In Renaissance art, as for example in Titian's *Venus Blindfolding Cupid* (1565) — otherwise known as *The Education of Cupid,* we see a Cupid figure being blindfolded by his mother as another Cupid-like but seeing figure, Anteros, looks on and while an unknown figure, perhaps a Grace, offers Venus Cupid's bow. Panofsky interprets the blinded Cupid as terrestrial love and the seeing Anteros as heav-enly love that seeks to raise earthly love to a higher level (fig. 2).[18] Francucci, in Titian's period, called the blinded Cupid of the painting "the perfidious Cupid of the bandaged eyes."[19] With its picture of the Grace with Cupid's bow and Venus pausing in binding or unbind-ing the blindfold of the perfidious Cupid, the painting may state, as Panofsky suggests, that the Venus of proper earthly and of heavenly love is seeking to educate the blind Cupid to a level where he har-monizes with the higher loves, as in standard love theory where he stands for married love.

As in Titian, the blinded Cupid in Shakespeare's plays is commonly contrasted with the seeing Cupid as signifying the difference between irrational and rational desire or love. The most common dictionaries of this language of myth are the emblem books. For example, we see a blind Cupid in Otto Vaenius's *Amorum Emblemata* (1608) who is said to figure the lack of wisdom that goes with love among men or among the gods, and this same figure occurs in a large number of other like books and in many editions and translations of van Veen.[20] We may also find subtle variations on this core usage. For example, in Shakespeare's *A Midsummer Night's Dream,* Helena says that "[l]ove looks not with the eyes but with the mind, / And therefore is winged

FIGURE 2. Titian (Tiziano Vecellio) (ca. 1488–1576), *Venus Blindfolding Cupid*, ca. 1565. Oil on canvas. Galleria Borghese, Rome. Scala/Art Resource, New York.

Cupid painted blind" (1.1.234–35).[21] Here she initially seems to assert that blind Cupid is a symbol of intellectual seeing in contrast to the usual versions that mark his blindness as intellectual blindness. We may be tempted to think that Helena is a Neoplatonist, saying that this blind Love rises above the intellect and its sight and fulfills one completely as do some Neoplatonic versions of the blind Cupid. But Helena is merely confused. Shakespeare gives us another twist of the knife. Helena's definition goes on to tell us that this version of Love's mind is an irrational one in that it has no taste for judgment and also in that its "[w]ings and no eyes figure unheedy haste." Love's mind is childish—often "beguiled" (*MND* 1.1.237–39). Helena's Love's "seeing with the mind," instead of with "blindness of mind," then becomes simply a variant of the old blindness usage: Love sees mentally but blindly, childishly, heedlessly, and without judgment. Thus, in one short passage Shakespeare invokes the conventional blind Cupid, then for a phrase ("but with the mind") tempts us to see him as a Neoplatonic Cupid of transcendent commitment, and then sends us crashing into the old world of mindless mind and hasty judgment.

Examining Shakespeare's other uses of blind Love reveals that in most if not all contexts, he is not one of the delicate *putti* Cupids on a cute Valentine suggesting something between infatuation and mild affection. He is a daemon and a powerful symbol. In one of Shakespeare's scenes filled with tragic dread, he appears as pulp-eyed Gloucester, blind and near Dover, addressed by Lear—"Dost thou squiny at me? No, do thy worst, blind Cupid; I'll not love" (*Lear* 4.6.134–35). Gloucester, done in by his own blind Cupid bastardizing, *becomes* a sightless Cupid to Lear, warning him against the Cupid that with his form of love will bring—indeed has already brought—children to destroy him. And the other blind Cupids in Shakespeare's works carry a family of meanings related to those briefly examined here (see chapter 3). A shift in meaning for the icon occurred from Shakespeare's time to ours that is not unlike other semantic shifts over time.

But how do we know that Shakespeare and his audience understood blind Cupid or blind Love (and the other iconic language we will examine) as the handbooks and commentaries say one should understand them? Perhaps he understood Cupid as we do when he talked about Love being blind—mechanically, as a cliché—or perhaps without saying so he understood Cupid in a Freudian way and anticipated Freud.

BLIND CUPID AS A CLICHÉ

In this case one could argue, along the lines of philosopher John Searle's "Chinese room" argument, that Shakespeare's use of blind Cupid, with the meaning "blindness of mind" or "irrationality of mind based on misdirected love," is semantically appropriate only accidentally. Searle's Chinese room argument is an effort to challenge the assertion that computers "understand" language. To simplify somewhat, a man who knows no Chinese is placed in a room where he is given a set of Chinese symbols, a set of rules in English for manipulating them, a set of questions in Chinese, and a set of instructions in English for how to give back answers in Chinese. The man gives back answers in what appears to be Chinese, but he answers wholly in uninterpreted formal symbols, even though they look like Chinese answers. He *does not understand* his answers, though they appear wholly coherent.[22] In the vein of Searle's opponents, we could argue that Shakespeare and his audience do not understand blind Love as Titian or van Veen do. Though he uses this Cupid in contexts where his characters *could well be thought* to be speaking about the irrationality of a certain kind of love, that apparent appropriateness is actually an accident. Neither Shakespeare nor his audience understands any of this.

Searle's argument has created a great deal of controversy (and I do not wish to subscribe to all that he has attributed to it), but its philosophic comedy does render improbable the argument that Shakespeare, his characters, or any other writer could use such a phrase as "blind Cupid" in the ways that the explanations of his time say it should be used, with a consonant family of meanings, in the contexts where the usage fits, or with the explanations normally given it, *and yet* that the words not mean what they were said to say.[23] Derrida speaks of the techniques of reading things outside the "lexicon" available at the time of writing as endeavoring to expose a "certain relationship, unperceived by the writer, between what he commands and what he does not command of the patterns of the language that he uses."[24] Derrida further argues that proper scholarship requires the scholar to know what language the author commands, in order to expose a meaning the writer is communicating through using locutions for which he does not command meaning. It is as if a writer were to say, "I was using 300 words, but I was only commanding 150 of them. You figure out the rest." Whatever the writer's intention, the speech and writing community of the author's time and place commands all of the language of the writer, or else it is gibberish.

ANTICIPATING FREUD

If we assume that human nature is always the same and that falling in love is always understood in the same way, we may believe that "blind Cupid" or "blind Love" has the modern meaning we find on valentines, or even that we can find this meaning if we look at the "language the author does not command"—an understanding possible now but not in 1600. For example, blind Cupid may have a meaning consonant with the conceptual world of psychoanalysis. Marvin Krims's interpretation says that the "blind Cupid" in *Romeo and Juliet* means that loving is hard for a young man like Romeo who has had—as part of the development of his human nature—a less than warmhearted wet nurse or mother in his childhood and has lost his sense of identity because of this. The passage in question involves a conversation in act 1, scene 1, between Romeo and Benvolio, where the two are joking about Romeo's sadness in love. Romeo says he is not sad because he does not love but because he is "Out of her favor where I am in love." Benvolio then observes solicitously:

> Alas, that love, so gentle in his view,
> Should be so tyrannous and rough in proof.

Romeo's reply-couplet turns to Cupid's blindness:

> Alas, that love, whose view is muffled still,
> Should, without eyes, see pathways to his will! (1.1.164–72;
>   lineation from Krims)

Krims's analysis of the passage goes straight to Romeo's childhood:

> From a developmental perspective then, Romeo's perception of his situation is accurate: a woman is the cause of his sadness but the perception is anachronistic. Romeo is unconsciously reliving his childhood, a time of helplessness and dependency on the will of another. At some time in these early years, a trauma might have occurred which he experienced as rejection and against which he defended himself by repression. This repressed trauma now expresses itself in his "choice" of a woman with whom he reenacts the trauma in disguised form.

Krims then finds that Romeo's "Out of her favor, where I am in love" (167) reflects memories from childhood that have been repressed, memories of when he loved a woman ("where I am in love") but suffered a traumatic rejection ("Out of her favor"). This type of woman has now reappeared in the form of Rosaline:

> The fact that Rosaline never appears in person in the text then becomes a dual metaphor for Romeo's inner life. On one level, her absence indicates that her identity is unimportant; her only role is someone with whom Romeo repeats his early trauma. (He refers to her by name but once and then only to deny his love for her in 2.3.45.) On another level, her absence symbolizes the loved woman (presumably his mother or perhaps his wet-nurse) who must have been unavailable to him—at least sometimes. Friar Lawrence recognizes the unreal nature of his love for Rosaline and chides him "For doting, not for loving." (2.3.47)[25]

Krims does not bother to show us that Shakespeare's time understood blind Cupid to be part of a person's psychology that included will, reason, and imagination. His world is the world of repression, trauma, and withheld affection. And he does not show us that Shakespeare's text does not provide us with an unavailable wet nurse, a cold mother, an early trauma, or a Rosaline who is a metaphor for an inner life. All of these have to be made up as part of a new universe of discourse to be imposed on the text. The text simply says that Romeo is out of Rosaline's favor, that he still loves her forlornly, and that the Cupid of his kind of love, though he looks so gentle, is really rough and tyrannous—rough because though he cannot see, he can infect the will and dominate the mind.

There is nothing puzzling in what Romeo says about blind Cupid if one studies what blind Cupid was conventionally said to mean, how he was thought to infect the will and destroy rational considerations. All of the figures that prop up Krims's interpretation have to be constructed from fictions that appear three centuries *after* Shakespeare in order to make the psychoanalytic hermeneutic work, since they are not part of the language that goes with blind Cupid in Shakespeare's discourse community. The passage's blind Cupid requires only that one remember the faculty psychology related to the will, found in almost every description from Shakespeare's time of how we are put together and recalled in the passage. That is not all. One could elicit similar examples from the hermeneutic practice of numerous critics, whether of the post-structuralist, cultural materialist, or New Historicist schools of interpretation. But we need not assume that every culture's sense of the usual or natural in human beings and their actions is like that of our culture in order to have the sense that we understand Shakespeare and his culture.

How to Read a Text

Though we cannot establish the meaning of a text by assuming a universal hermeneutic or a universal human nature, it does not follow that all historical reconstructions are simply and only artifacts of the place and time of the reconstructor. Can we argue, for example, that Edmond Malone's discovery of the office book of Sir Henry Herbert, Master of the Revels, 1622–42, derived either from ideology or resistance to ideology? Can we say the same for Malone's discovery of Henslowe's 1592–1603 diary? Where is the evidence for such an assertion? Few modern critics would argue that Malone's effort to find the variants in every known copy of Shakespeare's plays served only private interest or the interest of ideology or that most of his textual decisions were so driven, though we might plausibly argue that his edition of the sonnets reflects the time's interest in the artist's private biography. We can, however imperfectly, know other people, other places, and other times. Today we know of people who have fully adopted the languages, religious practices, artistic ways, and customs of persons who were not part of their nativity, and we can make something of the same leap into the past. We have an extensive record of how people said things and what they meant by them in various contexts in Shakespeare's time. Neither the solipsistic assumption nor the assumption that the past is unknowable will do. We accept all kinds of things about the structure of Shakespeare's company, his theater, his economic base, and the literal meaning and pronunciation of his words on the basis of historical reconstructions. We can do the same with the literal and figurative meaning of his works. We can discover whether the meanings that we find are conceivable in the universes of discourse that were available to his time. We do so by reading, watching how old language is used, and observing his and other authors' explanations of what they are doing, both in their works and in glosses, interpretations, and dedications.

Of course, we often do the same things that the Tiv did. We can make Shakespeare's duck into a rabbit and achieve a duck/rabbit seeing of Shakespeare. We can do so in both criticism and production. Such a transformation of the text as it could be understood in its own time undergirds many of the most popular of our cultural productions: Olivier's *Henry V* as World War II propaganda; Branagh's post-Vietnam antiwar versions of the same play; *Measure for Measure* as an assault on fascist regimes (as if it were *The Great Dictator* or *The Resistible Rise of Arturo Ui*); *Love's Labour's Lost* as critique of contemporary musical comedy; *Much Ado* as feminist statement; and *Merchant of Venice* as antidote to anti-Semitism. One could argue that what these significant directors and actors are doing is like playing variations on the theme of a popular song, as a jazz pianist might do, or as in Brahms's *Variations on a Theme by Haydn*. But in the case of the jazz pianist we know the original from which the variation is derived. Our pleasure arises from seeing the original moved around. In the case of the dehistoricized Shakespeare, we do not know what theme gives rise to the variations. We play the variation without the theme, and often we lose something.

Criticism that respects the past is not easy. By way of analogy, Rosalyn Tureck said of her performance of Bach: "I do what Bach tells me to do . . . I never tell the music what to do. I never make the decision, it makes the decision. But you have to delve deeply into a score. You can't just use your eyes; you have to use all your faculties of mind, heart, and body."[26] Perhaps we ought to seek a similar surrender to the score in playing Shakespeare.

The rationale for not letting the "music" tell us what to do in the case of Shakespeare may be that what he communicated to his original audiences is entirely irrecoverable. Some critics regard this as obviously true and even good. The past is a waste. In contrast, this book offers analyses designed to suggest that the myth of irrecoverability is not so much true as easy. If we are puzzled by a word, phrase, speech, or scene in a work from the past, it may be that we have not tried hard enough to get to the bottom of it. A second and more pragmatic rationale may be that were a historicized meaning recoverable, no one would want to read or see Shakespeare so recovered because he would be a dead duck or rabbit, a museum artifact. That argument may carry weight for some historical reconstructions, including some that this book makes. But it should be equally obvious that many variations on Shakespearean themes have not worked very well—the happy ending for *Lear*, the elaborate performance with curtains and pauses between acts and scenes on the nineteenth- and early-twentieth-century stages, use of the proscenium arch theater, or reliance on heavy-duty scenery. As historians of the theater have come to see what modern analogues for the historical presentation of the Shakespearean *mise-en-scène* could do to enliven Shakespearean drama and move it from the realms of cliché, so those who endeavor to render Shakespeare's *meanings* available to modern audiences may find uses in looking at what his language meant or probably meant in his time.[27]

In any case, one may ask if we understand Shakespeare at all if we do not understand him as his language was understood in his time. If, as Wittgenstein argues, a word's meaning is its use, a word's or a sentence's usage is defined by the time and place for which it is written or said. Some forms of language, such as legal language, endure across the centuries in a relatively stable state because the context in which they have force is recorded and kept relatively consistent. Others—such as parts of the vocabulary and usage in 1980s Valley Girl slang—have come and gone like the will-o'-the-wisp.

For most forms of talk and writing, including those that are most ephemeral, we can use the methods of historical linguistics to learn what the usages of other times and places have been, even if they lasted only for a summer's afternoon. We have the *Oxford English Dictionary* and concordances for the simplest things. For Shakespeare's time we have the dictionaries and interpretations of classical myths to tell us how people in his day used those stories. We have much the same thing in scriptural commentary coming out of a range of Jewish and Christian group traditions. We are beginning to know something about what different kinds of clothing and costume meant in the sixteenth and seventeenth centuries. We have English writers who tell us how they interpret Ariosto, Tasso, Spenser, and others, and we have Shakespeare's characters themselves making conventional—or comically and tragically mistaken—interpretations of the emblems they construct or encounter, supplementing what they have said. We have the emblem books, which give us a picture referent and a verbal explanation, both of which point to something outside the book. We know something about the range of interpretive methods that readers—explainers—of the time used.

At another level, we have a sense of how Shakespeare's London players pronounced words and how pronunciation affects how they can be taken, particularly where punning occurs. We also have evidence from within Shakespeare's plays as to what specific plots within the plays are supposed to do or suggest to their audiences. The Pyramus and Thisbe plot is designed simply to while away the time until bedtime, but *The Mousetrap* is to catch the conscience of the king, and the masque of Juno in *The Tempest* is to rehearse what a marriage is to be in the cosmic scheme of love. Shakespeare's own comments on playing within his plays show us that what a play means may depend on the kinds of players used and the entertainment or performance context—the specific "current events" context. We know that without Shakespeare's advice.

My aim is to reconstruct a few of the conventional languages in Shakespearean comedy as they reflect the languages of earlier comedies and as Shakespeare extends them to earlier plays. The route is to look at a few crucial areas where, in my view, the traditional language games are used and extended: (1) what the "syntax" and execution of comedic form are doing, (2) what the stories borrowed or extended from ancient Greek and Roman stories are doing, (3) what those from the biblical texts and biblical liturgies and festivals do, and (4) what the references to empire do. The assumption is that we can reconstruct these things enough to understand them—perhaps imperfectly but somewhat historically. This reconstruction may affect production for the producer who wants that, but it does not mean creating a fossil version of the plays. It means translating them in the fullest sense.

In all of this I assume that Shakespeare seeks to extend the realm of comedy so that, besides being funny, it also carries the *gravitas* of the most serious work. Florio in 1598 defines tragedy as follows: "Tragédia, a tragedie or moornefull play being a loftie kinde of poetrie, and representing personages of great state and matter of much trouble, a great broile or stirre: it beginneth prosperously and endeth vnfortunatelie or sometimes doubtfullie, and is contrarie to a comedie."[28]

Blount in his 1656 dictionary gives us essentially the same sort of definition:

> Tragedie is a lofty kinde of poetry. . . . The differences between a Tragedy and a Comedy are these; First, in respect of the matter, because a *Tragedy* treats of exilements, murders, matters of grief, &c. a *Comedy* of love-toyes, merry fictions and petty matters; in a *Tragedy* the greatest part of the actors are Kings and Noble persons; In a *Comedy*, private persons of meaner state and condition. The subject of a *Comedy* is often feigned but of a *Tragedy* it is commonly true and once really performed; The beginning of a *Tragedy* is calme and quiet, the end fearful and turbulent; But in a *Comedy* contrarily, the beginning is turbulent, and the end calm.[29]

Lodge says tragedy speaks of "the sower fortune of many exiles, the miserable fal of haples princes, The reuinous decay of many cou[n]tryes."[30] Other definers add that a tragedy is essentially historical in its content. On the other hand, comedy is said to be a picture of that which is not historical but verisimilar, of domestic and common life, of follies attendant on village or ordinary street reality, and a picture of such life as it moves toward happiness. Comedy treats of what is at home, nonviolent, middle and lower class, of love and marriage. Tragedy speaks of exile—spiritual and physical—of the historical struggles of kings and great ones, not of verisimilar ordinary blokes but of great men in history moving their nations toward destruction, of violence and war. I argue that Shakespeare takes comedy into realms formerly occupied by tragedy and epic tragedy—exile, history, great leaders, violence and war in the background, the fates of nations and leaders—and that it is this movement that makes his comedies so powerful.

Reconstruction of Shakespeare's usages and those of his age brings me to call into play many literary usages usually categorized as exemplary, allegorical, emblematic, or iconological. Such usages, it is commonly observed, lead to a wooden sort of acting in contrast to the brilliantly illuminating acting that tells us about universal human nature, such as we find in Olivier's *Hamlet*. But the Freudian subtext is surely an allegorization of Hamlet, turning him and his stepfather and mother into emblems or exempla "proving" some "universal truths" that lasted for about a generation. Another set of figurative constructions "in the language" of Shakespeare's time, and if we observe them, these constructions can become significant mockers of our twenty-first-century enterprise.

The point about Shakespeare's use of the exemplary, allegorical, emblematic, iconological, and the like is that it is almost never the case that a character simply "stands for" an abstract idea—an object, or an emblem.[31] The characters are generally representative of human beings struggling in their imperfection and incompleteness to embody ideals and ideal conditions or demons and demonic conditions. The struggle with the dream is the drama. That Ophelia carries emblematic flowers to give to the other characters does not make her mourning less. That Lear says that he "will be the pattern of all patience" on the heath does not make his struggle less. When Vincentio says a ruler should be as holy as he is severe, "pattern in himself to know," he is no wooden robot. He is the monarch of Vienna, struggling with his decision to place Angelo in power, struggling with his own former failure to govern the city well, struggling now to realize what good rule can be. Shakespeare's comic characters, as this book conceives of them, are no more wooden than Don Quixote struggling with his dreams and demons, and they are a good deal more various.

2

Shakespeare and the Invention of Grand Comic Form

When Ben Jonson writes his introductory poem for the First Folio, he casually mentions Shakespeare's outshining his contemporaries in tragedy and his parity with the ancients, Aeschylus, Euripides, and Sophocles. But when he speaks of Shakespeare's comedies, he claims for them an unrivaled place:

> [W]hen thy Socks were on,
> Leave thee alone, for the comparison
> Of all, that insolent *Greece* or haughty *Rome*
> Sent forth, or since did from their ashes come.
> Triumph, my *Britain*, thou hast one to show
> To whom all Scenes of *Europe* homage owe.
> He was not of an age, but for all time!
> And all the *Muses* still were in their prime,
> When like *Apollo* he came forth to warm
> Our ears, or like a *Mercury* to charm!
> Nature herself was proud of his designs,
> And joy'd to wear the dressing of his lines!
> Which were so richly spun, and woven so fit,
> As, since, she will vouchsafe no other Wit.
> The merry Greek, tart *Aristophanes*,
> Neat *Terence*, witty *Plautus*, now not please;

But antiquated and deserted lie
As they were not of Nature's family.[1]

The Jonsonian Shakespeare supersedes all that Greece, Rome, or sub-sequent cultures have offered in the mode of comedy, even outreaching Aristophanes, Terence, and Plautus. As he combines "Apollo's" wisdom with "Mercury's" eloquence, he writes Nature, or what natural wit dictates, according to Jonson's common use of the term *nature*: "Nature herself was proud of his designs, / And joy'd to wear the dressing of his lines!"

The New Comedy writers, Plautus and Terence, are obvious candidates for Jonson's list as Shakespeare writes a species of New Comedy from *The Comedy of Errors* on, and people like Francis Meres in his own time recognized him as claiming the mantle of the Romans. Even in *The Tempest* at the end of his career he continues to draw on Plautus for story lines and on Terence for the double plot.[2] But so pervasive is the influence of New Comedy on Shakespeare that critics have argued that tragedies such as Hamlet adopt the New Comedy masks—the old man, the matron, the young lovers, the parasite—for utterly non-comic purposes.

However, this chapter is not so much about the details of Shakespeare's adaptation from Plautus and Terence as about the broad outlines of how he developed the New Comedy and Early Modern comic form beyond the New Comedy to say things about the state and about the human community's construction of itself out of diverse materials. In this connection Aristophanes is the crucial name in Jonson's list, for he points to Shakespeare's larger-than-New-Comedy scope. The Old (or satirical) Comedy of Aristophanes attracted Jonson and appears to have formed partially the basis of the aesthetic of three of his early plays (*Every Man Out*, *Poetaster*, and *Cynthia's Revels*). Aristophanes also informed the great comedies of his middle period in a more subtle way.[3] Jonson knew that many of the plays labeled comedic in his time followed Plautus and Terence and observed only the complex webs that love weaves: "a duke in love with a countess, the countess in love with the duke's son and so forth with much cross-wooing."[4] Since

Shakespeare's plots are always such love-mongering constructions on the surface, Jonson could easily have placed him with the entertaining but lesser souls who give us much "cross-wooing." But what he saw in Shakespeare's comedies that went beyond cross-wooing—what raised them above conventional love-mongering and put them even above those of the most ambitious of ancients, Aristophanes—is, I think, their great subjects; Jonson says Aristophanes treats the "best men," that is, leaders, the usual subjects of Renaissance tragedy. At his worst, he treats them with scurrility and, at best, with a bit of salt.[5] Jonson would have us believe that great comedy can deal with emperors, specific great ones, as well as with the vast panorama of society and that it can bite so hard as to change people.[6]

What Jonson saw in Shakespeare, I suggest, is an analogously serious comedy that speaks of the actions of leaders and the fates of whole commonwealths. That Shakespeare saw comedy and tragedy as equal and related is suggested by his *Troilus and Cressida*, which, in the second version of the 1609 quarto, calls the play a history in its title and a comedy in its prefatory epistle. The work obviously comes from Homer's epic tragedy of the *Iliad* and Chaucer's tragedy of *Troilus and Criseyde*, and it deals with a great empire thought to be the predecessor of England in the transfer of empire from Troy to Rome to Britain. If we accept that Jonson's own understanding of comedy is basic to the greatness he finds in Shakespeare, what he finds there is a power of comedic analysis that reaches toward what he believes comedy ought to be: an imitation of life that persuades toward goodness and a mirror of manners that precisely images truth. Its grotesques are ridiculous, and its normative characters both pleasant and instructive. What Jonson in his general comic theory says comedy should do is not very different from what Hamlet would have playing do as he gives instructions for his *Mousetrap* "comedy": Hamlet would have comedians "hold as 'twere the mirror up to nature, . . . show virtue her own feature, scorn her own image, and the very age and body of the time his form and pressure" (3.2.16–22; see fuller quote, 3.2.1–40, early in chapter 1).

If we substitute the word "normative" for Shakespeare's word "virtue," we still in this time expect comedy to create laughter by surprising us with the comic violation of norms, whether in the unexpectedness of comic pratfalls, a shifting from the fluidity of normal behavior to the robotic actions of social pretenders, or the transformation of the world of ordinary social negotiation to the world of the self-appointed great man's utter egocentricity.[7] We laugh at Jacques Tati's Monsieur Hulot on holiday and Charlie Chaplin's "the Great Dictator" on crazed career for essentially moral and normative reasons.

Obviously, Shakespeare creates grand comedy by subtle means that do not require going back to Aristophanic bludgeoning (save perhaps in *Troilus*). He recreates the Plautine and Terentian New Comedy form so that—within its borders, seeming to center precisely in "a duke in love with a countess, the countess in love with the duke's son and so forth with much cross-wooing"—he can deal with the panorama of society from the top, the *dux* or leader, on down to street people. He moves the comedic action from the village or city street to the larger community or the nation to be able to rehearse how the whole panorama of society, the globe, can move toward civility and celebration. His settings are incredibly diverse—Venice, Vienna, Messina, the forest of Arden, Navarre, the Venetian Adriatic, Windsor, Troy, Athens—in contrast to those of his contemporaries in the art of comedy.[8] To add to or thicken this sense of the larger society created by the "[G]lobal" settings, Shakespeare reconstructs the character types of traditional New Comedy—the hero, heroine, braggart soldier, pimp, parasite, whore, eunuch, trade character—so that after *Comedy of Errors*, almost every major comic character represents a fusion of two or more traditional New Comedy character types into a new kaleidoscope. The characters created by this move invite us to inspect the shadowlands of their inner selves and the communities of which they are a part to spy potential for laughter and joy. Finally, the poet reconstructs the typical marriage and/or feasting conclusions of Roman comedy, making them into closings where benign judgment, celebration, and marriage prospects combine to carry a symbology for the potential unification and reconstruction of society.

The Introduction of the *Dux* or Leader

Shakespeare's first significant invention or expansion from the love-mongering comedy was the creation of the duke, or dux, who is a real national leader as the framing element in his New Comedies. Roman New Comedy, as it was described in Early Modern criticism, is essentially about the life of the street, the village, and the common, not about the commonwealth. Sidney elaborates the formula repeated by Florio and Blount (see chapter 1) as follows in the *Defense*:

[C]omedy is an imitation of the common errors of our life, which [the comic poet] represents in the most ridiculous and scornful sort that may be, so as it is impossible that any beholder can be content to be such a one. Now as in geometry the oblique must be known as well as the right, and in arithmetic the odd as well as the even, so in the actions of our life, who sees not the filthiness of evil, wants a great foil to perceive the beauty of virtue. This does the comedy handle so in our private and domestical matters, as with hearing it, we get (as it were) an experience what is to be looked for of a niggardly Demea, of a crafty Davus, of a flattering Gnatho, of a vain-glorious Thraso.[9]

The conventional medieval and neo-medieval critics of the Renaissance said a comedy is a village song, a *comos oda*, which treats of the mores and habits of villagers and shows the follies of the village's various character types. Stephen Orgel points out that when Sebastiano Serlio creates the comic scene in his *Architettura* (1545), it consists of the middle-class architecture of merchant's houses. His tragic scene has "palaces and temples, aristocratic and public buildings, and monuments."[10] Sidney and the other critics are really talking about New Comedy when they speak of comedy as "domestical." There are, save in one instance, no kings or significant leaders in Plautus and Terence. It could be argued that this is so because they were writing for audiences in the Roman republic, where authority was not quite as centralized as in the later Roman Empire or in Elizabethan and Jacobean England. But republics do not exist without leaders, and more important, there are no real civic authority figures in Plautus and Terence save for Amphitryon in Plautus' *Amphitruo*, who is called a dux or leader in the play's list of characters and is the commander of the Thebans. However, he never acts as a leader in *Amphitruo*'s action, as Shakespeare's ducal figures regularly do. There are almost no leaders in the Roman comedies because they are not about leadership.

Jonson, who knew the forms of Old Comedy, put the leaders of society among those who could play a role in comedy and praised Aristophanic comedy for its touching of the whole social order. In a somewhat similar vein, the elder Sir Francis Beaumont in Shakespeare's time saw Chaucer as a comic master who extended the range of comic characters beyond the usual list of pimps, whores, parasites, and braggart soldiers filling the pages of Terence and Plautus, but even he does not claim *The Knight's Tale*, with its central investment in the ruler figure and rulership, as a comic work, though it has a happy ending and enough irony and humor to qualify as a comedy in Aristotle's sense.[11] Since *The Knight's Tale* is the main source of *A Midsummer Night's Dream*, Shakespeare may have seen it as a comedy or comic epic. In any case, he used it with its great ancient hero as a central figure.

Jonson, with his roots in Old Comedy and his occasional concern for the comic aspects of the whole commonwealth, including the ruler, could appreciate what Shakespeare had done, and that, I think, is why he adds Aristophanes' name to the list of those whom Shakespeare so outshone in comedy that they "antiquated and deserted lie."[12] By inserting the ruler and his governing associates, Shakespeare moves comedy from the New Comedy's street to the simultaneous palace-and-street that makes up the panoply of human community.[13]

The dux or ruler of the place where the play is set (often the setting is a court as opposed to a city setting) is the Shakespearean icon for the functioning of the state, often in conjunction with religious authority. His is not, in my view, the aristocratic title that subordinates him to kings and emperors as John of Gaunt's title, the Duke of Lancaster, subordinates him to King Richard in *Richard II*. In most of Shakespeare's comedies, the duke is not the feudal vassal of anyone. He negotiates with kings, and he punishes treason to the state, as Vincentio does in sentencing Lucio (see chapter 6). He is not the holder of some distant ducal title that Shakespeare's audience might have known little about, such as "Archduke of Vienna" or of the Austrian Netherlands, as suggested as one option for Vincentio by Leah Marcus.[14] He is simply the leader of the civic unit of the play, and he generally initiates its movement by a harsh legal or quasi-legal judgment and then concludes the same movement by its annulment, reversal, or mitigation.[15] This is especially obvious in *Comedy of Errors*, *Midsummer Night's Dream*, *Measure for Measure*, *Much Ado about Nothing*, and *The Tempest*, but the same logic also appears in truncated form or reformulated in most of the other comedies. For example, the judgments that could come down on Duke Frederick and on Oliver in *As You Like It* are eliminated through their conversions and journey to the cave and the marriage, respectively.

The double movement does important work for an authoritarian state that the author and the sponsoring or allowing bureaucracies—whether the Lord Chamberlain, the Monarchy, or the Master of the Revels—wish to be construed to be happy. Elizabethan-Jacobean monarchy is endlessly paternalistic, and any parent knows that the first move of authority is to assert the rules; the second is to temper them, in administering them, with empathy, contextual considerations, and love. But Shakespeare also knew that in a setting where the centralization of authority is as extensive as it was in Elizabethan and Jacobean England, it is difficult to present a work as fully comedic if only the local social order, the neighborhood, is presented as funny, happy, or joyful. The spectator knows, unless told otherwise, that beyond the borders of the stage the legions are marching and holy innocents are being put to the sword. By showing the errors of monarchy at the beginning and having the monarchy's surrogate, the Duke, rectifying them at the end of the plays, Shakespeare reassures us that we know the worst and moves toward joy.

Not accidentally, Shakespeare's comic rulers—for example, Vincentio in *Measure for Measure*—appear in some of the criticism as Christlike or figures for Christ. These rulers *do* act to put the community together at the end of the play, but any benign ruler can be represented as doing that. Christ is not necessary. The view that the Shakespearean comic dux is an allegory for the historic or salvation-creating Christ ignores the paucity of such allegories in Early Modern allegorical explanations. One may find them in the moralizations of the fablelike stories in the *Gesta Romanorum* or in eccentric interpretations of the classical gods, such as those in the *Ovide Moralisée* or Alexander Ross's *Mystagogus Poeticus*. One will *not* find these sorts of explanations in mainstream Early Modern interpretations of classical poetry and narrative. They stick with moral, historical, or naturalistic interpretations of the works they treat (see chapters 3 and 4, especially resources sections).

However, there is also a common understanding in which the king is a Christ or god in a wholly secular sense.[16] The dux—the king or leader in Elizabethan and Jacobean society—is *rex imago Christi*, king in the image of Christ, with all of the limitations and possibilities that phrase carried in Early Modern ruler worship.[17] James's defenses of that idea are simply an unpacking, in extensive narrative detail, of ideas that Kantorowicz describes in *The King's Two Bodies* as extending back into the High Middle Ages and influencing Chaucer, Richard II, Elizabeth, and Shakespeare in *Henry V* and *Richard II*. The phrase never carried the idea that the ruler in all aspects—whatever he or she did—was a god. It implied that rulers mediate between natural and positive law in the state in the way that Christ and his clerical successors, in medieval ecclesiastical theory, mediate between eternal and divine law.[18] The leader begins with justice and ends with the construction of the good society, as Christ begins with law and ends with redemption. The dux must be both just and merciful or, more precisely, he must bear the sword in order to show the face of forgiveness and mercy when these are possible. When King James I writes his long meditation on the idea of kingship present in the crowning and robing of Christ before the crucifixion, setting forth the symbolism of earthly kingship, he culminates his argument as follows:

Temporall Kings must not likewise be barred the sword, though it bee not in this paterne ... for it is to be drawne for the punishment of the wicked in defence of the good: *for a King carries not his sword for naught.* But it must neither bee blunt: for lawes without execution are without life[;] nor yet must it be ever drawne: for a King should never punish but with a weeping eye. In a word, a Christian King should neuer be without that continuall and euer wakeriffe care, of the account he is one day to giue to *God,* of the good gouernment of his people, & their prosperous estate both in soules and bodies; which is a part of the health of his owne soule.[19]

Like James's monarch, following in the footsteps of Christ about to be crucified and holding back his sword (Luke 22:35–38), Shakespeare's comedic monarch begins with his sword drawn, but he eventually lowers his weapon and punishes with a weeping eye, or not at all. He ends the play caring for the prosperity of his citizens' bodies and souls. That is especially the myth of the comedies as Shakespeare moves into the last Elizabethan and Jacobean years (though New Historicist "reconfiguring" of any of these endings is possible).[20]

Even early in Shakespeare's comedic career the root of the myth is there. In *Comedy of Errors,* Solinus, Duke of Ephesus, would enforce the draconian Ephesian laws against Syracusans, whatever their appropriateness to a bereaved Egeon. At the end of the play he discovers Egeon's marriage to Emilia, the abbess of Ephesus and, enforcing no penalties, reconstitutes the family as both Syracusan and Ephesian, perhaps in some sense accepting Adriana's argument that husband and wife are literally one person (*CE* 2.2.121–46). However, here Solinus's identification of who Egeon is and his relation to Emilia changes his judgment; he does not suspend the law. Theseus, in *A Midsummer Night's Dream,* suspends what would have been seen as a false law. At the beginning of the play, contrary to Elizabethan law, he would force Hermia to marry Demetrius or, alternatively, to be killed or go to a monastery. The "dream"—the experience of the Midsummer Night—revises his judgment, and near the end of act 4 (4.1.174ff.), he conforms his ruling to the more temperate Elizabethan religious law requiring offspring to have choice of their spouses, whatever the parents demand.[21] Shylock's effort to enforce Venetian law mercilessly is prevented by the technicality that Portia discovers—that no blood can be shed. In the early plays, the ruler's revisions toward the logic of mercy tend to depend on the discovery of a technicality or mistake in the law that prevents its rigorous enforcement.

The same two moves, to rigor at the beginning and then to benevolence in the terminal judgment scenes, appear in *Much Ado, Measure for Measure, All's Well, The Winter's Tale,* and *The Tempest.* However, the second move in the later plays has the ruler extend mercy regardless of the quality—or the existence—of repentance.[22] In the case of Prospero's final comments on Antonio, he seems to extend a kind of pardon that does not include trust and does convey the threat of exposure (*Tempest* 5.1.126). He can do so without giving serious attention to Antonio's continuing danger to the commonwealth after he has regained his rulership (5.1.129–34).

Where the ruler does not explicitly frame the work as in the plays mentioned, he does so implicitly. For example, before the play, Duke Senior in *As You Like It* must have been the voice of even-handed authority (1.1.1, 3) contrasted with the paranoid Duke Frederick who kicks him into the golden world. At the end of the play, we naturally project upon the ending the idea that Duke Senior will return to golden rulership, the demonic figures of the play having either reincorporated themselves in the community of the play through the prospect of marriage (Oliver) or been removed from all community through going to the cave of contemplation (Duke Frederick; see 5.4.175–76). Again, in *The Merchant of Venice* the duke appears only toward the end (*MV* 4.1), partly because Venetian contract law functions to represent the "duke" in act 1 of the play. In a variation, *All's Well's* King of France moves from the impotent fisher king of act 1 to a healed and restored king who can become both strict judge and master of reconciliation in act 5. In *The Winter's Tale,* Leontes appears to have been an attractive enough ruler until struck mad by jealousy that leads to retributive and false judgment. He can only recreate his familial and social group through a sixteen-year contrition and search for restitution.

If *Merry Wives of Windsor* was written for Elizabeth and first presented to her and her retinue at the Garter Feast in 1597, then the framing of the drama by the demanding and then benevolent monarch would be enacted in the command of the monarch that the play be written in fourteen days and by her patron's plaudits at the end.

The dux frame for *Much Ado* is more complicated (for reasons treated in examination of the imperial theme in chapter 5). In this play Prince Don Pedro of Aragon, apparently the representative of Spanish hegemony in Sicily, is welcomed as the superior of Leonato, the governor of Messina (1.1), and seems to exercise quasi-judicial authority in the early portions of the play, especially on behalf of his knight, Claudio, in condemning Claudio's beloved, Hero, for infidelity at her would-be marriage ceremony. But his authority is unjustly used to destroy an innocent. Only as he begins to recognize that misuse, repents it, and implicitly returns to Leonato the authority of Messina's governor can the lucky and ignorant constables of Messina bring before the community of the play the true criminals—Conrad, Borachio, and the Spanish villain, Don Pedro's brother. When this has been done and the substitute rulers and their clients have heard challenges to their justice and manliness, both justice and mercy can be enacted by Leonato. He henceforth performs the dux role—as the just man and the ultimately merciful man. Shakespeare may be making a topical point about Spanish hegemony in Italy with this unique division of the authority of the dux in this play (see chapter 5).

Only *Twelfth Night* lacks altogether the framing of the ruler who begins as merciless judge and ends as the renewer of the social order and of the arts of celebration, mercy, and love, and this relates to the form in which the magi or kings come to this *Twelfth Night* play (see chapter 4). It is difficult to believe that Orsino—who is endlessly self-indulgent at the beginning of the play—embodies justice at its beginning, and it is equally difficult to believe that the order offered at the end of the play includes anyone who can act as the dux in reconstituting Illyria; its reconstruction is pure miracle, related to its title and that title's feast day (see chapter 3).

At the same time that Shakespeare's dux carries the *imago dei* or the *rex imago Christi*, the sword of justice, and the oil of forgiveness or reconciliation, he also increasingly images the hidden god or *deus absconditus* that so fascinated Renaissance theology, from Luther's *Bondage of the Will* onward (see Isaiah 45:15).[23] Commonly Shakespeare's comedic dux disappears from the court or city action of the play from early on until the time when the central resolution must occur. This, of course, allows him to set the problem at the beginning and solve it at the end while adding to the myth of authority: that the ruler should not be too common or dirty himself with the plaudits of the masses, "stag[ing] himself in the [people's] eyes, / . . . relish[ing] [t] heir loud applause and *aves* vehement" (*Measure for Measure* 1.1.68–70). But more is involved. In the earlier comedies, the occultation of the ruler is a stage device that allows for a reversal of judgment: Solinus makes a draconian judgment on Egeon and then disappears from the action until he can return a redemptive judgment on him and his family at the end; Theseus does the same thing with Hermia and Lysander and the other lovers. *The Merchant of Venice* has no such disappearing duke, but if we are part of the trading community of early modern London, we know that the Venetian state and duke lie behind the very reliable commercial contracts of Venice, including "pound of flesh" contracts, and so the duke need not be present throughout. He has to return in person in act 4 to discern, with Portia, the spirit beneath Venetian contractual law. As the playwright reconfigures his pattern in the middle and later comedies, we know with increasing emphasis that the ruler is always *there*, always observing the action, observing the whole action—like Joyce's God-artist within or behind or above his creation, a benign spy.

Beginning with Leonato we start to have a representation of the idea that the ruler knows more than the others in the play. At the beginning of the play Don Pedro tries to function as the always-there leader who can arrange all loves and all reconciliations, but though he succeeds as a Cupid with Benedick, he fails as the figure of Justice, as we have already noted. It is then that Leonato takes over as the dux behind the scenes. Leonato knows his daughter is alive, knows Hero's tomb is a penitential and redemptive hoax, that the mourning forced on Claudio and company is a hoax, and that the "niece" to be married to Claudio is Hero. He knows both of the *much ado* that the fiction of death creates and the *nothing* that the staged resurrection allows, and so he can forgive and expect forgiveness. The pattern of the succeeding *As You Like It* is a little different. Duke Senior, the hidden ruler in the forest of Arden, knows of his kingdom, or presumably does, from the "many young gentlemen [who] flock to him every day" (*AYLI* 1.1.101–2), but we can only project a fantasy that he will see to the marriage rites and create a just realm after he returns to his former honor, because we see none of this in the play. In *As You Like It*, there is little of justice yet to perform in the forest since the villains of the piece, Oliver and Duke Frederick, have both been converted by the green world's magic. However, the later comedies, *Measure for Measure* and *The Tempest*, complete the pattern begun in *Much Ado* and present the leader as the fully hidden god: Vincentio is always there in Vienna as benign spy, as is Prospero on his island. We even sense that Prospero can see the whole world of his enemies around the island. The increasing occultation and presentation behind the scenes of the god-monarch in the plays written during James's period represents an aligning of the myth of the god-monarch with the understanding of the hidden God in Protestant Early Modern Europe. The fabulation also assigns benignity to James's personal interest in spying on others and his creation of an elaborate and draconian spying apparatus.[24] Foucault has shown how important to the nineteenth-century liberal construction of authority was the hiding of the all-seeing eye of the state; the same all-seeing eye was crucial in the evolution of discipline in compulsory education in the same period.[25] However, the hidden and all-seeing ruler who "providentially" constructs not only education but culture itself is also a Shakespearean Jacobean fiction.[26]

As Shakespeare's comic dux becomes the "hidden god," he also becomes the *poeta*, the maker of a secular "providence."[27] He is the equivalent of Roman comedy's wily servant who creates device after device to control the final outcome of the play (see *Twelfth Night* 2.3.144).[28] In Plautus this character, master of disguises—Pseudolus or Libanus, or whatever—commonly procures erotic or material satisfaction for his master and so gains freedom at the end of the play. In Shakespeare, the *poeta* or playmaker—Tranio for Lucentio in *Taming of the Shrew*, Puck for Oberon in *Midsummer Night's Dream* (though Oberon himself partly plans the tricks)—begins as the wily servant; but in the later plays this character type, often female, is increasingly dissociated from the trickery that defies authority. He or she is the master of the play and the playing that creates legitimate power. Portia as a *poeta* begins this movement in her playing the role of Dr. Bellario's student, who constructs judicial redemption for Antonio in *Merchant of Venice*. Rosalind continues the process by arranging the marriages that recreate the final society of the forest. In *Much Ado* the rulers themselves are the *poetae*: Claudio and Don Pedro for Benedick, Leonato for Claudio and Don Pedro; and in *All's Well* the monarch's favorite, Helena, does the same things.

Finally, the better monarchs of the late comedies, such as Vincentio and Prospero, become the *poetae* and master the tricks that really do control the outcome of the action.[29] This shift envisages more than the reconstruction of a New Comedy "game piece," for it has a political-social significance. Shakespeare's age had of course seen the virtues of dissimulation advocated in Machiavelli and practiced by Elizabeth and James, though only Shakespeare had the moxie to make the dissimulative servant-*poeta* of the Plautine tradition into the monarch as master of disguises and constructive cheats—both the monarch in his own person, in the case of Vincentio, and in his own person combined with that of his Master of the Revels, in the case of Prospero combined with Ariel. The *poeta's* play as myth or propaganda constitutes the commonwealth. It represents how dissimulative superstructure serves infrastructure while "making everybody happy." Shakespeare's royal *mythos* is perfected when the ruler becomes both dramaturge and secular providence, the source of judgment and mercy both—the "hidden god" of the plot who knows all and, increasingly, the trickster who constructs the incorporation ceremonies that bring the society of the play together in some form of happiness.

The World of the Comedic Ruled

In Early Modern paintings of the coming of the magi, such as that by Fra Angelico and Fra Filippo Lippi (fig. 3) or by Benozzo Gozzoli (fig.

FIGURE 3. Fra Angelico (1400–1455) and Fra Filippo Lippi (1406–1469), *Adoration of the Magi*, ca. 1440–60. Tempera on panel. Image © Board of Trustees, National Gallery of Art, Washington DC, Samuel H. Kress Collection.

4), the painter shows the Christ child as the central focal point of the painting surrounded by the three kings (nativity not shown in fig. 4). Great crowds attending to the marvelous birth follow them.[30]

Similarly, Early Modern portraits of kings may show them surrounded by their temporal court, by the princes of the church, and by the emblems of the third estate, their people, the three together acting as a portrait of the *res publica*.[31] The *Pelican Portrait* of Queen Elizabeth shows her with a pelican pendant, presenting her as feeding her subjects from her own sacrifice, like Christ (fig. 5).

The Marcus Gheerhaerts the Younger's 1592 Ditchley portrait shows her as monarch standing upon the counties that are her realm (fig. 6).

A somewhat similar arraying of the monarch in relation to his subjects appears in Shakespearean comedy. Beneath the dux we see the courtiers as accouterments to the duke figure, and beyond them we see the commonwealth—the city or village of Plautine New Comedy—where Shakespeare reconstructs the character types of traditional New Comedy: hero, heroine, braggart soldier, pimp, parasite, whore, eunuch, trade character, and so forth. In each play he makes up a commonwealth for his own times and theme consonant with the setting, whether Arden or Vienna or the other places. In that place he conveys the complexity and richness of its possible society. The whole commonwealth is implicitly present—guilds, courtiers, rural people in some plays, and the persons who construct the legal machinery, not just Plautus's grotesques in the street outside a Roman house.

To feel that the leader counts, we must also feel that those he governs count, though they may be figures at whom we laugh. One of the reasons we may involve ourselves less deeply in *The Comedy of*

FIGURE 4. Benozzo Gozzoli (1420–1497), *Procession of the Magus Gaspar: Wall with Lorenzo the Magnificent*, ca. 1459. Fresco. Palazzo Medici Riccardi, Florence. Scala/Art Resource, New York.

FIGURE 5. Nicholas Hilliard (attributed to), *Pelican Portrait of Queen Elizabeth I* (detail), ca. 1574. Oil on panel. © Walker Art Gallery, National Museums, Liverpool.

FIGURE 6. Marcus Gheerhaerts II (1561/62–1636), *Queen Elizabeth I*, ca. 1592. Oil on canvas. Copy of Ditchley miniature by Henry Bone. Kingston Lacy, Dorset, United Kingdom, on loan to National Portrait Gallery, London. National Trust/Art Resource, New York.

Errors than in the comedies coming after 1594 is that the characters of that comedy do not count as much for us as do those in the other comedies. We may be concerned about their welfare but not *much* concerned. We do not love them as much as we do Beatrice or hate and fear them as much as we do Don John. My colleague Stephen Buhler has told me that one of the finest *Comedy of Errors* productions of which he is aware is that by John Rattalack in 1992–93, in which memories of film comedies are invoked to give the characters density. Perhaps Shakespeare created his fusions of character types based in New Comedy to evoke a similar desire to know and engage them at some deeper level because we remember what they are fusing from the relatively flat characters of Plautine New Comedy. The characters of *Comedy of Errors* are as close as Shakespeare ever comes to Roman New Comedy characters.[32] In the later plays we care more about the ruled as we are more caught up in their loves, folly, and danger. Their commonwealths, cities, and villages come from the materials of New Comedy but with this difference: New Comedy's original types were to some degree confined by their masks, by audience expectation, and—for Renaissance audiences—by what Donatus and the Renaissance commentators had said each character type had to be, but Shakespeare's characters have a shadowlands interior that does not come from Plautus or from Freud, or even from a psychologist of his own time, such as Thomas Wright (*The Passions of the Minde in Generall*).[33] Their interior dimension partly comes from us, especially if we have been raised on New Comedy in grammar school, on Latin theater, and on some New Comedy–based or *commedia dell'arte*–based vernacular theater. Commedia dell'arte was improvisational theater encountered by English tourists in Italy and imported in Shakespeare's time for a number of performances in England (see discussion in Resources section, this chapter). The depth of the characters comes from our watching the combining of "masks" and our projecting what must lie behind these combinations.[34] If we are Early Modern spectators, we half create many of Shakespeare's comic characters. We still do some of this in the twenty-first century, and that is why they have always been so labile in production.

Shakespeare in his own time was seen as doing New Comedy in its Roman manifestation. This is apparent in Meres's 1598 comments in *Palladis Tamia*: "As *Plautus* and *Seneca* are accounted the best for Comedy and Tragedy among the Latines: so *Shakespeare* among y' English is the most excellent in both kinds for the stage; for Comedy, witnes his *Ge'tleme' of Verona*, his *Errors*, his *Love labours lost*, his *Love labours wonne*, his *Midsummer night dreame*, & his *Merchant of Venice*."[35] John Manningham's 1602 comparison of *Twelfth Night* to the *Menaechmi* or *The Comedy of Errors* repeats the same generic insight.[36] And it appears in the 1609 prefatory epistle to *Troilus and Cressida* found in the second state of the 1609 quarto.[37] Jonson's comment quoted at the beginning of this chapter is only the last of a line.

That Shakespeare knew not only New Comedy plays but New Comedy and commedia dell'arte theory about character types is evident from some of his labels for his dramatis personae, labels that could be English translations from the lists of characters in Latin editions of Plautus or Terence: servants, courtesans, schoolmasters, pedants, pedagogues, old men, and merchants.[38] It is as if whoever wrote the dramatis personae lists wished us to remember that we are dealing with a version of Roman comedy. Again consider Jaques's "All the world's a stage" speech, naming both the grotesque and nongrotesque characters of New Comedy as central in the stagecraft of life: nurse, pedagogue, adolescent lover and "mistress," braggart soldier, advocate or "justice," and *senex*:

> JAQUES: All the world's a stage,
> And all the men and women merely players.
> They have their exits and their entrances,
> And one man in his time plays many parts,
> His acts being seven ages. At first the infant,
> Mewling and puking in the *nurse's* arms.
> Then the whining *schoolboy* . . . .
> . . . And then the *lover*,
> Sighing like furnace, with a woeful ballad
> Made to his mistress' eyebrow. Then, a *soldier*,

Full of strange oaths, and bearded like the pard,
Jealous in honour, sudden, and quick in quarrel,
Seeking the bubble reputation
Even in the cannon's mouth. And then the *justice*,
In fair round belly with good capon lined,
    . . . . The sixth age shifts
Into the lean and slippered *pantaloon*,
With spectacles on nose and pouch on side,
His youthful hose, well saved, a world too wide
For his shrunk shank . . . . Last scene of all,
That ends this strange, eventful history,
Is second childishness and mere oblivion,
Sans teeth, sans eyes, sans taste, sans everything.
 (*AYLI* 2.7.138–65; italics mine)[39]

Six New Comedy characters appear here. The schoolboy will, of course, meet the endlessly boring *paedagogus* when he reaches school.

But no dux appears in Jaques's list. Jaques does not care for Duke Senior or for the compromises of good rule that produce the comedic outcome. Because he does not care for rule with its messiness and contradictions, at the end of the play he leaves the court and society for the contemplative cave. But while he is in the exiled court and its related society, he—the incongruous melancholic of the play—is given the role of comedy's (and satire's) theorist, explaining the course of our life's playacting as taking us each on our disgusting downward trek (recall that Orlando has just told him of the pure love of Adam, the old man, one overcome not by childishness and oblivion but by age and the hunger created by his sacrifice for Orlando).[40] The nurse or *nutrix* of New Comedy and the *paedagogus* or schoolmaster rear us to adolescence.[41] We become in turn the *adolescens* or lover, the *miles gloriosus* or soldier, and the *advocatus* or justice.[42] And then we become the *senex* or pantaloon until, according to Jaques, our play ends in senile oblivion.[43]

For the melancholy comedic poseur, who wants to be both fool and satirist and does not quite succeed at either, the parade of comedy's characters marches to dirge music and no promise of marriage comes at the end.[44] But of course in the actual plays, the promises of marriage and betrothals do come as the biological and social antidote to the end of human life—"sans teeth, sans eyes, sans taste, sans everything" (*AYLI* 2.7.165). In short, though Jaques has the stock characters right, he does not have the comic story's ending quite right, or perhaps better, he has it right for the individual but not for the community or the species. Comedy celebrates the latter two.

Elsewhere Shakespeare refers to the New Comedy types rather directly: Dr. Pinch in *Comedy of Errors* is called a "Schoole-master" or pedagogue in a stage direction left in at 4.4.36, though he does not teach in this play. In *Love's Labour's Lost*, Biron makes of list of common commedia dell'arte and New Comedy types in protesting the tricks of the ladies of France on Navarre's court:

> BIRON: I see the trick on't. Here was a consent,
> Knowing aforehand of our merriment,
> To dash it like a Christmas comedy.
> Some carry-tale, some please-man, some slight zany,
> Some mumble-news, some trencher-knight, some Dick
> That smiles his cheek in years, and knows the trick
> To make my lady laugh when she's disposed,
> Told our intents before ... (5.2.460–67)

Biron's characters come either from New Comedy, or from commedia dell'arte, or both.[45] The tale-bearer and mumble-news are the comic messenger servants; the please-man is a parasite, as is the trencher knight; the zany is the clownish servant like Feste, a kind of commedia dell'arte version of the *poeta;* and the Dick who shows his years is the *pantalone* or *senex*.[46] For Biron all these comic grotesques are rolled into one in the person of the supposed tattler who told on the males of the court. Again Biron mentions the masks in his introduction of the players who are to play the worthies in *Love's Labour's Lost*: "The pedant, the braggart, the hedge-priest, the fool, and the boy" (5.2.536). At least the pedant and the braggart come from New Comedy as well as commedia dell'arte.

Some critics and scholars have wished to oppose Shakespeare's New Comedy stock characters to his commedia dell'arte ones, but this opposition seems unnecessary from the point of view of literary genetics since learned comedy so heavily influenced the commedia.[47] It is futile to distinguish the lists of stock characters that dominate New Comedy from those that dominate commedia. The standard characters of the commedia dell'arte overlap those of New Comedy: the *pantalone* is like the *senex*—the old man who is a greedy merchant, an overprotective father, a silly guardian.[48] The *dottori*—the doctor-lawyer-pedant types of the commedia dell'arte—are like the New Comedy pedagogues and vocational types, including doctors, lawyers, and craftspeople; the *capitano*, a cowardly braggart soldier, is like the braggart soldier of New Comedy; the *zanni* or bright and stupid servants have their parallels in the servants and fools in New Comedy, as do the female commedia servants. The *innamorate* and *innamorati*, the groups of lovers in commedia, had their counterparts in the various young women and their adolescent lovers in New Comedy.[49] The typology of stock vocations and stereotypical actions would have established itself soon enough after the beginning of the play for those who had no experience of Roman comedy or no sight of Italian improvisational playing. Those who had experience of the Italian players' groups would at some level have said to themselves, "Yes, we know this; we know more or less what is coming." For those who had read Plautus and Terence in grammar school, the same sorts of expectations would have been raised and fulfilled, and for many of the more educated and theatrically active of Shakespeare's audience, both traditions would have fused, as they had in Italy, in forming expectations to be confirmed *and* overthrown.[50]

If we were to have themes in symphonies without variations, we would have poor music indeed. We expect variation on the themes set by the comic masks. Yet Shakespeare, while moving the plays from the "domesticall" to the "commonweal," allows himself a flexibility in choosing his cast of characters that comic theory would not have allowed him. Almost all of the comedies include not only the dux but also aristocrats and pseudo-aristocrats not generally found in Roman comedy. They include shepherds and rural people in the cases of *As You Like It* and *The Winter's Tale*. There are soldiers or sea warriors who are not braggarts at core, such as Benedick in *Much Ado* or Sebastian and Antonio in *Twelfth Night*. There are the guild groups (craftsmen are barely mentioned in the Roman comedies)—the goldsmith in *Comedy of Errors*, the "confraternity" of guildsmen in *A Midsummer Night's Dream*, the "mysteries" of the executioners, whores, and pimps as entrepreneurs in *Measure for Measure*. Furthermore, Shakespeare gives considerably more emphasis than do the Romans to merchants and to the personages who make up the machinery of law, classes that dominated Early Modern London and made it a burgeoning capital city. Thus the range of civil society is there, stylized and transfigured, especially if one looks across the comedies. We are not faced only with Serlio's nondescript bourgeoisie.

Though Shakespeare knew the character stereotype building blocks from which one could construct the New Comedy's domestic unit, he does not often construct with such blocks taken integrally. After *The Comedy of Errors*, almost every comic character who is private and "domesticall" becomes, through the passage of the play, a fusion of several comic masks, a pastiche that invites us to inspect the inwardness of the character. They are, in the idiom of the still useful work of the Dutch psychotherapist J. H. Van den Berg, a pastiche of hidden selves, an enactment of differing roles for different social contexts beneath which may or may not lie a deeper self. Shakespeare does not give us pictures of "a *niggardly* Demea, of a *crafty* Davus, of a *flattering* Gnato, of a *vain-glorious* Thraso." He does not give us cardboard. (In teaching Shakespeare's comedies to undergraduates, I have had them read some Plautus or Donatus on Terence or Duckworth on Roman comedy and then asked them to classify the Shakespearean characters in terms of New Comedy standard masks. They almost always resort to fusions.)[51]

To give some examples: In *Twelfth Night*, Viola is a *puella* or marriageable woman of the comedy. She also pretends to be—and is, in some senses—the New Comedy plot's eunuch when she assumes male clothing as a eunuch and woos and does not woo Olivia (*TN* 1.2.52).[52] In the same play Sir Toby is the braggart soldier demonstrating the tricks of court-dancing and fierce dueling, but he is also the parasite living off Sir Andrew and Olivia.[53] Maria is the *poeta*, the wily servant, always in classical comedy a male, but she is also the female servant or *ancilla* and perhaps the *meretrix*.[54] After *The Comedy of Errors*, Shakespeare commonly constructs New Comedy characters who wear at least two of the masks of New Comedy or commedia dell'arte, the mask of their basic stage identity and that of one or more assumed identities that permit them to negotiate their way in a socially and sometimes physically unsafe world. It is not only in tragedy that improvisation is the route to power for the power seekers and to survival for the powerless. In comedy, in the course of improvisation, the ingenious characters often enact narratives that belong to other masks to protect themselves *and* to explore the new and strange social world that they confront when they come to Ephesus, Pisa, the Athenian forest, Arden, or wherever.

Shakespeare would almost surely have known of the masks, as Plautus's and Terence's plays refer to them (Plautus, *Amphitruo*, 458ff.; *Captivi*, 39; Terence, *Persa*, 783, *Eunuchus*, 26, 32, 35).[55] Robertellus in Shakespeare's time knew that the Roman comic actors wore masks, and perhaps everyone who studied comedy knew this.[56] Certainly Shakespeare offers us a number of scenes in which characters wear facial disguises at, for example, masked balls. However, for him, as comic constructor controlled by the conventions of the stage in London and without access to the masks (*persona* or *imago*) of Roman comedy, the tool equivalent to the standard mask is the disguise. He can give us the appearance of woman as man, ruler as cleric, servant as master, and the rest: "one man (or woman) in his/her time plays many parts." Thus, the playwright makes the issues of self and self-presentation in life into the multiple masks of each person in the drama. But the disguise permits many selves and many roles to make up the complex self, whereas the New Comedy mask or character type appears in Early Modern criticism as permitting only one stereotypic selfhood.

To give an example from one set of disguises or masks, consider the women of the comedies who are the sought-after *puella*-types—Hermia, Rosalind, Viola, Beatrice, perhaps even Isabella. Each in some scenes wears the brazen, witty mask of the Roman *meretrix* to discover lovers and husbands who will meet her own and society's needs.[57] Unlike the *puellae* of the Roman comedies, who are their chief female love interests and endlessly passive, Shakespeare's heroines go after their men with all the flirtatious and witty inveiglement skills of the Roman whore, especially when they are in male clothing or outside the standard family authority structures.[58] Often they have been rejected by their fathers or surrogate parents (e.g., Duke Frederick's rejection of Rosalind) or become orphans (apparently Beatrice's situation). Sometimes they believe that accident or religious choice has lost them the protections of dowry, family advice, and family property.[59] Those who have and accept parental protections in the comedies generally find an easily arranged betrothal and prospective marriage but not one in which personal desire and social expectation meet fully. The deepest female lovers are the least protected ones. Think of Kate, Hermia, Portia, Beatrice, Rosalind, Viola, and both of Shakespeare's Helenas in *Midsummer Night's Dream* and *All's Well*. Each is a woman of the margins. All are women who flirt, pretending to play the whore or the cuckolding wife of commedia dell'arte to gain a man. Sometimes they also wish to administer an Ovidian remedy for hot love to their suitors. Rosalind is an especially vivid example of this fusion when, as a boy playing a woman disguised as a boy, she promises to physic Orlando's love-sickness (3.2.355–86), to make him beholden to his "wives" for his snails horns (4.1.45–55), and at the same time to give him all of the torments that Ovid's remedies of love promise and more—to be jealous, clamorous, new-fangled, giddy, quick-weeping, and hyena-laughing (4.1.124–33).[60] Contemporary criticism may be correct. Shakespeare's construction of the "new woman" may be occasioned by a "feminism" of sorts, but its immediate root is his fusion of the *meretrix* and *puella* into a "woman" who relies on the strength of the boy actor in repartee to achieve her desire.[61] "She" can choose her male.

The Betrothal/Marriage Conclusion and Symbolic Marriage

New Comedy, at its most basic, appeals to what sociobiologists speak of as our desire to transmit our genes. Shakespeare's audience would not have put the matter in this way. Theologians would have spoken of the need that the human race has to convert concupiscence into a socially productive motion through marriage and the birth of children. Perhaps we could say, more neutrally, that the human race watches the infinite endless nothings that end in romance and coupling that populate our popular stage, and have done so perdurably since Shakespeare's time, to encourage itself in the view that life will go on. As already suggested in this chapter, we do not care for the comedies' individual characters alone but for their integrated and interdependent worlds, whether composed of the bawds and whores of *Measure for Measure*, the imported courtiers and local exploited rural people of *As You Like It*, the country estate people of *Twelfth Night*, or the Athenians of *Midsummer Night's Dream*. Shakespeare's comic landscapes take us to a "scene"—the city in *Measure for Measure*, *Much Ado*, and *Comedy of Errors*, the court or courts in *Midsummer Night's Dream* and *All's Well*, the city and the margin of the country in *As You Like It* and *Winter's Tale*. *Merchant of Venice* moves between the city and the country estate, as do *Merry Wives of Windsor*, with its implicit court frame, and *The Tempest*, with its remembered Milan and its island. Yet in these plays there is a blocking out of four groups of people circling about the issue of coupling that tells us we are close to a significant social world: (1) the ruler, (2) the courtiers or functionaries who administer the details of rule, (3) the lovers, and (4) the grotesques.

The lovers are the central group, caught between grotesquery and the establishment of a new generational stability, between rule and license, between frigidity and sexual abandon, and between neurotic melancholy and fruitless sanguinity. Conventionally, in Shakespearean comedy, it is the job of the ruler and his agents to assist society to reform or reject the grotesques. He must assist the lovers to achieve a marriage that promises social continuation and individual satisfaction. After *The Comedy of Errors*, the ruler is equipped to assist in social reconstruction by virtue of having reconstructed himself. He is like Theseus in Chaucer's *Knight's Tale*, who can say, "Who may been a fool, but if he love?" (A, 1799). He sees the lovers in his world foolishly fighting, but he then confesses that he was once such a lover. Similarly,

Shakespeare's rulers have in them the fool who has once loved and who has learned from the pains of misdirected love. The Theseus of *Midsummer Night's Dream* has just wooed and won Hippolita, doing her injuries like those the lovers of the play do each other. The mention of his tragic love for and abandonment of Ariadne (*MND* 2.1.80) suggests he has not fully escaped the thorns and briars of the woods that tear the mechanicals or guildsmen and the Athenian lovers (3.2.29; 3.3.31). He knows from his own experience that one form of seething-brain madness belongs to love (5.1.4). Again, at the level of the "epic" machinery of the play, where the gods or fairies play, the pattern of the construction of a leader who has learned repeats itself. Oberon tries to injure Titania as the queen and leader of the fairies by taking away her changeling boy. His first dominative efforts lead only to wrangling. He later finds that comic self-exposure, prompted by Love-in-Idleness, restores her to him and apparently makes the issue of the boy insignificant. A similar comic self-exposure in the woods that the lovers can only half-remember also brings them (4.1.138–95) to each other when aided by "Diane's bud."

The middle comedies' leaders are leaders not by virtue of stipulated power only but also by virtue of learning the ways of the heart. In *As You Like It*, Duke Senior has failed to defend his dukedom effectively on his first go with his brother, Duke Frederick, and lacks a strong proprietary sense that he "owns" his dukedom. He can therefore rule a modified golden age where, for his courtiers, the proprietary sense is lacking. They seem to share all things, including the animals they hunt and the food they eat. Against the background of this general brotherhood, Duke Senior can preside over the masque of Hymen, where his daughter as magician can bring in Hymen to commit the lovers of the play to marriage to each other.

In *Much Ado*, Leonato's plodding wit and wisdom in matters of the heart trains him for both the Hero crisis and the Beatrice game. *Measure for Measure*'s Vincentio, as the duke of Vienna, has by his own mouth been the Lord of Misrule or Carnival and, as Friar Lodovick, he sees what Angelo's perpetual Lent can do to a city. Hence his final judgment can mediate between extremes that he has created. Prospero has lost his wife, and then he forfeits Milan through his love of the contemplative life. However, he learns the tools both to recover it and to rule whoever would destroy him. In short, Shakespeare's comic dux is generally a man "tempted in all points" in matters of the heart, like his subjects, fallen in many of these points, yet now moving toward integration and, therefore, prepared to preside over the integration of his community in the symbology of marriage.

Although not all New Comedy ends with a betrothal/marriage or reconstitution of a family, or appearance of these, Shakespeare chose this as his preferred way.[62] He points to this in his elisions. Jaques's comedy of the seven ages does not end with marriages for reasons that I have explained. When Biron, near the end of *Love's Labour's Lost*, learns of the corporeal-works-of-mercy penance imposed on the academy of Navarre by the ladies of France, he says:

BIRON: Our wooing doth not end like an old play.
Jack hath not Jill. These ladies' courtesy
Might well have made our sport a comedy.
KING: Come, sir, it wants a twelvemonth an' a day,
And then 'twill end. (5.2.851–54)

The works of charity will cut off all courtship and marriage for a year (5.2.818ff.), and so, defamiliarizing generic convention, Shakespeare has Biron call attention to how the wooing in old plays, old comedies—presumably Roman New Comedies—ends. In them, *Jack has Jill.* This is of course a half-truth. Many New Comedy plays, especially plays by Plautus, do not end in a marriage.[63] But it is truth enough for Biron and enables him to contrast with the conventional New Comedy betrothal or marriage conclusion the death's head that appears at the end of this play—its announcing of the death of the King of France, its prescinding from courtship or marriage for a year, and its hospital charge.

As a matter of fact, the comedy-without-betrothal or marriage form of defamiliarizing in *Love's Labour's Lost* is the only one of that type that Shakespeare creates, and this ending may have been "corrected" by the ending of the lost *Love's Labour's Won*. At least the title of the latter suggests as much. All of Shakespeare's other comedies end either with the reconstitution of a family and marriage broken within the play, or at some previous time, or with the promise of a new marriage and family created between the young woman (*puella*) and the candidate boy or man (*adolescens*). The marriage promise also comes often to their friends or their servants. Shakespeare's solution to the social dislocation of the society of comedy is always the prospect of betrothal and marriage and more betrothal and marriage, accompanied by the state's or the dux's forgiving judgment on everyone else, or almost everyone else.[64] The marriages-to-be are not the familiar Plautine marriages but provide us with as clear an understanding of where the direction to wholeness might lie as does the service to the dying at the end of *Love's Labour's Lost*. Betrothals and the marriages anticipated are an emblematic statement of the spiritual and intellectual forces that will resolve the tension created in the love action, the turn and counterturn of the play, to use Terentian five-act terms.

Early Modern marriage is a complex phenomenon.[65] It is a system for the protection and control of biological inheritance, for the determination of land use, for the transmission or consolidation of property rights, for providing for the welfare of vulnerable members of society, and for the creation or manufacture of many of the products requisite for living: food, clothing, and revised shelter. The family in Shakespeare's time is, at some levels of society, the massive extended family of medieval Europe: grandparents, uncles and aunts and their families, parents, children, nurses and pedagogues, servants, field hands in the country, apprentices in town, plus any number of other dependents and short- or long-term guests. It is the fundamental unit of governance. At the same time, with the rise of the "middle class," mercantile capitalism, and city life centered in Calvinistic or other radical reforming Protestant tenets, a more nucleated family appears in the urban social sectors. Social centers outside the extended family, such as the guild and joint stock company, also become important.

Shakespeare's families come in all shapes and sizes. Consider the difference between the household of Leontes in Messina, with its adult offspring, servants, guests, priest, and laborers in the vocations, and that of Shylock, which appears to include only his daughter Jessica and servants. Theseus's *Midsummer Night's Dream* household may be composed only of himself, Hippolita, and Philostrate. The first stage direction in act 1, scene 1, gives us these three and adds "and others," who may or may not be from the household. Perhaps Theseus's household is all of the characters in the play save the guildsmen. He furnishes the other two couples with the nuptial entertainment, marries with them (*MND* 4.2.15–17), and has them stay at his place in the postnuptial fortnight (*MND* 5.1.340–53). Portia's household is Belmont, apparently with its servants and visitors, but what of Antonio's household? Is there one? What are we to make of the families in *As You Like It?* Some members of families envisage fratricide and reject the elderly. Despite Corin and Sylvius's traditional manorial responsibilities, their first landlord seeks to sell the land out from under them. Dynastic marriage such as that proposed for Ferdinand and Miranda lays on them a differing set of responsibilities from that known by mere landlords, as Gaunt makes clear in *Richard II* (2.1).[66] To understand what Shakespearean betrothal and marriage mean at the simplest social and infrastructural level one has to understand what it is marriage into—what sort of household is constructed in the putative marriage—and this varies from play to play. Yet whatever the marriage is, it is not the creation of a "relationship" in any sense conceptualized by the clichés of today's media, where the primary consideration is whether the unique sexual and personal identities of the proposed partners are served. It is the creation of a new society.

Even as Renaissance marriage is a complex and multiform social institution, it also carries complex symbology. That melancholy endeavors to destroy love and the aesthetic sense is implicit in Simon Vouet's 1627 painting of *Father Time Overcome by Love, Hope, and Beauty* (figure 7 is his 1646 version, with a slightly different title). Father Time is Saturn or melancholy, and his conquerors in the painting are Love, in the form of the seeing or celestial Cupid, a garlanded Hope, and Venus as Beauty. In the 1646 version the gods are presided over by angelic appearing figures, Fame and Fortune.

FIGURE 7. Simon Vouet (1590–1649), *Saturn Vanquished by Amor, Venus, and Hope*, ca. 1645–46. Oil on canvas. Photo by Gérard Blot. Musée du Berry, Bourges, France. Réunion des Musées Nationaux/Art Resource, New York.

As the institution in which sexual satisfaction is allowed, marriage was also considered a medical answer to melancholy.[67] The deepest melancholics in Shakespeare's comedies are not married: consider Jaques, Malvolio, and Don John the Bastard. Alternatively, they are forced into marriage as Angelo is. If Shylock is to be considered a melancholic, he follows the rule though he has been married. He is bitter and angry, and he is not presented as knowing love save when he remembers Leah's ring stolen by Jessica and traded for a monkey (3.1.100–102).

Religious differences also reinforce the emblemology of betrothal and marriage. In *Twelfth Night*, Shakespeare answers the Puritan enemies of the theater, who hold sway on the other side of the Thames in the city of London, by celebrating the marriage institution that they also uphold as sacred and by making it fundamental to the comic conclusion while presenting their melancholy ways as inimical to it. The betrothal/marriage conclusion may also answer Catholic polemics of the time. Catholic apologists accused Protestants of ignoring the apostolic counsels to perfection and celibacy, while Protestant polemicists accused Catholics of requiring clergy and people in the regular orders to submit to a discipline that had to be a gift of grace, given to some and not to others.[68] In the Protestant world, one could not legitimately compel celibacy if the grace or gift had not been given, and celibate people did not live in monastic houses but served in the community or lived with their extended families as bachelor uncles and aunts. It is a sign of the foolishness of Theseus in act 1 of *A Midsummer Night's Dream* that he tries to compel Hermia to become a celibate nun who sings to the "cold fruitless moon" (1.1.73), contrary to any vocation on her part. Marriage in Protestant eyes was not a lesser thing than celibacy, and it was regarded as preferable to concubinage.

When Shakespeare represents the challenge of celibacy, he commonly presents it as not a good prospect and often forced by authority, as Protestant polemicists also presented it. It is the route offered to and ultimately rejected by Kate, Hermia, the princes of Navarre, Beatrice, Olivia, and Isabella. Only for the melancholy, saturnine Jaques, among the principals in a play, is the contemplative cave offered as a good choice. The cave for Jaques must have to do with the transformation of his bitterness and despair into unitive detachment, as it does for Spenser's Red Cross Knight when he goes from the Cave of Despair to the Mountain of Contemplation or as the various aspects of Dürer's *Melancholia* attest.[69]

Marriage gets other symbolic resonances that have little to do with religious divisions, many of them used in court ceremonies and masques. Shakespeare's comedies almost always end with a set piece that endows the marriage or betrothal with a resonance beyond what appears on the surface.[70] Early Modern English marriage may be a metaphor for all sorts of nonsexual binding relationships. The monarch is married to the kingdom.[71] The bishop is married to the diocese, and the nun to God in the Catholic metaphor (as much *Measure for Measure* criticism observes).[72] In scriptural exegesis, the soul and God are married in the Song of Songs. Even the Calvinistic Geneva Bible makes the groom of that book into Christ and the bride into the faithful soul or the church.[73] Reason and passion, Adam and Eve, are married (reason controlling passion) when the interior spousal is done correctly. The scriptures contain "historical" marriages that have a figurative overtone in the scriptures themselves or were made to have such an overtone by the exegetes. Jacob's wives are emblems. Dimmed-eyed Leah represents the active life and the seeing Rachel the contemplative in Michelangelo's statues of them in San Pietro in Vincoli, Rome. Among the prophets, Hosea stands for God, and Gomer the Harlot, his wife, stands for Israel. Hagar is the Old Law and Sarah the New in St. Paul (Gal. 4:21–31). Early Modern Platonic theorists of love could conceptualize various levels of love from their study of Ficino's *Commentary on the Symposium*: the Uranian Venus being the highest and leading to contemplative love, the *Venus Vulgaris* being the reproductive Venus that leads on the one hand to loyal reproductive marriage and on the other to illicit love. Ficino also recognizes reciprocal love and unrequited love as varieties of Venus's action.[74] Similarly Harington, explaining *Orlando Furioso*, could postulate that four similar, differentiated kinds of love are represented in Angelica, Doralyce, Olympia, and Bradamante.[75] Finally, rafts of emblem books provide possible figurative meanings for marriage or for marriage situations.

Shakespeare develops a number of these or other emblematic or figurative interpretations of marriage in the comedies, often in a set speech or set symbolic scene at the end of the play. For example, at the end of *The Taming of the Shrew*, Kate turns the idea of the monarch's being married to the realm on its head by making the private and domestic husband into the monarch and the wife into the subject. She, at that time, turns the kaleidoscope of the play's narrative so that the pieces fall together in a new way, opening up the possibility that *Shrew* is primarily about rulership, about the art of creating devices and showings to redirect the Kates and Slys of the world:

> KATHERINE: Thy husband is thy lord, thy life, thy keeper,
> Thy head, thy sovereign, one that cares for thee,
> And for thy maintenance commits his body
> To painful labour both by sea and land,
> To watch the night in storms, the day in cold,
> Whilst thou liest warm at home, secure and safe,
> And craves no other tribute at thy hands
> But love, fair looks, and true obedience,
> Too little payment for so great a debt.
> Such duty as the subject owes the prince,
> Even such a woman oweth to her husband,
> And when she is froward, peevish, sullen, sour,
> And not obedient to his honest will,
> What is she but a foul contending rebel,
> And graceless traitor to her loving lord? (5.2.150–64)

The play that comes before this speech then becomes much more a play about passion and the governance of it in all of life and belongs before Christopher Sly as a silly drunken rebel but also before the silly Warwick lord who exploits Sly with his paintings and with devices he presents to deceive Sly into believing he is a Rip van Winkle lord. If the Griselda whom Walter abuses is made to be the symbol of the faithful soul, and Walter is a similitude for the testing God in Chaucer, then who is Kate?[76] The Kate who is a "second Grissel" (*TS* 2.1.284–88), whom Petruchio abuses, trains, and educates, can likewise, at the end, make herself and all "wives" emblems of the duties of the subject in a hierarchical society (though not without a parallel critique of the madness of coercive rulers cast in the mold of Petruchio at his worst).[77]

The Merchant of Venice ends with another set piece that resolves its tensions—the symbolic ring scene casting all the previous commercial and amorous covenanting into a shadow. Nerissa calls for the ring she gave to Graziano and, playing the page, demanded back after the court scene in Venice. The ring bears the motto "Love me and leave me not" (*MV* 5.1.149). Portia calls for what she has given to Bassanio (who supposedly has chosen to hazard all he has for Portia), but he has given it away to the mysterious lawyer who rescued his friend, Antonio. This ring supposedly contains a mysterious power and symbology from the person who gave it, a power and symbology that must be tied up with the act of complete sacrifice. Portia gave the ring with the statement that it symbolizes her giving Bassanio "this house, these servants, and this same myself" (*MV* 3.2.170). The women's giving of their rings reverses the symbolic movement of the conventional marriage ring in the 1558 *Book of Common Prayer*, where the husband's giving of the ring to his wife signifies the man's giving of his body and his worldly goods for his and his spouse's common reception of a "blessyng" on "thys man and this woman": "[W]e blesse [them] in thy name, that as Isaac and Rebecca lyved faithfully together: So these persons may surely performe and kepe the vow and covenaunt betwixte them made, wherof this ring geven, and received, is a token and pledge, and may ever remain in perfect love and peace together."[78]

Significantly, Shakespeare's marriage-symbolism scene follows the scene in which the women of Belmont play men's roles in the Venetian court and teach justice how to sit in a mercy seat. It shows how women are necessary to the full creation of either justice or love, something not explicit in the marriage ceremony. And finally, the ring scene itself is full of threats of female infidelity from Nerissa and Portia, threats that mimic male fears of female infidelity deriving from the commonness of male infidelity. When the women have fully exposed their husbands' failure to keep their ring oaths, they provide to them the same sort of unconstrained "quality of mercy" that they have extracted from the Venetian court, and they then show their husbands and the world of the play what a true covenant or contract is, carried even to risking one's life.

Perhaps the most complex symbolic betrothal/marriage, one that appears to represent four levels of love similar to those in Ficino or in *Orlando Furioso*, comes at the end of *As You Like It*. The set piece of the masque of Hymen has seemed contrived to many critics; Shapiro, who is generally brilliant on *As You Like It*, calls the masque of Hymen "over the top," an unnecessary divine intervention, and a gesture in the direction of musical comedy.[79] But Hymen is understandable if we accept Rosalind's claim that she is a magician and, like many magicians placed in a masque context, the presenter of the masque.[80] Magicians or their familiars can call down the gods; that is, the planetary powers or spirits. Prospero does this does in the marriage masque of Juno, Iris and Ceres in *The Tempest*. In *As You Like It*, Rosalind creates the masque of Hymen/Juno to embody Uranian love and celebrate its role in her betrothal and forthcoming marriage. Her love for Orlando is the highest love in Ficino's *Commentary on the Symposium* and in conventional Platonic treatises on love. Hymen's blessing that "no cross shall part" Rosalind and Orlando (*AYLI* 5.4.120) points to a love that is cruciform and transcendent in its care for the other's good. Further Jaques's blessing on the same prospective union—saying to Orlando that his "true faith doth merit" Rosalind's love—points to faith and not just fidelity (5.4.177). If this interpretation of Hymen is correct, then we may expect to find the conventional lower forms of love defined in the Renaissance Platonic treatises represented in the other marriages in *As You Like It*: in Oliver's and Celia's "heart in heart" love (5.4.121), a reflection of the nobler version of the *Venus Vulgaris* of reproductive love; in Touchstone and Audrey's relationship, the rutting and sluttish version of the same Venus; and, in Silvius's love for Phoebe, Ficino's unrequited love, which goes out and is not returned. Jaques's predictions about the loves reinforce Hymen's blessings: to Oliver, ordinary land and love; to Touchstone, wrangling; and to Silvius, a long and deserved bed that suggests rest more than requited love (5.4.173–82). The plot leading up to this final celebration is then a celebration of movement toward the perfect octave of loves. The lower notes of lust and the higher notes of the higher love now harmoniously blend in the hand-fasting of the eight hands of the four couples (5.4.118). The heavenly mirth announced by Hymen celebrates a making even of earthly things that is explicitly said to "atone," to be an "at-one-ment" together, that reconstructs the little community and makes all of the satiric and comic thrusts in the earlier parts of the play partial and fragmentary (5.4.97–100).

To conclude with some observations on seeing the plays: the important things for the viewer of Shakespearean comedy to ask are: (1) What endows the ruler—with his initial failures and his often unpredictable and unwarranted movement toward mercy—with comic or redemptive possibilities for his particular society? (2) What are the comic difficulties and conflicts of "the society of the ruled," concealed beneath its members' multiple comic masks, and how do these stand in the way of the society's forming a decent passage to the future? (3) How do the ruler's final judgment and forgiveness scene and the lovers' final betrothal and/or marriage restoration scene act as a symbolic unit to legitimize the ruler's actions and renew the society of the play? The final scenes are generally constructed so as to provide the sense that monarchy can work, that the social system can be redemptive, and that a reconstructive "marriage" and mercy may be at hand. They tell us that what is can be transformed to what ought to be—at least in part.

Resources on Shakespearean Comic Form

The best way to gain a sense of the patterns of New Comedy in Roman times and in the Renaissance up until Shakespeare is by reading as much Plautus and Terence as possible—at the very least Plautus's *Menaechmi*, one or two other plays by Plautus, and one double-plot comedy by Terence. New Comedy criticism and glosses were plentiful in the Early Modern period, beginning with the editions of Terence that included the commentary of the fourth-century Roman grammarian Donatus.

Unfortunately this commentary has not been translated save in part by Michael Hilger in a doctoral dissertation, "Rhetoric of Comedy."[81] Other commentaries created by Renaissance scholars and included in an edition of Terence and Plautus are listed and summarized in Marvin Herrick's *Comic Theory in the Sixteenth Century*.

Much of the understanding of comedy and New Comedy in Shakespeare's time is derived from short remarks about comedy in Aristotle's *Poetics* and in Servius's Roman commentary on Virgil's *Aeneid*. One significant commentary on classical comedy, partly growing out of Aristotle, is Robertellus's "On Comedy," a more learned version of what comedy is than Shakespeare is likely to have found useful.

The English theoreticians of comedy are Thomas Lodge, Sir Philip Sidney, and Ben Jonson, cited in this chapter and in chapter 1. In addition, although Thomas Heywood's *Apology for Actors* (1612) appeared late in Shakespeare's career, it contains many good insights from a practicing playwright.[82] Jonson is unique in relying less on New Comedy and its theory than do the other writers of comedy. He knew Aristophanes and his comic sweep, and he was clearly influenced by the new Aristotelian theoreticians of comedy, who wanted a comedy to take place in one action (no double plot), one place, and one day and night. It is the more remarkable that he declared Shakespeare to be the greatest.

The traditions of Italian learned comedy (*commedia erudita*) and Italian popular comedy (*commedia dell'arte*) certainly form part of the gestalt of what many in Shakespeare's audience brought to the theater. These are traditions to which he plays by naming some of his characters after commedia dell'arte types, such as the pantaloon, zany, and doctor. Even if one discounts the possibility that Shakespeare spent some time in Italy, commedia dell'arte troupes did go about in England from time to time, and many Italians were in London for trade and other purposes. Will Kemp, who played big comic roles in Shakespeare's plays up until 1599, apparently knew something about commedia dell'arte.[83] And although Shakespeare did not use stereotypical masks as did the commedia, save in scenes that are explicitly masked festival scenes, he recognizes the role of improvisation in his plays. Since a large number of paintings and sketches of commedia dell'arte performances from Shakespeare's period exist, most of them showing public square and improvised settings with a minimum of stage apparatus, these may assist us in thinking about how Shakespeare's comedies might have been staged.

Commedia dell'arte was improvisational drama put on by traveling companies of professionals who worked with a more or less set plot or *scenario*. The play was not written out, and the scenario allowed the actors to make things up as they went along. Giacomo Oreglia's *The Commedia dell'Arte* contains scenarios for many Early Modern plays, accounts and pictures of the character stereotypes and of the companies, and pictures of a variety of characters and scenes from the plays.[84] Another useful source of similar information is Pierre Louis Duchartre's *The Italian Comedy*.[85] Also wonderfully helpful is K. M. Lea's two-volume *Italian Popular Comedy*.[86] Two other books that are helpful are Leo Salingar, *Shakespeare and the Tradition of Comedy*, and Louise George Clubb's *Italian Drama in Shakespeare's Time*.[87]

One may gain some understanding of what Shakespeare does with comedy by producing a play like *Comedy of Errors* in the appropriate Roman masks or by doing a later play in the appropriate commedia dell'arte masks, just to see what moving the production in those directions does. One production of *The Taming of the Shrew* that uses many commedia production conventions—though not all of the masks and, unfortunately, without the Christopher Sly framework—is the San Francisco American Conservatory Theater's commedia dell'arte production of the play, available on DVD. It is worth a look.

The presence of the duke or dux in the comedies may come more from the epic that ends happily, such as the *Aeneid* or *Knight's Tale*. Queen Elizabeth's progresses often had a character, such as a Hermit, Squire, Soldier, or Wild Man, appear before the dux or monarch and ask a favor as she approaches a great house in the country. These may have preceded various pleasant shows for the monarch while she resided there, and she may then have granted a kindly boon or judgment as she left the place. One can study this structure in John Nichols's three-volume *The Progresses and Public Processions of Queen Elizabeth*.

3

Shakespearean Comedic Myths

James Shapiro speculates about whether Spenser refers to Shakespeare in "Colin Clout's Come Home Again" and whether Shakespeare was referring to Spenser in *Midsummer Night's Dream*. He concludes that whatever the case in these instances, the two poets knew each other's work.[1] Perhaps more important, the 1590 and 1596 publication of the *Faerie Queene* had taught a generation of lovers of literature one way of understanding myth based on ancient moral and religious understandings of how it works. This way of understanding was encoded in textbook, handbooks, and emblem books. Shakespeare used it as he used all things that lay at hand.

In writing about the nature of religion, anthropologists and students of religion talk about the priestly role and the shamanic, or vatic, role. The priest is the authority bearer, who tells us what the old codes are. The vatic, prophetic figure is the wild man who journeys into the world of spirits and comes back with a message. Although one must not be too literal minded about this distinction, if one defines the priest to be the officially ordained mediator of public ritual—and one includes among priests the dux in his role as an interpreter of law and moral/state leader—then Shakespeare's comedies may also be said to be divided between these two domains. The world of the city and of the organized community is the domain of the priest. Shakespeare's so-called "green world" where the gods and goddesses live, the invisible inhabitants of transcendent realms, is the world of the shamanic. The two realms tell us of the tensions between the bureaucratic and the mythic. If Shakespeare moves comedy from the domestic to the greater societal scene, he also moves it from the ordinary to the divine. He makes it enter the world of the sacred and enact versions of ancient Greco-Roman religious stories of love's ascents and descents. He does so not only in individual metaphoric references but in the general fabric and plots of his works as well. They become what Theseus called "antique toys," the stuff of Ovid's *Metamorphoses* and Homer's *Odyssey*, as these were given Platonic and Christian interpretations.[2] By Shakespeare's time the interpretation of myth in a figurative mode had dominated for centuries. But Shakespeare does not conceive of myth as do Sigmund Freud, Carl Jung, James Joyce, Ezra Pound, or any of our modern guides. He had his own conception, and we have to work at understanding it.

C. L. Barber has remarked that Shakespeare's approach to mythic reconstruction was not "so much to lift things gracefully from Ovid" as to make up fresh things in Ovid's manner.[3] Barber is precisely correct if one understands that Shakespeare made up fresh things using the semiology of myth as he and his audience found it in Ovid and in his interpreters in the late sixteenth and early seventeenth centuries.[4] Thus Shakespeare *does* think like a mythmaker but one who mined the mythic modes available to his time.

The main mythic sections of the plays usually come in mid-comedy. Shakespeare did not divide his works into acts and scenes in the quartos published in his lifetime—though modern Shakespearean scholars have argued that the comedies use the standard New Comedy five-act division into prologue, development, turn, counterturn, and catastrophe (or conclusion). Other scholars have argued that Shakespeare divided his comedies into three large movements: (1) a problem-setting beginning, usually one where authority imposes itself arbitrarily; (2) the main action; and (3) a final resolution scene. The main action section often comprises a theater of myth that moves in the realms of the imagination, where authority loses its bite in the face of invasions from the sacred world. In the final judicial and/or betrothal scene, authority and the realms of the sacred are brought together in a transfiguring moment.

Whether the plays are understood to have a five-act construction (perhaps reflecting the efforts of the Folio editors to give their author the classical respectability of the five-act comedies of the ancients) or to be in three movements as described, we still find in the middle of most of the comedies a mythic, highly imaginative section, perhaps containing the development, turn, and counterturn—a portion of the play that escapes from the world of authority to a world of dream, projection, fantasy, and spiritual construction. These sections comprise Ephesus as it appears to Antipholus of Syracuse, the *Midsummer Night's Dream* woods as these appear to all but Oberon, the *As You Like It* forest as it appears to Arden's exiles, and *The Tempest*'s island after the Neapolitans land. The mythic theater includes Illyria as it comes to appear to Viola, first sent a-wooing and then finding her brother saved, or Illyria as Malvolio thinks it to be when the letter sends him a-wooing in the world of erotic fantasy. In more subtle ways the imagination breaks lose in *Measure for Measure*, after the duke assumes the friar's garb and before he reassumes the ruler's. In *The Merchant of Venice*, in a kind of reversal, Belmont dominates the beginning and terminal scenes and Venice the middle ones. Sometimes the terminal setting is only suggested, as in *As You Like It*, and sometimes the middle is only a wildly grotesque version of the street world presented at the outset and terminus, as in *Measure for Measure*.

To understand the middle and end, then, we need to have a sense of how Shakespeare understands myth—sacred Greco-Roman myth and the sacred narratives of his own culture that come from Judaism and Christianity. The tragedy of *Titus Andronicus* tells us of Shakespeare's sense of the nature of Greco-Roman myth when Lavinia reveals the source of her destruction by pointing to Philomela's story in *Metamorphoses*:

TITUS: Lucius, what book is that she tosseth so?
YOUNG LUCIUS: Grandsire, 'tis Ovid's *Metamorphoses*.
  My mother gave it me.

MARCUS: For love of her that's gone,
   Perhaps, she culled it from among the rest.
TITUS: Soft, so busily she turns the leaves.
   Help her. What would she find? Lavinia, shall I read?
   This is the tragic tale of Philomel,
   And treats of Tereus' treason and his rape,
   And rape, I fear, was root of thy annoy.
MARCUS: See, brother, see. Note how she quotes the leaves.
TITUS: Lavinia, wert *thou* thus surprised, sweet girl,
   Ravished and wronged as Philomela was,
   Forced in the ruthless, vast, and gloomy woods?
   See, see. Ay, such a place there is where we did hunt—
   O, had we never, never hunted there!—
   Patterned by that the poet here describes,
   By nature made for murders and for rapes.
MARCUS: O, why should nature build so foul a den,
   Unless the gods delight in tragedies? (4.1.41–59)

The operative word for how myth works here is *patterned*. The wood in which Lavinia was raped is patterned after the mythic wood where Tereus raped Philomela in *Metamorphoses*, book 6. There Procne asks Tereus to escort her sister, Philomela, from Athens to Thrace. When Tereus arrives in Thrace, he rapes his charge, cutting out her tongue to preclude her witnessing against her ravisher. However, she weaves the rape into a tapestry to tell Procne her story, and when Procne learns of it, she murders her own and Tereus's son before feeding him to her rapist-husband.

The pattern woods in Ovid are described as "ruthless, vast, and gloomy" because of the human actions in them:

Tereus tooke the Ladie by the hand,
And led hir to a pelting graunge that peakishly did stand
In woods forgrowen. There waxing pale and trembling sore for
   feare,
And dreading all things, and with teares demaunding sadly
   where

His sister was, he shet hir up: and therewithall bewraide
His wicked lust, and so by force bicause she was a Maide
And all alone he vanquisht hir. (Golding's *Metamorphoses*
6:662ff.)

The "woods forgrowen" thus pattern out the woods in *Titus Androni-*
cus, where Lavinia endures her double rape and the double mutilation
of her hands and tongue. But the mentioned part of the pattern is not
its limit. The cloth of story that Philomela weaves to tell the source
of her suffering supplies the pattern for the book of stories in which
Lavinia locates the Philomela account that patterns her own story; the
book becomes her equivalent of the tapestry. Philomela and Procne's
making Tereus feast on his son becomes Titus's cutting the throats
of Tamora's sons, baking them and feeding them to her as the source
of the crime against Lavinia. Many events separate the two stories
from each other, but the pattern is there: the woods, the mutilation,
the artistic rendering exposing crime, and the cannibalistic revenge.
The architectonic physical events are reenacted so that *life lives out the*
narrative patterns of myth, repeating them with variations.[5]

Life in the drama also lives out the moral patterns of myth.
Golding's introduction to his *Metamorphoses* translation shows the
paradigmatic *moral* Philomela:

The tale of Tereus, Philomele, and Prognee dooth conteyne
That folke are blynd in thyngs that to their proper weale perteyne.
And that the man in whom the fyre of furious lust dooth reigne
Dooth run to mischeefe like a horse that getteth loose the reyne.
It also shewes the cruell wreake of women in their wrath
And that no hainous mischiefe long delay of vengeance hath.[6]

There is no shyness here about poetry and myth as construction. Myth shows what is. Myth shows what is to be. Myth creates.
Shakespeare often uses the term *pattern* in this way—that is, making a
mythic or fabulous paradigm that enables the construction of other like
individuals: for example, Lear's "I will be the pattern of all patience,"

71

or Vincentio's claim in *Measure for Measure* that the ruler "should be as holy as severe, / Pattern in himself to know ..." (3.1.483–84).[7] The first definition of *pattern* in the *Oxford English Dictionary* is: "the original proposed to imitation; the archetype; that which is copied; an exemplar." I do not wish to suggest that Shakespeare engaged in the obscure disputes over Platonic and Aristotelian metaphysics that occupied contemporary consideration of the heavenly paradigms and their relation to the physical world, but Shakespeare's use of language does suggest that he believed in the existence of a series of patterns enacted in myth and laid up in some transcendent realm. Furthermore, through moral struggle these patterns can be enacted in individual human beings. The patterns may be ideal or demonic in character, but in either case myth enacts the essential, the form or idea, in ancient and Renaissance metaphysics.

That myth patterns out the ethical or moral life of the individual was rehearsed endlessly in Shakespeare's time in the emblem books, mythographies, and commentaries; and Shakespeare has emblemologist myth-painters among his characters. As we will see later, he has mythographers also. For example, as an emblemologist, Fluellen, in Shakespeare's history of *Henry V*, gives us his Welshman's emblem of the Goddess Fortuna:

> FLUELLEN: By your patience, Ensign Pistol: Fortune is painted blind, with a muffler afore her eyes, to signify to you that Fortune is blind. And she is painted also with a wheel, to signify to you—which is the moral of it—that she is turning, and inconstant and mutability and variation. And her foot, look you, is fixed upon a spherical stone, which rolls and rolls and rolls. In good truth, the poet makes a most excellent description of it; Fortune is an excellent moral. (*Henry V* 3.6.26–33)

Let us return to the figure of Blind Cupid treated in chapter 1 but now from the perspective of the logic and semiology of Early Modern emblematic language: Helena, as she contemplates her love of Demetrius in act 1 of *Midsummer Night's Dream*, presents Cupid exactly as he is painted or, more precisely, as he is etched and analyzed in the emblem books—a less sinister version of that Cupid initially presented blind in book 3, canto 12, verse 22 of Spenser's *Faerie Queene*:

> HELENA: Things base and vile, holding no quantity,
>   Love can transpose to form and dignity.
>   Love looks not with the eyes, but with the mind,
>   And therefore is winged Cupid painted blind.
>   Nor hath love's mind of any judgement taste;
>   Wings and no eyes figure unheedy haste.
>   And therefore is love said to be a child
>   Because in choice he is so oft beguiled.
>   As waggish boys in game themselves forswear,
>   So the boy Love is perjured everywhere.
>   For ere Demetrius looked on Hermia's eyne
>   He hailed down oaths that he was only mine,
>   And when this hail some heat from Hermia felt,
>   So he dissolved, and showers of oaths did melt. (1.1.232–45)

Helena's Love, or Cupid, works blindly without judgment or reason, projecting things that have no basis in external reality while transforming base to noble and making and unmaking his foolish choices randomly. This Blind Cupid is the love-design for Demetrius's love for Helena and later for Hermia—the design also for virtually all the forest loves in the play. This same Cupid, played by Puck, comes from the Cupid of late medieval iconography and the illustrations of him in the emblem books, but he lives in this play as the architectonic of Demetrius's and Hermia's loves and, further afield, in the pattern of all of love-in-idleness loves.[8] It is notable that Helena can describe the iconology of Blind Cupid, though Shakespeare makes no suggestion that she is especially learned or trained in the classics. She carries the cultural assumptions of the time and, as I shall argue, her Blind Cupid becomes the Puck of the play.

Shakespeare uses several words to designate symbolic icons derived from classical myth. In his works, the words *imprese, device,* and *emblem* refer repeatedly to a configuration carrying a figurative reading that the spectator or reader has to fathom by putting together the parts.[9] In act 3, scene 1, of the history of *Richard II,* Bolingbroke speaks of Bushy and Greene as having "[r]azed out my imprese, leaving me no sign" (3.l.25)—that is, as having obliterated his heraldic allegorical motto. (Shakespeare assisted in the devising of an *imprese* for the Earl of Rutland in 1613.) The *imprese* or *impresa,* while not exactly an emblem, may be a classical tale that embodies the movement of the inner self. For example, in *Twelfth Night* Olivia carries as her emblem a representation of Lucretia or Lucrece ("soft, and the impressure her Lucrece" [*TN* 2.5.84]), and Maria in her trick letter makes this emblem into the "Lucrece knife" (*TN* 2.5.95) that embodies the enforced silence putatively destroying her relationship to Malvolio. For Olivia herself, the fate of Lucrece may symbolize her melancholy self-containment after her brother's death.

Emblems may not only typify the inner self but may be constitutive of new modes of being. In Shakespeare's history play concerning Henry VIII, Anne Boleyn becomes the queen by virtue of a series of emblematic gestures by the Archbishop of Canterbury:

THIRD GENTLEMAN: [B]y the Archbishop of Canterbury
She had all the royal makings of a queen,
As holy oil, Edward Confessor's crown,
The rod and bird of peace, and all such emblems
Laid nobly on her. (*Henry VIII* 4.1.88–92)

In short, the emblems, when laid on by Canterbury, make Anne a queen.

The most common word that Shakespeare uses for the figurative icon, whether static or developed by the action, is *device.* In *Pericles,* the six knights who pursue Thaisa all present shields bearing devices symbolizing their character and their love for her (act 2, scene 2). But a device may be more than a personal crest. It may be a play or trick acting out of the essentials of a whole situation. Theseus, in *Midsummer Night's Dream*, says that the play, "[t]he riot of the tipsy Bacchanals, / Tearing the Thracian singer in their rage" (5.1.48–49), is an old device played when he first came from Thebes, probably, by implication, in symbolic celebration of his conquest of Creon's wildness. After all, in his earlier encounter with Ariadne, he has been as much a fickle-hearted fool in love as Demetrius and Lysander are now in the woods of Athens. His counterpart in Chaucer's *Knight's Tale* observes as much when, looking at Palamon and Arcita fighting for an Emelye who neither knows nor cares about them, he reminds us that he too has been a lover and a fool (A, 1773–1825).

Again in *Twelfth Night*, Maria creates the play's device, the forged letter from Olivia that makes Malvolio act out his Puritan fantasies of sexual election by Olivia and of achieving rule over Toby and Andrew. He makes himself physically into a sign telling us what the moral emblem for his inner self, as controlled by Mal-Volio, or "Bad Will," should be. Falstaff's wearing the horns in imitation of Actaeon is a device that does the same thing (see discussion later in this chapter). In short, in the material action of the plays Shakespearean characters are constantly constructing and reconstructing themselves as would-be emblems, *impresa*, or devices; and they often base these pictures of the pattern they find in themselves or others on classical myth, sometimes consciously constructing a moral out of their own lives and sometimes unwittingly exposing themselves for what they are.[10]

Beyond the material and the moral, another level at which Shakespearean myth claims to lay hold on the paradigmatic is the vatic or heavenly level—what I have called the shamanic level, and what the Hebrew Bible would call the prophetic one. This level appears explicitly in Theseus and Hippolita's dialogue concerning the lovers' accounts of their "dream" in *Midsummer Night's Dream*:

HIPPOLYTA: 'Tis strange, my Theseus, that these lovers
  speak of.
THESEUS: More strange than true. I never may believe
  These antique fables, nor these fairy toys . . .

The lunatic, the lover, and the poet
Are of imagination all compact . . .
The poet's eye, in a fine frenzy rolling,
Doth glance from heaven to earth, from earth to heaven,
And as imagination bodies forth
The forms of things unknown, the poet's pen
Turns them to shapes, and gives to airy nothing
A local habitation and a name. (5.1.1–3, 7–8, 12–17)

The play's Theseus—parts of whose story had earlier appeared in the *Thebiad*, in *The Knight's Tale*, and also in Ovid's *Metamorphoses*—has just heard the story of what happened to the four lovers during their midsummer's night. He hears the "dream" as if it were a set of "antique fables," or "fairy toys," a series of myths like those in Ovid or Spenser. For him, the story's strangeness should create a vaguely familiar pattern, for the tale of the lovers repeats his own life in capsule form. However, their story is not so strange as his recounted in Ovid and elsewhere.

In the part of Theseus's story that occurs in and about Athens, his father, Aegeus—namesake of the Egeus of *A Midsummer Night's Dream* who would deny Hermia her Lysander—does not even recognize Theseus as his son, and the transformation-making stepmother, Medea—a greater transformer than either Puck or Titania—tries to poison him.[11] A woman named Pasiphae in a nearby country copulates with a bull to create a man-beast (far more dangerous than the man-beast Bottom) that devours all comers, including a tribute each year of youths from Athens. To conquer him Theseus has to wander in a labyrinth more bewildering by far than the madness-making woods of Athens. His female savior, Ariadne, teaches him to conquer the man-beast, and then, perhaps under a spell, he abandons her. Finally, he defeats a one-sex female society and marries its queen. That the Theseus of the play is also a creature of myth—an antique fable—is recalled in the play's references to his work in Crete and his relationships with Ariadne, Aegle, and Perigenia (*MND* 2.1.73ff.). He must know that his story belongs with the stories that Philostrate proposes for the prenuptial entertainment: the killing of Orpheus by the Bacchantes and the battle of the centaurs and Lapiths at which his friend Hercules defeated the centaur (*MND* 5.1.44ff.).

When Theseus enters the scene in act 5, scene 1, to give the speech I have quoted, a normal audience would presume that he has heard the tale of Bottom and Titania, since Bottom has also returned to Athens at this time. The lovers, too, may know of his story, parallel to theirs. In any case, the audience would at this point recall the whole dream, not just that which the lovers have experienced. The whole story is like an "antique fable" and "fairy toy" to Theseus, yet it contains in miniature the patterns of Theseus's own story: the unseeing father, the same Egeus, the labyrinths (now of the woods), the beast-man, the transformation-making "fairy" woman Titania (recalling Medea), and the unwarranted abandonment of loves who deserve better.

Ignoring altogether that he *is* an Ovidian story himself (*Metamorphoses*, books 7 and 8), Theseus, the man from myth, affirms reflexively that he *never could believe* Ovidian-style stories—"antique fables" and "fairy toys." He, or rather Shakespeare, is making a literary critic's joke: a fable, in Renaissance theory of fictions, is by definition false on the surface.[12] Ovid's *Metamorphoses* were often titled the fables of Ovid (Sandys, in the second decade of the seventeenth century, still says that his purpose is "to collect out of sundrie Authors the Philosophicall sense of these fables of *Ovid*").[13] Of course the ancient myths—the antique fables—were never to be regarded as literally true. They were metaphors for truth and for patterns of truth. But the stories that the lovers have told are also "fairy toys." The world of "fairy," in late medieval and Early Modern times in England, was primarily that of the Roman and Greek gods. Proserpina and Pluto are called "faerie" in Chaucer's *Merchant's Tale* (*CT*, Fragment 4, 2227–2229), and Spenser's *Faerie Queene* is about a realm where the gods and the shadows of the classical gods appear—Venus, Diana, Belphoebe, Britomart, and the like—and ride off to new adventures.[14] The fairies in *A Midsummer Night's Dream* function as the divine providence-producing machinery of comic epics like *The Knight's Tale* or the *Odyssey*, though they are a little more user-friendly.

Theseus, the fable, says one should not believe these metamorphic Ovidian antique fables or fairy toys. But we never take fables literally. As one of the standard Renaissance forms of narrative they are by definition not true; they communicate a truth metaphorically. However, Theseus also says one should believe that in creating such fables and toys, the poet's "eye, in fine frenzy rolling, / Doth glance from heaven to earth, from earth to heaven" so that "imagination bodies forth / The forms of things unknown" and "the poet's pen / Turns them to shapes, and gives to airy nothing / A local habitation and a name" (*MND* 5.1.12–17). The basic view undergirding Theseus's speech is that which undergirds all Renaissance visual images endeavoring to bring the patterns of the eternal Platonic forms into time. As I have observed in an earlier essay:

Theseus's lines have been interpreted in their context as a jocular degradation of the poet to the level of lover and madman. Poets do not often sell their craft so short, and Shakespeare is not ... doing so here. ... Theseus makes some implicit distinctions between the poet and his mad colleagues. It is only lovers and madmen who are said to exhibit fantasies, which descend beyond the comprehension of reason. ... Implicitly, poets, however much they are possessed by a *furor poesis*, may deal in imaginings apprehensible in more rational terms. [Theseus's] speech ... perhaps makes clear how this happens. Its syntax suggests that what the poet sees, in glancing to heaven, is the "ayery nothing" or "forme" which his imagination is then empowered to "body forth." In looking back to earth, he bequeaths to this Form a "locall habitation, and a name." In a similar vein, Neoplatonic criticism in the time spoke of the artist's duty to incarnate the universal (or "form") in the concrete visual emblem. Professor E. H. Gombrich ... used much the same language as Duke Theseus to summarize the rationale of such Renaissance visual symbols: "They are the forms, which the invisible entities can assume to make themselves understood to the limited human mind. In other words, the idea of Justice—be it conceived as a member of the celestial hierarchy or as an abstract entity—is inaccessible to the senses. At best we can hope to grasp it in a moment of ecstasy and intellectual intuition. But God has decreed in His mercy that these invisible and abstract entities whose divine radiance no human eye could support may accommodate themselves to our understanding and assume visible shape."[15]

The theory of poetic (or prophetic) frenzy as laying hold on the abstract universal and allowing the imagination to translate it into concrete patterns or emblems is to be found in Ficino, Pico, and Poliziano in Italy and in the thought of the French academies. Sidney, more Apollonian, less ecstatic in temperament than the continental Platonists, speaks of a "divine breath" that permits the poet to know the patterns of the golden world, the unfallen forms, and to create a fiction embodying them that will bring forth many resemblances to the exemplar.[16]

Shakespeare's comedies, like Renaissance and classical epic and tragedy, often move in this great world of myth as pattern, not simply at the level of the individual metaphors that he assigns his characters but also at the level of the plots at large, where a myth or several welded together become the plot's pattern, asking us to combine symbolic details and think like a Renaissance mythmaker. The comedies use different myths for different plays and use them in different ways. This chapter examines four such usages among the many that could be treated: (1) extended reenacted myth in the form of Titania reenacting Proserpina and Circe; (2) myth commenting on myth, with Cupid commenting on Hercules in the struggles of *Love's Labour's Lost*'s Navarre and elsewhere; (3) myth appearing in folk disguise, such as Falstaff appearing as a folk Actaeon; and (4) myth renewing myth, as in Ganymede's making a new golden age for *As You Like It*.

Extended, Reenacted Myth: Titania and Puck in *A Midsummer Night's Dream*

A Midsummer Night's Dream stays in the world of myth and the "vatic" in both its representations of Titania and of Puck as hobgoblin. Titania's name is used in myth to label both Hecate (Proserpina) and

Circe. Both descend from the Titans, the giant earth forces whom the Olympians defeated. Both pattern out the force of earthly passion. Hecate earlier has a major role in the life of Theseus, as recorded in Ovid, where she gives Theseus's stepmother, the sorceress Medea, her power, and in *The Knight's Tale*, where she appears as Lucina, the goddess of childbirth, one of Diana's (or the moon's) three phases.[17] The Titania-Hecate figure of *Midsummer Night's Dream* is not the chaste Diana used to pay tribute to Queen Elizabeth's "virginity." Indeed, Oberon is nearer the truth when he calls her "a wanton." Like Proserpina in *The Merchant's Tale*, she is the "queene of Fayerye" (E, 2316), and like her earlier counterpart she knows the world of flowers and the methods of seduction.[18]

Many of Hecate's characteristics overlap with those of Circe, also a Titan and earth spirit, who turned her lovers into beasts. Associated with the plant world, Circe was said to symbolize the sun mixing with moisture in the earth, enlivening the earth, and making it produce plants and herbs of all types. She too controlled the seasons. As Sandys argues, following Comes, Servius, and other commentators current in Shakespeare's time:

Others take [Circe's four handmaidens] for the foure seasons of the yeare, from this description in Homer:

Foure Damsels seru'd her, daughters of the woods,
Of sacred springs and sea ingulphed floods.
The first rich cloths of state hung ore their heads:
And on the floore faire-figur'd Carpets spreads.
One, siluer tables sets before the throne:
And Cates in golden dishes plac't thereon.
A third in flagons mixt mellifluous wine,
And pretious goblets fills to the diuine.
The fourth vpon a mighty Tripod sets
A Chaldron, and with fire faire water heats.

The first decyphering Spring; the second Summer, the third Autumne, & the forth Winter.[19]

Similarly, Titania, in her quarrels with Oberon, has seasonal connections when she makes summer into winter. So did Proserpina when
Pluto ravished her down to Hades.

Titania does not literally change Bottom to a beast, as Circe does to
her admirers in the Renaissance Homer. However, if the emblematic
Circe uses cupidity, or Cupid-attraction, directed toward her to make
her admirers into beasts, Puck as a kind of Cupid uses love-in-idleness
to do the beast-making job on Bottom. The effect is the same. And
when the man becomes a beast, Titania allows herself to be his Circe.
She invites her lover-ass for playtime to a bower reminiscent of Circe's
in Homer or Acrasia's in book 2 of *The Faerie Queene*.[20] Sandys's meanings for Circe summarize a thousand-year-old tradition:

Seruius will haue Circe not onely an Inchantresse, but a notorious
strumpet; and therefore feigned the daughter of the Sun, in that
nothing more apparant; who by her lasciuious arts drew many
from a morall life to a brutish; and therefore said to haue changed
them. . . . . [L]ust proceeds from heat and moisture, which naturally
incites to luxury; and getting the dominion, deformes our soules
with all bestial vices; alluring some to inordinate Venus; others to
anger, cruelty, and euery excess of passion: the Swines, the Lyons,
and the Wolues, produced by her sensuall charms; which are not
to bee resisted, but by the diuine assistance, Moly, the guift of
Mercury, which signifies temperance. . . . For as Circes rod, waued
ouer their heads from the right side to the left: presents those false
and sinister perswasions of pleasure, which so much deformes
them: so the reuersion thereof, by disciplines, and a view of their
own deformity, restores them to their former beauties.[21]

Bottom is not so much a sinister as a silly follower of pleasure, responding to the "quaint mazes" (2.1.99) that Titania offers, reacting as-
ininely to her "entrall[ment]" to his shape (3.1.123), and coming with
tied-up tongue to her "bower," a place over which the moon weeps
for violated chastity (3.2.178–82). When he sleeps there, Titania also
sleeps as ivy twisted about his elm (4.1.40–41). In the comic strategy

of *Midsummer Night's Dream*, the flower, love-in-idleness, acts as both the Circe's rod and the Cupid's arrow that twists the queen and the ass about each other. In act 4 of the play, Diane's bud acts as the contrary force, the Mercury's *moly* that returns an element of sanity to the lovers.[22] Though Bottom in the presence of the fairy queen never becomes more than an "inordinate" follower of "Venus," his semblances—Lysander and Demetrius—under the spell of love-in-idleness move from inordinate Venus to the lionlike and wolfish anger and cruelty of Circe's followers in the woods until Oberon, through Puck, uses the juice of what is apparently Diane's bud (4.1.36–47; 41.1.65–71) and cures Lysander of his madness, returning him to his true love, Hermia.

Puck as a minor devil enacts the Cupid-force that brings Bottom down to Titania and his own beastly form. The Renaissance Cupid is a devil, as Armado witnesses in act 1, scene 2 (153–157), of *Love's Labour's Lost*:

> ARMADO: Love is a familiar [i.e., a familiar spirit]; *love is a devil.* There is no evil angel but love. Yet was Samson so tempted, and he had an excellent strength. Yet was Solomon so seduced, and he had a very good wit. *Cupid's butt-shaft is too hard for Hercules' club,* and therefore too much odds for a Spaniard's rapier. (italics mine)

What can a mere Bottom do against such force?

The notion that the ultimate evil angel is misdirected love is almost as old as Christendom. In many Renaissance paintings of the Fall, the serpent is a fully breasted female creature having a distinct erotic appearance (not a statement about women but about male desire).[23] He may also be a Cupid-like creature with a serpent's tail, as in Titian's *Temptation of Adam and Eve* in the Prado Museum in Madrid (fig. 8).

While Don Armado is hardly a theologian, his bravura communicates an insight concerning the Cupid of self-centered love. In conventional theological terms, "he"—self-centered love—is a devil, and *Midsummer Night's Dream*'s Puck is a tricksterish configuration of

FIGURE 8. Titian (Tiziano Vecellio) (ca. 1488–1576), *Temptation of Adam and Eve*, ca. 1570. Oil on canvas. Museo del Prado, Madrid. Scala/Art Resource, New York.

the Cupid-Devil icon who, like Cupid flies, brings people to desire against their better will, and produces strange permutations in their characters.[24] From Cupid's arrow touching a western flower, Puck receives the love-in-idleness flower, his equivalent for the arrow that created it. Oberon describes the origin of the flower:

> OBERON: That very time I saw, but thou couldst not,
> Flying between the cold moon and the earth
> Cupid all armed. . . .
> Yet marked I where the bolt of Cupid fell.
> It fell upon a little western flower—
> Before, milk-white; now, purple with love's wound—
> And maidens call it love-in-idleness.
> Fetch me that flower; the herb I showed thee once.
> The juice of it on sleeping eyelids laid
> Will make or man or woman madly dote
> Upon the next live creature that it sees. (2.1.155–57, 165–72)

Before he receives this weapon, Robin Goodfellow or Puck acts as a hobgoblin who causes minor erotic grief: arousing stallions, mocking the "laps" of old crones, and making old women fall from their *sitzplaces* (*MND* 2.1.43ff.). After he receives his flowery tool, he is gifted with the power of a spiritual transformation that drives men mad. He is comic exactly as the devil who wears a firecracker in his fundament in late medieval drama is comic.

The flower he bears is the flower that creates him, for, as Ovid asserts in the *Remedia Amoris*, Love/Cupid is born and nurtured by Idleness, who in some accounts also makes Cupid's shafts and torch—using sleep, gambling, wine, and aimlessness. Love-in-idleness is not the pansy perfume synthesized by experimentally minded British chemists, only to fail in its aphrodisiac purpose. It is the entanglement of the woods, the sleep, and the doing-nothing amid the brambles that releases the self-centered imagination. It is perfect for the comic exploration of follies (and crimes) in that one falls under its spell in a somewhat passive attitude, not through the plotting ratiocination of a

Macbeth or an Iago. The flower releases the descending imagination that reigns in the woods to begin the comic destruction of the lovers, but the grace-filled imagination that begins with the dawn also enables their comic re-creation as persons who can love fixedly and socially when, as reintegrated persons, they learn to love and live in Athens.

As I have argued in my 1957 essay on MND, Oberon is a grace or providence figure, based both on his previous history in literature and on his use in *Midsummer Night's Dream*. Like Puck, he is a trickster but an ultimately redemptive one. If Puck scatters love-in-idleness in the wrong places, Oberon undoes this by having him apply the *remedia amoris* of Diane's bud to the lovers so that they achieve the correct pairings. Oberon commands the release of Titania from her bondage, and in act 5 he leads the blessing of the houses and beds of the three couples to be married.

In our twenty-first-century melodramatic and Manichean world, if Oberon were a grace figure, Puck as a minor devil could not serve him. But the devil and his hobgoblins did serve God in medieval and Early Modern culture. The hobgoblin type in Chaucer's *Friar's Tale* tells the tale's Summoner:

> [S]omtyme we been Goddes instrumentz,
> And meenes to doon his comandementz,
> Whan that hym list, upon his creatures . . .
> And somtyme, at oure prayere, han we leve
> Oonly the body and nat the soule greve;
> Witnesse on Job, whom that we diden wo.
> And somtyme han we myght of bothe two,
> This is to seyn, of soule and body eke.
> And somtyme be we suffred for to seke
> Upon a man, and doon his soule unreste,
> And nat his body, and al is for the beste.
> Whan he withstandeth oure temptacioun,
> It is a cause of his savacioun,
> Al be it that it was nat oure entente
> He sholde be sauf, but that we wolde hym hente. (D, 1480–96)[25]

Early Modern commentary on Job made the same point concerning the devil's work in that heroic tragedy that Chaucer's hunter-devil makes in a comic tale. So also does Faust in Marlowe's *Dr. Faustus.*

As a hobgoblin, Puck can do mischief, some of it unintended by Oberon, but the ruler of fairies ultimately controls the mischief. Grace (Oberon), as God's messenger, tests with love-in-idleness and grants relief through Diane's bud. With the lovers' imaginations released and their loves unconstrained by parent or magic (save in Demetrius's case, and he moves back to his former love for Helena), the sighted Cupid can triumph in the play's culminating show of amorous and civic unity. The structure parallels the similar iconic structure in Sir John Harington's contemporary *Orlando*, where Atlas as Cupid has a "castle" of delight, reached through wandering-in-idleness and coming to the wandering wood of the palace-labyrinth where would-be lovers paint the fantasy of their beloveds as idols everywhere, until reason and eloquence dissolve the enchantments of the place and move the idle to useful civic activity.[26] Both Titania and Puck, as they reenact the patterns of their mythic models, Circe and Cupid, give us a sense of the comedy of wild desire and the witchery of the woods. They may speak also, armed with new insight, of the need for a return to a rule-governed Athens and marriage, in which the household is cleansed by Oberon and the awakened Titania as they spread "fairy grace" (5.2.21–52).

Myth Commenting on Myth:
The Labors of Cupid and Hercules

The flag that hung outside the Globe reputedly depicted Hercules bearing the globe on his shoulders with the motto: *Totus mundus agit histrionem* (the whole world plays the actor). Hercules, replacing Atlas, was said to bear the world on his shoulders in Seneca's *Hercules Furens* (69–74), so the globe is not entirely out of place on the flag, though the myth usually indicates the sky. In the scene, Hercules acts in the place of Atlas, holding up the world so that Atlas can recover the apples of the Hesperides for him; he then feigns that he needs to make his cloak more comfortable in order to trick Atlas into relieving him of the burden of the world and taking it back permanently. Hercules has the power of the actor to assume roles and also the power to lay them aside. Since in both Roman and Renaissance emblemology he was often made an emblem not only of physical strength but of the strength of eloquence, he must on the Globe represent the power of playing that makes the world of social interaction go round.

But within the Globe Theater, when comedy played, one far more powerful than Hercules acted, and that was Cupid. In *Love's Labour's Lost*, *Taming of the Shrew*, and *Much Ado about Nothing*, Shakespeare calls on the notion that Cupid is counterpart to Hercules but a far more powerful creator of feats of strength. The idea is that desire is more powerful than strength or eloquence in creating the human world. In *Love's Labour's Lost*, Cupid and Hercules are twice compared, much to the disadvantage of Hercules in the matter of strength (*LLL* 1.2.156 and 4.3.314). Any educated person in Shakespeare's audience would probably have recognized that the title of *Love's Labour's Lost* glances at Hercules's labors. But Hercules's labors are not lost. They win him immortality (*Metamorphoses*, book 9). However, Cupid's labors are lost in this play, though as suggested in chapter 2, they may have been won in the lost play that Shakespeare is said to have written subsequently, *Love's Labour's Won*. So how are Cupid's labors like those of Hercules and how are his labors lost?

When Hercules appears in *Love's Labour's Lost*, he appears ironically inverted and played by the Cupid-like imp-page, Moth, in the pageant of the Nine Worthies that ends the play. Holofernes, the play's pedagogue, makes clear that his labors do not win much:

HOLOFERNES: Great Hercules is presented by this imp,
Whose club killed Cerberus, that three-headed *canus*,
And when he was a babe, a child, a shrimp,
Thus did he strangle serpents in his *manus*.
Quoniam he seemeth in minority,
Ergo I come with this apology.
[To MOTE] Keep some state in thy exit, and vanish.
(5.2.577–83)

In contrast to Moth's Cupid-like Hercules, the real Love or Cupid in this play plans Herculean labors that he eventually loses, as the title of the play suggests. These would-be labors begin with the Navarrese princes' choice of asceticism over hedonism at the Pythagorean Y of their lives, a choice that the young Hercules also made.

The story of Hercules's choice between Virtue and Pleasure, so often the source of Early Modern paintings—for example those by Carracci and Veronese—is best told in Xenophon's *Memorabilia* (2.1.21ff.):

> Heracles was passing from boyhood to youth's estate . . . he went out into a quiet place, [22] and sat pondering which road to take. And there appeared two women of great stature making towards him. The one was fair to see and of high bearing; and her limbs were adorned with purity, her eyes with modesty; sober was her figure, and her robe was white. The other was plump and soft, with high feeding. Her face was made up to heighten its natural white and pink, her figure to exaggerate her height.

The sexy woman offers an easy life of pleasure, sensory satisfaction, and neither war nor worry. After Pleasure has completed her story, Virtue makes hers, beginning by assessing the hero's birth and education, asserting his capacity for noble deeds, and his need for discipline:

> [I]f you are fain to win the admiration of all Hellas for virtue, you must strive to do good to Hellas: if you want land to yield your fruits in abundance, you must cultivate that land: if you are resolved to get wealth from flocks, you must care for those flocks: if you essay to grow great through war and want power to liberate your friends and subdue your foes, you must learn the arts of war from those who know them and must practice their right use: and if you want your body to be strong, you must accustom your body to be the servant of your mind, and train it with toil and sweat.

Pleasure then reminds Hercules how difficult is Virtue's road to joy, while hers is easy and short, and Virtue accuses Pleasure of "eating before thou art hungry, drinking before thou art thirsty, getting thee cooks, to give zest to eating, buying thee costly wines and running to and fro in search of snow in summer, to give zest to drinking." Pleasure is a connoisseur of the sensate, rousing "lust by many a trick, when there is no need, using men as women . . . waxing wanton by night, consuming in sleep the best hours of day."[27]

For Early Modern people, the story was one of the best-known classical stories and the subject of magnificent works by Dürer, Veronese, Carracci, and numerous other artists. In Carracci's painterly elaboration of the story (fig. 9), the tough, sinuous road that goes with the figure of Virtue on the left apparently leads to Helicon and the poetic achievement of the man in the left foreground, who is crowned with a laurel. Pleasure on the right, on the other hand, has her flowers, her forest (as in *MND*), her symbols of the music of pleasure, and her playing cards. In Veronese (fig. 10), Pleasure, this time on the left, has sharp nails that tear at Hercules's stocking with an obvious sexual connotation; the sphinx that steadies her throne appears with a knife, perhaps for dueling; and art historians have said that she stands for Ignorance or Fraud. Veronese's Hercules seems already to have made the choice to take the upward path toward which Virtue tugs him gently. The entablature above the statue on the left reminds the viewer: *[Ho]nor et virtus/[p]ost morte floret*—(honor and virtue flower after death).

The princes of Navarre make a choice similar to that of Veronese's figure—Hercules's choice of Virtue before Pleasure—when they absent themselves from women, forming a celibate academy and determining to pursue the contemplative life of study and meditation. But Love, rather than Hercules, is Shakespeare's silent hero and the story is the story of Love's labors, not those of Hercules.

Love also has to choose between Virtue and Pleasure in Renaissance love philosophy, which commonly posits a Uranian Venus, or heavenly love leading to virtue, and a Venus Vulgaris, who stands for earthly or physical love, leading to reproduction but also, in her degenerate form, to all sorts of shameful abuse of the self and the other. Though at the beginning of the play Navarre's princes make Hercules's choice of Virtue over Pleasure, each surreptitiously falls under the influence of Cupid, or Love, and together they perform Cupid's unheroic labors (Hercules too was in love—see 1.2.61) to attain their women: writing secret love poetry for them; describing them as books that outrival conventional books in inspiring learning; anticipating revels, dances, and masks that will win their hands; and dressing up in Russian disguise to woo them. As C. L. Barber remarks, "what the lords give sway to is, in a general sense, the impulse to love; but the particular form that it takes for them is a particular sort of folly—what one could call the folly of amorous masquerade, whether in clothes, gestures or words . . . [t]he folly of acting love and talking love without being in love."[28] Love's labors are sonnets and puns and euphemisms and masquerades and oath-swearing and oath breaking, but they are not love itself. And these efforts, as love's labors, come to nothing. The males appear altogether to have abandoned their choice at the crossroads until the women, full of satiric play at the masked meeting and after,

FIGURE 9. Annibale Carracci (1560–1609), *Hercules at the Crossroads*, ca. 1596. Oil on canvas. Museo Nazionale di Capodimonte, Naples. Scala/Art Resource, New York.

FIGURE 10. Paolo Veronese (1528–1588), *The Choice between Virtue and Vice*, ca. 1565. Oil on canvas. Copyright © The Frick Collection, New York.

make them promise to perform in the future genuine labors of love, such as works of mercy for the dying. Meanwhile, they must wait a year for the women.

In short, the lovers choose the path of Pleasure rather than Virtue, only to find that the women of France whom they seek require that *Pleasure [be] reconciled to Virtue*, in Ben Jonson's phrase (used to title a later masque).[29] Love's labors are lost in this play in that no Herculean labors are done. None of the real labors of genuine Love appear—no romance, marriage, love-sacrifice, or apotheosis, and no Christian charity save that promised after the end of the play. Perhaps in Shakespeare's lost successor play, *Love's Labour's Won*, Love did win and attain to fusions of Virtue and Pleasure. Perhaps Love's labors are those works of mercy exacted from Biron by Rosaline (5.2.831–61). The significance of all this is that in Shakespearean comedy, Hercules is never far from Cupid.

In performing his labors following the path of Virtue, the emblematic Hercules was also driven by the Love or Cupid that suggests the love of Virtue. In the *Amorum Emblemata*, for example, Emblem 17 (fig. 11) shows Hercules conquering the hydra, Cupid having struck Hercules with his bow. The motto of the emblem reads *Virtutis radix amor* (Love is the root of virtue), and the accompanying material tells us that heroic action comes out of Love; that is, the love of Virtue.[30]

The same struggle for ascendancy between Cupid and Hercules appears in a number of other plays, though not as elaborated as in *Love's Labour's Lost*. Wherever Blind Cupid appears in Shakespeare, we may suspect a useful appearance of spontaneity, but we may also suspect the loosing of that hobgoblin of the imagination that can lead anywhere from destructive falls off milk stools to forest loves. Whenever his Herculean alter ego appears, we may search for the reconciliation of pleasure and virtue. Don Pedro, in *Much Ado*, knows how the paired great powers work:

DON PEDRO: Come, you shake the head at so long a breathing, but I warrant thee, Claudio, the time shall not go dully by us. I will in the interim undertake one of Hercules'

FIGURE II. Otto Vaenius, *Amorum Emblemata*, Emblem 17. Image scan used courtesy of the Emblem Project Utrecht (http://www.let.uu.nl.emblems).

labours, which is to bring Signor Benedick and the Lady Beatrice into a mountain of affection th'one with th'other. I would fain have it a match, and I doubt not but to fashion it, if you three will but minister such assistance as I shall give you direction. (2.1.315–21)

Later in the same scene, Don Pedro announces that if the group can perform this trick, previously described as Herculean, they will be the only Cupids: "Cupid is no longer an archer; his glory shall be ours, for we are the only love-gods" (*MAN* 2.1.335–36). In *Taming of the Shrew*, after hearing Petruchio's initial boast of his great labors in war and peace (1.2.193–205), Gremio says his labor with Kate will be greater than Hercules's twelve (1.2.253–54), and Portia in *Merchant of Venice* cheers on the Bassanio she would have as a husband with the cry, "Go, Hercules" (3.2.60). She does so as he approaches the three caskets left by her father and has to make his Herculean choice between love, avarice, and pride, anachronistically represented in a choice among metals. He has to choose between loving virtue (lead), possessive mass culture (gold), and narcissism (silver). Hercules in big and Cupid in little are the same figure when they love the path of Virtue rather than Pleasure, or when they find a path to combine the two through Uranian Love.

Human love, in all the comedies, is caught between the Herculean and the Puckish or Cupidean, sometimes with an admixture of each and sometimes with uncertain consequences until near the end of the play. The love-trappers in *Much Ado* perform the labors of Hercules and Cupid in getting Benedick to love Beatrice, but only in the final scene of the play do we know whether that love will lead to honor or to another fall. Petruchio accomplishes Herculean labors in taming Kate, reversing the embarrassment of Hercules's captivity to Omphale and Artegall's to Radigund in the *Faerie Queene*, but at the end one does not know who is the shrew and who the tamer, whose individual wiles—or whether both lovers' wiles together—produce the witty love that ends the play.

Orlando, Jaques's Monsieur Love, becomes the Cupid of the Forest of Arden (or Ardenne; see note 36 in this chapter) after his appearance as a hunter:

> CELIA: There lay he, stretched along like a wounded knight—
> ROSALIND: Though it be pity to see such a sight, it well becomes the ground.
> CELIA: Cry 'holla' to thy tongue, I prithee: it curvets unseasonably.—He was furnished like a hunter—
> ROSALIND: O ominous—he comes to kill my heart.
> CELIA: I would sing my song without a burden; thou bringest me out of tune.
> ROSALIND: Do you not know I am a woman? When I think, I must speak.—Sweet, say on. (*AYLI* 3.2.219–28)

Earlier in *As You Like It* (1.2.175–76), Rosalind has said to Orlando as he goes out to battle with Charles the wrestler: "Now Hercules be thy speed, young man!" And he wins with Herculean speed. He is, by turns, both Cupid and Hercules's understudy in her mind. However, his silly love—until he receives Rosalind's (or Ganymede's) cure—only fills the tree bark with praise of her as Diana, and his affections bear more the marks of love-in-idleness than of Herculean strength, no matter how deftly he overthrew Charles the wrestler. But he ascends to the top of the hierarchy of loves in both Hymen's and Jaques's blessings after Ganymede has taught him his Ovidian remedy for puppy love, after the serpent and lion have struggled over his and Oliver's fate, and after he extends his forgiveness to Oliver (see chapter 2).

Myth in Folk Disguise: Falstaff as Actaeon in *The Merry Wives of Windsor*

Shakespeare's mythic world is almost always near to the world of English beliefs, whether it be the Warwick of *Taming of the Shrew*, visited by a type of commedia dell'arte troupe that puts on a play about Italy; a *Midsummer Night's Dream* that takes place in ancient Athens but includes some very English maying and perhaps references to the Kenilworth celebration; or an *As You Like It* with its Arden visited by a female Ganymede and a mysterious Hymen. *Merry Wives of Windsor*, set in and near Windsor, acts out a comic version of the Actaeon myth, as *Titus* reenacts a tragic version of the Philomela one. But in *Merry Wives of Windsor*, Actaeon does not actually appear. His folk equivalent, Herne the Hunter, does, and we know we are to look for Actaeon in him only because earlier references in the play have set up that search. Falstaff's final appearance in the Windsor woods as Herne the Hunter—crowned with the horns of the stags that he might have hunted and that imitate Actaeon's own horns after his metamorphosis—and his pinching by a mock Diana, and her "fairy" associates, patterns itself after the Actaeon story in a comic incongruity that not only bears physical resemblances to the original story but offers comic moral understandings like those provided by contemporary mythic commentary.

A version of that mythic commentary appears in Shakespeare's own work when *Twelfth Night's* Orsino offers an explanation of the Actaeon story using the same mode of interpretation that Helena uses for Blind Cupid. Thinking of Olivia, he sees himself as Actaeon, Olivia as Diana bathing and turning him to a hart, and his own dogs of desire as nearly destroying him:

> ORSINO: O, when mine eyes did see Olivia first
> Methought she purged the air of pestilence;
> That instant was I turned into a hart,
> And my desires, like fell and cruel hounds,
> E'er since pursue me. (1.1.20–24)

Arthur Golding, whose translation of Ovid Shakespeare used often, makes Actaeon into an almost identical general allegory for those whose desires consume them:

> All such as doo in flattring freaks, and hawks, and hownds
> delyght,
> And dyce, and cards, and for to spend the tyme both day and
> nyght
> In foule excesse of chamberworke, or too much meate and drink:
> Uppon the piteous storie of Acteon ought too think.
> For theis and theyr adherents usde excessive are in deede
> The dogs that dayly doo devour theyr followers on with speede.[31]

Sandys also makes Actaeon into a man devoured by his own appetites and his hangers-on. Actaeon as the voyeur devoured by his own desire is a common type in Renaissance art and in mythological explanations of Ovid in Shakespeare's time. This figurative Actaeon, mentioned twice and then glanced at indirectly but fully in the last act of the play, forms the central myth of *Merry Wives of Windsor*.

The Actaeon ending of the play is set up early on. In act 2, scene 1, of *Merry Wives* Auncient Pistol tells the jealous Ford that Falstaff loves his wife and that if he does not prevent the effort, he will end up like a cuckoldry horned Actaeon:

FORD: Love my wife?
PISTOL: With liver burning hot. Prevent,
Or go thou like Sir Actaeon, he,
With Ringwood at thy heels.
O, odious is the name! (2.1.103–7)

Pistol, knowing the horn reference of cuckoldry, makes Actaeon into the emblem of a cuckold, and Ford then picks up this mistaken allegory and applies it to Page when he finds out that Falstaff's boy has been with Mistress Page, who plans in turn to be with Ford's wife:

FORD: Has Page any brains? Hath he any eyes? Hath he any thinking? Sure they sleep; he hath no use of them. Why, this boy will carry a letter twenty mile, as easy as a cannon will shoot point-blank twelve score. He pieces out his wife's inclination; he gives her folly motion and advantage. And now she's going to my wife, and Falstaff's boy with her. A man may hear this shower sing in the wind. And Falstaff's boy with her. Good plots—they are laid; and our revolted wives share damnation together. Well, I will take him; then torture my wife, pluck the borrowed veil of modesty from the so-seeming Mistress Page, *divulge Page himself for a secure and willful Actaeon*, and to these violent proceedings all my neighbours shall cry aim. (*MWW* 3.2.25–37ff.; italics mine)

Neither Mistress Page nor Mistress Ford is a cuckold maker, and so there are none of Ford's Actaeon cuckolds in the play.

But the last scene gives us another Actaeon, the real one of the commentaries and of Orsino's musings, one torn by "desires, like fell and cruel hounds"—Falstaff himself. Here, playing Herne the Hunter to seduce Mistresses Ford and Page, he precisely reenacts the Actaeon legend as Orsino and the mythographers had interpreted it. He is the real voyeur and the hopeless "cuckold" deceived by the women, who punish him for his endless voyeuristic coming on to them (*MWW* 5.5.106). The folk Herne legend makes Herne, like Actaeon, a hunter who is given the horns of his former prey, and Falstaff, playing his role, lives out the mythic pattern of his medieval predecessor in that he has his prey's horns. But the completion of his pattern requires the classical predecessor. In the medieval story that passed down into Shakespeare's time, Herne was Richard II's favorite huntsman, nearly fatally injured while saving Richard from a stag. When a "fairy" stranger cured Herne of his injury, she placed the stag's antlers on his head and made him pay for his life with his skill at the hunt. Despairing over this loss, he hanged himself in Windsor Forest and ever after haunted it, antlered, and leading a ghostly hunt.[32] Herne the Hunter, however, is never accused of lechery or voyeurism or misdirected desire and is never punished or threatened with tearing apart by Diana's servants. Playing the role of Herne as he is told to do by the women, Falstaff is only the pathetic victim of a prank. But as Actaeon torn by Mistress Quickly (Diana) and her helpers, he is a moral emblem: Actaeon and Actaeon alone.

In preparing for his assignation with the wives of Windsor in the disguise of Herne, Falstaff imagines himself one of the metamorphosed Joves of ancient myth:

FALSTAFF: Now the hot-blooded gods assist me! Remember, Jove, thou wast a bull for thy Europa; love set on thy horns. O powerful love, that in some respects, makes a beast a man; in some other, a man a beast! You were also, Jupiter, a swan, for the love of Leda. O omnipotent love! How near the god drew to the complexion of a goose! A fault done first in the form of a beast—O Jove, a beastly fault!—and then another fault in the semblance of a fowl—think on 't, Jove, a foul fault! When gods have hot backs, what shall poor men do? For me, I am here a Windsor stag, and the fattest, I think, i'th' forest. (*MWW* 5.5.2–11)

If both gods and men can turn beast for desire, then so also can Falstaff with his great gut sloshing around. Yet the Jovelike patterns that Falstaff proposes for himself do not come into the action. Actaeon does. Falstaff, turned to a deer and waiting to seduce the chaste wives

of Windsor, encounters the "chaste" aspect of the triple Diana, the
Fairy Queen—ironically played by the very fast Mistress Quickly (and
her actually chaste followers, the wives and husbands of Windsor).
He receives his punishment: possible transformation from a stag to
"a piece of cheese" (*MWW* 5.5.78–79), burning as he burns, "cuckolded"
and deceived as Actaeon was by his own dishonest desires:

MISTRESS QUICKLY: Fairies, black, grey, green, and white,
  You moonshine revellers, and shades of night,
  You orphan heirs of fixed destiny,
  Attend your office and your quality—
  Crier hobgoblin, make the fairy oyes.
HOBGOBLIN: Elves, list your names. Silence, you airy toys.
  Cricket, to Windsor chimneys shalt thou leap.
  Where fires thou find'st unraked and hearths unswept,
  There pinch the maids as blue as bilberry.
  Our radiant Queen hates sluts and sluttery.
FALSTAFF: They are fairies. He that speaks to them shall die.
  I'll wink and couch; no man their works must eye.
  [*He lies down, and hides his face*] (*MWW* 5.5.34–45)

The pretend fairies seek to eliminate all unchaste acts and desires from Windsor Castle with their chants, juices, and references
to Edward III's *Honi soit qui mal y pense*, the motto of the Order of
the Garter, for whom the play was putatively performed. That motto
would license the undoing of the unashamed Falstaff, who has worked
to defeat chastity:

FALSTAFF: God defend me from that Welsh fairy,
  Lest he transform me to a piece of cheese!
HOBGOBLIN: Vile worm, thou wast o'erlooked even in thy birth.
MISTRESS QUICKLY: With trial-fire, touch me his finger-end.
  If he be chaste, the flame will back descend,
  And turn him to no pain; but if he start,
  It is the flesh of a corrupted heart.
HOBGOBLIN: A trial, come!

EVANS: Come, will this wood take fire? [They burn him with
their tapers]

FALSTAFF: O, O, O!

MISTRESS QUICKLY: Corrupt, corrupt, and tainted in desire.
About him, fairies; sing a scornful rhyme;
And, as you trip, still pinch him to your time.

FAIRIES: Fie on sinful fantasy!
Fie on lust and luxury!
Lust is but a bloody fire,
Kindled with unchaste desire,
Fed in heart, whose flames aspire,
As thoughts do blow them, higher and higher.
Pinch him, fairies, mutually.
Pinch him for his villany.
Pinch him, and burn him, and turn him about,
Till candles and starlight and moonshine be out. (*MWW*
5.5.78–99)

The dogs do not leap on Falstaff. The gods (here fairies) do. The
emblemology of the mythographers gets him. As this is mock epic,
comedy turns him less to dog food than to ass head. The question of
how the dogs became fairies can easily be answered. In interpretation
the myth has many explanations, some of them as demythologized as
Falstaff's pain among the burning fairies. Sandys writes that Diana,
the "fairy" or god, tied Actaeon into a stag's skin where he was devoured by his own dogs or by the "fairy" power of the moon as it
possesses the imagination:

Actaeon thus transformed, is deuoured by his owne hounds.
Stesichorus writes that she sewed him within the skin of a Stag,
and set his dogges vpon him: others, that he was neither turned
into a Stag, nor clothed in his skin; but that she possessed his dogges in their madnesse with such an imagination. And perhaps they
ran mad in the Canicular dayes through the power of the Moone,
that is, of Diana; augmented by the entrance of the Sunne into

Leo and then what force or knowledge could resist their worrying of their master? Scaliger reports that the like befell to diuers hunters of Corsica in his time: and some auerre that Lucian, the Apostata and Atheist, came to that end.[33]

Mistress Quickly (Diana) with her canicular power turns her fairies on Jove's votary. The old bucket of flesh earlier disguised both as dirty laundry and as the witch that follows the Hecatish Diana finally sees the dogs of appetite turn on him. Their objective correlatives are the fairies. Ostensibly speaking of the young lovers following Anne Page but also speaking reflexively, he remarks in his last words in the play, "When night-dogs run, all sorts of deer are chased" (*MWW* 5.5.215). He is chased, objectively, by disguised fairies but more substantially by his "desires like fell and cruel hounds." By this time, the hounds have pretty much torn him apart, and he stands in comedy, as Actaeon does in tragedy, for the pathetic funniness of aged voyeurism and incompetent lust.

Myth Renewing Myth: Ganymede and the Golden Age

Finally, a figurative pattern may fulfill or complement another figurative pattern, so as to make both develop a sense that neither would make independently, whether understood literally or figuratively. In *Richard II*, John of Gaunt speaks of England as an "other Eden, demi-Paradise" (2.1.42). In *As You Like It* Shakespeare presents us with an Arden/Ardenne set in England or France that is also a demi-Paradise or partial golden age, obviously imperfect in many ways and irresponsible in its indifference to the genuine woes of civil society at its centers. He completes the incomplete promise of that place with a celebration of ascent to a better spiritual place—a better love, a better society, and the better unity represented by Ganymede and Hymen.

At the beginning of *As You Like It* Charles the wrestler says that Duke Senior's forest society reenacts the golden age:

CHARLES: They say he is already in the forest of Ardenne, and
a many merry men with him; and there they live like the old
Robin Hood of England. They say many young gentlemen

flock to him every day, and fleet the time carelessly, as they did in the golden world. (*AYLI* 1.1.99–103)

Arden (Ardenne) should be Eden, as many critics have suggested. Mythographers in Shakespeare's time assumed that the story of the golden age and the story of Adam and the garden were essentially the same story. As Sandys describes Saturn's golden age, it is Eden:

> The Golden Race of many languag'd men
> The Gods first made, who heauen inhabit, when Age
> The Scepter Saturne swaid: like Gods they liu'd,
> Secure in minde; nor sweat with toile, nor greiu'd ...

> Then was there neither Master nor Seruant ... Vnforced Nature gaue sufficient to all; who securely possest her vndiuided bounty. A rich condition wherein no man was poore: Auarice after introducing indigency: who by coueting a propriety, alienated all; and lost what it had, by seeking to inlarge it. But this happy estate abounding with all felicities, assuredly represented that which man injoyed in his innocency: vnder the raigne of Saturne, more truly of Adam, whereof the Sabaticall yeare among the *Iewes* was a memoriall: wherein they neither sowed their fields nor had a propriety in the fruits of the Earth, which she voluntarily afforded. ... Saturne was the first that inuented tillage, the first that euer raigned; and so was Adam: Saturne was throwne out of Heauen, and Adam out of Paradice: Saturne *is* said to deuoure his owne children, and Adam ouer-threw his whole posterity.[34]

However, we are not exactly in Eden; rather Arden has multiple layers of reference to the first place. Duke Senior, when he first speaks to his little community, recognizes that Arden is like Eden but also radically unlike it:

DUKE SENIOR: Are not these woods
More free from peril than the envious court?

Here feel we not the penalty of Adam,
The seasons' difference, as the icy fang
And churlish chiding of the winter's wind,
Which when it bites and blows upon my body
Even till I shrink with cold, I smile, and say
'This is no flattery. These are counsellors
That feelingly persuade me what I am.'
Sweet are the uses of adversity
Which, like the toad, ugly and venomous,
Wears yet a precious jewel in his head;
And this our life, exempt from public haunt,
Finds tongues in trees, books in the running brooks,
Sermons in stones, and good in everything.
AMIENS: I would not change it. (*AYLI* 2.1.3–18)

At one level, the place seems Eden. It is relatively without peril. The "penalty of Adam," the changing of the seasons and bad weather, are not felt as evil because they providentially tell one the truth about one's limitations. However, the seasons' differences do come to postlapsarian Arden as they did not to Eden. But according to the Duke, the pain of the forest—as in Boethius's *Consolation of Philosophy* (translated by Queen Elizabeth at about this time)—makes one know oneself. In Arden the cold that tells the truth substitutes for the court flattery that mythologizes the self at Frederick's court. Absent in Eden, and difficult to bear in Frederick's court, pain becomes providential in Arden. Visible things become the emblems of invisible ones as adversity finds sweet uses and the world about the forest speaks as a tongue, a book, and a sermon. The duke's essential message is later converted into song when Amiens tunes his song to that of the birds—in another version of the Eden metaphor—which also tell their sermon of good in everything: "Here shall he (*whoever comes here*) see / No enemy / but winter and rough weather" (*AYLI* 2.5.6–8).

The new situation offers one a world forested with symbols, though no unified perception of the meaning of the symbolism exists among the disparate inhabitants of the place. The wood that is around the duke is a sermon-making vehicle that speaks to almost everyone with differing messages according to their temperaments (*AYLI* 2.1.44). That is, of course, part of the solipsism of Eden after the Fall. To Jaques, the forest makes symbols of the stricken deer, the herd that ignores it, the bourgeois pretense of caring. To him, Touchstone as fool becomes the true satirist, Adam as *senex* becomes the emblem of the end of the New Comedy stages of life (see chapter 1). On the other hand, for Rosalind, Orlando as a forest hunter becomes the Cupid who slays hearts rather than what he is for Jaques, a contemptible Monsieur Love. Jaques almost always preaches, but in moralizing everything, Jaques is not so different from the duke, Orlando, or Rosalind, though Rosalind's interpretations are more constant. All are emblem makers, all tirelessly moralizing whatever spectacle appears, often in apparently contradictory ways. To various of the characters at various times the world is providential, the world is a path to senility and death, the wood is a paradise, a usurper's hell, a place of endless love-longing. Arden is no unified sermon in stone or wood. Its various figurative interpretations reflect the tensions available in a fallible but decent society, governed not by the ambition of Duke Frederick's court but by natural law and natural conscience.

In Arden at the beginning of the play, natural law and natural conscience are not yet illuminated by any special grace or love. People are still trivially mean to each other—to Jaques, to the shepherds, to Audrey, to Orlando. Unlike the busy and fratricidal world outside, the social condition of Arden speaks partially of human love and friendship. It has no marriages until the end, and its society seems a little like the society of a men's locker room. Arden does not experience the divine as Eden did in the lives of Adam and Eve (certainly as Milton's Eden does in book 4 of *Paradise Lost*). It will take a further mythic move to direct the community toward a reconciliation and unity with each other and perhaps with the One, the moves accomplished by Ganymede and Hymen culminating in the Juno-song of act 5 in praise of marriage (*AYLI* 5.4.130).[35]

Arden is not so much Eden as Eden's shadow and only so for a few people. The courtiers in the forest, like the innocents in Ovid's golden age, seem to live without much sense of "mine" and "thine" and with little explicit attention to class. However, class is in fact operative in the separation between the hunters and the shepherds; the shepherds have to worry about having their fields sold out from under them, traditional manor rights no longer being theirs.[36] As James Shapiro has observed, four scenes in the play celebrate the courtier's deep woods, "the forbidding terrain where Orlando and Adam stumble upon the Duke and his men," a place of "ancient oak, streams, caves, and herds of deer, . . . men dressed as outlaws," Robin Hood–like. Twelve other forest scenes reveal to us a farmer's and shepherd's "world of enclosure, of sheep and shepherds, landlords and farmers, . . . peasants and . . . wage earners," a place where crops have replaced the hunter-gatherers and where exploitation is rife.[37] As in the golden age, the courtier's forest has no military, but the lesser weapons of the hunter exist there (though Renaissance chronology affirmed the apparent biblical assertion that no eating of meat existed until after the flood [see Genesis 9–10]). In Arden the hunters pursue the hunted, much to the consternation of Jaques, who, perhaps as a Saturnine melancholic, glimpses the golden world before arms existed.[38] But if Arden is not Eden, it is also for the courtiers not Jaques's endless Tartarus of malice, vanity, ruination of nature, and mutual human exploitation. It cannot be measured by some unreachable standard of perfection, but it is all right for most of the exiled court, somewhere east of Eden. In it the Saturnine Jaques, who bases his satire in what appears to be a wish to turn the world golden, is endlessly melancholy, preparing to go to the abandoned cave and to learn from the ducal "convertite" of the contemplative life.[39] He thus sums up the meaning of Dürer's *Melancholia* by representing the humor's depressed, dry, cold, languid character at its lower reaches in most of his idle hours. Only at the end of the play does he reach toward the artist's and prophet's melancholy also suggested by Dürer—that pure contemplative state or Saturnine contemplation that makes for artistic and religious greatness.

Apart from Jaques's satiric invective against the fallen and foolish aspects of this world, the deep part of the forest does seem to have regenerative effects. It is not sin-free like Dante's sacred wood at the heights of the *Purgatorio*, but it is renewing. Into it come two fratricidal brothers, Oliver and Duke Frederick, who wish to kill their siblings, as Cain wished to kill Abel. One is converted by his brother's rescue of him from the lion *and* the serpent, the other by an "old religious man" (*AYLI* 5.4.149) who leads him to put off fratricide and put on the religious life of the cave.[40] The Eden–golden age metaphor of this part of the forest continues in some of the characters. Accompanying Orlando into Arden/Eden comes the Adam/*senex*, who, outside the forest, recalls a genuinely Edenic time when people served each other for love and not for "meed" (reward). He still so serves his master, Orlando, upon his return to the forest (*AYLI* 2.4.32ff.). In book 1 of *Metamorphoses* Ovid describes the golden-age life without search of "meed," exploitation, tillage, war, government, or exploration.[41] It is of just such a world, free of the search for money, that Adam seems to remind Orlando in his description of an "antique world" where human beings served each other for duty and loyalty (2.3.57–77); Shakespeare almost always uses the word *antique* to speak of early mythic times like the golden age.

But the Adam who comes from the hell of Oliver's household and goes with Orlando to the new Eden or Arden disappears from the play (or dies) after the scene where he is fed. Adam's goodness to people such as Orlando may palliate the misery caused them by the Olivers and Duke Fredericks of the world. But it is not enough to make the world a joyous place, nor is Arden by itself enough to give us full delight, though it leads the courtiers back to a college fraternity type of community and a self-knowledge of sorts. The end of the comedy has to be more—full joy, joy beyond a common joy—and in Shakespeare such joy is never gained through a utopian grasping for the golden age's commune or for a permanent escape from the evils attendant on governing.

Standard Renaissance political theory taught that the first paradise was lost in Eden as part of the Fortunate Fall.[42] Arden is the shadow of that first paradise. It reminds us of what was and what has been lost. When one grants the theory of the Fortunate Fall, one assumes that a second more joyous paradise can be regained in a world characterized by the eternal contemplation of God. Further, within the fallen world of property and selfishness, though the first commune is lost, unselfish love of the other can be gained through grace and the practice of neighborly and married love.

If there is a paradise that surpasses the demi-paradise of the overaged fraternity boys who play at Robin Hood and the golden age in the Arden of *As You Like It*, it is the world of love and its higher reaches explored by a Ganymede/Rosalind in the reenacting of the Ganymede/Jupiter pattern in Ovid's *Metamorphoses* 10, 152ff. There, as the story is told by Orpheus and elaborated by the commentators, Jove takes the form of an eagle to kidnap Ganymede, bring him to the divine realms, and make him Jove's cupbearer and lover. To Rosalind, Orlando is a reminder not only of Cupid but of Jove, and he is first discovered under "Jove's tree" (3.2.211–14). Like the heroine in Shakespeare's source story, Lodge's *Rosalynde*, Shakespeare's Rosalind calls herself Ganymede, and like her ancient forebear she has a shepherd's role. Unlike Lodge's Rosalynde, who claims only to have a friend who is a magician, Shakespeare's Rosalind claims to have *learned* the arts of magic from a magician uncle who lives in the forest (5.2.54; 5.4.28–34; see act 3, scene 2); that the uncle nowhere appears in the play does not mean he is Rosalind's fiction. She does work a sort of magic as the *poeta* of the play and presenter of its masque.

She apparently cures her lover of writing bad puppy-love poetry and fouling the tree's bark with doggerel through the nonmagical techniques of Ovid's remedies of love:

'From the east to western Ind,
No jewel is like Rosalind.
Her worth being mounted on the wind
Through all the world bears Rosalind.
All the pictures fairest lined
Are but black to Rosalind.
Let no face be kept in mind
But the fair of Rosalind.' (3.2.77–84)

Ovid says those who wish to be cured of love need to stay away from poetry and that magic will not help. After act 3, scene 2, where Rosalind begins to administer her version of Ovid's cures, Orlando writes no more bad verse. But Rosalind only cures Orlando of infatuation. She tells him at first that he is a liar about his love. He has none of the signs of love sickness on him, the signs of unrequited obsession that Ovid purports to cure and against which the medical books from Galen to Burton warn. She promises or threatens to provide their sorts of remedies — prison, whipping, reimagining the beloved in many unflattering physical and psychological poses, promising jealousy, infidelity, hyena-laughing at sleep time, and all the imaginable ills that a relationship can have (3.2.338–80; 4.1.125–51). His heroic imagination of himself as dying for love of Rosalind becomes mock-heroic when Rosalind assures him that even love's heroes — Leander and Troilus — did not die for love (4.1.81–94). As an Ovidian satirist, she teaches her Orlando the cosmic stupidity of the deifying idolatry of his poems.

As satire is usually regarded as a rationalistic mode, one might expect that Rosalind's satire would leave her and her lover with only the light of common day, without desire or energy. But such is not the case. When Orlando leaves her after the mock marriage, she declares her love bottomless; when she learns of his gratuitous rescue of his unkind brother, Oliver, from the serpent and the lioness, and hears that he has given up some flesh in the process betokened by his sending his bloody napkin to her as emblem of fidelity, she faints in her commitment. She has given him her *remedia amoris* and knows, from the way that he takes her cure, that he is ready for a marriage that "no cross shall part" (5.4.120).

But the magic that is to produce Rosalind for Orlando described in 5.3.54 is only the pretend magic of Ganymede's taking off his disguise. Even so the magician uncle and magic she mentions to Orlando (5.4.30–35) may not be altogether a lie. For Rosalind/Ganymede promises what Hymen, who seems to appear magically, delivers at the end of the play (one must suppose that it is Rosalind's art that produces Hymen). She promises — and he delivers — betrothal and promised marriages for each of the four pairs of lovers; she, in a sense,

FIGURE 12. Correggio (Antonio Allegri) (1489–1534), *The Rape of Ganymede*, ca. 1525–30. Oil on canvas. Photo courtesy of Kunsthistorisches Museum, Vienna.

promises a reunified society, and Ganymede and Hymen deliver on the promise. Ganymede is after all a figure in alchemy and hermetic magic, an allegory for the stable part of the matter to be changed, with which the eagle of volatile matter unites to form the new, transformed, and purified matter that is Jupiter—gold, the gold of the golden age. Rosalind/Ganymede is both transformer and transformed in the last scene of the play.[43]

Recent scholarship has emphasized the degree to which her sexuality allows her to play both the male and female roles in same-sex flirting, both with Orlando and with Celia. She is an androgynous magician of love to almost everyone she meets. As such, she also bodies forth the emblematic meaning of the love that rejoices in God, that love recorded in Alciati's fourth emblem about Ganymede, in Dante's ascent with Ganymede's wings from the ante-Purgatory to Purgatory proper. However, several early Renaissance paintings and drawings of Ganymede by Michelangelo, da Vinci, and Correggio seem to emphasize Ganymede as same-sex more than mystical love (fig. 12).[44]

The Hymen whom she calls down tells us that "Wedding is great Juno's crown"—that is, she is the symbol of Uno, the unitive experience, or unity in all things. She is used so in Ben Jonson's parallel *Hymenaei*. She gives us the marriage with the One that Jaques must be seeking as a convertite and that even a partial golden age cannot offer.[45] The text asserts that Hymen brings Rosalind *from heaven* (*AYLI* 5.4.102), surely a magical act and one stage-possible if, as Shapiro suggests, "Hymen appears from above, descending in a throne from the cover of the Globe's stage."[46] As noted in the preceding chapter, he comes announcing the heavenly mirth created by the "at-*one*ment of earthly things made even" in the octave of the four couples about to be wed (*AYLI* 5.4.97–104) and the oneness of the crown of Juno, the goddess of the unitive experience.[47] He grants to Rosalind and Orlando the higher love that Jove gives to Ganymede, and he offers it to the community. Every town honors the Hymen of wedlock; every town seeks the Juno's crown of wedlock and unity. In the betrothal, the vatic power of divine breakthrough and the priestly aspect of community custom are joined.

As a mythmaker, Shakespeare shows disintegrative and frenzied forces undoing individuals, households, and commonwealths. Hobgoblin malice can be propelled by an apparently innocent self-centeredness, and quotidian psychological idleness can turn to a destructively unbridled appetite that destroys the community. At the level of *both* the commonwealth and the household, uncontrolled, solipsistic desire may erase others' goods and needs (e.g., Falstaff-as-Actaeon, Titania). Shakespeare is concerned equally with the burning with which we destroy ourselves and with the brute force with which we endeavor to destroy others (Theseus initially, Ford, Frederick, Oliver, Charles the wrestler).

But the daemonic frenzy is not all destructive. The Cupid/Love of service to the needy at the end of *Love's Labour's Lost*, the Oberon who blesses the household of *Midsummer Night's Dream*, the pinching fairy housewives who torment their Actaeon at the end of *Merry Wives of Windsor*, and the Hymen who brings Ganymede at the end of *As You Like It* are also forces that create and direct intense passion, forces that integrate the vatic and the rule-governed and create the comic conclusion. Such forces reach beyond mere solipsism and violence. In his expansion of New Comedy to reenact figurative versions of household and commonwealth myth, Shakespeare continues the work that began with his addition of the dux and commonwealth to the foibles of the street and the middle-class citizen seeking love and marriage. He recreates the pain and the comedy of our deepest breakthroughs into daemonic and sacred territory.

Resources on Classical Myth

This chapter has examined in depth only four of Shakespeare's explorations into mythic territory. One can explore mythic metaphoric dimensions in the middle sections of other comedies, especially the Hercules pattern in *Taming of the Shrew* and *The Merchant of Venice*, the pattern of Virgilian myth in *The Tempest*, Chaucerian versions of the Venus-Mars-Diana-Saturn stories in *Two Noble Kinsmen*, and a variety of mythic dimensions in *Measure for Measure*, partially explored in chapter 6. Readers will see other possibilities. The masques of the period are variously printed, but the most revealing ones are those by Ben Jonson, which contain extensive annotations to the mythographies to assist readers in understanding the language game; these are published in *Ben Jonson*, edited by Herford, Simpson, and Simpson.

The idea of myth as pattern or, in Latin, *exemplum*, is virtually universal in Renaissance mythography, and one can approach this idea through Boccaccio's commentary on the pagan gods (see the theoretical section, translated as *Boccaccio on Poetry*). Similar explanations are found in the English theorists Lodge, Sidney, Golding, and Sandys.

One useful introduction to the medieval and Renaissance use of myth is to be found in H. David Brumble's *Classical Myths and Legends in the Middle Ages and Renaissance: A Dictionary of Allegorical Meanings*. Other useful beginning books are Jean Seznec, *The Survival of the Pagan Gods*; Erwin Panofsky, *Studies in Iconology* and *Meaning in the Visual Arts*; and Philipp Fehl's essays on the history of the classical tradition in *Decorum and Wit: The Poetry of Venetian Painting*. Also see Fehl's article "The Rocks in the Parthenon Frieze" and subsequent articles by Fehl on the "invisible" gods in Renaissance painting. For a modern discussion of scholarship on these matters, see John W. Veltz, "Shakespeare's Ovid in the Twentieth Century: A Critical Survey."

Roman comedy includes only one play that rests wholly on an ancient myth about the gods, Plautus's *Amphitryon*. Of course, Aristophanes frequently plays off classical myth and legend in his plays, but it is doubtful that Shakespeare and his audience knew Aristophanes or used him as an interpretive frame.

One goes to Ovid's *Metamorphoses*, a universal grammar-school text in its Renaissance embodiments, to know the common significance of myths in Shakespeare's times, especially to Golding's translation, with its brief exemplary explanations of the myths in its prefatory materials, and to Sandys's translation, which, though published a little after Shakespeare, translates into English the time's common Latin understandings of the Ovidian myths. Students familiar with Latin can pursue the Renaissance Ovid in the various editions of and commentaries on Ovid at http://etext.virginia.edu/latin/ovid/about.html; they may also wish to read in Pierre Bersuire's *Ovidius Moralizatus*, an Ovid quite popular in the Renaissance (Berchorius, *De Formis Figurisque Deorum: Ovidius Moralizatus*).

A fine Web site that is expanding regularly covers Johann Spreng's 1563 interpretation of Ovid at http://etext.virginia.edu/latin/ovid/ovidillust.html (sometimes English translations of Spreng are available at http://etext.lib.virginia.edu/latin/ovid/book1.html or elsewhere at this site). The 1563 version of Spreng and the later versions contained on this Web site also allow one to look at the Virgil Solis illustrations for Ovid from the 1563 and later editions—illustrations that may suggest ways of staging scenes in the comedies. For example, the Solis woodcut of the golden age shows nearly naked people conversing innocently and gathering fruits from the trees in an open forest. The open forest and the languor of the people suggest *As You Like It*, but the absence from the picture of any suggestion of seasonal differences, cold wind, or hunting suggests the limits of *As You Like It*'s reenactment of the golden time. The Spreng explanation says the movement from gold to iron times signals the departure of faith, piety, justice, and honesty, and the iron time, like Oliver's and Frederick's households, is filled with greed, envy, avarice, and murder—including the absence of brother love.

Solis's Actaeon turned to a stag shows a picture of a human being with a stag's head walking toward Diana and her nymphs as if coming on to them, his dogs at his feet. In the distance, his dogs are tearing the stag man to pieces, a configuration that may suggest some details of how to stage Falstaff in act 5 of *Merry Wives of Windsor*.

It may seem silly to treat of epic materials in a book on comedy, but Aristotle treated *The Odyssey* as in some sense a comedy and so did Servius in commentary on the *Aeneid*. *A Midsummer Night's Dream* owes its fairy world (the realm of fairy meant the realm of the classical gods) to Chaucer's *Knight's Tale*. Shakespeare's similar fairy machinery in *The Tempest* draws on the *Aeneid*, so it is not idle to look to epic versions of the myths for understandings of how they function semiologically in the comedies.

In exploring myth, one should probably start with Homer. However, there is not much evidence that Shakespeare makes extensive use of

Homer in his comedies (I follow the Folio in treating *Troilus and Cressida* as a tragedy). When Shakespeare used Homer, it seems likely that he used some combination of the Greek text and Latin translations and Chapman's 1598 translation of seven books of *The Iliad*. Homer, like Ovid, had been given extensive figurative interpretations, some of which continue in the Spondanus commentary that Chapman used. Spondanus is to some degree incorporated into Chapman's translations of both *The Iliad* and *The Odyssey*. However, no great illumination of Shakespeare is likely to come out of pursuing the Renaissance Homer. Another source of interpretation of *The Odyssey* is the concluding part of book 2 of *The Faerie Queene*, which tells of Guyon's journey to a place like Circe's island but imitates Homer's fabulous places as allegorical loci. For an excellent account of the emergence of the figurative version of Homer and later epic figurative work, see Robert Lamberton, *Homer the Theologian: Neoplatonist Allegorical Reading and the Growth of the Epic Tradition*. See also Paul A. Olson, *The Journey to Wisdom: Self-Education in Patristic and Medieval Literature*, for the role of this sort of interpretation of Homer and related interpretation of Virgil in medieval and Renaissance literature relating to education and scientific pursuits.

Of course, Shakespeare and the more learned members of his audience also got their understanding of ancient myth from the figurative versions of the *Aeneid*, a standard grammar-school text. Virgil, in editions widely available in Shakespeare's time, was often accompanied by Servius's fourth-century commentary on Virgil and Fulgentius's sixth-century one, both of them heavily figurative, especially in the treatment of Virgil's sixth book as a parable about education. In all likelihood, Shakespeare used Fabricius on Virgil for the identity of the Harpies and Furies played by Ariel and her troupe in *The Tempest*. He *may* also have used Badius Ascensius and Manutius. One translation that gives a sense of how people read Virgil in Shakespeare's time is that of book 6 of the *Aeneid* by Sir John Harington, with an elaborate marginal and end commentary and full-blown advice on how one is to read Virgil. See Sir John Harington, *The Sixth Book of Virgil's "Aeneid"* (1604), edited by Simon Cauchi (New York: Clarendon, 1991, especially pages 95–101).

One would like to be able to point to similar work that should have guided Shakespeare and his audience in their readings of Chaucer's *Knight's Tale*, but one has only a few suggestions in Sir Francis Beaumont's letter to Thomas Speght in Speght's 1598 edition of Chaucer and in Francis Thynne's 1598 *Animaduersions vppon the annotacions and corrections of some imperfections of impressiones of Chaucers workes*, a critique of Speght's edition of Chaucer. It seems likely that the machinery of the gods in *The Knight's Tale* would have been readily accessible since Saturn makes clear that the gods in the tale are personifications of the planets and their influences (A, 2453ff.), and people in the time were well acquainted with how the gods or planets could influence a life course and behavior. Though we tend to dichotomize our understandings of the gods, favoring either literal or allegorical readings, figurative readings were as common as dirt because of the presence of figurative interpretations of the planets: Mars as the planet of righteous or unjust rage; Venus as that of heavenly or earthly love; Diana as the moon governing chastity, the hunt, or witchcraft and magic. The planets and their houses influenced but did not determine how one behaved, and one could appropriate one's "birth" in a variety of ways, positive and negative.

The myths were also popularly explained in mythological handbooks that were widely read. The main non-English explicators popular in Shakespeare's time were, in Latin, Lilio Gregorio Giraldi (Gyraldus), *De deis gentilium libri*; Natale (Natalis) Conti (Comes), *Mythologiae sive explicationis fabularum libri decem*; and, in Italian, Vincenzo Cartari, *Le imagini degli Dei degli antichi*. All kinds of handbooks like these followed in most of the western European nations. One easily available handbook of myth in English from Shakespeare's time is Abraham Fraunce's *The Third Part of the Countesse of Pembroke's Yvychurch* (1592), which retells many of the myths and explains them. Another published after Shakespeare's death but reflecting older lore from the Latin sources is Alexander Ross's *Mystagogus Poeticus, or The Muses Interpreter* (1647). A somewhat unusual mythography is that by Sir Francis Bacon, *De Sapientia Veterum, 1609 and the Wisdom of the Ancients*, translated by Arthur Gorges.

One of the most accessible routes to an understanding of classical myth is through the emblem books, beginning with Alciati. Many of these are on the Internet. Alciati's emblems, first published in 1531, were enormously popular throughout Europe for over a century. Alciati, in Latin and English, appears at http://www.mun.ca/alciato/. One can get some sense of the complexity of Shakespeare's use of myth in *Comedy of Errors*, for example, when Antipholus of Ephesus tells Luciana:

ANTIPHOLUS OF SYRACUSE: Sing, siren, for thyself, and I will
   dote.
Spread o'er the silver waves thy golden hairs,
And as a bed I'll take them, and there lie,
And in that glorious supposition think
He gains by death that hath such means to die.
Let love, being light, be drowned if she sink. (*CE* 3.2.47–52)

Antipholus is clearly a fool for making Luciana into a siren, and the siren myth in Alciati suggests that the siren is monstrous lust and that learned men (i.e., Ulysses) have nothing to do with prostitutes (Emblem 116). Luciana is hardly a prostitute.

Geoffrey Whitney's *A Choice of Emblemes* (1586), much of it indebted to Alciati, is also helpful. For instance, if one is exploring the Hercules at the crossroads myth, Emblem 40 presents a Hercules deciding between two women, one Venus and Cupid and the other clearly Minerva. The poem that goes with the emblem is as follows:

When HERCULES, was dowtfull of his waie,
Inclosed rounde, with vertue, and with vice:
With reasons firste, did vertue him assaie,
The other, did with pleasures him entice:
They longe did strive, before he coulde be wonne,
Till at the lengthe, ALCIDES thus begonne.
Oh pleasure, thoughe thie waie bee smoothe, and faire,
And sweete delightes in all thy courtes abounde:

Yet can I heare, of none that have bene there,
That after life, with fame have bene renoum'de:
For honor hates, with pleasure to remaine,
Then houlde thy peace, thow wastes thie winde in vaine.
But heare, I yeelde oh vertue to thie will,
And vowe my selfe, all labour to indure,
For to ascende the steepe, and craggie hill,
The toppe whereof, whoe so attaines, is sure
For his rewarde, to have a crowne of fame:
Thus HERCULES, obey'd this sacred dame.

The last few lines perhaps furnish an intertextual explanation of why the women in *Love's Labour's Lost* impose the hard work of the works of charity on the play's lovers before they will consider entering into a virtuous love relationship with them. Whitney contains myriads of explanations of classical stories, explanations, and pictorial representations.

One of the most interesting of the emblematic myth books, used in England in Shakespeare's time by Ben Jonson, is Cesare Ripa's *Iconologia*, first published in Italy in 1593 but only translated into English in 1709. The 1709 English edition can be found online at http://emblem.libraries.psu.edu/Ripa/Images/ripatoc.htm. For example, the picture of the Fury that inspires poetry is figure 132, *Furor Poeticus*, which is described as follows:

A brisk young Beau, of a ruddy Complexion; crown'd with Laurel; bound about with Ivy; in a writing Posture, but turning his Head backward toward Heaven.

The wings declare the *Quickness* of his Phansie, which soars aloft, and carries an Encomium with it, which still remain *fresh* and *green*, as Laurel and Ivy intimate: Looking upwards, the Ideas of *supernatural Things* which he writes down.

One could hardly have a better framework for looking at Theseus's speech on the fine frenzy of the poet.

Another place to examine the uses of classical myth is in the progresses and masques put on for the monarch, while he or she was traveling to rural estates or at court. These have been edited by John Nichols and have the advantage of specifying somewhat the occasion on which the myth was used and why. See John Nichols, *The Progresses and Public Processions of Queen Elizabeth* (1823); and John Nichols, *The Progresses, Processions, and Magnificent Festivities, of King James the First, His Royal Consort, Family, and Court* (1828). The masques of the period are variously printed, but the most revealing ones are those by Ben Jonson, which contain extensive annotations to the mythographies edition. Anyone interested in this area should follow articles, past and present, in the *Journal of the Warburg and Courtauld Institutes*, an incredible source of mythographic knowledge concerning the Early Modern period, especially as it applies to art. A very useful entry to Early Modern art, though seldom English art, is to be found in the *Web Gallery of Art* at http://www.wga.hu/index1.html—which contains a large number of paintings based on classical subjects that can be used to help one understand Shakespeare. For example, serious study of Agnolo Bronzino's *Venus, Cupid, and the Time* (c. 1545) or Vouet's *Father Time Overcome by Love, Hope, and Beauty* (1627) will certainly assist one to understand the relationship between love and time, Venus and Saturn, and Orlando and Jaques in *As You Like It*.

Perhaps one should not intrude on other Shakespeareans' joy in exploring figurative Renaissance myth and how it plays into Shakespeare's hands, but a few suggestions for exploration may be in order: the story of Ariadne and Theseus as an intertext for the Julia and Proteus story in *Two Gentlemen of Verona*; the Hercules-Omphale story as parodic introduction to *Taming of the Shrew*; the general figurative mythology surrounding Diana/Cynthia/Hecate and the Rosalind figure in *As You Like It*; the intertextual reference to whole books of Cupid's emblems in *Much Ado about Nothing*; the Pluto/Proserpina and Pygmalion/Galatea myths in *The Winter's Tale*; and the whole range of *Aeneid* mythic structures, asserted or inverted, in *The Tempest*. These should give one enough fun for a lifetime.

4

Biblical Story and Festival Enter Shakespearean Comedy

The ultimate prophetic or vatic book for Shakespeare's contemporaries was the Bible—both the Hebrew Bible (or Old Testament) and the New Testament. The Bible was the center of the prophetic visions studied by Elizabethan Bible readers, and its prophecies offered possible visions of the future in an unstable age. It also offered prophetic testimony, admonishing the age and its individuals to reform. Thinkers from Ficino down to Shakespeare, following Socrates' analysis of the Furies in *Phaedrus* 244–56, spoke of a prophetic or Apollonian Fury that rivaled the other furies: the poetic or Muses' fury; the love or Venus' Fury; and the Dionysiac Fury, the fury of superstition or of genuine religious revelation. Theseus speaks of the last three of these Furies or frenzies in the great *Midsummer Night's Dream* "fine frenzy" speech analyzed in chapter 3 when he speaks of the poet, the lover, and the madman. In *Othello*, Shakespeare goes on to have Othello name the fourth, the prophetic fury, in his second extended speech about Desdemona's handkerchief:

> 'Tis true. There's magic in the web of it.
> A sibyl that had number'd in the world
> The sun to course two hundred compasses,
> *In her prophetic fury* sewed the work;
> The worms were hallowed that did breed the silk;

> And it was dyed in mummy which the skilful
> Conserved of maidens' hearts. (3.4.68–73; italics mine)

Othello's sibyl with her prophetic seizures and her magic is sister to Virgil's Cumaean sibyl and, as we shall see, to Prospero.

With the prophetic Cumaean sybil Shakespeare combines the related prophetic furies of the biblical prophets such as Isaiah, and he also uses the New Testament prophets such as John the Baptist and the Magi. This does not mean that the Shakespearean biblical mythos draws only on the conception of the prophetic fury. In writing of comedic families, he also employs biblical family struggles—Jacob-Laban, Cain and Abel, the family in Ephesus—and draws in a few Christological stories. He uses all these biblical stories as he uses the sacred stories of the Greeks and Romans—for their figurative application within the drama on the stage. The biblical text, taken as a unit extending from Genesis and the Fall to the Apocalypse and final rejoicing, appears to be a vast cosmic comedy beginning with the adversity of a Fall in a garden, descending into history with its wanderings, and ending happily with the prophecy of a divine marriage and group unification in the activity of the "the Spirit and the Bride" (Rev. 22:17). At some very general level every Shakespearean comedy emulates that pattern.

At the level of more precise biblical intertexts, as early as 1594 one of the first of the comedies, *The Comedy of Errors*, plays with the Ephesian settings in Acts or Ephesians, and as late as 1611–12, the last of the comedies, *The Tempest*, does much the same thing with the Isaiah setting. Between these lie significant uses of extended biblical intertexts in almost every play that the Folio treats as a comedy, almost all focusing on the renewal of the individual and the social order.[1]

Figurative Exegesis, Hamlet's "Tropical," and Biblical Pattern

Biblical texts do not come into the comedies as something in the mode of which Shakespeare creates anew, as he does with the myths.[2] His handling of the biblical intertext is as cautious as one would expect from a public entertainer writing in a time when no topic was more likely to promote controversy than how one used the Bible. This chapter does not catalogue Shakespeare's allusions to the Bible; previous scholars and critics have addressed this task repeatedly and well. Using this earlier work, however, I look at a few situations where a biblical story, biblically based feast, or feast-text (and sometimes its popular commentary, especially in the Geneva Bible) becomes a controlling or significant reference or intertext, and suggest a method for approaching these Shakespearean biblical intertexts.

This discussion of method does not attend much to the detail of disputes about Early Modern biblical hermeneutics. For example, Erasmian and post-Erasmian Catholic exegesis may appear to be more literalistic than its medieval equivalent, although Erasmus loved Augustine's allegory-making *De Doctrina Christiana*. The common modern accounts make Luther and his followers appear literalistic and render Calvinistic biblical explanation intensely literalistic. However, most of the differences between Early Modern exegetes aside from the Calvinistic ones are more terminological than real, and even today's descriptions of Early Modern biblical interpretation often become sticks with which to beat a modern opposition. While it is true that the marginal commentaries in the Geneva Bible are nothing like as heavily metaphorical as those in the *Common Gloss* or Nicholas de Lyra's *Postilles*—both used heavily in the later Middle Ages and into Shakespeare's period—they are still quite metaphorical in dealing with works like the Song of Songs. Erasmus is, in fact, very traditional. The exegetical practice of John Colet is "medieval."[3] The explanations of Luther owe much to the medieval glossators, though he often fulminates against them.[4] Further, William Whitaker's *Disputatio de Sacra Scriptura* and the biblical explanations of Lancelot Andrewes and John Donne all testify to a consistent tradition of complex and metaphoric use of the Bible in Shakespeare's time.[5] Further, the older explanations continue to be read down into the Protestant period, and while they are not often part of published scholarly explanations, they often inform the writing of religious poetry, such as Spenser's or Herbert's, and the construction of emblem books for popular consumption.[6]

Shakespeare is no different from these other writers. As he uses the conventionally accepted solvents of myth in his age to build the strata of his comedies (see chapter 3), so he also uses the figurative solvents that were thought to lead to biblical understanding. He uses the terminology of biblical exegesis, its strategies, and its emblems and figures (or those appropriated in literature and the emblem books) to build a series of "biblical" comedies based on the grand comedy of the original text, often using the biblical-vatic to make his drama but applying it to the situation in England and in Europe. Often the most revealing passages for the application of interpretive strategies to the comedies come from the tragedies—see, for example, in chapter 3, the use of the word *pattern* in *Titus Andronicus* to explain how Ovidian story works. In the biblical arena, Hamlet's use of the word *tropical* explains how a comedy full of biblical resonance is to be understood.

In framing *The Mousetrap* the Prince of Denmark answers the king's question about the name of the play by describing its function for him in the context in which he has it put on. To describe this function, he uses a piece of conventional exegetical terminology having to do with figurative scriptural levels—"tropical" from the conventional scholarly levels of interpretation, tropological or tropical, allegorical, and anagogical:

> HAMLET: *The Mousetrap.* Marry, how? *Tropically.* This play
> is the image of a murder done in Vienna. Gonzago is the
> Duke's name, his wife Baptista. You shall see anon. 'Tis a
> knavish piece of work; but what o' that? Your majesty, and
> we that have free souls, it touches us not. Let the galled jade
> wince, our withers are unwrung. (*Hamlet* 3.2.217–22; italics
> mine)

The word *tropical* and the biblical, exegetical term *tropological* had the same meaning in Shakespeare's time, and both point to an ethical or tropish application of a story, especially appropriate to a comedy with its ethical obsessions. Hamlet calls *The Mousetrap* a comedy (3.2.269).[7] And he has said that he will catch the conscience of the Danish king with the Vienna play, as we have shown that comedies in general were expected to catch people's consciences (see chapter 2).[8] When he skittishly points to *The Mousetrap* as tropological metaphor for Claudius's action, we know that the tropology of the scene prompts his twisting of the knife: "we that have free souls, it touches us not. Let the galled jade wince, our withers are unwrung."

If one examines the dumb show and the Gonzago play as "tropical" in relation to Claudius's actions, they tell us that the "tropical" or "tropological" use of the Bible or of biblical reference works in the same way as does pattern in myth (as in Sandys or *Titus Andronicus*). The ghost of Hamlet Sr., whether ghost or devil or some other apparition, has told Hamlet the story that, Adam-like, he was stung by a serpent while sleeping in his garden. The serpent was Claudius with his poison, though Gertrude seems not to have been wholly innocent in the matter. If Claudius was the serpent, Gertrude has to have been his Eve. In the dumb show the king lies on a bank of flowers, the queen acts out deep affection, the poisoning occurs, and then she easily accepts the poisoner's love. The reflexive scene as played by the itinerant players is more ethical in its content and more suggestive of the Edenic biblical intertext in its meaning than any historical assassination would have been. Assassinations in history always come out of complex motives and an ambiguous historical matrix. In the player's play reshaped by Hamlet, the poisoner is simply diabolical. He is explicitly in league with Hecate and the powers of evil, and the motive of the poisoning—"his estate" (*Hamlet* 3.2.239); that is, the crown—is explicitly declared. The effectiveness of the tropological mirror in what Hamlet calls his comedy (3.2.269) depends on his bringing the action of the great Edenic narrative that rehearses recurrent patterns in life to bear on the evil of a specific event in the life about him. Ethical pattern is everything, as it is said to be in the theories of comedy. *The Mousetrap* also appears to Hamlet to be a kind of twisted comedy in the sense that it recounts a love affair and ends with the prospect of a new married life.

Claudius apparently understands the Genesis Edenic metaphor implicit in the Mousetrap device, but he finds another and more cogent

FIGURE 13. Titian (Tiziano Vecellio) (ca.1488–1576), *Cain and Abel*, ca. 1570–76. Ceiling painting at S. Maria della Salute, Venice. Erich Lessing/Art Resource, New York.

biblical analogy to his own life in the story of Cain and Abel. However, in the biblical narrative and in typical Early Modern painting, that story contains no element of seduction, only pure envy and rage (see, for example, Titian's Cain and Abel painting, fig. 13).

Claudius continues by applying the Cain and Abel analogy to his own life: "O, my offense is rank! It smells to heaven" and "[i]t hath the primal eldest curse upon't" (*Hamlet* 3.3.36–37). Claudius seems to speak here both of the curse of Original Sin and of the curse on Cain, Claudius's fratricidal killing of his brother resembling the killing of

Abel. Though the differences between the two plots are gaping (e.g., the reversal of the anxieties of primogeniture in the Cain story, where the younger brother is killed—here Claudius kills his older brother), they have their similarities. A king is, of course, like Abel, an anointed or blessed being in Renaissance ruler mythology. Both Hamlet Sr. and Abel were the God-favored brothers, Hamlet Sr. favored with the blessing of the crown and Abel with an acceptance of his sacrifice. In both stories the unfavored brother kills the favored, both killings happening in a tilled place—a field or garden. In both the "blood" of the victim cries out, Abel's to God and that of Hamlet Sr. (or the ghost that bears his person) to Hamlet. Then both Cain and Claudius try to placate God, the former by pretending that he does not know where his brother is, the latter by pretending to pray when he cannot. And both become outsiders through their crime, Cain protected by God in his fugitive status, Claudius apparently protected when he tries to pray but unprotected when he tries to make Laertes kill Hamlet as the rightful heir.

That an anointed king who is killed may be compared to Abel in Shakespearean mythology is confirmed when Bolingbroke speaks to the man who, on his behalf, murdered Richard II and by indirection also speaks to himself:

KING HENRY: With Cain go wander through shades of night,
And never show thy head by day nor light.
Lords, I protest my soul is full of woe
That blood should sprinkle me to make me grow. (*Richard II*
5.6.43–46)

In the same scene, Bolingbroke promises to go to Jerusalem to cover his sin. The closest he gets physically is the Jerusalem Chamber in which he dies (in *2 Henry IV* 4.5.305–68), and the closest that he comes spiritually is the quoted gesture toward repentance in *Richard II*. In Claudius's case, his being "mousetrapped" leads to his anger and murderous intentions rather than to his repentance. The Geneva gloss makes clear that the tropology of the Cain story suggests that reprobates do not accept responsibility when rebuked for their hypocrisy (i.e., Claudius at *The Mousetrap*; Cain before God) and that God avenges the wrongs against his saints though no human agent acts (Hamlet apparently does not believe this).

But the pattern seems to continue. Concerning the Cain story, the Geneva Bible—the most widely used Bible in England and the Bible that Shakespeare used most often—asserts, "God reuengeth the wrongs of his Saints, though noon complaine: for the iniquitie it selfe crieth for vengeance." It appears that the pattern repeats itself in Hamlet's killing of Claudius in his duel with Laertes when chance, or providence, gives him the poisoned weapon.[9] The poisoned sword, ironically, may be part of the providence in the fall of the sparrow to which he has committed himself when he talks with Horatio. At least an Elizabethan playgoer immersed in biblical lore might so have viewed it.

The Merchant of Venice: Exegesis and Jacob-Laban

If scripture creates a pattern that tropologically legitimizes or undercuts action in the world outside the scriptural text, the exegete's motive in constructing how the biblical pattern applies is also a relevant consideration in any Shakespearean examination, as is particularly evident in one of the more "tragic" passages in *The Merchant of Venice*—Shylock's explanation of Jacob and Laban's division of their flock in the book of Genesis. Everyone acquainted with medieval and Renaissance exegesis knows of Augustine's *On Christian Doctrine* requirement that all biblical interpretation be governed by the motive of charity, the love of God and of neighbor.[10] Admonitions like Augustine's continue to appear in Early Modern theory, and of course the precepts of love were seen to be as forceful and fully governing in Protestant England as they were in patristic Rome.[11] We may then properly ask whether exegesis by a specific Shakespearean character or his or her related action observes charitable motives.

Consider the extended piece of scriptural interpretation that appears in *The Merchant of Venice*, when Shylock uses the example of Laban to justify his usury:

SHYLOCK: Methoughts you said you neither lend nor borrow
  Upon advantage.
ANTONIO: I do never use it.
SHYLOCK: When Jacob grazed his uncle Laban's sheep—
  This Jacob from our holy Abram was,
  As his wise mother wrought in his behalf,
  The third possessor; ay, he was the third—
ANTONIO: And what of him? Did he take interest?
SHYLOCK: No, not take interest, not, as you would say,
  Directly int'rest. Mark what Jacob did:
  When Laban and himself were compromised
  That all the eanlings that were streaked and pied
  Should fall as Jacob's hire, the ewes, being rank,
  In end of autumn turnèd to the rams,
  And when the work of generation was
  Between these woolly breeders in the act,
  The skilful shepherd peeled me certain wands,
  And in the doing of the deed of kind
  He stuck them up before the fulsome ewes
  Who, then conceiving, did in eaning time
  Fall parti-coloured lambs; and those were Jacob's.
  This was a way to thrive; and he was blest;
  And thrift is blessing, if men steal it not.
ANTONIO: This was a venture, sir, that Jacob served for—
  A thing not in his power to bring to pass,
  But swayed and fashioned by the hand of heaven.
  Was this inserted to make interest good,
  Or is your gold and silver ewes and rams?
SHYLOCK: I cannot tell. I make it breed as fast.
  But note me, signor— (*MV* 1.3.65–93)

Antonio cuts off the discussion with what has since become the bro-
mide that the devil can quote scripture.

Shylock's explanation reflects Puritan, commercial exegesis at its
most sophistic, and Shakespeare's anti-Semitic thrust in assigning

the speech to Shylock is wholly indefensible, especially given modern and postmodern criteria for understanding racism and respect. The portrait of Shylock, whatever its post–World War II humanitarian explanations, cannot but have fed Elizabethan hatred of the Jews. But Shylock's explanation of the Bible does not target Jewish interpretations of the Laban and Jacob story since Jewish interpretations of the passage did not make it justify usury.[12] On the other hand, Puritan—and specifically Calvinistic—exegeses of the Bible in general *did* justify Early Modern Protestant usurious banking practices so that they needed none of the inconvenient subterfuges that bankers who charged interest required in the medieval Catholic world.[13] The Shylock who charges interest in Venice is a metaphor for the Puritans of London *as well as* for the Jews of Venice, and the references to Puritans under the metaphor of Shylock continue in other sections of the play. Shylock's hatred of masques and pretend festival makes him more like the Puritans than any other sizable group in Shakespeare's England. He is a harsher version of *Twelfth Night*'s Malvolio as a killjoy, and like Malvolio, he criticizes Puritan greed and hatred of expensive shows and showings that create eidola for the imagination. However, even the Puritans' Geneva Bible upholds Antonio's argument that Jacob's act, unlike usurious lending, was not deceit but involved a special act of God that cannot be generalized. The pattern is limited to a sample of one and cannot become the foundation of scripture-based institutional practice.

Shylock's exegesis makes Laban's sheep, magically transformed by Jacob, describe usury as ethical or tropologically ideal. The criterion that Antonio applies to it in his response is not whether the exegesis is "accurate." Both he and Shylock accept a figurative reading of the passage. Rather Antonio's criterion for judging Shylock's exegesis is whether it is governed by a good heart *and* by a recognition of the limits of the pattern (1.3.87–93). Having offered the text of Laban's speckled sheep as an allegory, either for the right to engage in usury or for the logic of obedience to divine command, the rest of the play becomes an exercise in scriptural and legal interpretation that turns over the issue of figurative and literal interpretation. Shylock, having in act 1, scene 3, vested his lending practice in a *metaphoric* interpretation of Genesis, in act 4 wishes to rest his case against Antonio on a *literalistic* interpretation of Venetian law.[14] The play, in contrast, argues for hermeneutic consistency. In the court scene in act 4, Shylock's new literalistic interpretive strategy allows the charging of interest *and* a pound of flesh, but it does not anticipate the even more literalistic interpretation of Portia (she herself is not the letter of what she appears to be when she comes disguised to court). She has enough sense to know that blood would be included in a pound of flesh and seizes on the letter of the law excluding the shedding of Christian blood in the city.[15]

Ironically, however, Venice, more than Shylock, is condemned by the allegory—if allegory there be. Shylock is not what he appears or claims to be in the metaphoric pattern—a dehumanized and bitter Jew or a one-dimensional representative of the Old Law.[16] He is more than the Jacob who generates speckled sheep with the wands of moneylending at usurious interest. More centrally, he is metaphorically or intertextually a new Laban who loses his daughter, Jessica, to a Lorenzo who takes her from him as surreptitiously as Jacob takes Leah and Rachel from the biblical Laban (Genesis 31). As an outsider to Christianity, he is a mirror of the Laban whom medieval and Early Modern exegesis presented as an outsider to the God of Abraham, Isaac, and Jacob.[17] He loses his ducats as Laban loses his idols. But although Laban reconciles with Jacob as a representative of the God of Abraham, Isaac, and Jacob (Gen. 31:43–52), Shakespeare's Venice/ London authority system offers no reconciliation between the play's Shylock and the Christians of the city. It proffers only Shylock's forced conversion, an action that any person who follows the grammar of the word "faith" in Hebrews 11 must find dubious, since faith is there treated as the voluntary stance of such figures as Noah, Abraham, Jacob, and Moses. Forced conversion also represents a theoretically dubious practice under Christian canon law and a crazy one to anyone with a modicum of common sense.

Yet the possibility exists that the scene of Shylock's conversion was played for laughs, however cruel. One of the persons who read this book in draft form remarked to me that my argument violates the general historicizing tendency of this book. As he puts it, "Here is Shylock with his beak nose, his exotic Jewish dress, the stereotype of the Jewish money lender—a Christian! For Shakespeare, I think, the moment is analogous to that wonderful moment in *Twelfth Night* when Malvolio decides he is going to smile. It is a splendid moment for a comic actor." Even if the forced conversion was so played, it must have raised the bittersweet question of whether a Jew forced to convert to Christianity, an Elizabethan Catholic forced to express allegiance to the Church of England, or a Puritan forced to conform in the vestiarian or edification crises had indeed given more than a meaningless formalist adherence. The expression of the actor's face would, I think, have determined whether pure comedy, pure pathos, or something between, like Chaplin's expression in the last scene of *City Lights*, would prevail.

Indeed the general scriptural pattern calls into question the whole logic of Venetian dealing with Shylock: in the Bible, neither Jacob nor Laban is forced to worship against his will, but Shylock is; and this "Christian" departure from the biblical pattern in his treatment constructs the play's deepest irony.

In using the Cain and the Jacob-Laban patterns, Shakespeare metamorphoses the Bible, but he does so considerably more cautiously than he does in making new the classical myths. He uses the biblical intertext either as an extended literal analogy, subverted or embellished in his text, or he uses it as a tropological basis for a scene or scenes.[18] It is as if he is showing how the tropology of the Bible works by *referring to it* in his fiction rather than *creating new fictions in its mode, his practice with classical myth.*

The Tempest, the Prophetic Fury, and the Biblical Pattern

One aspect of Shakespeare's use of biblical intertexts shows more fire than his cautious use of scriptural patterns, or fires his use of scriptural patterns when they are not cautious, and that is his interest in the diabolic and divine furies that construct the scriptural and prophetic. The divine fury in this instance is not the Platonic poetic fury that makes myths but the prophetic one that anticipates future patterns and teaches tropologically with such patterns. If Shakespeare represents scripture as mandating tropological interpretation from the perspective of a generous heart, he also presents some scripture as coming from a Fury, like classical myth. The vatic element is most evident in *The Tempest*, but the prophetic possibility also influences our reading of texts claiming less obvious prophetic roots.

Shakespeare's prophetic fury follows in the tradition of the prophetic fury described by the Socrates of Plato's *Phaedrus* and the Florentine Platonists. Like the Florentine Platonists he apparently assumes that the prophetic fury governs biblical prophets and those who follow their pattern. Biblical story may thus have the same vatic dimension that the poetry of the ancients has.

The Tempest's magus/ruler constructs the play's story so that it reenacts the supposed End Time pictures of Isaiah 26–32, and he does so through the Ariel/Fury (see 3.3), whom he governs but who also governs him. Through his use of Isaiah's Ariel and a series of Isaiah episodes, Shakespeare invites his audience to see portions of the *Aeneid* as a controlling intertext behind his spectacle.[19] But he also invites us to see Isaiah superseding Virgil.[20] It is as if the monarch can materialize an apocalyptic and millenialist archetype present in Isaiah to promise union and eschaton while reforming his subjects and enemies.

Shakespeare's conflation of Isaiah and Virgil is not surprising, for Isaiah and Virgil were conventionally related in Virgilian commentary. Lancelot Andrewes, who was already preaching at court when Shakespeare's company was appearing there, calls attention in a 1622 sermon to the similarity between Virgil's cognizance of prophecy and the Magi's understanding of Isaiah. As he puts it, toward "the end of Augustus' reign . . . a star was seen" and Virgil "would needs take upon him to set down" whose star it was: "[v]erily there is no man that can without admiration read his sixth Eclogue [error for fourth eclogue] of a birth at that time expected, that should be the offspring of the gods, and that should take away their sins."[21] Andrewes's Virgil, however, made the mistake of attributing the star to Caesar—to little Salonine—when he should have attributed it to Christ. Andrewes's

Magi following Isaiah know for whom the star shone and, coming to worship Him, find their world transformed.[22] It is not by accident that Isaiah's and Virgil's Cumaean sibyl both sit among the prophets of the new dispensation in the Sistine chapel (though Michelangelo sees fit to pair Isaiah most closely with the Erythraean sibyl).

The biblical Ariel is the center of *The Tempest*'s prophecy (see Isaiah 29). Prospero's Isaianic familiar, Ariel, protects his kingdom as the biblical Ariel protects and tempests "the city where David dwelt," and he enables Prospero to see what is happening and what is about to happen (Isaiah 29:1).[23] *The Tempest*'s storm destabilizes Milanese-Neapolitan political relationships in imitation of Ariel's storm in Isaiah as it tempests Zion in unstable times.[24] If Prospero's Ariel is a familiar, Isaiah's Ariel speaks to Zion with a "voice [that] shall be, as of one that hath a familiar spirit" (29:4).[25] If in *The Tempest* he lions it for a godlike ruler, in the Geneva Bible, he is "the lyon of God."[26] As the Isaianic Ariel protects and inspires the holy rule-place of Zion and acts as its agent who can mingle with thunder, earthquake, whirlwind, tempest, and "the flame of devouring fire" (Isaiah 29:6), so Shakespeare's Ariel, performing his errands for Prospero, mingles with the same elements and protects Prospero through his use of them.[27] As the voice of Isaiah's Ariel comes from the ground (Isaiah 29:4), so must that of Shakespeare's sprite when he performs Prospero's "business in the veins o' th' earth / When it is baked with frost" (1.2.253) or when he speaks from the earth to bewilder the villains (1.2.387).[28] Lest it be argued that Ariel comes from the magic books, one should note that the biblical Ariel, as the lion of God, is not different from the one found in the lore of the magicians: both are spirits of air, lions of God, and protectors of monarchs.[29]

Prospero and Ariel reenact Isaiah by sponsoring patterned emblematic events that come from Isaiah but also from Virgil in the same way that the Puck of *A Midsummer Night's Dream* as a little devil reenacts events from the classical Cupid's pattern. The primary Isaianic events in *The Tempest*, aside from Ariel's name and the tempest, are the play's tropological teaching shows: the recapitulation of the banquet in Isaiah 29, the drunkards' events described through the Isaiah 26–32 sequence, Prospero's reflection of the just king who restores right order in Isaiah 32, and his iteration in act 4 of the End Time promises found throughout Isaiah.

Isaiah, in *The Tempest*, is at the Harpy banquet in act 3, scene 3, though it also relates intertextually to the similar scene in book 6 of the *Aeneid*.[30] *The Tempest*'s banquet is not only, as in Virgil's book 6, a reaching for the food and a failure to take it away because the harpy/fury intervenes; it comes in a kind of trance. Gonzalo speaks of those who have seen the banquet as in a "strange stare," while Alonso tells of a dreamlike experience where the winds and thunder bespeak his sins and the doom of his son. Both trancelike descriptions follow the King James and Geneva intertexts of the banquet narrative that comes after the introduction of Ariel:

It shall even be as when an hungry man dreameth and, behold, he eateth; but he awaketh, and his soul is empty: or as when a thirsty man dreameth, and behold, he drinketh, but he awaketh, and, behold, he is faint, and his soul both hath appetite: so shall the multitude of all nations be, that fight against mount Zion (Isaiah 29: 8, King James).[31]

And it shal be like as an hungry man dreameth, and beholde, he eateth: and when he awaketh, his soule is emptie: or like as a thirsty man dreameth, and loe, he is drinking, and when he awaketh, beholde, he is faint, and his soule longeth: so shal the multitude of all nations be that fight against mount Zion. (Isaiah 29:8, Geneva)

The Geneva Bible's commentary makes Isaiah's waking/sleeping event the repast of those who have waged war against Zion (i.e., the Davidic king's dwelling).[32] Similarly, *The Tempest*'s banquet pictures what happens to those who war against Prospero's divine kingship and the emptiness of their reaching for authority without legitimacy.[33]

The second emblem that comes from Isaiah is the drunkards. The first set of "drunkards" is the Alonso/Sebastian/Antonio group who are drunk for power and crowns, but Shakespeare doubles these sins by creating his second set of usurpers in Caliban and his drinking companions. Their counterparts in Isaiah are the drunkards of Ephraim, filled with vomit and filthiness (Isaiah 28:1–9), reeling drunkenly while confusing alcohol with vision.[34] Renaissance commentary makes them into those who are drunk with power and pride but also into those literally drunk on wine and/or hypocritically drunk on would-be New Age religious vision (28:7), the situations of Caliban, Trinculo, and Stephano (2, 2).[35] In the Shakespearean mythos, this second pair of "drunks" seems to combine the chiliasts and enthusiasts, who will later lead to the Commonwealth, with the Catholics who swear by the book and worship wine as God in the form of the transubstantiated wine that the priest drinks. As Isaiah's drunkards think they are divinely inspired prophets, so a drunken Stephano, Trinculo, and Caliban—in a parody of the Prospero, Ariel, and Caliban relationship—pretend to be god/king, minister, and worshiping servant (2.2; 3.2; 4.1; cf. 5.1.295ff.). Isaiah promises to the drunkards that they will be trodden underfoot, which is what the fury-dogs do to *The Tempest*'s drunkards (Isaiah 28:3).[36]

If, as I have argued, through his studies Prospero as the just king has been unified with the One in the rapture of which he speaks at the beginning of the play (1.2.77), his successors, Ferdinand and Miranda, appear to follow him in finding a vision of unity and Paradise in the masque. Preparing for their marriage by excluding the lower Venus, Prospero has his spirits perform the masque of Juno, Ceres, and Iris to reconfigure Virgil's vision of how the Roman Empire has been and will be sustained by Venus. He transforms Rome's venereal god to a marriage god, and her founding dynastic political marriage of Aeneas and Lavinia into the love-marriage of Ferdinand and Miranda, and his masque shows how this dynastic marriage—presumably that between Elizabeth Stuart and Frederick of the Palatinate in 1612—will serve the nation and the One symbolized by Juno.

But Prospero abruptly dismisses the masque before it is complete. He enters into his most Isaianic mode—a prophetic fury. Ferdinand observes to Miranda that he is in a passion that works him "strongly" (4.1.143–44). *The passion works him*; he does not work it up. It is like the Fury that rides its intoxicants in Greek and Renaissance Platonic lore, and Miranda notes that never before has she seen her father so "distempered"(4.1.144–45), a strange remark in view of Prospero's continuous rage against the crimes that have previously been perpetrated against him. Prospero describes his own mind as "beating" (4.1.163). Then he utters what his prophetic fury has given him to utter: that his masque's actors are spirits, that their revels are over, that their being melted into "thin air" (4.1.150) is a metaphor for the eschatological dissolution of the whole globe:

[L]ike the baseless fabric of this vision,
The cloud-capped towers, the gorgeous palaces
The solemn temples, the great globe itself,
Yea, all which it inherit, shall dissolve,
And, like this insubstantial pageant faded,
Leave not a rack behind. We are such stuff
As dreams are made on, and our little life
Is rounded with a sleep. . . . (4.1.151–58)

The Globe Theater may be implicated in the meltdown, but when Prospero speaks of the destruction of the cloud-capped towers, the great globe, and its inheritors, he surely speaks of universal dissolution.

Prospero's and Ariel's reconstruction of the Isaiah pattern adds to the Virgilian prophetic mode of the sixth book an eschatological sense. Isaiah is ultimately an eschatological writer. He treats the material world as a veil, as does Prospero when he returns from his sibylline moment to announce that the world will dissolve as dreams do into a sleep (4.1.146ff.). He, in fact, uses the same word as the Geneva Bible when he speaks of the dissolution of the world: "dissolve" (Isaiah 34:4). The word is used elsewhere in the Bible, especially in King James, to signify End Time, but it is used with a special power in Isaiah 34:4. The world's transient prospect may be what leads Prospero ultimately to the forgiveness and incorporation scene that ends the play (5.1.172–Epilogue, 20). It is as if he is saying, "Why sweat these things when they will vanish?"

When the Bible comes into Shakespeare's comedies, it does what myth does. It adds an element of fire and moral patterning. It may be that Shakespeare had the sense that a prophetic fury governed his own writing, supplying biblical iconology appropriate to the contemporary world and giving that writing energy and point, as the Ariel fury using Isaiah gives Prospero's constructions energy and point. But to suggest so much is merely to speculate. We do know that Shakespeare's use of biblical pattern to speak to the paradigms of his own age gives us a Bible that is more than a moralistic tool—it is one that carries the fire of breakthrough.

Other biblical intertextual patterns appear, most of them having to do with comedic reversal or renewal, and in them the furious also appears, either the daemonic fury of witchcraft and diabolism or the benign fury of the Apollonian. *Comedy of Errors* uses its inversion of the proleptic biblical Ephesian setting and the continual fear in Ephesus of witches to heighten its picture of materialism's failures in spiritual discernment. *Much Ado* and *The Winter's Tale* present feigned proleptic resurrections to talk about the renewal and innocence coming from forgiveness. Among the festival comedies, *A Midsummer Night's Dream* uses Feast of St. John symbolism and *Twelfth Night* the propers of Epiphany and its lore to valorize the search for renewed light. In each there is the fury of witchcraft or feigned witchcraft overcome and the dawning of a light prophetic of the future.

Comedy of Errors: The Ephesian Setting and the Extended Inversion of Intertexts

Ephesus, in Shakespeare's day, was the living image of an ideal Christian society, especially for the Puritans. As described in Acts 18–20, it was the New Testament model of individual resistance to the forces of evil. The Ephesian church of Ephesians 1–2 is proleptically related to the eschatological church, so that what the Ephesian church is and can become in Paul's vision is a kind of forecast of what the eschatological church is to become (see Geneva Bible and commentary,

Ephesians 2, 1ff.). It is a church to be viewed in prophetic or vatic sight, both predictive of the heavenly church and of the pattern of proper practice in developing a this-worldly Christian social order. In the ordinary world, masters and servants, parents and children, husbands and wives—indeed the whole Christian community—are, in Paul's eyes, to be properly related to one another in a hierarchical fashion. In the church militant, as Paul understands things, the former parties in the pairs listed are to dominate the latter but do so with a complete love for the subordinate and a willingness to sacrifice for them, however unlikely this may seem from a commonsense perspective. In the heavenly world, Christ is the only power, so far above all other rulers or powers or authority systems in Paul's view that other authority no longer matters and peace is all (1:15–2:22). St. Paul's program for the organization of the church militant powerfully interested the Calvinists and other Puritans in Shakespeare's time because of their wish to recreate, in their communities, the social practices of the early church and to anticipate a church that exists in the eternal world (Ephesians 2:6–7).

The proper context for reading Ephesians was thought to be Acts 18–20, where Paul goes to Ephesus to found a community, an event receiving significant attention from Calvin, Bucer, and the Geneva Bible.[37] In Acts 18–20 Paul comes to the city, disputes with some Jews, and then leaves for Galatia and Phrygia with a promise to return. Following Paul in the conversion business is Apollo, who preaches about Jesus and converts many but who knows only the penitential baptism of John the Baptist. Afterward, Paul returns to complete Apollo's work by baptizing people into Christ's "Holy Spirit" baptism and granting charismatic gifts. On this visit Paul again disputes in the synagogues and performs a sufficient number of miracles to encourage some Jewish exorcists also to attempt to cast out demons in Christ's name. However, as the story goes, one demon, irritated at Jewish exorcism, decries the effort and makes the man he possesses fall upon his fake exorcists and beat them, a bit of comedy in a not-very-funny biblical chapter.

Afterward Demetrius, an Ephesian silversmith, raises a riot against

the Christians for converting too many people, spoiling the local silversmith business that made statues of Diana, and diverting devo-
tees from the goddess of the local temple. Demetrius creates a tough
situation for Paul and his group until the town clerk says that Paul's
bunch is not particularly dangerous and that the courts instead of the
streets should provide venues for the resolution of such accusations.
After Paul goes into Greece for a bit, he returns to Miletus, not far
from Ephesus, and calls the Ephesian elders to him, asking them to
continue to teach what he has taught and direct their "flock" to per-
sist in righteousness until they receive their "inheritance." Sometime
after, Paul addresses to this same flock his epistle's advice about resisting evil spirits, preserving unity in Christ, and creating a sort of
hierarchy-respecting love between parents and children, masters and
servants, and husbands and wives. At least that is the conventional
Early Modern view of the relationship between Ephesians and Acts.
The work is essentially a picture of how a community behaves while
awaiting the eschaton.

In *The Comedy of Errors*, the proleptic vision of community is gone,
and in the externals of its plot the play reflects a series of comic inversions of the narrative in Acts 18–20—glancing at exorcism, magic, the
temple of Diana, metalsmiths, and the rowdy crowd. At another level,
it treats of the fictional city's comic perversion of Paul's proleptic or
eschatological advice to the Ephesians on what a Christian society
should be; the only prophetic fury in the town is the specious fury
of men deemed mad or women deemed witches. In both Acts and
Ephesians, fear and irrationality are the comic targets that prevent the
appearance of any tropological, individual renewal that might renew
the city. Fear and irrationality create the comedy.

In transforming its Plautine source, the *Comedy* self-consciously
removes the story of the confusion of the twins from the *Menaechmi*'s
Epidamnum to Ephesus, the place where, according to Acts 19, Paul
encounters versions of Judaism attentive to the early Jesus movement
and also meets alternative versions of early Christianity.[38] Ephesus is
particularly relevant to the probable date of the play's first performance
in 1594. At that time Shakespeare's plays were still being acted at The

Theatre, in the neighborhood of Shoreditch on the London side of the Thames, on land owned by the increasingly Puritan Giles Allen. It seems likely that the entire neighborhood was also increasingly Puritan in its persuasions. The Ephesian setting should have appealed to a neighborhood looking for Puritan righteousness. However, if London is Ephesus, the play's social comedy must also have stung, for Shakespeare's Ephesus is not the partially pagan Ephesus of Paul's epistle to the Ephesians, where the Christians are an underground movement seeking renewal, or the similar Ephesus of the passages dealing with the city in Acts. It is also not the ideal pagan Ephesus of the later *Pericles Prince of Tyre* whose temple of Diana protecting the chaste Thais appears to be parallel to Emilia's *Comedy of Errors*'s nunnery. It is certainly no prolepsis of the City of God.

Shakespeare's stage Ephesus is a nominally Christian city that is a sinkhole of superstition, abuse, family disintegration, fear, anger, and wholesale stupidity. If *Comedy of Errors* is imagined in a historically coherent time, it must be a patristic Christian or early medieval era. The town has an abbey and an abbess, and the speech of the citizens is filled with references to Christian figures and biblical passages. Islam does not threaten this place, so it is not yet 781 AD. Remaining, however, is the fear of what appears to be the Greco-Roman witchcraft that Paul combats. One Ephesian character, Dr. Pinch, engages in exorcisms like that of the false Jewish exorcist in Acts, a little sexual vice appears, the precious metalsmiths are there but working gold instead of silver, and the propensity for hubbub when the civic leader is not at hand continues. The imagining of a pagan Ephesus is predictably active in the middle sections of the play and among the Syracusans, who seem to know the city's ancient reputation for sorcery and witchcraft (though not the actuality of these). Finally, the abuse of wives and servants against which Paul's epistle warns the Ephesians appears commonplace. The whole ethos of the place runs counter to Pauline teaching.

These Acts and Ephesians themes are pertinent to a North London audience's concerns in the 1590s in that much of the period's discussion surrounding the direction of the English and Continental

Reformation church had to do with what it meant to follow the pattern of early Christianity in the household. If Ephesus in *Comedy of Errors* is in part a picture of London, as some of its place names suggest, part of the irony is that those Londoners who seek to follow an early Christian model are themselves the victims of the irrational error and superstition that Puritan reform efforts hoped to abolish when they sought to control the arts of entertainment and imaginative construction.

To turn to what I have called the externals of the play, an analogy to the Acts 19:13–17 episode of the victim who falls upon his exorcist appears in the *Comedy* in Antipholus of Ephesus's falling upon Dr. Pinch. Pinch earlier creates a furious "drama" with Antipholus by pronouncing him mad and bewitched. In this set of episodes, we can see in some detail how Shakespeare uses the Acts intertext. First, Adriana, Antipholus's wife, describes her husband's madness (that is, "his incivility") to Pinch:

ADRIANA: His incivility confirms no less.—
Good Doctor Pinch, you are a conjurer.
Establish him in his true sense again,
And I will please you what you will demand. (*CE* 4.4.41–44)

Then Luciana notices how fiery and "sharpe" Antipholus appears, the courtesan sees him as in some sort of ecstasy, and Pinch tries to feel his pulse (4.4.48–50). When Antipholus tries to punch out the good doctor, Pinch tries his pseudo-Catholic exorcism routines:

PINCH: I charge thee, Satan, housed within this man,
To yield possession to my holy prayers,
And to thy state of darkness hie thee straight:
I conjure thee by all the saints in heaven. (*CE* 4.4.49–52)

Later Antipholus and his man fall upon their conjurer as the possessed Ephesian man does in Acts. The messenger describes the event:

MESSENGER: O mistress, mistress, shift and save
yourself!
My master and his man are both broke loose,
Beaten the maids a-row, and bound the Doctor,
Whose beard they have singed off with brands of fire,
And ever as it blazed they threw on him
Great pails of puddled mire to quench the hair.
My master preaches patience to him, and the while
His man with scissors nicks him like a fool;
And sure—unless you send some present help—
Between them they will kill the conjurer. (*CE* 5.1.169–78)

This is not, as in Acts, a case of *false* conjuring. Pinch's conjuring is
fake. The Geneva Bible makes explicit the distinction between true
and false exorcism in its comments on Acts 19:13 and 16, where Satan
is said to give witness against himself in the case of the false exorcism and where the difference between Pauline and other exorcism
is indicated by the fact that those who do genuine exorcisms "cast
out devils by conjuring them in the Name of God."[39] In the play no
demon speaks out against Pinch. Here the masks of the world of the
spirit lie about, but no one fights a serious spiritual battle. Pinch's
undoing edifies no one, for—and this sets the theme of the *Comedy*'s
use of Paul—Antipholus has no demon.

In Acts, after the conjurors have been put to flight, many Jews
and other Ephesians convert to Pauline Christianity. They burn their
magic books, worth fifty thousand silver coins. None of this happens
in *Comedy of Errors*. In contrast, what is attributed to the supernatural
in Shakespeare's Ephesus is always the result of purely human error
and irrationality. Only in imagination is this place haunted by witches
and enchantments, in the same way that Shakespeare's London was
haunted. In the early 1590s the Anglican apologists Samuel Harsnett,
John Deacon, and John Walker attacked the claims of the Puritan
John Darrell and the Jesuit William Weston to have rid England and
London of demons. Both were tried for fraud.[40] Thomas Hennings
has argued, with other critics, that Ephesus is portrayed as made up

of "tedious and/or oppressive restriction: Draconian legalism and its concomitant legalese; financial obligations; punctuality; beatings reinforcing hierarchy; innocent men bound in chains, imprisoned and threatened with execution" and the like.[41] Shakespeare, in perhaps his most brittle comedy, points to the "measuring out of lives in coffee spoons" in a world where neither witchcraft nor prophecy, neither heroic evil nor good exists, in a milieu characteristic of commercial urban society anywhere, certainly of late sixteenth-century London.

It was not so in Paul's Ephesus. Early Modern people understood—at least Erasmus understood—the identity between the Ephesian community in Acts and the community that Paul addresses in Epistle to the Ephesians and saw Paul's letter as a counter to wild Ephesian folly. The Diana of the Pauline story is obviously the triple Diana whom we treated in writing of Titania as Hecate. She is the patron of chastity. She is also—as Hecate—the patroness of the magicians, witches, and exorcists—as Erasmus says, the Diana Polymaston, who is "the nource [nurse] of all maner of beastes" and followed by men who gave their "whole studies unto curiouse artes and sciences: as we may gather where we reade, that at the preaching of the Apostles, they brought in theyr bookes of enchauntmente, and burned them in the fyer." Erasmus further argues that concern with these arts led Paul to work with the Ephesians for a longer period of time than was usual for him in his visits to Near Eastern cities, and they are the reason why, in his epistle, he makes frequent mention of devils and spirits, encouraging the people to remember what they were like when they served "wicked" spirits and what they have became as "engrafted unto Christ."[42] Indeed, Paul's admonitions are part of his sense that he is moving the Ephesian community from domination by one set of spirits to domination by a new being that anticipates the eschaton. But there is no eschaton in prospect in Shakespeare's Ephesus and no real battle of the spirit.

As the fear of magic in Ephesus that Antipholus of Syracuse and others express has a basis in the biblical Ephesus, so also does the metalsmithing. The silversmith's statues of Diana in Acts become in *Comedy of Errors* the goldsmith's golden chain. In Renaissance London, *the goldsmith's guild handled both silver and gold.*[43] And, as mentioned, Diana's temple is replaced by the nunnery in *Comedy of Errors*, both of them dangerous and foolish places to London's Protestants.

But the ironies go deeper than the use of intertextually related plots to furnish the norm and the departures from the norm. The deeper comedy of *Comedy of Errors*, having to do with the spirit, structure, and use of social institutions, derives from the social program of the Epistle to the Ephesians. Its norms concerning husbands and wives, but also fathers and sons and masters and servants, require replacing fear and anger with affection, reason, and anticipation of the eschatological. *Comedy of Errors* is funny to the degree that these are lacking in an Ephesus that is supposed to be the model for all. Sidney advises that "in Geometrie, the oblique must be knowne as well as the right, and in Arithmetick, the odde as well as the even" and that "in the actions of our life, who seeth not the filthinesse of evill, wanteth a great foile to perceive the bewtie of vertue." This metaphor applies to *Comedy of Errors*' use of the precepts of Paul's letter to the Ephesians.

The folly of the citizens of Shakespeare's Ephesus and its visitors arises out of their passions, combined with their rigidity and irrationality in adhering to these passions. These together threaten to make a wasteland. Fear is especially important—fear of wives and husbands, fear of masters, fear of witches and enchantments, fear of debt and fear of prison, all of which create a world of an endlessly violated protocol governed by no rationality. The irrationality is such that a brother looking for his twin does not recognize that something may be up when people speak to him or act upon him as if he were someone else.[44] Fear and anger are rehearsed in the stichomythia of the lines, the endless running around to find what has been given to the wrong persons, the constant servant beatings, and the fake formality of the speeches when the characters have quieted themselves enough to speak with *gravitas*.

Of course the alternatives to fear and anger, in Ephesian terms, are hope in the coming kingdom of God and, in this world, patient, rational analysis of disturbing appearances, self-control in responding to these appearances, and proper love of and respect for the other. For example, if the gold chain made by its poor goldsmith is parallel to the Bible's silver Diana statuettes, then marriage is to replace celibacy in this town. The golden chain, contrasted with the rope of abuse, represents whatever binds husbands, wives, and families together. Though the chain is for a time promised to a courtesan and for a time given to the wrong Antipholus, its power returns to Adriana when the comic conclusion comes at the end.[45] This power of married fidelity valorized by middle-of-the-road Protestants contrasts with that of the asceticism of the Diana of *Pericles* or the dark enchantments of the Diana-Hecate worshiped in the Ephesus of Acts. Paul's city of Ephesus is not to be reformed by corporate reform but by inner transformations in its households—reciprocal service from those in command of each social unit, whatever its size, the elimination of anger, and kindness between all plus a willingness on the part of superiors to sacrifice for subordinates.[46]

The grotesqueries of comedy appear in *Comedy of Errors* because Shakespeare's Ephesus, as a would-be Christian city, still has all the problems of witchcraft, disorder, and domestic strife of the pagan city (or thinks it does). They also obtrude because those authorities who are supposed to direct the city are stupid and impractical. The duke enforces stupid laws about illegal immigrants. No one seems to know how to make a good household without making an ass of himself or herself. At the level of fathers and brothers, Egeon, as the father of the twins, seems to be a good Pauline father, caring for his lost child, but he really does nothing fatherly aside from search—and that long after he has lost his wife and child. As a brother, Antipholus of Syracuse also searches, but he does so without reminding himself *that he is looking for an identical brother who has a servant identical to his.* When confusion swirls over his and his servant's identities, he thinks the city full of witches. Constantly afraid of that which is not familiar, the twins do not recognize that they are "altogether castaways and aliants [sic]" in the spiritual sense of Geneva's Ephesians.[47]

As to marriages, among the women Luciana, *who has no experience in marriage,* advocates the Pauline marriage hierarchy described in Ephesians and enforces it in the most literalistic terms. She never remembers that Paul also says husbands are to love their wives as Christ loved the church (see Ephesians 5:25–33 and the Geneva gloss).[48] Adriana, her sister and a wife, in turn demonstrates how difficult subservience to an unfaithful husband can be and has no reform strategy to bring him into line. Though Emilia is a nun long separated from marriage, she can give know-it-all advice on proper marriage that seems at first to follow Paul and then to oppose him. No one recognizes how Ephesian husbands are to love their wives and that, as Hennings has argued, the Anglican doctrine of the affectionate marriage provides for more than either Adriana or Antipholus of Ephesus envisages in their anxieties and angers about love.

Again with the servants, Ephesian masters do not forbear threatening. Geneva, commenting on Ephesians 6:9, commands that they should. Master[s] should "use the authoritie that they have over their servants, modestly and holily, seeing that they in another respect have a common master, which is in heaven, who will judge both the servant and the free."[49] *Comedy of Errors* is an endless silly servant beating.

In the end Paul's letter proposes a new social order in Ephesus based on a motivational structure where an inner selfish Self has died and a New Man has appeared. But contrary to Paul's understanding of the New Man, Dromio of Syracuse thinks that this Adam is the opposite of the *Old Adam* (a central metaphor in Paul for the unregenerate human being) who keeps the local prison. In the view of Dromio of Syracuse, the New Adam is simply the local Ephesian officer clad in a new skin. He is a person still ready to take one to the prison that denies the Pauline liberty of the new Self:[50]

DROMIO OF SYRACUSE: Master, here's the gold you sent me
   for. What, have you got redemption from the picture of old
   Adam new apparelled?
ANTIPHOLUS OF SYRACUSE: What gold is this? What Adam
   dost thou mean?
DROMIO OF SYRACUSE: Not that Adam that kept the
   Paradise, but that Adam that keeps the prison—he that goes

in the calf's skin, that was killed for the Prodigal; he that
came behind you, sir, like an evil angel, and bid you forsake
your liberty.

ANTIPHOLUS OF SYRACUSE: I understand thee not.

DROMIO OF SYRACUSE: No? Why, 'tis a plain case: he that
went, like a bass viol in a case of leather; the man, sir, that
when gentlemen are tired gives them a sob and 'rests them;
he, sir, that takes pity on decayed men and gives them suits of
durance; he that sets up his rest to do more exploits with his
mace than a Moorish pike.

ANTIPHOLUS OF SYRACUSE: What, thou mean'st an officer?

DROMIO OF SYRACUSE: Ay, sir, the sergeant of the band: he
that brings any man to answer it that breaks his bond; one
that thinks a man always going to bed, and says 'God give
you good rest.' (*CE* 4.3.12–31)

The Pauline New Man (Ephesians 4:24), the tropological New Adam
who anticipates the new world to come, is an inner spiritual state, not a
newly suited constable or sergeant—not the old Keystone cop decked
out in a new uniform, even one made from the Prodigal's calf.

The confusion about the New Man is a touchstone. One finds
no "new spirit" in nominally Christian Ephesus—read Puritan
London—until the duke decides for mercy at the end of the play
(5.1.130ff.). Greeting one instead are the spirits of superstition,
lust, pride, greed, and the failure to think. Even the ducal resolution of the problem in act 5, the restoration of Emilia to Egeon,
and the giving of the two sets of twin brothers to each other come
more as accidents (or rather superficial "providential" events) than
as products of thought and strategy.[51] Authority finally rescues the
plot, but it is a meager and insufficient authority that casts a harsh
light on Early Modern London and its claims to reformation. As
Don Quixote's chivalric dreams shipwreck when the reality of Early
Modern Spain surfaces in the countryside, so the Pauline Ephesian
dreams in *Comedy of Errors*' run aground in a commercial city's stupidity, vanity, and hypocrisy.

Resurrection in *Much Ado About Nothing*
and *The Winter's Tale*

If the issue of how the New Man largely *fails* to emerge is central in *Comedy of Errors*, how "he" might emerge is central in *Much Ado About Nothing*'s and *Winter's Tale*'s literally fake and figuratively real anticipations of renewal and resurrection. He comes through a proleptic forgiveness. It is difficult to watch the final scene of Kenneth Branagh's *Much Ado* without seeing Hero's return as a resurrection of some sort. The closed chapel, Hero's coming out of it in her white veil, and her luminous presence could create that sense even if it were not in Shakespeare's lines. Almost any production of *Winter's Tale* has to convey a like sense when Hermione-the-statue comes to life. In this section I argue that if there are resurrections in *Much Ado About Nothing* (or in *Winter's Tale*, briefly treated), they are not hokey reenactments of the Bible story. Rather they are resurrections of an innocence lacking from *Comedy of Errors* and created through Hero's and Hermione's goodness. Their actions combine to restore a like innocence to their lovers and to the ruling characters of the works in which they are found.

As mentioned, in the Branagh production of *Much Ado* Hero returned emerges radiant in white, with her face covered, from a chapel that has the appearance of a Renaissance version of the tomb of Christ. Resurrection is everywhere. But is this staging correct? And what does it mean? The language that Shakespeare provides for the scene in part confirms the impression that Branagh's production conveys:

CLAUDIO: Give me your hand before this holy friar.
I am your husband if you like of me.
HERO: [*unmasking*] And when I lived, I was your other wife;
And when you loved, you were my other husband.
CLAUDIO: Another Hero!
HERO: Nothing certainer.
One Hero died defiled, but I do live,
And surely as I live, I am a maid.

DON PEDRO: The former Hero, Hero that is dead!
LEONATO: She died, my lord, but whiles her slander lived. (*MAN*
5.4.58ff.)

The Hero that lived before being put away by Leonato and the friar's decision was another wife who died "defiled." Found innocent, she now "live[s]" and is "a maid" (5.4.60–64). When "The former Hero! Hero that is dead!" lives, the action seems either a resurrection or a parody of resurrection.

Certainly the crucifixion-resurrection topos is anticipated in the mourners' song at Hero's "grave," appealing to Diana to forgive the slaughter of her knight: "Graves yawn, and yield your dead / Till death be utteréd, / Heavily, heavily" (5.3.19–21). Graves do not normally yawn save in miraculous times; the preeminent biblical time when graves yawned appears in Matthew 27:52, which tells of graves opening and giving forth their dead in anticipation of the End Time during the day of Christ's crucifixion. The Geneva version says:

> And the[r] graves did open themselves, and many bodies of the Saints which slept arose.
>
> r. That is to say, the stones clave in sunder, & the graves did open themselves to shew by this act that death was overcome: & the resurrection of the dead followed the resurrection of Christ, as appeareth by the next verse following.

Other language suggests a sacred context. For example, Hero's remark about defilement and maidenhood (5.4.63) sounds a little like the tropological crucifixion rehearsed by St. Paul in 2 Corinthians 5:21 and its gloss in the Geneva Bible:

> For he hath made him [i.e., Christ] *to be*[q] sinne for us, which[r] knew no sinne; that wee should be made the[s] righteousnesse of God in him.
>
> q. A sinner, not in himselfe, but by imputation of the guilt of all our sinnes to him.

r. Who was cleane void of sinne.

s. Righteous before God, and that with righteousnesse which is not essentiall to us, but being essentiall in Christ, God imputeth it to us through faith.

As in the Christian mythos, wherein Christ endured attributed defilement in the crucifixion, so also did Hero in her confinement and "death" as an unfaithful slut. As Christ returned to make righteous those who had offended against him and felt penitential grief, so Hero does with Claudio. The language of defilement and lack of defilement that Hero attributes to herself, in 5.4.62 and beyond, describes the sacrifice of Christ in Geneva's version of Hebrews 7:26: "For such an hie Priest it became vs to have, *which is* holy, harmelesse, *vndefiled*, separate from sinners, and made higher than the heavens" (italics mine).

Christ as the white lamb or maid and the "virgins" who follow him are central in the mythos of the Revelation of John and much of Paul, and this language is projected back, using erotic terminology, in the relationship of bride and bridegroom in the Song of Songs in Christian commentary. That a maid, an innocent, dies with defilement attributed to her, that after her death graves are commanded to open, that she "comes back to life" an innocent, and forgives those who cause her suffering is at the very least suggestive.

If we accept the suggestion, what then? The play may still be much ado about nothing. No graves have opened save in the song at Hero's supposed grave. Nothing has happened in the play. The events that end it are entirely a *poeta*'s trick. Hero has not died. Benedick has challenged Claudio for creating a death that has not occurred. Claudio and Don Pedro have done a one-night repentance that is as much formality as anguish, and Leonato, who has had as much to do with the forgiveness and resurrection as anyone, ends the play almost as much the "good old boy" parvenu as when he began it. Hero is certainly not Eliot's "infinitely suffering, infinitely gentle thing."

In this hall of mirrors, the death and resurrection that we seem to witness have disappeared as a plausible historical allegory. But the tropological pattern assigned in Shakespeare's time to the historical resurrection of Christ has its beginning in Paul's notion of a daily tropological crucifixion and resurrection. As the *Homilies* say:

> *As we be buried with Christ by our baptism into death, so let us daily die to sin,* mortifying and killing the evil desires and motions thereof (Romans 6:2–4). . . . *If we then be risen with Christ* by our faith to the hope of everlasting life, let us rise also with Christ, after his example, to a new life, and leave our old. We shall then be truly risen, if *we seek for things that be heavenly, if we have our affection on things that be above, and not on things that be on the earth.*[52]

Pauline Christians are to be resurrected to leave behind the fierceness, malice, bad speech, and lying of the Old Man. They are to aspire to "mercy, kindness, meekness, patience, forbearing one another, and forgiving one another," the kind of resurrection that Hero represents, if any.

What has happened by the end of the play for all but Don John is forgiveness, "mercie, kindenesse, meekenesse, patience." It may be that the play represents fake resurrection as a metaphor for "real" End Time events and as a pattern of regeneration—ignoring the question of what can be historically authenticated, ignoring the much ado about what may be nothing. The play concentrates on what is *something*: the quality of forgiveness. An inner application is crucial. Perhaps by the end of the play, because of the Hero cycle, Don Pedro, Beatrice, and Benedick are more innocent, less given to the defensive repartee, more transparent in their professions, and more authentic than they were at the beginning of the play and are so without losing their wit. This interpretation appears to ignore the Beatrice-Benedick plot, which in all stage performances dominates the action, but it need not. The absolute sacrifice that is Hero after her marriage rejection is lived out, minute by minute, in the increasingly "sacrificial" witticisms of Beatrice and Benedick. The saint's life that is Hero's story frames and makes meaningful the sacrifice that is Beatrice and Benedick's tale—their willingness to take and give testing insult to know and love each other.[53]

A somewhat similar "resurrection" occurs in *Winter's Tale*, which I discuss only briefly because this theme has often been treated before. Much of the symbolism in the play reenacts the springtime motif that surrounds all resurrection festivals, pagan and Christian. The story satisfies our common intuitive wish for the dead to be alive and extends the Flora and Proserpina stories of life returning into the celebration of pastoral Floralia, with Perdita (the lost one) playing the Flora role of lost life returning and with Florizel acting as her cult's follower. Her flowers' return in Bohemia and her own return to Sicily both extend into the return of Hermione from the life of a statue to civic life in Sicily after the reconstitution of the friendship of the royal houses of Bohemia and Sicily.

In the crucial scene Paulina calls upon Leontes to awaken his faith before Hermione can come to life, then reassures the group that Hermione's resurrection will draw on no demonic powers and asserts that life redeems Hermione from death. The statue moves and woos the tropologically dead figure that is Leontes. Paulina's call to Leontes to awaken faith is to be taken at the deepest level. We are to see in Leontes's mien as he responds that he has awakened faith—his tropical innocence, his New Man. Then, as an objective correlative, Paulina can bring back Hermione:

PAULINA: It is required
    You do awake your faith. Then, all stand still;
    On those that think it is unlawful business
    I am about, let them depart.
LEONTES: Proceed:
    No foot shall stir.
PAULINA: Music, awake her; strike!
[*Music*]
[*To HERMIONE*] 'Tis time; descend; be stone no more; approach;
    Strike all that look upon with marvel. Come,
    I'll fill your grave up: stir, nay, come away,
    Bequeath to death your numbness, for from him
    Dear life redeems you. You perceive she stirs:

[*HERMIONE slowly descends*]
Start not; her actions shall be holy as
You hear my spell is lawful. Do not shun her
Until you see her die again, for then
You kill her double. Nay, present your hand.
When she was young, you woo'd her. Now in age
Is she become the suitor?
LEONTES: O, she's warm!
If this be magic, let it be an art
Lawful as eating.
POLIXENES: She embraces him. (*WT* 5.3.94–112)

Hermione apparently forgives Leontes as she embraces him, and Paulina tells why the scene requires incarnate representations of Hermione's resurrection:

CAMILLO: She hangs about his neck.
If she pertain to life, let her speak too.
POLIXENES: Ay, and make it manifest where she has lived,
Or how stol'n from the dead.
PAULINA: That she is living,
Were it but told you, should be hooted at
Like an old tale: but it appears she lives ... (*WT* 5.3.113–19)

Hermione, like Hero forgiving Claudius, forgives Leontes and thereby makes her resurrection into another making new. However, as doctrine rather than stagecraft, her coming to life is as much a case of "much ado" as Hero's, and one that reflects Paulina's regenerative devices (is she a mirror of St. Paul?) more than the historical "divine drama." The existence of a new life physically and a new kind of spirit in society, replacing the old malice and jealousy at the Sicilian court, may have appeared to Early Modern audiences to be the sort of outer and inner miracle that figurally anticipates final resurrection. To us the outrageous claims of the plot—a statue coming to life, a woman hidden for a generation—may appear laughable, as biblical resurrection claims appear outrageous. They awaken in us the simultaneous senses of skepticism about and hope for the too-good-to-be-true.

This is not the end of Shakespeare's use of resurrection motifs as proleptic devices. One could apply the same modes of analysis to *All's Well* by looking at Diana's first appearance in Paris and her regeneration of the monarch and at her second appearance in France, when she has apparently resurrected herself and begins to work at the renewal of Bertram. The "fake" resurrections of *Much Ado about Nothing, The Winter's Tale,* and *All's Well That Ends Well*—with their presentations of reconciliation where reconciliation seemed impossible—may or may not have struck Shakespeare's audience as figurations of End Time and as comic utterances of the prophetic fury. Whatever their conscious appeal, unconsciously they must have appealed to some sense of comic and cosmic proleptic possibility that virtually everyone in Shakespeare's era anticipated.

A Midsummer Night's Dream and the Feast of St. John the Baptist

The sense of inner renewal in comic protagonists, potentially correlative to the spectator's inner renewal, has its dramatic counterpart in the coming and retention of seasonal light. One great festival marks the effort to retain the light of summer at its peak, the Feast of St. John the Baptist on Midsummer's Day. Another, Epiphany (Twelfth Night), marks the effort to bring back the light from near its low point in winter. In either case the light celebrated is both physical and spiritual in the Early Modern English liturgical year. Shakespeare attaches his two great comedies bearing the names of feasts to these complementary days where light is at issue. His use of biblical passages, together with shadows of their feast days as intertext, gives these plays their profound sense of hopefulness.

Across the last half-century we have had excellent studies of the relationship between Shakespeare's comedies and the folk festivals of the year.[54] In reading these studies we may forget that Shakespeare was not a folklorist or an old warlock humming his spells in the Cotswold countryside. He was an entertainer before a theologically sophisticated court and in a theologically divided London. The festivals in Early Modern Europe that inform the comedies carry the names of the cult of a biblical saint or an event in the life of Christ himself, however much they also echo popular celebrations as old as antiquity. Indeed one can hardly extricate "popular" from "worshiping" acts in the celebration of these days.

For instance, the Midsummer Night's eve of *Midsummer Night's Dream* occurs on the eve of the birth of St. John the Baptist, and I submit that both the eve's celebration and the biblical saint's story furnish the most significant intertexts of the play. Barber has argued that the title of the play does not imply specific associations with the customs of Midsummer's Eve save for the suggestion of magic associated with that time.[55] But it seems probable that an audience attending a play titled *A Midsummer Night's Dream* would expect something to do with the customs of the day—its rehearsal of Misrule, its liberation of the light and the mythology of its saint's time, and the feast of the last pre-Christian prophet, St. John the Baptist.[56]

The scriptural John the Baptist lives in the wilderness, calls his contemporaries to repentance, baptizes Christ, and proclaims him as the Lamb of God who takes away the sin of the world. He witnesses to Christ as the light coming into the world (John 1), and he suffers the first martyrdom because of Salome's whims and Herod's lust. Based on this slim story, his cult often included scenes of enthusiasm and rapture. St. Jerome, when he visited John's tomb, saw furious demonic group raptures, as did later observers, so it is not surprising that the night of his saint's day includes a certain expectation of madness.[57] But *The Golden Legende* also describes John more soberly as "a prophete; frende of the spouse; lanterne; angell voys, hely (Elias) as baptyste of the savyour; messenger of the Juge; and foregoer of the Kynge."[58] The lantern, we are told, signifies bringing "noblesse of holynesse," the angel bringing the "prerogative of virginity," the voice "nobleness of mekenes," and Elias the "noblesse of brynnynge loue."[59]

In short, John's story suggests the abandon of his feast day but also a calm association with light and ordered love. Even in Protestant England John the Baptist, represented as this kind of person, retains a

significant place in sermon.[60] Both because of the tradition of the summer solstice festivals and because of the tension in John's story between
the force of the ascetic prophet and his murderess, Salome, in medieval
Europe John's feast became both an orgiastic event and a celebration
of the fire and rituals that would keep out the darkness.[61] John the
Baptist's night is the kind of night in which Puck, a minor devil, can be
turned loose, in which love-in-idleness can exercise its power, in which
a witch-goddess like Titania can bewitch the local guild bumpkin, and
in which lovers run after each other in higgledy-piggledy fashion. On
such a night, Bottom's observation that "reason and love keep little
company together nowadays" is perfectly plausible (*MND* 3.1.128–29).
But the light of the last part of act 3 and act 4 also follows it.

Christian writers explained the solstice ritual on St. John's Eve as a
celebration of John the Baptist's pointing to the true Light that comes
into the world, as the Gospel of John would have it (John 1:5–8). The
dancing of the night was sometimes related to the sinister dance of
Salome. In the end, in the celebration, it was John's Light, not Salome,
that would emerge the stronger, but the eve was still very troubling to
Puritans like Stubbes, who were afraid of its evocation of the Salome
forces of instinct and imagination in its celebration.[62] The subjugation
of darkness by light, of course, is valorized by Oberon's placing the
force of Diana's bud on the eyes of Titania and the lovers to conquer
their love-in-idleness as the dawn comes on. As dawn or "vaward of
the day" arrives, Theseus praises it and its natural music in anticipation
of his own "St. John's" morning observation on the mountaintop:

THESEUS: Go, one of you, find out the forester,
    For now our observation is performed;
    And since we have the vanguard of the day,
    My love shall hear the music of my hounds.
    Uncouple in the western valley; let them go.
    Dispatch, I say, and find the forester.
    We will, fair Queen, up to the mountain's top,
    And mark the musical confusion
    Of hounds and echo in conjunction. (*MND* 4.1.100–108)

Hippolita then tells of her experience in Crete with Hercules and Cadmus when their hounds "bayed" a bear and filled the skies and the whole world around with a *concordia discors*. Theseus responds:

> THESEUS: My hounds are bred out of the *Spartan* kind,
> So flewed, so sanded; and their heads are hung
> With ears that sweep away the morning dew,
> Crook-kneed, and dewlapped like *Thessalian* bulls,
> Slow in pursuit, but matched in mouth like bells,
> Each under each. A cry more tuneable
> Was never holla'd to nor cheered with horn
> In *Crete*, in *Sparta*, nor in *Thessaly*.
> Judge when you hear. But soft: what nymphs are these? (*MND*
> 4.1.116–24; italics mine)

The morning comes on with a fresh innocence—wonder at the hounds baying a harmony in discord and recollections of the Herculean time. Then the lovers are found, and the reincorporation of Athens begins with people who are new.

In *A Midsummer Night's Dream* we have a full St. John's Eve event: the young people who stay up almost all night, the mad behaviors of the night, the Hecate-Circe witch figure in Titania, the animal-man Bottom, the dawn events with Theseus going on his hunt and discovering the sleeping lovers, and finally the herbs that bewitch and restore the lovers. In the "fury" sections of *Midsummer Night's Dream* all the furies save for Oberon are shape-destroying daemons whose antitheses are the wild saint of the day on which they appear and the reformed Duke of Athens. However, the dawn recognition brings the lovers back into Athens knowing fully the meaning of passion and equally fully recognizing the significance of the "Diane's bud" to their renewal (whether they remember the flower or not). With the coming of the light, an uncaring and dominating Egeus and his for-the-moment mouthpiece, Theseus, no longer control them. When they have seen the light they can come home to a marriage that is as appropriate for them in Protestant England as asceticism is for John. When dawn comes, the lovers see with the double vision of night wildness and Athenian clarity (*MND* 4.1.185ff.). However, the authoritative dream is the light of rational and witted love and warm concern for the other, even if marred by supercilious remarks about the guildsmen's play. It is this light that is not consumed by the prenuptial entertainments with their parody of the potential tragedy of the lovers (after all Starveling is there as Moonshine). This light leads the fairies to anticipate the daybreak of the second day as they bless the house. The deepest dream is not Bottom's pseudo-Pauline "vision" (1 Corinthians 2:9) of an erotic Titania and an inverted epiphany that has no bottom.[63] It is morning when the woodland lovers come back to Athens with renewed love.

Epiphany and *Twelfth Night*

Twelfth Night conventionally appears in contemporary criticism as reenacting the battle between Carnival and Lent. My argument is that the prospect of renewal lies beyond the powerful forces of both these observances. Renewal means moving from playing at love to serious sacrifice for it. Renewal means abandoning posturing melancholy for innocent and uncalculated choice, and renewal happens at the end of *Twelfth Night*'s journey.

At the other end of the festival year of the church from *Midsummer Night's Dream*'s Feast of St. John occurs the period from Christmas to Twelfth Night, or Epiphany, near another solstice. As a festival time, one of the things that the day celebrates is the prophetic sight of the Magi who followed the star and came to the cradle to recognize the embodiment of God in man. The play *Twelfth Night* was early—perhaps first—performed in February of 1602 in the Middle Temple Hall of the Inns of Court, during the Twelfth Night or Epiphany season defined in the Book of Common Prayer (though not on the night of January 5–6, technically Twelfth Night). This Middle Temple performance entertained lawyers and would-be lawyers, many of whom were probably would-be social climbers like Malvolio or pursuers of the arts of dancing, fencing, and drinking, like Sir Andrew and Sir

FIGURE 14. Sandro Botticelli (1445–1510), *Adoration of the Magi*, ca. 1478–82. Tempera and oil on panel. Image © Board of Trustees, National Gallery of Art, Washington DC, Andrew Mellon Collection.

Toby.[64] (There is, of course, Hotson's theory that the play was first performed on the twelfth day of Christmas, January 6, 1600–1601, before Elizabeth and an Italian aristocrat, Orsino, but one has to ask why anyone would want to portray a distinguished guest as such a fool as is the play's Orsino).[65] Interestingly Barber, in writing on Shakespeare and festival, makes little effort to relate the play to the Twelfth Night religious festival after which it is named, or to the Epiphany season's Misrule, although he treats of its festive qualities and elsewhere treats the Lord of Misrule figure sometimes associated with Twelfth Night celebrations at great length.[66]

Early Modern Christmas feasting extended from the Nativity on December 25 to the appearance of the Magi on Twelfth Night. The time during and after the winter solstice was celebratory, heralding hope for the return of the sun, just as the summer solstice celebration supposedly kept the summer season's light from being wholly swallowed by the next midwinter's darkness. While traditional Christians in writing of this season emphasized Christ as the Light that would

FIGURE 15. Leonardo da Vinci (1452–1519), *Adoration of the Magi*, ca. 1481–82. Oil on wood. Uffizi, Florence. Scala/Art Resource, New York.

renew the spiritual world, the Puritans emphasized the continuities between the winter solstice period's Saturnalian pagan feasting and the Christian feasting during the Christmas season. They hated both. Following from this critique, modern criticism has made the play a dialogue between Carnival—of a Bahktinian sort—and Lent.[67]

However, winter rejoicing is not all Saturnalian. Indeed one suspects that few of the country folk who kept up the Christmas period feasts knew anything about their roots in another culture. They were told in Gospel, prayer, and homily that what they were celebrating was the appearance of God, the innocent child who would eventually make the crucial sacrifice.[68] The feasting that went with Epiphany celebrated the manifestation of God from behind the mask of material flesh—the appearance of the divine child to the Magi, of the divine adult to those present at His baptism, at His feeding of the five thousand, and at His making of the wine from water at the marriage at Cana.[69]

The feast of St. John tells us of an early dawn's midsummer light that subdues the darkness. Epiphany, set in the darkness of midwinter, tells of late dawn's new light beginning to come into the world, reaching from the Jews to the Gentiles. Epiphany's celebration moves beyond the battle between Carnival and Lent—pure abandon and pure asceticism—to honor the manifestation of the divine in human flesh, making the flesh a potential vehicle of the beauty of spirit glorified in Early Modern Magi paintings.[70] In the period's art persons regarded as historical, but also as symbolic, witness the event: Joseph and Mary standing for humankind, Mary representing womankind, and the Magi representing human wisdom coming to encounter its divine counterpart (figs. 14, 15).[71]

In Early Modern understandings, the Magi come from the three ages of humankind—youth, middle age, and old age—and sometimes from humankind's three races—Jews and Semitic peoples, European peoples, and Africans (or Shemites, Japhethites, and Hamites).[72] Their gifts of gold, frankincense, and myrrh symbolize that Christ's appearance as the divine in mortal flesh entails a series of attributes in him that require reciprocal responses from his followers: gold for his kingship requiring obedience; frankincense for his worshipfulness requiring adoration; and myrrh for his suffering, implying his sufferings and the pain of those who come to him.[73] The medieval and Early Modern paintings of the whole world coming to the cradle at Bethlehem show a fantastic rejoicing in processional, for example in Filippo Lippi's painting of the scene or Benozzo Gozzoli's *Procession of the Magus Gaspar*.

As the feast of St. John celebrates the retention of light, the emphasis of Epiphany—particularly evident in Early Modern Magi paintings from just before, during, and just after Shakespeare's time—goes to light returning, often shining out into darkness. Indeed, the paintings by such chiaroscuro predecessors of Rembrandt and his school as Leonaert Bramer offer us a very dark stable with a mighty

FIGURE 16. Leonaert Bramer (1596–1674), *The Adoration of the Magi*, ca. 1628–30. Oil on canvas. Founders Society Purchase, Joseph M. de Grimme Memorial Fund; and gifts from Mr. and Mrs. Edgar B. Whitcomb, Harriet Scripps, and Mr. and Mrs. Sol Eisenberg by exchange. Photograph © 1993, The Detroit Institute of Arts.

luminescence coming from the cradle (fig. 16). If the painting is set during the daytime, the light of the Nativity casts a special light on the worshipers' faces.

One painting that summarizes much of the tradition of the Magi paintings and gives us a sense of what to look for in Shakespeare's *Twelfth Night* is Rubens's *Adoration of the Magi*, painted for St. Michael's Abbey in Antwerp (fig. 17).

Here Christ-the-Child lies on the Virgin's lap on a coverlet that also has a sheaf of grain with it, the Wise Men approaching with their gifts—one old, one young, and one of middling age. The birth takes place in a rough building, apparently a stable symbolizing the New Law, placed near a Corinthian pillar, behind which stands a large, apparently Roman building, symbolizing the Old Law. Quite undisturbed by the crowd, an ox looks out from the foreground. The crowd

FIGURE 17. Peter Paul Rubens (1577–1640), *The Adoration of the Magi*, 1624. Oil on panel. Royal Museum of Fine Arts, Antwerp. Photo courtesy of Reproductiefonds Vlaamse Musea NV.

includes Roman military officers who seem to show admiration for Christ. Light radiates from the center of the painting, whether from the star or from the presence of divinity is not clear.

Barbara Haegar has argued that the scene, painted for a Catholic audience, is a rehearsal of the sacrifice of the Mass and an anticipation of the Crucifixion (as is the myrrh in conventional accounts). One Magus wears an explicitly priestly robe as he offers the gift of frankincense recognizing Christ's divinity, a recognition that in Haegar's view is reinforced by the light dominating the center of the painting, and announces the new day of the Incarnation: "Arise, O Jerusalem, be bright, for thy light is come" (Geneva Bible, Isaiah 60:1–4). Haegar shows that the Corinthian column in the painting also signifies the New Law or the Virgin/church as its representative. She sees the sheaf as Eucharistic, the Magi as the New Law seekers for the Eucharist, and the ox as a figure for the sacrifice of Christ.[74] The painting is more emphatically Catholic in its theology than a comparable painting in England would have been in 1604, but it introduces the standard symbolism.

Some of this painting's kind of symbolism is present in the much less explicitly religious *Twelfth Night*, and the painting's imagery without the Eucharistic emphasis is a touchstone to what Twelfth Night, the festival, meant in exegesis, painting, and sermon. Consider for instance the painting's movement from darkness in the back part of the scene to light in the foreground. The early condition of most of the characters in the play is either physical or psychological darkness or both: Toby and Andrew's celebration in the night, Orsino and Olivia's contrasting forms of melancholy, Malvolio's would-be solemnity in the presence of Olivia's sorrow, and Viola and Sebastian's supposed drownings. One speculates that the early viewers of the play would not have been insensitive to Sir Toby and Sir Andrew spending their first Misrule hours in the dark. Concomitantly, Orsino begins in the blackness of melancholy love and self-absorption and Olivia with the fake black of perpetual mourning for her brother:

FESTE: Good madonna, why mournest thou?
OLIVIA: Good fool, for my brother's death.

FESTE: I think his soul is in hell, madonna.
OLIVIA: I know his soul is in heaven, fool.
FESTE: The more fool, madonna, to mourn for your brother's
soul, being in heaven. Take away the fool, gentlemen. (*TN*
1.5.57–62)

The end of the play with the return of the twins and the unions of
Sebastian and Olivia, and Orsino and Viola, celebrates light and airi-
ness, the reunion of the spiritual and the physical. The play goes from
domination by the fleshly Toby and would-be fleshly Andrew, by the
secretly flesh-bound Malvolio, and the speciously spiritual Orsino and
Olivia, to epiphanic celebration as Viola and Sebastian come together
and reach their final loves.

The feast of Twelfth Night or Epiphany is represented in the play in
two forms, first in the forms of the Magi-beggars, Viola and Sebastian,
who are cast up seeking for each other and a place, and then receive
gifts from Illyria. Second, and by way of inversion, it is represented in
the persons of the three fools, Sir Andrew, Sir Toby, and Feste, who,
abusing the imagery of Epiphany and its motions, find nothing aside
from a little fun. Between them appears Mal-volio as "bad will," who,
thinking he has found everything, finds nothing but the *consequences*
of bad will and of specious belief in erotic election.

Treating these two appearances of Twelfth Night's idea in the play
in order before returning to their knotting together, I argue that Viola
and Sebastian answer the failures of the other characters. Viola does
so by demonstrating to those narcissistic characters who are possessed
of melancholy love—Orsino and Andrew—what sacrifice in love is;
Sebastian by demonstrating to those afflicted with black melancholy
(or pretending so)—Olivia and Malvolio—what innocent choice in
love that is beyond posturing can be. The end of the Twelfth Night
journey is innocence and sacrifice.

In the person of Viola, the play moves the possibilities for love from
the self-centered to the willingly sacrificial. She has wooed Olivia for
Orsino through most of the play in order to be near him, and at the
end she is willing to die to be his love:

DUKE ORSINO: Why should I not, had I the heart to do it,
Like to th' Egyptian thief, at point of death
Kill what I love. . . .
Come, boy, with me. My thoughts are ripe in mischief.
I'll sacrifice the lamb that I do love
To spite a raven's heart within a dove.
VIOLA: And I most jocund, apt, and willingly,
To do you rest a thousand deaths would die.
OLIVIA: Where goes Cesario?
VIOLA: After him I love
More than I love these eyes, more than my life,
More by all mores than e'er I shall love wife.
If I do feign, you witnesses above,
Punish my life for tainting of my love. (*TN* 5.1.113–15; 125–34)

Both Orsino and Viola describe the proposed killing of Viola in the language of willing sacrifice. The doves and lambs are there, and the scene calls more for altars than for the masks of homicide.

Sebastian, the other twin, provides an image of masculinity with his swordplay with Sir Toby, but even more, he embodies the image of sudden, innocent choice in love. Sebastian's quick union with Olivia comes with a eulogy to light and an innocence that has few rivals in literature. An ecstatic Sebastian throws himself upon the delight of his unexpected love for Olivia:

SEBASTIAN: This is the air, that is the glorious sun.
This pearl she gave me, I do feel't and see't,
And though 'tis wonder that enwraps me thus,
Yet 'tis not madness. (*TN* 4.3.1–4)

The Geneva Bible says that the pearl signifies the "most precious heavenly doctrine" and the riches of the kingdom of heaven redeemed with the "losse of all his goods."[75] Sebastian, losing everything, has found a kind of sudden love. The sun and the pearl shine with it in a feast of light.

The twins are the characters who see beyond the surfaces in the play—Viola sees both Olivia's and Orsino's real capacities for love amid their posturing at melancholy and passion, and Sebastian recognizes Olivia's eagerness for marriage. We have in them the phenomenon described by Richard C. Trexler in his brilliant *The Journey of the Magi: Meanings in History of a Christian Story.* Trexler shows that during the Early Modern Twelfth Night celebrations beggar children, often two of them, went from door to door and requested gifts at the houses instead of offering them. The beggar-Magi played gift-seekers rather than gift-givers, and the purpose of their processional, in turn, was to compel the consciences of the rich to assist the poor.[76] In *Twelfth Night*, the beggar children are Viola and Sebastian—assuredly not Magi and not exactly beggar children, but boy actors presenting young, shipwrecked, and bereft persons, going from Orsino's to Olivia's door and back again and finding gifts. Viola depends on Orsino's kindness and gift of himself, and Sebastian on Antonio's protection and Olivia's gift of herself. Their need, and the benefit to the Illyrians of respecting that need, produces Viola's gift of sacrificial love and Sebastian's bright innocence before Olivia's proposals.

The other side of the play—that which inverts the Twelfth Night story—is darker, depending as it does on separation of the material from the spiritual and on mistaken or silly uses by the grotesques of the play of the literal or tropological meaning of the Magi visit. These uses occur in the drinking scenes and in Malvolio's mistaken projection on Maria's "epistle" of a meaning making him predestined to sexual bliss. Malvolio is a Puritan in the revelers' eyes (*TN* 2.3.131), and like the Puritans of five decades later who abolished all religious holidays and the theater, he hates festival. In retaliation, in the letter-dropping scene, the hedonists arouse his erotic attraction to Olivia by using the very Puritan convictions that have made him a good steward for an Olivia pretending melancholy. That is, they appeal to his literalism and his sycophant's attention to his lady's commands. To these Maria adds his Puritan belief in acronyms and acrostics as revelatory, his love of the epistle that brings good news (e.g., St. Paul), and his belief in this-worldly manifestations of other-worldly grace and predestination that promises present material and sexual advantage. The Malvolio who comes in to pick up the epistle is so utterly humorless, even when contemplating sex followed by masturbation—playing with "some rich jewel" or "wind[ing] up" his "watch" (2.5.52–55)—that he thinks the epistle promises the fulfillment of his every fantasy of sex, power, and wealth. He is the perfect Puritan, probably of a Calvinistic variety.[77]

Malvolio is wrong. He converts egocentric fantasy to religion, and it has no spiritual content. Epiphany is, par excellence, the feast of those who perceive the translucence of the "general in the special, the eternal in the temporal," as Coleridge puts it.[78] By definition, it can carry no meaning to those for whom such seeing is impossible. The Epiphany feast privileges the revealed knowledge that comes from divinity over the natural knowledge of wise men. It celebrates the integration of body and spirit in the Epiphanic moment over the dichotomizing of flesh and spirit. Luther, in one of his sermons on Epiphany, makes an extended analysis of the difference between the darkness and light that various actors in the Epiphany story have. He sees this as the difference between diabolic knowledge, which ordinary sorcerers have (and which the Magi could have been taken to have); natural university-style knowledge, which the Magi had; and the revealed knowledge that Christ gave. For him Epiphany, as the marriage of flesh and spirit in Christ, shows the error of those who consume or do not consume food and drink because they regard such actions as contributing to salvation. Neither consuming nor abstaining is salvific by itself, but the spirit that informs either may be.[79] In an attack on Catholic asceticism that is part of this Epiphany sermon, Luther would have whoever "fasts, labors, wears the garments of monks or priests, or keeps the rules of his order, consider this just as he considers eating and drinking, not as making him holy by doing it, or as making him unholy by omitting it" because he can "become holy only through faith."[80] In *Twelfth Night* Toby eats and drinks and relishes both, and he flaunts his relishing before Malvolio: "Dost thou think because thou art virtuous there shall be no more cakes and ale?" (2.3.103–4). In contrast, Malvolio appears to abstain. At the beginning of the work he would appear to regard himself as holy in just the sense that Luther attacks.

In his "deepest" inwardness, Malvolio senses only that life consists of trivial household order for others and gratification for himself. He has no real depth that feels the movements of the spirit.[81] Malvolio's repressive mask comes off with his effort to approach Olivia as a lover (3.4.16ff.), but he never encounters Viola in a real way and Sebastian not at all. He ends up cast in the role of one possessed by a demon or lower fury while being ill with love melancholy. He is angry with the "exorcizing" Sir Topas (modeled comically after Chaucer's fleshly Sir Thopas who pursues the faery Oliphaunt), never recognizing that he needs some sort of exorcizing for his fury and that comedy could be his exorcist.

Toby's, Andrew's, and Fabian's world of hedonistic abandon conquers Malvolio's world of false asceticism. The party in act 2, scene 3, is a most egregious distortion of the Epiphany feast night, twisting both its letter and its meaning as set forth in Matthew and his commentators. At the drinking bout we begin in the dark, literally and figuratively. The soft feasting that is to go with Christmas and Epiphany has, among the play's party boys, especially Toby and Andrew, become the wild rumpus of the denial of the eternal in the temporal. Feste's part in the rumpus is partly participatory—"Yes, by Saint Anne, and ginger shall be hot i'th' mouth, too" (2.3.105–6)—and partly parody of Sir Toby and Sir Andrew—"Sir Toby, there you lie" (2.3.96). The trio's spirit of Misrule does not mock Misrule but celebrates it.[82] For Toby, the genius of the festival—to drink all night—is health, pure nonsense is "Pigronomitic" wisdom, and with his approval the "wise men's" sons of Feste's song are lovers who seize the day and not those who follow their Wise Man fathers to epiphany:

FESTE: (*sings*)
O mistress mine, where are you roaming?
O stay and hear, your true love's coming,
That can sing both high and low.
Trip no further, pretty sweeting.
Journeys end in lovers meeting,
Every *wise man's* son doth know.

SIR ANDREW: Excellent good, i'faith.
SIR TOBY: Good, good.
FESTE: (*sings*)
  What is love? 'Tis not hereafter,
  Present mirth hath present laughter.
  What's to come is still unsure.
  In delay there lies no plenty,
  Then come kiss me, sweet and twenty.
  Youth's a stuff will not endure. (*TN* 2.3.35–48; italics mine)

But Love clearly is and is not hereafter. The revelers have no love save in song, and the journey ends less at Mary's cradle than at Maria's "buttery bar" (1.3.59)—or at Maria's device to trick Malvolio. The three merry men who celebrate in the night (2.3.69) become the three fools who could see themselves in the mirror of Feste's wit (2.3.15). They hint at their obverse models from the Epiphany story—the Wise Men—by distorting the narrative so that it becomes time-bound drunken chatter. Toby's "twelfth day of December" (2.3.76) mangles the idea of the twelfth day of Christmas, his "man in Babylon" (2.3.71) shadows the thought that the Magi came from the "east"—from Persia or some similar region. Toby's denial of death in this scene (2.3.95) also denies the meaning of eternal light coming into the world. While the festival of the season neither denies the goodness of the time-bound world in which incarnation happens nor asserts its absolute separation from divinity, Toby's hope rests on the hope of permanent material satisfaction (contrast 2.3.43–48):

SIR TOBY: But I will never die.
FESTE: Sir Toby, there you lie. (*TN* 2.3.95–96)

The story to which this twisted morsel from Elizabethan song probably refers is Luke 12:16–21, where a rich man says to his soul, "Soule, thou hast much goods laid vp for many yeeres: liue at ease, eate, drinke, and take thy pastime," and God says, "O foole, this night will they fetch away thy soule from thee: then whose shall those things be which thou hast prouided?"—an exemplum to those rich to themselves and "not rich to God." Christ's follow-on advice is that one should consider the ravens and the lilies.

When Sir Toby extends his rich man's fantasy from many years of living to never dying, he acts as the successor to all those medieval "Epicureans" who imagine permanent pleasure—lords of Cockaigne, Belaise monastics, and Chaucerian Januarys who see material satisfaction as their life's goal. He, among all of these heroes of the consumer world, is best at his job, wittier and less bombastic than Jonson's Sir Epicure Mammon, more endearing than Chaucer's January, and more perfectly realized than any of the inhabitants of special pleasure gardens. Toby—and to some extent his allies—can only gain their joy from the cannikin or from the destruction of, or effort to destroy, others—Malvolio or Andrew or Viola.

The yearning for love and pleasure of Sirs Toby and Andrew parallels and satirizes the similar yearning of Orsino. The will to the pretense of austerity and repression of Malvolio matches Olivia's mourning mood. The play's Illyrian characters divide the world between the dogmatic egotists and the hedonists. Nothing of Epiphany remains without the twins—without Viola and Sebastian's coming ashore as Epiphany's beggar children seeking gifts. The *Menaechmi*-like aspects of the play bring in the possibility that there is more than never dying or failing to read the letter and the spirit of the text. There is more than repressing others to gain self-satisfaction. There is life, a miraculous renewal of life. Prior to and without Viola and Sebastian, all that we have are a series of masks with nothing under them. Olivia keeps Malvolio as a steward because he expresses her posture of mourning and acts as her mask to ward off suitors. (Real mourning, in a Church of England world, would be in order if she believed her brother damned, as Feste suggests she does [1.5.56–62].)

Until help comes from Viola as would-be duelist and Sebastian as master of the sword, Sir Toby and Sir Andrew continue as useless parasites in Olivia's house and allow her endlessly to put off sexual and other consummations. Without the help of Viola and Sebastian, Sir Toby continues as the successful braggart soldier and patron of his niece. He endlessly exploits Andrew, and he sees to it that Olivia has no one serious to marry. When Viola/Cesario comes to Olivia's household, some of its masks are removed, Olivia's of sorrow and Sir Andrew's of lover and duelist. When Viola/Cesario comes to Orsino's household as a eunuch, Orsino can no longer be fully the love-melancholic fool, the straight version of a Sir Andrew who knows nothing of love as sacrifice. On the other hand, when Sebastian comes to Olivia's house, Sir Toby can no longer pretend to be the pattern of knighthood and Olivia can no longer flirt with Viola without commitment. When the twins begin to manifest themselves, integrity enables genuine and sacrificial love to achieve its epiphany. Viola, patience seated on a monument, martyrs herself for Orsino to allow him to reach Olivia. She then is willing to martyr herself again to give Orsino peace (5.1.112–34). Sebastian comes ashore to a world of light, innocence, and marriage made possible by Viola. The miracle of love has cosmic and epiphanic implications in Viola's understanding. When she hears Antonio call Sebastian's name, she begins to believe that he is alive, not destroyed by the storm, and cries out:

> VIOLA: He named Sebastian. I my brother know
> Yet living in my glass. Even such and so
> In favour was my brother, and he went
> Still in this fashion, colour, ornament,
> For him I imitate. O, if it prove,
> Tempests are kind, and salt waves fresh in love! (*TN*
> 3.4.344ff.)[83]

Cosmic love stands revealed. The love that brings the twins ashore permits the unmasking of everyone else in a plot where they appear to gather darkness in a world of light. The twins are not so much Magi as beggar children who deserve gifts, but they also give gifts in that they see what needs to be done to create a different order of love that will alter society. The unmasking of love as sacrifice and epiphany comes as suddenly as light shining to Viola and Sebastian and their partners.

Shakespeare's "tropicall" patterns reveal something about his sense of what comedy is. Insofar as comedy is satiric and based in scriptural hermeneutics, it tells us of the *failure of ideals* and the *failure to achieve ideals*,—the failures that disturb such comic cities as Ephesus, Illyria's city and country, Messina, Venice, and *Measure for Measure's* Vienna (to be discussed later). Comedy also observes that the hermeneutics of selfishness dominating every interpretive culture, our own included, fails its practitioners in the end, because in reading and interpreting texts we practice a social art and lead life in community. For Shakespeare, Bible narrative-based comedy is often the comedy of the encounter with true or fake daemonic furies. It may also be something else—an encounter with the energy of the higher furies. This encounter may go beyond common joy and laughter because it tells how light and renewal, in coming, anticipate or are prophetic of happy End Time conclusions. The comedies tell us how laughter and joy arise through our exercising our commonsense rationality but also through our—or our society's—acts of extraordinary mercy, sacrificial love, and luck-finding ability (in the Early Modern period, a capacity to discover the providential). At a daily level, Shakespeare's higher fury's comedy tells of the light of civility dawning slowly. It may tell of miracles of transformed perspective that allow us to treat one another with affection and decency.

Resources for Biblical Story and Festival

Elizabethan and Jacobean people were expected to know the Bible from home reading, church reading, sermons, and all kinds of occasional references in popular culture. That does not mean one can assume some uniform response to biblical stories. The period in which Shakespeare worked is a period in which biblical interpretation was everywhere up for grabs. The question of whether the so-called apocryphal books should be included divided Catholics from Protestants, the latter eliminating them (interestingly Shakespeare's daughters were named after the apocryphal heroines Judith and Susannah). Whether one accepted the apocryphal books could affect whether one believed in, say, the doctrine of purgatory, an important point in assessing the authority of the ghost of Hamlet's father.

How one worked at interpretation was also up for grabs, especially all forms of figurative interpretation and hermeneutics. Protestant exegetes of the Calvinistic and "Puritanical" stripe would inveigh against the Catholic interpreters for ignoring the "clear meaning" of scripture in their pursuit of allegorical meaning. Conversely, interpreters like Cardinal Bellarmine defended the old tropological, allegorical, and anagogical approach to the search for possible biblical meaning.[84] Actually much of this controversy was more heat than light. What both sides were fighting against were figurative interpretations that legitimized institutions and doctrines that the other side deplored. Exegetes from both sides sometimes used the standard medieval explanations of the whole of the scriptures, the *Common Gloss* (or *Glossa Ordinaria*) and Nicholas de Lyra's *Postilles in Sacram Scripturam*, both commonly included as marginal glosses in Early Modern Bibles in Latin. Protestants, especially Lutheran and Church of England Protestants, turned to figures like Bernard of Clairvaux, Augustine, and Origen for exegeses. And both sides, save for the Calvinists, used differing versions of the tropological, allegorical, anagogical approaches—Protestants generally saying that their figural approaches were applications of the letter and Catholics that the figurative meanings were concealed beneath the letter and therefore not simply applications.

For those who wish to study Early Modern biblical hermeneutics, the works to study are St. Augustine's *On Christian Doctrine* (still very influential) and Erasmus's *Enchiridion Militis Christiani*, especially chapter 14, rule 5. One should also read John Colet's *Two Treatises On The Hierarchies Of Dionysus*, chapter 5, with its explanations of how scripture should be understood.[85] Also essential are Luther's remarks in his commentary on the Psalms, his prefatory material for the Song of Solomon, and William Whitaker's *Disputatio de Sacra Scriptura*.[86] The preachers of the day such as John Donne or Lancelot Andrewes also implicitly or explicitly suggest exegetical approaches. Though John Calvin and Theodore Beza in their approaches to the biblical text often deemphasize figurative readings, the Geneva Bible, which Calvin's relative William Whittingham supervised, includes a fairly heavy suggestion that figural readings of some sorts be sought.

Shakespeare's own biblical citation of the letter of scripture goes mostly, as one would expect, to the most widely read Bible of his time, the Geneva Bible. English exiles from England produced Geneva during Queen Mary's restoration of Catholicism to England, and it is a revision of Tyndale's 1534 Bible. The translation was also checked with Theodore Beza's Greek and Latin New Testaments. It was published in one version on the continent in 1560, with a dedication to Queen Elizabeth, and in England in 1575 and thereafter. There it was intensely popular until the King James Bible was mandated in 1611. One need not be concerned about the influence of the King James Bible on Shakespeare or his first audiences as it was published only as his career concluded.

The Geneva Bible tells us a great deal about the hermeneutic assumptions shared by Shakespeare and his audience. It contains marginal glosses explaining hard words and literal Hebrew usages that require a figurative translation for the English text to make sense. Its margins also provides references to other parts of the Bible to illuminate literal or metaphoric meanings when the text seems to require these, and it frequently gives a periphrastic sense of what a passage "says." Since the Geneva explanations may be expected to have their roots in Calvinistic thought—that is, what Calvin and Beza had to say about the Bible—and since both were professed literalists, one may expect the marginal explanations to be endlessly literalistic. However, many marginal comments point to types or metaphors in the Old Testament that look forward to the New Testament and imply a moral or tropological meaning for the reader: for example, the Song of Solomon ("Salomon's Song") begins with a note that gives the work a tropological and allegorical meaning. The work is an allegory and parable for the perfect love of Christ for the soul *and* for the church.

In using the Geneva Bible's marginal notes to reconstruct the nuances of intertextual references to the Bible that would have influenced Shakespeare's audiences' construal of meaning, one needs to look both at the marginal explanations and at the cross references to other parts of the Bible. For example, the Cain story references that we have used in talking of *Hamlet* go to Matthew 23:35, 1 John 3:11, and

Jude, verse 11. These passages in turn give further metaphoric explorations of Cain's lineage and the dichotomies between brother-love and brother-hate, passages that are germane to the Cain imagery in *Hamlet* and the related fratricidal themes dominating the Roland-Oliver and Duke-Frederick relationships in *As You Like It.* Again the Geneva's introductions to individual biblical books and to parts of individual books may help one understand what Shakespeare's audience would have understood in looking at Shakespearean imagery. For example, if one were looking at *The Comedy of Errors,* one might as an Elizabethan recall that the book of Ephesians, from Ephesians 4 on, contains that part of the book most relevant to Pauline social ideology. Geneva says this part deals with "precepts of Christian life."

Of course, primary understandings of the Bible for Church of England people in Shakespeare's time (officially everyone) also came from the Book of Common Prayer, the Anglican Church's official guide to worship. The student should look through the BCP to note any Shakespearean subtexts represented in it and examine what other texts are read in parallel. Frequently the reading from the Psalms, the Collect, the Epistle, and the Gospel are related thematically to one another and to a Shakespearean theme in a figurative way. For example, the texts for Christmas Day for the communion service of the day are related. The Psalms text speaks of the perfection of praise in the mouths of babes, the Collect prays for regeneration and new being in the parish, the Epistle speaks of the incarnation and glorification of Christ, presumably as a model for the worshiper, and the Gospel tells how Christ as the Son of God enables all to become sons of the same father. Taken together, the texts place the hearer topologically in the position of being both the new being—the Christ—that can appear on Christmas Day and the worshiper with those who come in hope to adore that new being.

Examining the array of texts that accompany the relevant texts in Shakespeare will often be productive. Following such an arraying of texts, the great preachers of the time, especially the court preachers from Elizabeth's time (such as Edwin Sandys or Richard Curteys) and from James's courts (such as John Donne or Lancelot Andrewes) may assist one in reconstructing the commonplace biblical semiology of the period.

There are, of course, other routes to understanding biblical narrative. There are the other versions of the Bible that were available in the late sixteenth and early seventeenth centuries, especially the Tyndale, Bishops, and Douay bibles (though there is not a lot of evidence that large numbers of people in the London of 1590 to 1610 derived their understanding of the biblical texts from these versions). We may assume that the churches in Shakespeare's time still contained large numbers of wall paintings and stained glass windows organized according to the logic that Emile Mâle sets forth in *The Gothic Image*, though many of these were destroyed in the Commonwealth period.[87] Certainly a study of the windows at such cathedrals as York or Gloucester is worth a go even if one cannot establish that their kind of interest in the saints or biblical typology had much power in Shakespeare's London.

Less generous pictorial sources are available. However, the *Biblia Pauperum*, a book of printing blocks that showed all sorts of biblical allegories and typologies widely used by critics of Early Modern Bible–based poetry (such as that of Herbert or Spenser) probably is not a good entryway to Shakespeare. It was somewhat passé in Shakespeare's time and probably of interest primarily to specialists in biblical poetry.

On the other hand, the biblical illustrations of Lucas Cranach, Jost Amman, and Albrecht Dürer, though Shakespeare did not know them, are well worth studying. They tell how biblical scenes were portrayed in his time and are frequently suggestive for latent, exemplary meanings. For example, discussion in chapter 6 addresses how Vincentio, the duke in *Measure for Measure*, acts as king-in-the-image-of-Christ and as the figure of Justice in the play's last scene. Dürer, in illustrating Malachi 4:1–3, where the prophet speaks of a *sol justitiae* or "sun of righteousness" that will arise for those who fear God, creates a figure with a sunlike face riding on a royal lion and bearing the emblems of justice, the scales and the sword, in hand.[88] To pursue a biblical motif such as the Adoration of the Magi so as to be able to explore its literal or figurative dimensions in art, one can visit the Web Gallery of Art by using the search function at http://www:wga.hu/index1.html. This provides dozens of variations on the basic theme, and looking up good iconological studies of these works can supply much help. Few of these are English, because so much English work has been lost or destroyed. As regards lost English work, we know that large numbers of biblical scenes and emblems were pictured in at least some aristocratic households on tapestries, painted cloths, and paintings. For a sample, see Peter M. Daley, ed., *The English Emblem and the Continental Tradition*, 11–13 and 18–19. These works were not as well preserved as were oil paintings in sixteenth-century Italy or Venice, for example.

Emblem books also provide a pictorial way of getting into biblical symbology. One popular book is Georgette de Montenay's *Emblemes, ou, Deuises chrestiennes*, which includes many emblems based on biblical passages, such as the Tower of Babel, "You cannot serve two masters," and other symbolic passages. Some modern critics also see Montenay as a proto-feminist. Another biblically based emblem book published in Shakespeare's time, widely read and used, is Andrew Willet's *Sacrorum Emblematum Centuria Una*. Willet divides his biblical emblems (which are not given pictures) into three kinds: (1) types presented in traditional passages where the biblical metaphoric dimension is explicit or had long been seen, like Jacob's ladder as the traditional figure for contemplation or looking for God; (2) historical emblems—those events that are presumed historical and have a typological and tropological dimension, such as the explanation that Israel needed to gather the manna in the morning or it would spoil as signifying that the soul has to lay hold on salvation as soon as it is available or lose it; and (3) emblems using plants and beasts, a section that engages in the construction of moral emblems from everything in the natural world in a technique similar to that used by the characters in *As You Like It*.

The Willet emblems from the 1590s are well worth examining even if the poetry is sometimes painful. The work is often suggestive. For example, consider Old Adam's remark to Orlando in *As You Like It*:

> Take that, and he that doth the ravens feed,
> Yea providently caters for the sparrow,
> Be comfort to my age. Here is the gold.
> All this I give you. Let me be your servant. (2.3.44–47)

Willet, earlier than Shakespeare, uses the feeding-of-the-ravens passage from Luke 12:24 to tell us of the providence of God toward his faithful, Adam's device also.

One late indication of the liveliness of the tropological tradition of interpretation in the visual arts is Francis Quarles's 1635 *Emblems*.[89] These emblems may not tell one directly how Shakespeare's first audiences would have understood him save that they reflect older traditions, current before and during his time. Quarles includes extensive figurative commentary on numerous biblical scenes, provides us with pictures illustrating his meaning, and draws on patristic and later exegetical tradition, especially about the Song of Solomon and the Psalms. Quarles's emblems are based on two Jesuit emblem books having an earlier publication date, *Pia Desiderata* (1624) and *Typus Mundi* (1627). Though Quarles is deeply indebted to Catholic tradition, he went through eleven editions in Protestant England in the seventeenth century and many more in England and the United States in later periods.

BIBLICAL FESTIVAL

Biblical festival is perhaps the most difficult area to explore in treating Shakespeare's biblical figuration. The sociology of festive celebration is quite various depending on the community and performative context, and it can change quickly as people act out their devotion and/or their passions. It is difficult to know which aspects of holy day celebration came into the figurative language and performance of Shakespeare's plays. It is also difficult to know to what extent the performance of a play on a specific holy day influenced what its audience saw in the play. The usual interpretation of the holiday or holy day frames of Shakespeare's comedies is that they are in some sense Carnival and resistant to the pious frowning of the Lenten-faced Christians.

One source that gives both countenance and refutation to this attitude is James I's 1618 "Declaration . . . Concerning Lawful Sport." It sees nothing impious in feast day recreation but also admits that it appears impious to some:

Whereas we did justly in our progress through Lancashire rebuke some Puritans and precise people, and took order that the like unlawful carriage should not be used by any of them hereafter, in the prohibiting and unlawful punishing of our good people for using their lawful recreations and honest exercises upon Sundays, and other holy days, after the afternoon sermon or service, we now find that two sorts of people wherewith that country is much infected, we mean Papists and Puritans, have maliciously traduced and calumniated those our just and honourable proceedings: and therefore lest our reputation might upon the one side (though innocently) have some aspersion laid upon it, and that upon the other part our good people in that country be misled by the mistaking and misinterpretation of our meaning, we have therefore thought good hereby to clear and make our pleasure to be manifested to all our good people in those parts. . . .

[W]e heard the general complaint of our people, that they were barred from all lawful recreation and exercise upon the Sunday's afternoon, after the ending of all divine service, which cannot but produce two evils: the one the hindering of the conversion of many, whom their priests will take occasion hereby to vex, persuading them that no honest mirth or recreation is lawful or tolerable in our religion, which cannot but breed a great discontentment in our people's hearts, especially of such as are peradventure upon the point of turning: the other inconvenience is, that this prohibition barreth the common and meaner sort of people from using such exercises as may make their bodies more able for war, when we or our successors shall have occasion to use them; and in place thereof sets up filthy tipplings and drunkenness, and breeds a number of idle and discontented speeches in their ale-houses.

For when shall the common people have leave to exercise, if not upon the Sundays and holy days, seeing they must apply their labour and win their living in all working-days? . . .

[O]ur pleasure likewise is, that after the end of divine service our good people be not disturbed, letted or discouraged from any law-ful recreation, such as dancing, either men or women; archery for men, leaping, vaulting, or any other such harmless recreation, nor from having of May-games, Whitsun-ales, and Morris-dances; and the setting up of May-poles and other sports therewith used: so as the same be had in due and convenient time, without im-pediment or neglect of divine service: and that women shall have leave to carry rushes to the church for the decorating of it, ac-cording to their old custom; but withal we do here account still as prohibited all unlawful games to be used upon Sundays only, as bear and bull-baitings, interludes, and at all times in the meaner sort of people by law prohibited, bowling.

And likewise we bar from this benefit and liberty all such known as recusants, either men or women, as will abstain from coming to church or divine service, being therefore unworthy of any law-ful recreation after the said service, that will not first come to the church and serve God: prohibiting in like sort the said recreations to any that, though [they] conform in religion, are not present in the church at the service of God, before their going to the said recreations.[90]

To the king, the recreations and sports of Sunday and of feast days are a complement to the worship of the day and may induce con-version. The meanings of play and of worship are consonant, and it takes no great wit to conclude that the meanings of individual acts of worshiping on a holy day and playing festively on that day ought to be consonant. Obviously, to the Puritans these festivities meant something very different.

Whatever the meaning, Shakespeare certainly uses the festivals of the church year and related folk festivals as the center of the action in many of his plays: the Feast of St. John for *Midsummer Night's Dream*, Epiphany for *Twelfth Night*, and May Day in *Two Noble Kinsmen*. Other feasts are suggested in other plays. May Day is the night of Saint Walpurga in Scandinavia and Germany and of St. Philip and St. James the Less in the Church of England (though it is difficult to show that anything other than the celebration of spring, Flora, and the return of green is the center of this day). *Love's Labour's Lost* seems more vaguely poised between winter and spring, *Hiems* and *Ver*, death and life—perhaps at the vernal equinox.

Again, the feast day on which a Shakespearean play is performed, according to the records, seems to give the play additional significance. For example, *The Comedy of Errors* is first recorded as having been played amid the Christmas Revels at Gray's Inn as part of the *Gesta Grayorum*, where a sort of "mock-epic" government was created —largely self-parody for the lawyers and lawyers-to-be who constituted the Inn as well as for their rivals, those at the Inner Temple. The *Comedy* with its inversion of order would have fit in. That it was performed on December 28, the Feast of the Holy Innocents, is not insignificant. Duke Solinus comes on like a Herod at the beginning of the play, ready to execute perfectly innocent people. But December 28 is not only the day of the massacre of the children of Bethlehem. It is the day of the Feast of Fools—the feast of the ass. On this day, human foolishness is celebrated, a time perfect for the *Comedy*. Characters call themselves or someone else asses at least six times in the *Comedy*, reminding us of the wearing of the ass head on the feast of fools and of the human foolishness implicit in this feast day.

To explore the meaning of the feast days one needs to explore the meaning of the village celebrations as these are recounted in local stories. The literary nuances given to such days as May Day in other writers also help one to know the story. Beyond such explorations, one can examine what the feast day may have meant in traditional culture by looking at the older accounts of the saints whose days are celebrated—such as *The Golden Legende*, no longer used in Elizabethan England—or older explanations of the liturgical year, such as that found in William Durandus's *Rationale Divinorum Officiorum*. Durandus was frequently reprinted in the Early Modern period, though one cannot know that he had much influence in Shakespearean England outside of recusant circles. One should of course examine what the Book of Common Prayer psalms, prayers, epistles, and Gospels are for the feast days. Some of the extant sermons for particular feast days assist one in understanding the spirit of the day and the imagery that went with a day with which a play is associated. For example, John Donne's sermon preached at St. Paul's Cathedral on Midsummer's Day, 1622, develops the motifs of John the Baptist as authority, the light coming, the infusing of knowledge similar to "poetic furor," contrasted with the dimensions of darkness, death, lostness, and wilderness. We have explored these motifs in connection with *Midsummer Night's Dream*, though obviously Donne looks at the Feast of St. John in a more didactic, austere form than does the play.[91]

5

Empire and Conquest in the Comedies

Shakespeare's public theater after early 1599 was the Globe. Here his company laid its claim to being able to talk about the entire globe. When Prospero speaks of the world's (or globe's) dissolving in an apocalypse, he deliberately leaves open the question of which globe would vanish (*Tempest* 4.1.153), but there is little doubt that one meaning of the "great globe" is the whole world, verified to be round only a little over a hundred years before the Globe opened. Shakespeare in the comedies talks about the entire known world. As I have mentioned, outside the Globe hung the sign of Hercules supporting the circle of the world with a Latin motto telling theater goers that all the world is a stage. And the globe as a world, as a community of national communities, or as a series of empires, comes to us vividly in the comedies. The histories are all England; the tragedies are primarily England and Scotland, ancient Rome, and Italy. But the great globe itself, insofar as it was available as something knowable to Shakespeare and his age, is the domain of the comedies (especially if one allows for the fact that Asia and the Americas were not available for Shakespeare or his audiences in forms that would permit serious verisimilitudinous narration). Even given the distance of Africa, the Far East, and the Americas, Shakespeare seems to refer to America in *The Tempest* and occasionally refers to India, China, and Africa in short passages, such as Benedick's reference to Prester John, the pigmies,

Kingdom of Denmark

North Sea

United Provinces
(Holland)

Kingdom
of England

Holy Roman
Empire

London •

Spanish
lands[1]

(without Austria,
Palatinate,
and
Spanish
lands)

Prague •

The Channel

Paris •

Palatinate

*Atlantic
Ocean*

Kingdom
of
France

Spanish lands

Switzerland[2]

Duchy
of
Savoy[2]

Spanish lands[1]

Venice

Papal

Navarre

Rousillon

States

K i n g d o m   o f   S p a i n

Kingdom
of
Portugal

Kingdom
of
Castile

Kingdom
of
Aragon

Mediterranean

Algiers

Tunis

Kingdom
of
Fez[3]

Kingdom
of
Morocco

Notes:
1) Spanish land holdings within the Holy Roman Empire
2) Contested territories within the Holy Roman Empire
3) Contested between the Ottoman Empire and the Kingdom of Morocco

MAP 1. The Europe of Shakespeare's Comedies, about 1600

Imperial borders are ambiguous because empires had a tendency to claim more land than they actually controlled. The Ottoman Empire, Holy Roman Empire, the kingdoms of Spain,

France, and England, the Venetian Republic, the Commonwealth of Poland and Lithuania, and Russia (the Tsardom of Muscovy) all claimed descent from the Roman or Eastern Roman Empire.

MAP 2. Shakespeare's Central and Northern Italy in 1600

and the great Cham's beard in *Much Ado*, act 2, scene 1. The references to these places do have the air of the exotic, however. Europe, the Mediterranean, North Africa, the Ottoman Empire, and Russia were available as real places to the citizens of a great port city, and Shakespeare wrote about them (see map 1). And his global interest does not begin with the erecting of the Globe. Even before he came to his new theater, around 1594 he parsed the body of the kitchen maid, Luce, in *Comedy of Errors* as a representation of Europe and America.

The center of Shakespeare's global world for the comedies includes the English empire, the Venetian one (see map 2), the Turkish Ottoman hegemony, the Holy Roman Empire and related Habsburg domains, especially the Spanish possessions, possibly the New World in *The Tempest*, and the Russian Empire.

Of Russia Shakespeare has little to say that reflects much knowledge. Ivan the Terrible had just completed his reign and claimed the title of "czar" or Caesar. The country was in turmoil with a succession of claimants to the throne after Ivan's death, and England's commerce with Russia was limited; voyages there had begun in 1553. Though the Russia Company, a trade organization, was somewhat active in Shakespeare's productive period, it was not a great company like its East India counterpart. The Russian Empire was terra incognita, barbaric, cold, and bloody.[1] The "Muscovites" who appear in *Love's Labour's Lost* are somewhat exotic parody figures placed in a masked courting ritual, and the other allusions to Russia largely have to do with cold.

The imperial centers of Shakespeare's global attention are a little closer to home: the Ottoman empire, extending over to Persia and across North Africa to Morocco; the Venetian empire, extending along the Adriatic coasts with many islands in the Mediterranean and trade routes deep into Persia and the subcontinent of India; and the Habsburg territories, including Germany, much of eastern Europe not controlled by the Ottomans, most of Italy, Spain, and the New World. Sir Walter Raleigh refers to all these empires save the Venetian when he writes that "[s]ince the fall of the *Roman* empire (omitting of the *Germaines*, which had neither greatnesse nor continuance) there hath beene no State fearful in the East, but that of the *Turke*; nor in the West any Prince that hath spred his wings farre ouer his nest, but the *Spaniard*; who since the time that *Ferdinand* expelled the *moores* out of *Granada*, have made many attempts to make themselues Masters of all *Europe*."[2] The German empire is, probably, the Holy Roman Empire. The fall of Rome may mean the fall of the Western Roman Empire in the 400s or of the Eastern Roman Empire in the 1400s. Raleigh goes on to say that the Turks seek to root out Christianity altogether and the papacy to root out sincere Christianity; one empire seeks to join Europe to Asia and the other to join it to Spain.

Raleigh's was the view of at least well-traveled English warriors in Shakespeare's time (1613). It is not unusual that he leaves out England. England was small fry, growing rapidly toward empire in the period 1590–1612 but not yet the wonder we are inclined to make it when we think of Elizabeth. Though England identified with Venice and negotiated with both Spain and the Turk, it feared them all, especially Spain and the Ottomans. Their worlds are not at first glance the worlds of comedy but of war, sea rivalries, religious difference, and territorial aggrandizement. So we must ask why Shakespeare made them the stuff of comedy. Perhaps he believed, with Yeats, that at the individual level, "all [persons] perform their tragic play," but that at the level of groups and history in general—and especially history in England and Christendom—all things move toward happy ends: to paraphrase Yeats again, "Their ancient glittering eyes are gay." Perhaps he also thought he could best treat the great globe by treating its empires and the implications of domestic relations for their great events.

This book has examined how Shakespeare's comedies rehearse potential movements toward rejoicing, in the household and in the commonwealth, and how they do so through altering New Comedy form and employing classical and scriptural intertexts to give the form a larger dimension. Shakespeare's plays in this genre additionally give us pictures of the potential for movement toward joy in the largest units of human governance known to his time—empires. Sometimes the joy tells us how to transcend or subvert empire. When we deal with Shakespeare's history plays, we are likely to see them, whether we are Marxists or not, addressing the consolidation of the nation-state and Tudor hegemony in England. We may observe the beginnings of colonialism in the Irish references in works like *Henry V.* However, Shakespeare's time is no simple nation-state period. It comes at the end of a long evolution from a feudal system that still held on in parts of the country *in fact* and in all of the country *in myth.* Beyond the nation-state there were the great empires, descendents of a Rome still alive in the imagination of Europeans.

As in England, in many parts of Europe and in the Middle East a range of governing systems competed. From at least the thirteenth century, several entities resembling nation-states came into being, beginning with Frederick II's Sicily and continuing through Edward III's England, Charles V's France, and Ferdinand and Isabella's Spain. France, Spain, England, and Sweden are on the edge of statehood in Shakespeare's time, but Elizabeth's and James's England is not really a *stable* nation-state unit yet, as the dynastic and religious conflicts preceding their time, and those following their reigns, testify. Further, national units in Shakespeare's time were parts of supra-national ones: England, Scotland after Elizabeth's death, and the parts of Ireland under English control had one ruler. The Holy Roman Empire included many nations and petty sovereigns. So did the Ottoman and Russian empires. And, quite unremarkably, many of Shakespeare's plays occur in the imperial contexts either of ancient Rome or of Europe and the Middle East in Shakespeare's century. The Roman imperial myth was still alive in Europe—in Czarist Russia, in the Habsburg Empire, and in the Ottoman world (through its imitation of Byzantine Rome). Other nations, such as Venice or England, claimed descent from imperial Rome. Given the locations of the comedies and, as we shall see, the governing issues that they raise, one can properly ask the question: What does Shakespeare say about empire and about England-and-empire in the comedies? He assuredly speaks of both.

Though Shakespeare, as a member of the Lord Chamberlain's and King's Men companies, received protection and support from the propaganda mechanisms of the English throne in the 1590s and early 1600s, he also had access to other sources of information and imagery. He lived in a great port city where the fluidity of political and commercial transactions both in his immediate environment and in the larger world, especially the Mediterranean, was apparent. People in London trade and government were as interested in Spain, Italy, Ottoman Turkey, Venice, and the Holy Roman Empire as we are in the European Union or in the Islamic world. In this larger world,

centering in the Mediterranean, the imperial unit is primary. If tragedy and epic sit at the pinnacle of the Early Modern period's literary
forms, if the Hebrew scriptures and the Greco-Roman myths as allegories carry its final religious and moral authority, empires sit at the
peak of its sense of political authority.

As Shakespeare's career progresses, the comedies reach increasingly for the grand themes and myths and come to touch on the
fates of empires. They do not touch them directly through portraying
their battles or conquests—these are only dragons on the margins of
the plays. They rather reach into imperial matters indirectly through
portrayals of the private and public interactions of people who can be
imagined to have constructed imperial turning points. Like the *Aeneid*,
in Roman times regarded as a sort of comedy, Shakespeare's comedies
tend to move toward marriages that solve or temporarily diminish the
great imperial struggles or point to something beyond empire. The
Virgil who so influenced Shakespeare furnished him with the model
of a "comic" work that ended in a "providential," destined marriage
and an imperial triumph uniting several nations. Shakespeare explored
the meaning of ancient empire in at least two of his tragedies, *Julius
Caesar* and *Antony and Cleopatra*. He also did so more indirectly and
politically in *Cymbeline*, and following Cymbeline he imitated the
Aeneid in his final *Tempest*.[3]

A host of entities in Shakespeare's world claimed to succeed Rome
or its predecessors in one way or another: Ottoman Turkey said it suc-
ceeded the eastern Roman Empire, Czarist Russia the eastern Roman
Empire again, the Holy Roman Empire the whole of Rome, Britain
all of Rome again. England's Roman claims are envisaged in Geoffrey
of Monmouth's Brutus-the-Trojan story supposedly behind Britain's
name. Even Venice claimed to be a New Rome. *Empire*, as understood
by Virgil and as used in Shakespeare's time, means the ultimate governing unit comprising a centralized "peace-making" authority and
ruling a polyglot group of nationalities and identity groups coerced
into accepting its rule in the interests of peace.

The prominent empire known to Shakespeare was obviously the
nascent British one celebrated by Spenser and, during Elizabeth's

time, active in Ireland. After James's coronation, it came to Scotland, North America, and, through the East India Company, to the Indies. Shakespeare uses *Cymbeline* to suggest that Britain is properly part of the Roman Empire or the Roman Empire of Britain. Though Cymbeline at the end of the play has won his war with the Roman Empire, he submits to it in a compromise (5.6.458–85). Leah Marcus has presented good evidence that James considered Great Britain—combining England and Scotland and the other territories that his monarchy controlled—a second Rome. For Marcus, Imogen resurrected becomes a Roman attached to the Roman commander, Lucius. In contrast, Posthumus, once a Roman, becomes a British peasant, and each becomes a precursor of a new peace between Rome and Britain at the time of the birth of Christ and the return of Astraea.[4] Indeed, the last lines in *Cymbeline* celebrate the fusion of the flight of the Roman eagle into the British sun:

> SOOTHSAYER: The fingers of the powers above do tune
> The harmony of this peace. The vision,
> Which I made known to Lucius ere the stroke
> Of this yet scarce-cold battle, at this instant
> Is full accomplished. For the Roman eagle,
> From south to west on wing soaring aloft,
> Lessened herself, and in the beams o'th' sun
> So vanished; which foreshowed our princely eagle
> Th'imperial Caesar should again unite
> His favour with the radiant Cymbeline,
> Which shines here in the west.
> CYMBELINE: Laud we the gods,
> And let our crooked smokes climb to their nostrils
> From our blest altars. Publish we this peace
> To all our subjects. Set we forward, let
> A Roman and a British ensign wave
> Friendly together: So through Lud's town march,
> And in the temple of great Jupiter
> Our peace we'll ratify, seal it with feasts.

Set on there. Never was a war did cease,
Ere bloody hands were washed, with such a peace.
(5.6.466–85)

Though *Cymbeline*, as Marcus argues, probably had a relation to James's project for an English-Scottish union, one cannot read these lines without feeling that they also make a larger claim that Britain is Rome and Rome Britain in a sense legitimized by history.

The Soothsayer's claim is at least as old as the Brutus story in Geoffrey of Monmouth, and it had been resurrected in Spenser's *Faerie Queene.* James I's analysis of the passion of Christ, as described in Matthew, makes His being given a purple robe and His crowning before the praetorium symbolize emperors inheriting Christ's mantle; he observes that many "Romane Emperours (his shadows and substitutes) should soon after his death [be] inaugurated and invested in the Empire" with a like procedure. James especially emphasizes the importance of Augustus as the first real emperor and peacemaker. He regards Julius Caesar as only a shadow first emperor, unworthy of the title because of his war-making proclivities. Since James valorized his own peacemaking skills, he certainly uses this passage both to suggest that Christ is the model of empire and that he, James, is cast in the form of Augustus as the substitute for Christ.[5] In the same treatise, the king mentions the Ottoman Empire as resembling the Roman in that the role the Janissaries play in it is like the role the military played in Rome.

In 1612 the Protestant Union within the empire was formed to protect Protestant interests, and James joined that union in 1612.[6] He had a continuing interest in relating his "empire" to the Holy Roman Empire through marriages and negotiations, culminating in the 1613 marriage of his daughter, Elizabeth, to the Palatinate elector, Frederick. There is no reason given in any other play to believe that Shakespeare did not believe Britain was in some senses "Rome," a New Rome, *and* a continuation of classical Rome and the Holy Roman Empire.

The other great empires with activities that touched the port of London and grabbed the English government's attention were the

Spanish Habsburg dominions in the Mediterranean and North and South America; the Ottoman Turkish area in the Middle East and the Balkans; and Czarist Russia, the European part of the territory that we identify with modern Russia. Russia is not prominent in Shakespeare's eye save for the lovers' masks as Muscovites in act 5 of *Love's Labour's Lost* and the references to the emperor of Russia in *The Winter's Tale* (3.2.119) and *Measure for Measure* (3.1.337). Crouched among these great powers, the empire of the Venetian Republic—minor in territory but very wealthy—traded in the Indian subcontinent and Persia, despite Turkish conquests in the Middle East and Portuguese rivalry in the Indian Ocean.[7] Given Russia's distant and unstable state, the struggle for imperial dominance in Europe in Shakespeare's time centered in the Mediterranean and engaged Ottoman Turkey, the Holy Roman Empire, Spain, and Venice. As Fernand Braudel has demonstrated in *The Mediterranean and the Mediterranean World in the Age of Phillip II*, the Mediterranean remained the center of European and world trade through the sixteenth and well into the seventeenth century, and Shakespeare's comedies behave as if this were the case. The great power struggles appeared, to contemporary eyes, to be working themselves out there, and access to the Orient remained primarily a Mediterranean matter despite the presence of the Ottomans as a partial barrier and the development of Portuguese oceanic routes.[8]

As Shakespeare treats of Mediterranean empires, he also uses them as the mirror of an England that was on the way to restoring Arthur's realm, as Spenser had represented things.[9] If playing is to "hold . . . the mirror up to nature," as one of Hamlet's metaphors argues, it is also to show the "very age and body of the time his form and pressure" (*Hamlet* 3.2.20–22). The face in the mirror in Shakespeare's mature comedies is alternately the *spezzato* face of England, of empire, or more often both mirroring each other. This double image is not outside the tradition of New Comedy. Plautus wrote *fabula palliatae* in the Greek garb that allowed him to refer to sensitive aspects of the Roman scene and avoid censorship.[10] Hamlet's *Mousetrap* is a version of the *fabula palliatae*. As I have noted, Hamlet calls it a comedy (3.2.269). When Shakespeare goes to Hamlet's mode and holds up the mirror, he almost never holds a flat mirror. It is a concave or convex one, never naming specific contemporary or recent rulers in his plays, always presenting the "other places" of his comedies in a slightly garbled way. However, his Mediterranean and Central European comedies do not garble things ignorantly but give his fictions a useful ambiguity in an authoritarian time while getting across a powerful political or social point.

Shakespeare's interest goes to the four geographic areas where dominance was contested among the imperial powers: Venice's borders with the Ottoman Turks (*Merchant of Venice* and *Twelfth Night*), Spain and the Holy League's struggles with the same Ottoman power (*Much Ado*), Austria and the Holy Roman Empire's wars and negotiations with the Ottomans and Hungary (*Measure for Measure*), and finally, the new English empire's rivalry with the Habsburgs in the Mediterranean and in its New World territories (*Tempest*).[11] Some aspects of the Habsburg hegemony may be treated in *The Winter's Tale* with its concentration on Bohemia, where the Austro-German Habsburgs lived at times, and Sicily, where the Spanish ones held sway, but how the tale works politically is not clear to me.[12] As I have said, *Cymbeline* simply legitimizes the idea that Britain is the Roman Empire or is a part of it. Leah Marcus has given authority to this general critical direction with her argument that James had a project to create a new empire called Great Britain and that, following this project's dream, Imogen becomes Roman after her burial of Cloten, and Posthumus becomes British in his disguise as a peasant. Further Posthumus's tablet tells us that "[t]he eagle of empire will pass from the Rome of Augustus Caesar to a reunited Britain."[13] With that background from *Cymbeline* in mind, this chapter treats the comic imperial theme in the order in which we believe the plays to have been written.

Venice and Turkey: *The Merchant of Venice* and *Twelfth Night*

The imperial struggle between the Ottomans and Venice developed the general political tensions underlying the battle at Lepanto and led to the hardening of the Catholic-Turkish struggle for the Mediterranean. The Levant Company had been formed in 1592 to trade with the eastern Mediterranean Turkish domains, and Elizabeth had sent William Harborne there to arrange a commercial treaty with the Ottomans.[14] In 1581 Harborne also negotiated with the Turks about English piracy. The issue concerned two Greek boats (owned and sailed by subjects of the sultan) headed from Patmos to Venice, which an English boat, the *Bark Roe*, had captured and taken to Malta, much to the consternation of the Venetians and the Ottomans. The two Greek boats had been captured near the island of Sapienza, near the Adriatic possessions of Venice.[15] While the English feared the Turks, they generally respected Venice because of its sea-trading position and its tolerance for Protestants, and writing about Venice was common from King James on.[16] The settings for *Merchant* and *Twelfth Night* are thus important to London's rulership and business.

However, Venice cannot be understood apart from the Ottoman expansion. After its defeat of Constantinople and the Eastern Roman Empire in 1453, Ottoman Turkey tightened its control over the lower Balkans and moved up the peninsula under a succession of able monarchs. The most important of them was Suleyman the Lawgiver, other-wise known as Suleyman the Magnificent (1520–55), who brought the Turkish forces to the gates of Vienna in 1529 and created one of history's greatest land empires, extending at its height from the Persian Gulf to Vienna and to modern Russia's borders. It stretched across North Africa to the borders of Morocco.[17] In order to destabilize the rival Holy Roman Empire, Suleyman gave financial support to the Protestant rulers in Germany, and he expanded Turkish dominance in Europe and in the Near East in counterpoint with the Spanish and Holy Roman Empire's expansion in Mediterranean Europe and the New World.[18] While Suleyman expanded militarily, he also gave Turkish culture an architectural and artistic development that brought it attention from the European courts and from as far away as China. In the Near East, he battled the Turkic-derived dynasty of Safavid Shiite rulers of Persia (the "sophy": *MV* 2.1.25ff.) and reduced the Mamluk dynasty in Egypt to Ottoman dependency.[19] His successor, Selim II (1566–74), on the other hand, mainly expanded the Ottoman bureaucracies and took little more interest in his empire than did his contemporary, Rudolph II, in the Holy Roman Empire, though Selim's underlings did initiate Ottoman efforts to expand into Russian territory. Late sixteenth- and early seventeenth-century Turkey, now largely ruled by a hereditary bureaucracy rather than the great sultans, continued to acquire land in the Balkans throughout Shakespeare's lifetime. It recovered quickly from defeat by the Europeans at Lepanto to gain control of the eastern Mediterranean. Its land extended to Tunis and Algiers on the south coast of the Mediterranean and ran up the Balkan peninsula to include parts of Hungary and to threaten Venice's territory on the Adriatic eastern shore. Istanbul now held the Arabic holy lands of Islam. Its navy now rivaled that of Venice.

Venice, on the other hand, like England and the Netherlands, was primarily a sea republic, controlling a small imperial land base extending toward Milan in the Po Valley at the head of the Adriatic and dominating coastal territory down the eastern Adriatic and Balkan coast to where the Battle of Lepanto had been fought. Venice extended into island territories in the eastern Mediterranean that were important for trade there and, by extension, for the Orient trade—that is, Cyprus, until losing it in 1571, and Crete, until this was lost in the seventeenth century. The Venetian empire grew powerful commercially because of the strength of its navy; because it tolerated many trading cultures—Islamic, Jewish, Christian—from many parts of Europe and Asia; because it had a good system of spies; and finally because it possessed sophisticated commercial law that was enforced systematically and on all persons, subjects and aliens alike.[20] With this wealth, Venice also grew powerful culturally. Its greatest painters appeared just before and during Shakespeare's time: Titian (1485–1576), Veronese (1528–88), and Tintoretto (1518–94). Through Palladio (1508–80), it influenced English architecture late in Shakespeare's life and in the period immediately thereafter, especially through the work of Inigo Jones.

Venice was the great Christian power in the eastern Mediterranean. Spain was the great western Mediterranean power, and the two had uneasy relations throughout the period—allies in the Holy League for a time but generally uneasy rivals on the Italian peninsula. Spain was more absolutist in its Catholic political commitments, Venice more pragmatic because its trade interests required a more cosmopolitan religious stance. Venice was willing to ally itself with almost anyone to limit Turkish and Spanish power in the Mediterranean. For example, it had diplomatic relations with Morocco, its natural ally in that both had to fear the Turkish power encroaching on their territories. Morocco was the only Arab Mediterranean power remaining in 1578. In the Battle of the Three Kings (1578), Morocco did Venice and England a favor by defeating at sea the Portuguese, who were increasingly under Spanish domination. Portugal, which was to come completely under Spain in 1580, was of course Venice's great rival in the East Indian area for the trade with that subcontinent. Because of geography and religion, Venice was increasingly a military rival of the Ottoman Turks after 1500, but it also depended on Ottoman good offices and protection in times of peace in order to continue its trade with Persia in silks and other commodities and with the Indian subcontinent in spices, jewels, and drugs.[21] Thus Venice created elaborate open and secret agreements in times of peace with the Mamluks in Egypt and with the Ottoman Turks, while occasionally seeking to strengthen Ottoman rivals in Safavid Persia.[22]

All of this is relevant to *The Merchant of Venice* (1596–97) and *Twelfth Night* (1601). The suitors who approach Portia's caskets in *Merchant of Venice* include Spain ("Aragon") and its two non-Ottoman rivals in the Mediterranean world, Morocco and Venice. The casket scenes do possess a topicality that is suggested before we actually see these scenes on stage. The processional of wooers for Portia that has come before Morocco, Aragon, and Venetian Bassanio is made up of political caricatures. We are told that the Prince of Naples—whoever he is—has been dismissed from the love competition for his horse fetish, the prince from the Calvinistic Palatinate has lost because of his puritanical frowning, the Englishman for his provincialism, the Frenchman for his fey and irresponsible character, and the Scotsman for his cowardice and dependence on France. All of these characters exist as political/cultural caricatures.

Shakespeare then makes the casket choice point to the balance of power among the anti-Turkish forces in the Mediterranean, a second level beyond the London anti-Puritan commentary developed in chapter 4. The Mediterranean terrain of the casket choice would have been familiar enough to Londoners of the period: Spain because the Armada had occurred not long before, and efforts to disrupt the Spanish trade in silver were in process; Venice because of its trade and perceived cultural similarities to London (see James I's poem on Lepanto later in this chapter); and Morocco because of England's relations with it through Leicester's Barbary Company.[23] The company leaders were persons familiar to Shakespeare. The Levant Company also had Moroccan knowledge, as did English Mediterranean privateers.[24]

Given Morocco's connections to Venice, the presence of a Moroccan at Belmont is not surprising. Beyond Venice's and Morocco's common diplomatic and military interest, both shared Jewish communities descended from those Ferdinand and Isabella had expelled from Catholic Spain. The expulsion sent them first to Morocco and then on to Venice, Istanbul, and other Mediterranean port cities.[25] In *Othello* we are asked to believe that a Moor—that is, a Moroccan or a sub-Saharan African identified as a Moor—has come to be Venice's military leader against the Turks in Cyprus. *Merchant's* Morocco likewise has a historical dimension in that he recalls his battles against Suleyman, the Persian "Sophy," and another Persian leader:

MOROCCO: Even for that I thank you.
  Therefore I pray you lead me to the caskets
  To try my fortune. By this scimitar,
  That slew the Sophy and a Persian prince
  That won three fields of Sultan Suleiman,
  I would o'erstare the sternest eyes that look,
  Outbrave the heart most daring on the earth,
  Pluck the young sucking cubs from the she-bear,
  Yea, mock the lion when he roars for prey,
  To win the lady. But alas the while,
  If Hercules and Lichas play at dice

Which is the better man, the greater throw
May turn by fortune from the weaker hand.
So is Alcides beaten by his rage,
And so may I, blind Fortune leading me,
Miss that which one unworthier may attain,
And die with grieving. (2.1.22ff.)

The Sophy is one of the Safavid leaders of Persia who fought the Ottoman Empire nearly to a standstill for a time.[26] Suleyman died in 1566, but the Ottoman wars with the Safavids continued, on and off, for generations, and Shakespeare appears to distance the comedy from his time deliberately with his mention of Suleyman, perhaps to facilitate deniability, should any reference be taken as making a controversial assertion.[27] Still the present mirrors the past.

Another of Shakespeare's Hercules types pushed into Cupid's wars, the Prince of Morocco, chooses the gold casket to get Portia. He does so on the basis of his sense of the authority of popular choice: "what many . . . desire" (*MV* 2.7.36). But though in choosing gold he seeks to claim what belongs to popular desire, he does only what he may think expected of him as a cultural outsider and a Moroccan, since Morocco's wealth and golden coins were legendary in Shakespeare's time.[28] He makes his choice on the basis of an outsider's objectification of Portia that makes her a Midas prize (3.2.102), the coveted treasure of peoples from all over the Islamic world, from the Caspian to Arabia (2.7.41–42). But as the golden casket affirms, if the only criterion is popular choice, many men also desire death, and the casket's skull comes with a scroll telling Morocco that worms and death live in gilded tombs.

The parchment combines the sentiments of Matthew 6:19–20 and 23:27–28 in the Geneva Bible.

6:19   Lay not up treasures for yourselves upon the earth, where the moth and canker corrupt, and where thieves dig through and steal.

6:20   But lay up treasures for yourselves in heaven, where neither

the moth nor canker corrupteth, and where thieves neither dig
through, nor steal.

23:27 Woe be to you, Scribes and Pharisees, hypocrites: for ye are like
unto whited tombs, which appear beautiful outward, but are
within full of dead men's bones, and all filthiness.

23:28 So are ye also: for outward ye appear righteous unto men, but
within ye are full of hypocrisy and iniquity.

Spain (or Aragon), on the other hand, assumes that the casket bearing "Who chooseth me shall get as much as he deserves" is the winning one (*MV* 2.9.35). He receives the fool's head. The message within the casket says that the fire has tried the casket seven times and that good judgments come from the seven-times trial in contrast to the quick judgments of fools who choose and kiss shadows. The seven-times tried reference probably echoes Psalms 12:6, in the Geneva Bible, and means that the judgments are to be like "word of the Lord" judgments. ("The words of the Lord are pure words, as the silver, tried in a fornace of earth, fined sevenfold.") The rejection of the silver-loving Spaniard also perhaps refers to Spanish silver from the New World, which by this time had supplanted gold as the New World's colonial staple.[29] Giving the ego-obsessed Spaniard a fool's head turns aside a man who wills to get as much as he deserves, almost certainly a reference, in Aragon's mouth, to Protestant contempt for Catholic "works righteousness." The biblical text often refers to the arrogant or those proud of their own works as fools.[30]

Finally, with Venice/Bassanio, England's counterpart in the Mediterranean offers the love that requires "hazarding all [one] has," an absolute gamble on love and faith.[31] In choosing among the classic three temptations—the lust of the eye or gold, the pride of life or silver, and the lust of the flesh or lead—Bassanio chooses to reject the first two and takes the lust of the flesh as a lover should. But he takes it as lead, hazarding all that in the alchemy of love it might be transformed to the gold of marriage. Bassanio hazards nothing to gain simple physical beauty.[32] He chooses nothing by sight and acquires the prize he requires for married love and the faith that supports it.

Implicit in the representation of Bassanio's gamble as the right one in love's realms is perhaps a Protestant political polemic valorizing the marriage estate over the ascetic ones and privileging the hazarding implicit in faith and love over reason and good works.[33]

The debate over the three caskets is a debate among Mediterranean powers and a fictive debate about the paths to wisdom and love. Venice, probably as a surrogate for England, wins it through hazarding everything for love. But Venice is also the Shylock who wishes to hazard as little as possible even when he lends out money. Shylock is Venice's radical outsider, more the outsider even than a black Othello. He is the subhuman usurer who loves his ducats, not his daughter, and seeks nothing other than Christian flesh as his reward if he does not get his money.

It was, of course, the case that Venice tolerated Jews as few other supposedly Christian European cities did. However, the notion that Jews in Italy, or Jewish moneylenders anywhere in Europe, could charge usury, meaning any interest, and that Christians could not, had gone by the wayside at least by the fourteenth century. The notion became archaic as a descriptor of behavior, as opposed to a mark of prejudice, with the appearance of fictions legitimizing Christian charging of interest. These fictions usually required currency exchanges that were, in fact, ways of charging interest, brotherly "chevysaunces" that did the same thing, letters of credit, and the like.[34] Indeed it would have been impossible for a merchant to conduct commerce on the grand scale that Antonio pursues, in the Venetian or in the Elizabethan-Jacobean world, without borrowing, lending, and charging interest using some rationalizing fiction.[35] Shakespeare's audiences were a commercial bunch, and they would not have been naïve about Venetian Christians and their lending-borrowing practices.

Antonio's open lending to Bassanio out of friendship so that the latter can secure his love in Belmont seems to tell us that trade among Christians *ought to be* different from that among Jews, not marked by the commodification of money or people, and that it can be different in certain friendship and love contexts. It does not, I think, extend to Antonio's whole career as a "merchant venturer." As I have argued in chapter 4, insofar as Shylock's part of the play holds the mirror up to England in the sixteenth and seventeenth centuries, it probably thrusts at the Calvinists and Puritans in London as well as at England's few Jews, though Jewish issues also lie at the heart of the play insofar as Venice is taken literally to be Venice in Italy.[36] Most of England's Jews had been expelled three centuries earlier, and although Shakespeare certainly explores the depth of Jewish-Gentile relations in the play insofar as it applies to Venice, he also brings the play home to the new "Jews" in England, the Puritans—those who hated masques, play, and feasting almost as much as Shylock does:

> SHYLOCK: What, are there masques? Hear you me, Jessica,
> Lock up my doors; and when you hear the drum
> And the vile squealing of the wry-necked fife,
> Clamber not you up to the casements then,
> Nor thrust your head into the public street
> To gaze on Christian fools with varnished faces,
> But stop my house's ears—I mean my casements.
> Let not the sound of shallow fopp'ry enter
> My sober house. By Jacob's staff I swear
> I have no mind of feasting forth tonight.
> But I will go. (*MV* 2.5.27ff.)

Calvin and other Puritans had argued that interest and usury were all right, that the biblical proscriptions against them applied only to certain biblical times and places, not to Early Modern Europe.[37] Even English law allowed the charging of an interest rate of 10 percent on loans. In contrast to the Calvinists and the mainstream moneylenders, Shakespeare's story of Bassanio's wager, through the casket scene, tells us that Portia's love requires a complete hazarding, a gamble with faith, apart from commerce. In Shakespeare's *mythos*, some Venetians—or some English—when in love, know how to separate the acts of love and friendship from the acts of buying and selling and do so on the basis of the spirit of charity.

The Merchant of Venice's twin, *Twelfth Night,* is set in Venetian Illyria. If we must affix a locale to the play, we probably should say that it is set among the Italian peoples who settled the Dalmatian coast and who were affiliated with Venice in the sixteenth century. The names in the play are often Italian. Ortellius's 1624 map shows Illyria located on the eastern shore of the Adriatic where Venice had her dependencies.[38] This is also where the pirates' community of the Uskoks, refugees from the Turks, lived and had a hand in the redevelopment of the war between Venice and the Ottomans, of which Lepanto was later a part.[39] Antonio in *Twelfth Night,* though claiming not to be a pirate, has had some role in theft from Orsino's galleys, and for the sake of keeping trade alive, his unnamed city has repaid Orsino's territory for what it took (*TN* 3.3.30–37). Antonio is later accused of having fought with the ship, the *Phoenix,* near Crete, a Venetian territory, and Orsino says, apparently incorrectly, that he is a pirate (5.1.57–69).[40] In any case, the odor of the Mediterranean and English or Uskok piracy clings to the play.

The Mediterranean and Adriatic Dalmatian areas were full of pirates. The empire supported the Uskoks as a buffer against the Turks, Elizabeth and later private investors encouraged English pirates in the area, and there were pirates who were encouraged by the Ottoman Empire and other North African powers. One cannot assign a national origin or affiliation with a client state to Antonio. His name is Italian, but Italians served with all sorts of naval forces in the Adriatic and Mediterranean. What we do know of the setting for *Twelfth Night* is that it is a Venetian territory sufficiently distant from Venice to be unconcerned with the goings-on in the center but sufficiently part of it to be involved in the Mediterranean piracy issues.

One may ask why Shakespeare imports Illyria into a play that appears to deal with Puritans and Cavaliers and the management of English loves and English country estates. Perhaps he does so only to say that, in a commonwealth at war or in tension, even the hinterlands are important. Through employing Illyria, he is also able to defamiliarize the conflict between the English aristocrats and Puritans by placing it in the Venetian empire, where *The Merchant of Venice* is also located. When Malvolio is compared to a rare "turkeycock" (2.5.26), the reference goes to more than a bird. He is, at it were, the enemy of a celebratory and festive Venice, not just an image of the Puritans in England. The epiphanies of *Twelfth Night* come to a Dalmatic country on the edge of the violence of colliding civilizations, as England was to collide with itself in the 1640s. In *Merchant*, love comes to commercial Venice through wholly uncalculated acts of self-sacrifice, though it is troubled by a puritanical Shylock and a prodigal Bassanio. In *Twelfth Night*, it also comes to rural Illyria, troubled by a puritanical Malvolio and a worthless knighthood, through similar acts of uncalculated sacrifice on the part of the country-less magi/beggars cast up on its shores. The solution to the problem of empire, in Shakespeare's myth, begins with giving—not what empire was then or what it became in the next few centuries.[41]

The Spanish and Ottoman Empires:
Lepanto and *Much Ado*

The Turkish-Venetian theme from *Merchant* continues in *Much Ado about Nothing* (1599), which opens in Messina and includes as primary characters members of the principal nations that fought at Lepanto. They appear to have just come back from the war, as some of the victors at Lepanto came back to Messina after that battle. Messina was not a famous city to the English. It derived what fame it had from the fact that the combined Catholic Holy League fleet composed of representatives from Spain, Spanish Italy, and Venice, sailed from there to fight the Battle of Lepanto.[42] This fleet won the battle, reputedly the most important battle of the time. The fiction of *Much Ado* is that Don John, the Bastard of Aragon, and his brother, Don Pedro, have completed their wars and returned for relaxation to Messina. As Spaniards they would have been part of the Holy League. They bring soldiers with them, principally Claudio from Florence—historically in the Holy League—and Benedick from Padua, part of the Venetian Republic's territory and also part of the Holy League. The persons who come to Messina have been in a war where by all accounts they have borne themselves courageously. Beatrice's unauthenticated taunting of Benedick, at the beginning of the play, for cowardice or incompetence receives no confirmation from anyone else (*MAN* 1.1.32–48). Venice furnished the genius that won Lepanto (see later discussion), and that Beatrice puts down a Venetian from Padua for cowardice or incompetence may heighten the irony. Nothing absolutely requires that a Messina related to Lepanto be imagined as the background of the play. But Spain, especially Don John the Bastard, Florence, and Venice would hardly all have gathered in Messina independent of Lepanto and the Holy League. Indeed Spain, Florence, and Venice rarely pulled together in the period and never at Messina, aside from Lepanto.[43]

Much Ado's references to Lepanto come out of concerns over power and values in the imperial Mediterranean world that also underlie the earlier *Merchant of Venice* and the later *Twelfth Night*. The primary European anxieties that led to Lepanto were Catholic and general European anxiety about the progress of the Ottoman military in diminishing Europe's great empires—Habsburg Germany (or the Holy Roman Empire) and Habsburg Spain. Venice was the most immediate victim of Turkish expansion. For over a hundred years the Ottomans had constructed their empire throughout the Balkans, Central Europe, and the Mediterranean, and by the 1570s Ottoman Turkey was the great thorn in the Catholic empires' side. Earlier in the sixteenth century, the Schmalkaldic War had allowed the powerful Holy Roman Emperor, Charles V, to weaken the Protestant princes in Germany. His later battles with the Turks (who quietly supported the Protestants, especially over Hungary) and with France, as the sometime supporter of the empire's Protestant principalities, left him somewhat impotent. Without the tools to impose a settlement disadvantageous to the Protestants *or* to conquer the Turks, Charles abandoned his imperial throne for a monastery in 1556 and turned over the imperial title to his brother, Ferdinand I. He, along with his Habsburg successors, generally ruled from Vienna. Charles V gave the crown of Spain and control of Spain's New World lands to Philip II (1556–98), his son and the husband of Mary I, "Bloody" Mary, who was England's queen just before Shakespeare's birth. Philip was also for a time Elizabeth's suitor.

As Europe's most powerful Catholic nation, Spain preserved Habsburg power in the Mediterranean in Shakespeare's time, especially the territories of Sicily and southern Italy that so dominated eastern Mediterranean traffic. (Philip also held most of Central and South America, though they were not at the center of the European gaze until after his reign.) Philip fought and lost the Spanish war against the Protestant Low Countries, in which the Protestant paragon Knight, Sir Philip Sidney, died, but he also expanded and consolidated the Spanish empire in the New World and intensified Spanish domination of Italy, aside from Venice and the Papal States. Most important for the purposes of this chapter, his Spanish navy participated with the Holy Roman Empire, the Papal States, Venice, and the rest of the Holy League in the naval Battle of Lepanto against the Turkish fleet in 1571, the first significant European victory against the Ottoman Turks since their invasion of Europe in the fourteenth century.[44]

Lepanto lies at the heart of the myth of sixteenth-century Spain and the papacy: the motto could have been "Protect Christendom from the Turk, or all is lost," and this version of the myth of Lepanto is still alive in some modern Catholic circles. The push for a confrontation with the Ottomans came from the papacy and the Spanish monarchy, especially from Pope Pius V. It came in the wake of the partial Ottoman conquest of Venetian Cyprus beginning in 1570. The Turkish landing there on July 1, 1570, led to the quick investing of Famagusta. This event's arousal of European fears may be partially reflected in the Cyprus scene of *Othello* but with a happy conclusion for the Christian forces that Cyprus never experienced after 1570. The great fear for 1570s Europe was that Venice—which had earlier often cooperated with the Ottomans in trading agreements that gave Venice access to the Middle East and the Orient—was now in danger of losing its prized colony and the source of Venetian and European control of the eastern Mediterranean. It took only a step to imagine that the control of the western Mediterranean was up for grabs and even that the survival of Christianity and of European civilization was at stake. The collective failure of the Mediterranean nations to control piracy in the Aegean, the Mediterranean, and the Adriatic were minor issues compared to Cyprus. Given these fears, in 1570 Pope Pius V proclaimed a crusade against the Ottomans and successfully promoted the Holy League composed of Spain, the Spanish possessions in Italy, and Venice (Genoa also had a small role) to fight the Turk. These are the forces represented by the central characters in *Much Ado.*

Drama was part of the preparation for Lepanto. When the details of the Holy League were proclaimed in Venice in July of 1571, the announcement was accompanied by officially sponsored celebrations typical of Venetian public ceremonials at the time in their fusion of civic and religious elements and in their use of drama as a political tool. In the July procession, Venice explained the purpose of the league to the onlookers through a series of dumb shows mounted on platforms. The first group showed the Great Turk as a ferocious dragon emerging from a cave, easily identified by a pyramid surmounted by a crescent moon. In front, three richly dressed youths attacking the dragon with swords symbolized Saints Peter, James, and Mark. Saints Peter, James, and Mark were respectively the patron saints of the papacy, Spain, and Venice. Later in the procession, the three Holy League leaders were equated with the theological virtues of faith, hope, and charity. Further displays showed the members of the league represented by the figures of pope, emperor, and doge, each distinguished by dress. Toward the end of this section of the display, Charon's boat transported the Turk to Hades.[45]

When the war turned to more than play acting, the Holy League fleet—under the historical Don John the Bastard, brother of Rudolph of Austria, now the Spanish commander—sailed from Messina in Sicily with more than three hundred boats and more than sixty thousand men.[46] Though the Venetian forces fell ill prior to the battle and were considered unfit by some of the Holy League leaders, Venice furnished the superior military tools that created success for the Catholic forces. Especially crucial to the victory were six huge galleasses armed with unusually heavy movable cannons capable of blowing apart the Turkish ships.

On October 7, 1571, the fleet that had sailed from Messina went via the Ionian Sea to the island of Cephalonia, across from the opening to the Gulf of Lepanto (see map at http:www.nafpaktos.com/battle _of_lepanto.htm).

At the Gulf of Lepanto, the Turkish fleet was coming from the Gulf of Corinth into the Gulf of Patras. The Holy League's aggressive tactics and use of the unusual boat cannons quickly imposed significant losses on the Turkish fleet.[47] In the battle the Holy League lost seventeen of its more than three hundred ships and lost about seventeen hundred men. In contrast, the Turks had fifteen ships sunk and more than 170 taken, and they lost four times as many soldiers and sailors as the Christians and more than ten thousand galley slaves (both sides used ships propelled by galley slaves, the last time these were so used in a major battle).

The victory at Lepanto became symbolically important in England and Scotland. For example, James I wrote a poem about Lepanto that was published in 1603. His introduction says the poem was written earlier and misconstrued as praising Don John the Bastard. Indeed the poem does praise Don John and the Catholic forces, but then in its published version it concludes with an application section saying that if God so protects the erring Catholic Christians against the Turks, He will the more protect Protestants against the papists. James's curious introduction, designed to deliver the poem from blame for papist tendencies, refers to the common disdain for Don John the Bastard as a bastard and a papist, and James appears here not to approve him either.[48] Strikingly he praises Venice as a town prompted to resist the Turk by the Archangel Gabriel, a "wondrous sight / A Towne to stand without a ground," whom a "Duke with Senate ioynd doth rule." Each year this town, in James's eulogy, marries the sea.[49] Toward the end, we hear the Venetian celebration song after Lepanto's news has arrived.

That the chief characters of *Much Ado about Nothing* are soldiers rather than sailors does not diminish the shadow of Lepanto. Indeed this makes it more likely. It was the firepower developed by the cannons, controlled by the soldiers who worked from the decks of the Christian ships, that won Lepanto. And Lepanto makes Margaret's banter with Beatrice about turning Turk ("Well, an you be not turned Turk, there's no more sailing by the star" [*MAN* 3.4.47]) more pointed.

That Don John the Bastard is from Aragon in the play is understandable since Don John the Bastard in history, though technically an Austrian, was the leader first of the Spanish forces and then
later of the whole assemblage of Holy League ships that went to
Lepanto from Messina. The play does not purport to reflect history,
but the historical Don John also returned to Messina after Lepanto,
was feted there, and is remembered permanently by a statue by
Andrea Calamech placed in the square of the ancient church of the
Annunziata dei Catalani.

Finally Don John pairs with a good legitimate brother, Don Pedro,
whose only sin is his naïveté in accepting Don John's version of Hero.
None of this is a literal allegory for Lepanto; rather it is a kind of
playing with name and place to remind us of the good-face/bad-face
character that the Catholic power in the Mediterranean had in the
English government's eyes and even in James's poem. Don John may
be the villain he is for the reasons that underlie James's vilification of
him in the introduction to *Lepanto* and for the reasons that the monarch assigns to those who criticized him. The Protestant world could
not endure a long celebration of a Catholic hero.[50]

In contrast, Don Pedro is literally the Petrine brother. Since England was in 1598–1600 moving toward the peace with Spain that was
realized in 1604, Shakespeare probably needed a good-prince/bad-
prince Spanish dichotomy as part of his strategy of creating ambiguity
in a play set against the background of Spanish Italy and Lepanto.
Though Lepanto, according to the Venetian processional, was to be
fought by powers representing faith, hope, and charity, *Much Ado* offers us a picture of a set of households that may have won the war
for "Christian civilization" but that have lost the battle for or sense
of the war's ostensible purpose. We see a Messinan governing household nearly destroyed by Don John the Bastard's choler and Iago-like
malice, malice often attributed to the Catholic powers in Elizabethan
drama. Though Lepanto was supposedly a just battle in a just war,
the pursuit of Messinan justice is tarnished by the incompetence of
its slightly dotty governor and its faithful but incompetent constabulary. Only accident or providence produces the just arrests and a just

outcome. Tellingly, the redemption of Messina as a site for the exercise of mercy, hope, and love does not come from crusading ships but from a pragmatic friar, from witty women, and from innocent Christlike ones who are willing to name the truth and suffer to create love.

Vienna, Austria, and the Holy Roman Empire in *Measure for Measure*

Shakespeare continues the Ottoman/imperial theme in *Measure for Measure*. In the time when he wrote it (1604; first acted at Christmas 1604), Germany—that is, the empire—was a crazy quilt of Protestant and Catholic principalities caught up in internecine religious struggle that, soon after Shakespeare's death, would erupt in the Thirty Years' War, which killed an estimated 30 percent of the population in parts of Europe's heartland. The politics of the empire were tied to Catholic Austria and the Habsburg family, but within the empire lay also the Protestant parts of Bohemia, the Protestant Palatinate, and most of the northern German-speaking areas. On the empire's border also lay Hungary, much of its free area having become Protestant but some of it also under the thumb of the Ottomans, who periodically supported the Protestant leaders. In the several decades after Charles V left the imperial and Spanish thrones, the empire's disputes with the Turks over Hungary (1556) continued, as did the Protestant-Catholic tension that eventually led to the Thirty Years' War. Charles's imperial successors were the less dynamic Ferdinand I (1556–64), Maximilian II (1564–76), and Rudolph II, who reigned during Shakespeare's period of creating plays.

That period also saw the formation of the central European Protestant League containing the Protestant princedoms in the empire and led by the Palatinate, a formation countered by a Catholic league of similar petty princedoms led by Bavaria. At the same time, the empire had to continue its war over a Hungary that had come to be partly under Turkish and partly under Habsburg rule. The significant thing is that Transylvania—a mostly Protestant part of Hungary—remained free under Transylvanian rulers from the Zapolya line.[51] Because of the usual dynastic claims and counterclaims, rival kings from the

Habsburg and Zapolya lines claimed the crown of Hungary from 1526 through 1571. The Ottomans supported the Zapolya right to the throne, and that weakened the Habsburg imperial opportunity. Habsburg opportunities were further weakened when the Habsburg rulership divided itself so that only the chancery that administered the empire remained in Vienna, while the nominal Habsburg ruler Rudolph II (1576–1612)—a recluse, an astrologer, and later insane—hid himself among the learned in Prague.

Those parts of Hungary that the empire did rule were not well ruled. When the Habsburgs tried in the early 1600s to form a rapprochement with Transylvania (or free Hungary) and the Hungarian Protestants, they so thoroughly botched the job of ruling that Transylvania revolted in 1604 and made István Bocskay, a rebellious Habsburg general, its prince.[52] Knolles's 1611 history of the Turks places the revolt after October 24, 1604, and says that Bocskay "stil[ed] himself the Prince of Transylvania" from the beginning. Later the Ottomans gave him the Hungarian kingship that had belonged to the Zapolyas, a kingship confirmed by both the Hungarian estates. He cast himself in the role of protector of the Protestants.[53] Only in 1606 did Hungary work out its peace with Emperor Rudolph in the Peace of Vienna, and this peace recognized what Bocskay had fought for: that is, the right of Protestants to religious freedom. The peace also gave Hungary a sort of autonomy. The fight against and negotiations with Bocskay were carried out by all kinds of representatives of the Habsburgs who might properly be styled "dukes," and the outcome of these negotiations was of no small importance to Protestant England, as they had everything to do with whether Protestantism would survive on the continent in central and eastern Europe.

The Duke of Vienna represented in *Measure for Measure* (1604) would probably have been seen by Shakespeare's audience as glancing, at least part of the time, at Vienna's ruler, the Holy Roman emperor, perhaps a semblance of Rudolph II (1558–1612) practicing his rule *in absentia* in Prague. The kinds of negotiations that went on over tripartite Hungary and over the rights of Protestants appear vaguely in Lucio's conversation in act 1, scene 2:

LUCIO: If the Duke with the other dukes come not to composition with the King of Hungary, why then, all the dukes fall upon the King.

FIRST GENTLEMAN: Heaven grant us its peace, but not the King of Hungary's!

SECOND GENTLEMAN: Amen.

LUCIO: Thou concludest like the sanctimonious pirate, that went to sea with the Ten Commandments, but scraped one out of the table.

SECOND GENTLEMAN: 'Thou shalt not steal'?

LUCIO: Ay, that he razed.

FIRST GENTLEMAN: Why, 'twas a commandment to command the captain and all the rest from their functions: they put forth to steal. There's not a soldier of us all that in the thanksgiving before meat do relish the petition well that prays for peace.

SECOND GENTLEMAN: I never heard any soldier dislike it.

LUCIO: I believe thee, for I think thou never wast where grace was said.

SECOND GENTLEMAN: No? A dozen times at least.

FIRST GENTLEMAN: What, in metre?

LUCIO: In any proportion, or in any language.

FIRST GENTLEMAN: I think, or in any religion.

LUCIO: Ay, why not? Grace is grace, despite of all controversy; as for example, thou thyself art a wicked villain despite of all grace. (*MFM* 1.2.1–25)

Though the Oxford Shakespeare editors believe that this passage comes from a Middleton revision done shortly after Shakespeare's death and before the First Folio, we cannot know for certain when someone penned the passage. Shakespeare may have written it in 1604 or later, given the development of the situation in eastern Europe. It fits the situation in the Hungarian end of the Habsburg domains in 1604–6—that is, the effort to achieve some sort of peace among the non-Turkish forces and the fight among Catholics, Lutherans, and Calvinists in that part of the world over the doctrine of grace. The dukes who would have to come to composition with the King of Hungary (i.e., Transylvania) would be the Catholic leaders of the empire.[54] Lucio's "Grace is grace, despite of all controversy" (*MFM* 1.2.23) glances at the kinds of discussions that were part of all such Catholic-Protestant disputes in the early seventeenth century. Finally, the First Gentleman's phrase, "in any religion" (22), may suggest the further Islamic-Christian controversies that came with the movement back and forth of the sultan's armies. Certainly word of the Hungarian situation could have come back to England between October and December when the play was performed. Further, the situation with István Bocskay and the empire was not radically different from that which had obtained until 1571 with the Zapolya kingship. If this conflict is the context, then the dialogue within the play between Isabella, as ascetic Catholic, and Angelo, as a kind of Puritan, reflects the Catholic-Calvinist dialogue and war that was afflicting Hungary and the empire.

Though the disappearance of Duke Vincentio from Vienna probably has to do with the religious and political symbolism of the play and with James I's view of himself as a master spy rather than with any historical reference to Austria, Vincentio's disappearance from rulership in Vienna would also not have been surprising to Jacobean audiences who knew of the Emperor Rudolph's disappearances from the life of his chancery to do astrology in Prague.[55]

The battle for the soul of the Austro-Hungarian band of nations then appears to be collapsed into the fierce Catholic asceticism of Isabella and the equally fierce Calvinistic legalism of Angelo. The plot of the play is a thought experiment in how these superficially contrary forces work in a world needing reform, especially when the monarch is absent—really absent in imperial history and pretending to be absent in the fiction. Though there was little Calvinism of Angelo's type in historical Vienna, Calvinism had spread rapidly in the Hungarian part of eastern Europe, and it is not wholly an exaggeration to see the conflict in central Europe as one between Catholic discipline, represented by Isabella with her asceticism, Calvinist theology, twisted by Angelo, and some sort of moderation, perhaps represented by Vincentio in his better moments. Vincentio's final forgiving judgment on everyone save Lucio, guilty of the crime of *lèse-majesté*, may suggest that compromise is the only constructive outcome for the Calvinist-Catholic struggle in eastern Europe as both parties face the Turks.[56]

The Tempest and the Mediterranean World

The Tempest appears historically to be set in the Habsburg Mediterranean *and* in a New World where there are indigenous inhabitants. It is set metaphorically in the world of Virgil's *Aeneid* but also at the gates of the Christian and Virgilian entry to the spirits' afterworld.[57] Through Prospero it forecasts a world-ending event that will dissolve empires and make all of history appear to be a dream (*Tempest* 5.1.33–57). Prospero, when he occupies the role of the Duke of Milan, would in 1611–12 have had his historical counterpart in the Habsburg king of Spain, Philip II. The Treaty of Cateau-Cambrésis (1559) confirmed Philip as the duke of Milan. His successors who ruled after he died in 1598 could likewise be referred to as dukes of Milan. But the Spanish kings were also monarchs of the Kingdom of the Two Sicilies, which included Naples, and Antonio's placing Milan under the authority of Naples seems a little like what happened to Milan in 1559 when it was subordinated to Spain. However, if we are to believe this, are we then to imagine Habsburg usurping Habsburg, Naples destroying Milan? Such a theory would make Shakespeare pit Habsburg against Habsburg in a silly conflict.

One alternative construction might be that he reminds us in *The Tempest* of a past when Milan was free and the Sforzas governed it without the empire's domination.[58] Certainly the Treaty of Cateau-Cambrésis was virtually forced upon Elizabeth, and Elizabeth did not hold herself bound by it. The idea of a return to an independent Milan may have been attractive to the English imagination, however unlikely it may have been in history.[59] A Milan that was independent from Spain would also have carried an appeal for James, who had his eye on acquiring a role in the empire through his daughter's 1612/13 marriage to the Palatinate elector.[60] The 1612/13 marriage festivities with the future ruler of the Palatinate, at which *The Tempest* was performed for the second time, situated the Stuarts in a place where they could expect to be future imperial electors and perhaps even emperors.[61] Alternatively, Shakespeare may be presenting the happy and sad faces of Spain's Italian dependencies in the form of the wronged king of Milan and his usurpers from Naples, using a technique similar to his presentation of the two faces of Catholicism in Don Pedro and Don John in *Much Ado*.[62]

The imperial/colonial theme so often remarked by critics of *The Tempest* makes sense in relation to Spanish suzerainty in the New World and the Mediterranean and the debate over whether Europeans should seek to colonize, where, and how. Shakespeare seems to combine the Mediterranean and the New World by locating his play on a Mediterranean island but naming his antihero, Caliban, after the Carib Indians (and Montaigne's essay related to them, "Of Cannibals"). The Caribs lived on the northern shore of South America and the Caribbean, places that the Spanish dominated as colonialists. The debate over empire existed in Spain as well as in England.[63] Given the terms of the debate, one can see Prospero as the conqueror who unwittingly conquers the New/Old World of the Mediterranean island and learns the limits of conquest when he meditates on his masque for Ferdinand and Miranda and then goes back to Milan to be a proper ruler there. In the terms of the same debate, one can see the Neapolitans as the forces of untrammeled colonialism seeking only European expansion and seeking it wholly conspiratorially.

Caliban the Carib is crucial in this debate. Spain ruled most of the Carib territories by the early seventeenth century. It had killed Native inhabitants mercilessly and forced many of the remainder into slavery while requiring them to convert or feign conversion. It is not accidental that Caliban's rulers through much of the play are the servants of a bunch of Neapolitan—presumably Habsburg-based—ruffians who resemble their masters in their usurping intentions and who demand that Caliban kiss the book of their God/wine. The satire directed against Catholic kissing of the book and belief in transubstantiation is fairly heavy-handed, but that directed against a cynical religious and alcoholic manipulation of Native peoples is even more forceful.

CALIBAN: I'll swear upon that bottle to be thy true subject, for the liquor is not earthly.

STEFANO: Here. Swear then how thou escapedst.

TRINCULO: Swum ashore, man, like a duck. I can swim like a duck, I'll be sworn.

STEFANO: Here, kiss the book. Though thou canst swim like a duck, thou art made like a goose.

TRINCULO: O Stefano, hast any more of this?

STEFANO: The whole butt, man. My cellar is in a rock by th' seaside, where my wine is hid. How now, moon-calf? How does thine ague?

CALIBAN: Hast thou not dropped from heaven?

STEFANO: Out o'th' moon, I do assure thee. I was the man i'th' moon when time was.

CALIBAN: I have seen thee in her, and I do adore thee. My mistress showed me thee, and thy dog and thy bush.

STEFANO: Come, swear to that. Kiss the book. I will furnish it anon with new contents. Swear.

TRINCULO: By this good light, this is a very shallow monster! I afeard of him? A very weak monster! The man i'th' moon? A most poor, credulous monster! Well drawn, monster, in good sooth!

CALIBAN: I'll show thee every fertile inch o'th' island, and I will kiss thy foot. I prithee, be my god. (*Tempest* 2.2.116–41)

However stupid and brutal Caliban is portrayed as being for accepting such treatment, he is not so evil as his drunken cargo-cult-creating masters.

An attack on Spanish Catholic colonialism and so on any English effort to emulate it seems suggested by the occasion. The first recorded performance of the play is at Whitehall on Hallomass Night in 1611, a night when the spirits from the other world were supposed to come into this one and a time appropriate for the presentation of a play where spirits come and go regularly. If the play was intended for some celebration in the life of James's son, Prince Henry, the jabs would still work since Henry was expected to be the hope of Protestantism.[64] The play may or may not have been revised for the 1612/13 marriage of Frederick, the Palatinate elector, and James's daughter, Elizabeth, but it was certainly presented there. It was apparently not an accident that this satiric thrust would be presented at the quintessentially Protestant marriage, which was accompanied by many entertainments celebrating the prospect of empire for Britain. The Stuarts and the Palatinate rulers were among the most powerful Protestant houses in Europe, though James himself vacillated about how he should relate to Catholic Spain.[65] If Protestantism was to have an empire at all, it probably had to begin with the noble houses that were celebrating the 1612/13 union.

As part of the imperial theme, we have the whole drama placed against the *Aeneid*'s imperial setting, first in Gonzalo's conversation and then in the plot itself:

GONZALO: Methinks our garments are now as fresh as when
    we put them on first in Afric, at the marriage of the King's
    fair daughter Claribel to the King of Tunis.
SEBASTIAN: 'Twas a sweet marriage, and we prosper well in
    our return.
ADRIAN: Tunis was never graced before with such a paragon to
    their queen.
GONZALO: Not since widow Dido's time.
ANTONIO: Widow? A pox o'that! How came that 'widow' in?
    Widow Dido!
SEBASTIAN: What if he had said 'widower Aeneas' too? Good
    Lord, how you take it!
ADRIAN: 'Widow Dido' said you? You make me study of that:
    she was of Carthage, not of Tunis.
GONZALO: This Tunis, sir, was Carthage.
ADRIAN: Carthage?
GONZALO: I assure you, Carthage. (*Tempest* 2.1.68–84)

What I think we are to imagine is the Mediterranean of the ancient Roman Empire made new in an England/Milan that, as a kind of empire, is inscribed over the conflicting legitimacies of pre- and post-Sforza Mediterranean, both to reinforce the claims of James and the Palatinate in 1612/13 and also to qualify them as ultimately nothing more than material dreams.

At the betrothal and marriage festivities in 1612/13, masques, plays, and other entertainments were presented celebrating the marriage, Protestant hegemony, the conquests of "Indian" people in other worlds, and the coming of future millennial rule or utopian time. It is in this context among others that the play raises the question of what legitimate and "civilizing" empire is in a world of usurping and illegitimate monarchs, Catholic idolaters, and rough aborigines. Gonzalo imagines his islanders to be what More's are in the realm of King Utopus and what Montaigne imagines Caribbean Indians to be. That is, he pictures them as wholly obedient to natural law. The passage echoes Montaigne (and perhaps More):

The lawes of nature doe yet command them [the Indian nations]. . . . It is a nation, would I answer *Plato*, that hath no kinde of traffike, no knowledge of Letters, no intelligence of numbers, no name of magistrate, nor of politike superioritie; no use of service, of riches or of povertie; no contracts, no successions, no partitions, no occupation but idle; no respect of kindred . . . no apparell but naturall, no manuring of lands, no use of wine, corne or mettle. The very words that import lying, falshood, treason, dissimulations, covetousness, envie, detraction, and pardon, were never heard of amongst them.[66]

Gonzalo's form of natural-law-based utopian vision quickly dissolves in the minds of the play's spectators, because once they see Caliban, they realize that the "good old lord Gonzalo" (*Tempest* 5.1.15) is quite wrong about the innocence of the "native" life on this island and its capacity to create communal benefit.

If the play presents a harsh view of Catholic Neapolitan–Spanish colonialism, it presents an almost equally austere picture of the Carib. Of course, Caliban is not as responsible for what he does as are

Trinculo and Stefano, and they are not as responsible as the masters whom they imitate—Alonso, Sebastian, and Antonio. However this may be, Shakespeare gives us an extremely stark view of the ubiquity of original depravity in indigenous peoples as well as in empires. His view contrasts with that of Montaigne, who argues in the same essay already quoted that the Caribbeans may be unfallen "golden age" people whom Plato and Lycurgus, as envisagers of the ideal state, should have known.

Shakespeare's point, surely, is that—were Gonzalo's dream of removing from society all structure to be seriously pursued—removing all commerce, rulership, and sovereignty, all distinctions of poverty and wealth, mastership and service, all hereditary succession, property and conventional agriculture, and most labor and letters—the Calibans from the island and the barbarians from Naples (along with a Milanese traitor) would rule absolutely and wholly destructively, given the terms of Shakespeare's *mythos*.

While Gonzalo's utopia echoes both More and Montaigne, at the level of substance it denies them. The corrupted Caliban cannot create a golden-age world because in a fallen world he has no sense of what is really his and what is not and therefore attempts rape. As a grotesque construction of an indigenous man and a reflection of Europe's nightmare before the different, Caliban, in the Shakespearean frame, knows no worship of an "Author and Maker of nature" that can constrain his libido. His own cargo-cult religion, encouraged by Trinculo and Stefano, offers him a drunken Stefano as a material idol. It gives him alcohol transubstantiated into the book he kisses as his Word. Ultimately Caliban receives his punishment for worshiping the garments of power rather than legitimate power. He and his allies flee the hell dogs that are legitimacy's tools in *The Tempest* and in its *Aeneid* subtext. The rulers of Naples who seek to usurp the realm of "Milan" from Prospero end up destroying not only legitimate authority in their own realm but the Prosperan authority that can control Shakespeare's rabble. The Neapolitans are punished for their usurpations by Harpy/Fury tempests like those found in the *Aeneid* and by banquets that punish those who betray their kin, again like that in the *Aeneid*. As noted in chapter 4, versions of this tempest and storm are also found in Isaiah 26–32, confirming the authority of the divine fury directed against those who betray the God/king, who happens to be very like James.

The legitimate alternative to the Neapolitans and to Trinculo and Stefano is Prospero. He is not kind to his servants when they counter his commands; the play is utterly absolutist and governed by the assumptions of divine right. Prospero does, however, claim that he punishes to bring people to civility, just as he produces his devices and showings for the same purpose. Prospero's education of virtually all of the play's persons through Ariel's devices and showings improves almost everyone, as the play would have it.

In the end, when things are back in place, Prospero abandons empire with its insubstantial promise, not a withdrawal respectful of other peoples and cultures but still a withdrawal. The duke's forgiveness and withdrawal from empire and its magic are all justifications for a static role system in the state and a static preservation of the natural world, all mystifications of the need for colonial power and empire for limited purposes. The historical king or emperor outside the play has no magical powers beyond brute control of the instruments of propaganda. While the dream of the play is with us, his powers all seem possible because of Ariel's potent songs, music, and the mise-en-scène Isaianic/Virgilian events in his control. The play tells us that the monarch *could* educate us toward ideal community; that directed by him we all could set aside aspiration and forgive one another, know one another, and grant indulgence to one another (Epilogue 1–20; 5.1.205–73). The monarch could be sibylline, possessing a frenzied prophetic brain. He might thereby know what empire's limits must be. The final dissolution of the cloud-capped towers and of the great globe of the material world are serious signs of the limits of empire in the play. They were not *effective* signs to historical England any more than they were to Spain. The English in New England treated those they saw as Calibans at least as savagely as did the Spaniards in Mexico. The historical monarch of England sought empire as cats seek mice or seals seek fish. Literature's king can, through his control of the revels, give temporary material form to ancient intertexts such as the *Aeneid* in order to send his reformed people back to the old order, but history's kings never looked back as they constructed the colonial order.

The Tempest indicates that legitimate imperial power derives from the ordered dynastic household ruled by the orderly, yet vatic, imperial leader who is the tool of God. This dux must be the channel of divine power and forgiveness—what Naples, as the Spanish Catholic power, what Trinculo and Stefano, as idolaters, and what Caliban, as the natural aborigine, cannot be. That leaves Milan/England, the patron of marriage and civility, to carry the burden of empire, marriage, and love. But it is an empire that will soon dissolve in an eschaton as the "cloud-capped towers" (*Tempest* 4.1.152) go. In the long run, Shakespeare, the imperialist, plays out from under the imperial dream. His comedies save Venice and its territories through marriage and sacrifice, Messina through marriage and a wit that restores civility, Vienna through marriage and the arts of justice, and Milan through a promised eschaton.

Most of Shakespeare's best comedies take place on the edge of grand imperial events. Similarly, the domestic events of the life of the little barber in Tomania in Chaplin's *Great Dictator* take place on the edge of the rise to power of the dictator of Tomania, Adenoid Hynkel or Hitler, and the comedy and pathos of the barber's world tells us of the comedy and madness of Hitler's world. So also the events of Shakespeare's grand comedies take place on the edge of great events and near efforts to create domestic civility within the barbarous world of empire—whether that of the Turks, the Venetians, the Mediterranean Catholic powers, or the Holy Roman Empire. In each play, they say a variant of: "It doesn't help to win Lepanto if we can't preserve city order, love, decent families, respectful hospitality." Shakespeare may be reflecting something like the insight found in Augustine's *City of God*, Book XIX, that the empire or any civic order—if it is to work at all—requires order and love in the household. Shakespeare seems to add that the ruling households in the *imperium* especially require such love and order. From them flows the image of what civil government is to be for the rest of the realm. The imperial households in Shakespeare's comedies are the reverse of his tragic royal households, the households of Macbeth, Othello, King Lear, Antony and Cleopatra, and the rest. In Shakespeare's sense every household is an imperium, every person within the household the author of comedy or tragedy.

Resources for the Study of Empire in the Comedies

Each of the empires that Raleigh mentions in the passage quoted at the beginning of the chapter, plus Venice, claimed the mantle of ancient Rome. The Ottomans claimed succession to Rome through their conquest of the eastern Roman Empire in 1453, the Holy Roman Empire through the foundational work of Charlemagne, and the Venetians through an elaborate literary myth. England, though a marginal country in that time, also claimed Roman hegemony through Geoffrey of Monmouth's story of Brut and successor versions of the same story.

Of the other continental claimants to empire, France was not yet a serious empire, though it was beginning to occupy territories in the New World and elsewhere. For the most part in the 1590s and 1600s it was occupied with achieving a unified kingdom and keeping the Holy Roman Empire at bay by supporting the Protestant powers.[67] Shakespeare treats it in *Love's Labour's Lost* and in *All's Well*. The former of these two plays appears to arise out of a very particular historical context provided by the rivalry of coterie groups at the English court and the rise of the French academies and Henry of Navarre.[68] The latter play, at least on the surface, reflects the time of the Florentine-Siennese struggle in Italy, two centuries earlier, especially as this struggle is represented by Bocaccio and his successors. As such the struggle is largely irrelevant to Shakespeare's time since Spain controlled the territories of both city-states.

The great classical comedy of imperial, would-be global domination is, of course, the *Aeneid*, as it is interpreted by Servius.[69] This sense of the *Aeneid* was strengthened in its happy and comic thirteenth book, added long after Virgil was gone. The successor story that made like claims for England was *The Faerie Queene*, especially book 5, which legitimized Elizabethan England's oppression of Ireland and its wars on the continent and again ended happily.

A work useful for its methodology and placement of the imperial theme within the policy parameters of James I through the examination of a large number of literary works is Tristan Marshall's *Theatre and Empire: Great Britain on the London Stages under James VI and I.* Marshall provides a good context for Shakespeare's explorations of the themes of empire in his later plays by showing how the idea of the creation of a "British Empire" was central to the idea of the unification of Scotland, England, and the rest of the "British" domains that obsessed King James. It is not accidental that Shakespeare makes Britain into a part of Rome in *Cymbeline* and writes a new *Aeneid* for a Milan that is very like James I's England in *The Tempest.* There is no comparable book for Elizabeth's reign.

Where the creation of empire involves the resettlement of one's own citizens in a new land, the process was called "plantation" in Shakespeare's time. It was later called colonization and the policy, pejoratively, "colonialism." In modern political theory, colonialism and imperialism are virtually synonymous. However, they were not so in Shakespeare's time. Gonzalo imagines himself as supervising the "plantation" of *The Tempest*'s island and creating a Utopia there in which the people's innocence is their governor (*Tempest* 2.1.142). Prospero finds it anything but easy to rule the island, with its older inhabitants, Ariel and Caliban, and its recent visitors, suggesting that Shakespeare understood the bubble factor in Gonzalo's dream. However, though colonialism became a form of theft, some British leaders in Shakespeare's time did not see "plantation" as coming about at the expense either of other lands or of the people indigenous to those lands. Bacon, the lord chancellor from 1618 to 1621, when colonialism and "plantation" were just beginning to be British policies, says in his essay "Of Plantations":

I like a plantation in a pure soil; that is, *where people are not displanted, to the end to plant in others; for else it is rather an extirpation*

than a plantation. ... Planting of countries is like *planting of woods;
for you must make account to lose almost twenty years' profit, and expect
your recompense in the end: for the principal thing* that hath been
the destruction of most plantations hath been the base and hasty
drawing of profit in the first years. It is true, speedy profit is not to
be neglected as far as may stand with the good of the plantation,
but no further. It is a shameful and unblessed thing to take the
scum of people and wicked condemned men to be the people with
whom you plant; and not only so, but it spoileth the plantation;
for they will ever live like rogues, and not fall to work, but be lazy,
and do mischief, and spend victuals, and be quickly weary, and
then certify over to their country to the discredit of the plantation.
*The people wherewith you plant ought to be gardeners, ploughmen,
labourers, smiths, carpenters, joiners, fishermen, fowlers, with some few
apothecaries, surgeons, cooks, and bakers.*[70] (italics mine)

The late sixteenth- and early seventeenth-century idea of empire,
save in Venice, does not begin with a center with far-flung colonies
across the sea, similar to the Victorian British Empire. It begins with
a contiguous land base similar to that of the Roman Empire. The
place to start for an insider's understanding of how leaders viewed
the Roman Empire in Shakespeare's England, especially in its court-
ly circles, is with the biblical picture of Rome as the peaceable empire into which Christ chose to be born. Complementing this for
Elizabethans was the *Aeneid*'s portrait of Rome as the creator of the
Pax Romana and successor to Troy in the succession of great empires. The Roman Empire, especially from around Christ's time, is
still the grand keeper of peace and justice. It is the model of what
empire should be. A somewhat similar picture of what Rome should
be emerges from Shakespeare's four Roman plays—*Coriolanus, Julius
Caesar, Antony and Cleopatra*, and *Cymbeline*. The image of Rome developed in Elizabethan-Jacobean court ceremony, play, and propaganda
makes England part of the Roman Empire, or legitimate Rome, or the
Protestant successor to the old Holy Roman Empire.[71]

The place to begin one's study of Shakespeare's understanding of empire in his own time is with Fernand Braudel's *The Mediterranean and the Mediterranean World in the Age of Philip II*. Normally the bibliographies and study aids in this book do not recommend going to secondary works at the beginning of one's explorations, but Braudel's work on the Mediterranean and its cultures is so rich in detail about commerce, topography, and the relationship among various systems in that world as to provide a wonderful sense of the interaction of the Mediterranean civilizations known to Shakespeare's world and also of the physical features of landscape and economic life sustaining those interactions.

Then one can go to a few crucial accounts. The reader who wishes to know of the Venetian empire as it was seen in Shakespeare's time should read the relevant sections in William Thomas's *History of Italy* (1549). Fynes Moryson's fine account of his Elizabethan/Jacobean travels on the continent, many of them undertaken in the 1590s, is available in *Fynes Moryson, An Itinerary*; though not published until 1617, his observations show a great deal of what an intelligent traveler would have seen and known of Venice, Italy, the Mediterranean, and the Empire (Germany/Austria) in Shakespeare's day. They tell what such a traveler could bring back to London. Venetian, Messinan, and general Mediterranean and imperial political lore are detailed in King James I's poem, *Lepanto*, discussed in this chapter (see note 42). Of course, England included a sizable number of Italians who were present there as part of diplomatic missions, business ventures, and theatrical companies.

Moryson's account of the Holy Roman Empire is full in its examination of the character of the German, Bohemian, and Austrian governance systems and the characters of the leaders of those systems (see *Moryson, An Itinerary* 4:238–383). For example, in relation to *Measure for Measure*, Moryson (4:250–53) says that Ferdinand, the emperor succeeding Charles V, caused his son Rudolph, later Emperor Rudolph II, to be chosen king of Hungary while his father lived. This conceivably could be what the King of Hungary is in *Measure for Measure*, but it does not seem likely that the passage referring to the King of Hungary in the play refers to Rudolph as the king of Hungary. The reference seems to go to István Bocskay, titled Prince of Hungary in this period and about to be attacked by the leaders of the empire and Austria. But the "King of Hungary" title may also have had multiple and ambiguous references for a 1604 audience.

For the Ottoman Empire, Richard Knolles's *The Generall Historie of the Turkes: From the First Beginning* contains a magnificent amount of material about the Turkish Empire's history, Venice, Lepanto, Italy, and the Mediterranean. Shakespeare apparently used the first edition of the work (1603) for *Othello*, but it is principally of interest in studying the Shakespearean milieu in that it gives a detailed and plausible Englishman's view of the Mediterranean and the Ottoman Empire. Abraham Holland's *Naumachia, or Hollands Sea-Fight* also tells of Lepanto. The 1626 revision includes an epistle that tells of the English court's enthusiastic response to the victory at Lepanto.

One should always be alert to the possibility that Shakespeare is also talking about England when he portrays the continental empires and vice versa. He distorts the names of places, their histories, and titles enough to escape the censor, placate foreign dignitaries who might be offended by what he says about their nations (he doesn't mind attacking Turks), and distorting their geographies. He generally does his obfuscation by substituting a part for the whole (Aragon for Spain), a lower title for a higher one (the Duke of Vienna for the emperor), or altering geography ("the coast of Bohemia"). There is, I think, very little evidence that Shakespeare, living amid the tales of the port of London and the court of Westminster—living, as George Buck put it, in the "third universitie"—did not know what was going on or what the geography of his globe was. After all, he knew of such remote things as the battle between Suleyman and the Shiites.

There is an enormous amount of travelers' literature and history of the continent from this period, and I have not tried to summarize it at all fully. The travelers' accounts are listed in Marjorie Reeves, *Elizabethan Explorers: Illustrated from Contemporary Sources*. The histories available to Elizabethans and Jacobeans are listed in F. J. Levy, *Tudor Historical Thought*; Annabel Patterson, *Reading Holinshed's Chronicles*; and, by the same author, "Rethinking Tudor

Historiography" in the *South Atlantic Quarterly*. Further sources can be found in Robert Watt, *Bibliotheca Britannica*. For detailed and useful modern histories of the period with detailed bibliographies in many historical areas of inquiry relevant to this chapter, read J. B. Black's *The Reign of Elizabeth: 1558–1603* and Godfrey Davies, *The Early Stuarts*.

6

Measure for Measure as Form, Myth, and Scripture

Throughout his comedies Shakespeare presents us with a New Comedy world reordered so that the comedy includes a model of the whole of society, and in no play is this more apparent than in *Measure for Measure*. Oscar Campbell has described it as a "comicall satyre," like those mounted by Marston and Jonson—a play that moves between the gazes of a wise satiric spectator, the Duke, and a buffoonish one, Lucio, both of whom comment on a parade of grotesques from many parts of society such as might appear in a formal satire by Horace or Juvenal.[1] In a typical formal satire or dramatic "comicall satyre," these gargoyle characters are first shown, then displayed in a typical grotesque action, and finally exposed and punished at the end. But even Campbell admits that *Measure for Measure*'s form would have to be twisted considerably to fit this satiric formula. Though Vincentio and Lucio may be seen respectively as the wise and the buffoonish satiric spectators, the play does not present us with an initial parade of grotesques as in a formal satire, and some of the grotesques appear late. For example, Abhorson does not appear until act 4, scene 2. Furthermore, the two satiric spectators do not function in a neat tandem. Vincentio announces his absenting himself from the throne as the play opens, but he does not become a spectator of his city's follies until act 2, scene 3, when he comes as a friar to the prison. At the beginning of the play we hear of Claudio and Juliet's arrest and

Lucio's appeal to Isabella, and the full plot is under way, plotted much as any other New Comedy might be. No systematic presentation of grotesques comes in the first movement of the play, and no systematic exposure of foolish or villainous actions comes in the second movement. Though the end, as in Marston and Jonson, threatens punishment to most of the grotesques, it never comes for most of them. As to form, it may be more productive to regard *Measure for Measure* as an experimental New Comedy that includes a "comicall satyric" element distorting the grotesque masks to an unusual degree and that calls into play both the resources of classical and biblical myth and those of the imperial struggles of the time to give the grotesques profundity and scope. The play does this to make a political/religious statement as powerful as that in Orwell's *1984* and pertinent to every generation.

In the turning toward political/religious statement, some traditional New Comedy formal elements suffer. For example, psychologically, the apparent betrothal of Isabella and Vincentio at *Measure for Measure*'s end seems almost as artificial as the marriage of Pip and Stella in the second version of *Great Expectations*. Like Dickens creating Pip's marriage out of few preparatory materials, Shakespeare here seems primarily to satisfy his audience's formal expectations without giving us an amatory or erotic runup, though he does provide us with a few subtle preparatory speeches. At the wholly different level of comedic final betrothal as symbolic tableau, the betrothal asserts a Protestant valuing of marriage over asceticism and the Anglican view of the monarch as head of state and church.[2] Given the play's political context, it is no surprise that the duke moves so easily from ruler to friar and back to marrying monarch.

Form

In the matter of form, like many of the earlier comedies and especially like *The Tempest*, which came later, *Measure for Measure* includes the *poeta* who is a duke, Vincentio. The play makes him occupy a position that, outside the play, would have been that of the Holy Roman emperor. As such he would have had a pale claim to wide rule in central and southern Europe.[3] In playing *poeta* he also plays New Comedy "pimp" for Mariana, adolescent lover to Isabella, and the priest to Claudio, Juliet, Isabella, Barnardine, and the prison officials. As a priest during the central acts of the play, he plays a role a little like that of the priestess of Venus, Ptolemocratia, in Plautus's New Comedy *Rudens*: like Vincentio in friar's garb, she protects the virtue of innocent women. Finally, he is the comic *advocatus*, or legal advocate, that part of the judicial system represented in New Comedy by the lawyers and by the judicial and court system.[4] His shadow semblance is Angelo, who is almost as successful as he is at improvisational playing with sex and power.[5]

Several renderings of the play have made Vincentio into more than a ruler or *poeta*. He is also a God or Christ who saves Claudio by arranging for a substitute sacrifice to rescue him from death and who rescues Isabella from coerced sex or rape through arranging a parallel sacrifice that spares her. In this version he comes in the last scene to judge and forgive humankind, separating the goats—namely Lucio—from the sheep. Isabella and Mariana are Mercy itself in the logic of redemption. The sheep are all of the penitents who go on to forgiveness in the restored duke's realm. But this is to stretch things a little. Vincentio can only play Christ or God as any legitimate ruler in Shakespeare's time could play him, by being a *rex imago Christi*. He is the image and not the thing itself. The *rex imago Christi* figure, which every king is supposed to be, acts out in his secular role Christ's role of mediation between God and man. The king mediates by interpreting eternal and natural law into positive law and produces final temporal justice (as a friar or priest he may have a role in eternal justice also). Though Angelo says Vincentio's "grace, like power divine / Hath looked upon my passes" (*MFM* 5.1.361–62), the statement comes from Angelo's subjective state in act 5. Further, even Angelo knows that he is expressing an analogy: Vincentio has looked "*like* power divine," not "*with* power divine." The recognition of the analogical mode is crucial. Vincentio has *not* in fact looked on Angelo with power divine. Angelo only thinks he has looked with something *like* such power. And although Angelo describes his own hypocrisy as diabolic ("Let's write 'good angel' on the devil's horn— / 'Tis now the devil's crest"

[2.4.16–17]), he is no devil either. For he can be forgiven and receive pardon at the end of the play as no Renaissance devil can.

Indeed, everything that supposedly relates to the representation of Christ's judgment, grace, or mercy in the play fits the role of the king as *image* of Christ in Tudor/Stuart ruler worship. None of it fits the historical or soteriological Christ, a role critics from Roy Battenhouse in 1946 on have claimed for Vincentio.[6] As the pedagogue of the realm who sees much from behind the scenes, he is no more than what James aspired to be through his spy system. As the ruler away from government who can return to set everything right in Vienna when he bothers to "return" there, he combines the Habsburg Empire's Rudolph, famously absent from Vienna in Prague with his alchemists, and the Stuart James I, famous for his absences from the English court while on hunting trips or other royal dalliances. James also thought himself the "great schoolmaster of the whole land" and acted as if he could remedy the kingdom with an occasional wise return to the court.[7] Vincentio extends the dux figure in *Measure for Measure* into religious and surveillance realms only to the degree that James made the same extensions in his own reign.

To test the ruler's mettle in creating a community, we have the old Shakespearean fusion of masks in a heightened and more unpredictable form. We have the standard New Comedy figures—the persons from the legal world, like Escalus and Elbow; from the world of sexual trade, such as Pompey the Pimp, Overdone the Whore, and Lucio the Parasite; from the world of "adolescent" love in Vincentio, Claudio, Angelo, Isabella, Juliet, and Mariana. We have the guilds—Overdone and her guild of sex industry women and Abhorson and his guild of the executioners (*MFM* 4.2.22–37). Yet each of these characters is more extreme in his or her deviation from social norms than the grotesques in the early and middle comedies. Each has more than one mask: Elbow is both the legal establishment's constable and the *senex* trying to protect his wife from whoring. If he cannot prevent vice in his wife, how will he do so in others? Pompey is both the pimp and the philosopher for the guilds of tapsters and of executioners. Isabella is both the *puella* and the Portialike advocate, though she advocates in less formal contexts than does Portia. As the masks are fused and defamiliarized, they achieve a new, Hogarthian power. The depth of the play comes from the comic awkwardness with which those in the underworld assume the New Comedy bourgeois masks *and turn crime into business.* Satirical comedy here is only New Comedy pushed to the depths and the heights.

But the satiric tone does not allow much room for love in the gentle mode of the middle comedies. Of course love also had a satiric overlay there.[8] But now all matters of love seem to be harsh. The marriage conclusions come from Claudio and Juliet's mutual seduction, from the dirty tricks that Angelo and Mariana have played on each other, from the duke's command to Lucio to take Kate Keepdown, and from his request to Isabella to be his consort. Though it is possible to play Isabella as somehow searching for some dream Vincentio for much of the play and Vincentio as playing the "redemptive Machiavell" throughout, sacrificing himself to gain Isabella, that production style is not easy. It is not what the majority of the relevant lines of the play suggest. We have a conclusion in which the marriages are ordered both by Vincentio as playwright and *poeta* and by the requirements of the form, something that rarely happens in the other comedies save perhaps in *All's Well.*

Myth

Of all of the plays we have treated, *Measure for Measure* seems least to use the realm of myth. Or rather it seems as a whole to be a kind of parable. Yet two mythic or near mythic reference realms construct the inner structure of the play: (1) references to Themis, or Justitia, the goddess of Justice, and to her descendent Astraea; and (2) references to Pompey the Great as a near mythic Roman general and to his role in reenacting the Pygmalion-Galatea story. The former advance the claims and obligations of the ruler to manifest the heavenly idea of justice and seek its restoration to the terrestrial world. The latter present the pragmatic world of profit that turns people into moneymaking objects and destroys ethics for opportunity.

Justice has a double story: the story of Themis or Justitia and the story of Astraea. The first story appears in Whitney's emblems in an account of how the elements were confused and chaotic before the creation and how the appearance of order produced the creation—the earth, sea, rivers, crops, and the green world of the Golden Age. In this world hate did not exist, nor war, nor pride, nor ambition. During the Iron Age other forces appeared and recreated chaos—armies, crime, oppression of the poor, class distinctions, and tyranny covering itself with glory through propaganda:

> But GOD, that of the former heape: the heauen and earthe did frame.
> And all thinges plac'd therein, his glorye to declare:
> Sente IVSTICE downe vnto the earthe: such love to man hee bare.
> Who, so survay'd the world, with such an heauenly vewe:
> That quickley vertues shee advanc'd: and vices did subdue.
> And, of that worlde did make, a paradice, of blisse:
> By which wee doo inferre: That where this sacred Goddes is.
> That land doth florishe still, and gladnes, their [sic] doth growe:
> Bicause that all, to God, and Prince, by her their dewties knowe.
> And where her presence wantes, there ruine raignes, and wracke:
> And kingdomes can not longe indure, that doe this ladie lacke.
> Then happie England most, where IVSTICE is embrac'd:
> And eeke so many famous men, within her chaire are plac'd.[9]

In short, justice is the principle of order that makes the cosmos orderly in the natural law sense, and it is also the principle of civic law that orders societies. Whitney's version simplifies the myth somewhat. In the original Greek and Latin versions, Themis or Justice is one of the few Titans who sides with the gods in the war of the supernatural beings, and she executes order in the natural world. During the Golden Age her daughter, Astraea, works on earth to assist humankind in establishing a just order, and she becomes the last of the gods to leave earth—to become the constellation Virgo—as the Golden Age turns by steps to iron, and injustice dominates. Part of Queen Elizabeth's political mythology was that she was Astraea returned to restore the Golden Age and justice to English society. Whitney seems to combine the Justitia myth associated with the creation in classical literature generally with the version of the Astraea myth promoted by Elizabeth. In a fallen world, what Justice is—how the principles of law derived from the natural order are to inform human law—must be contemplated; law is a human construction based on thought about the order of things, and the monarch is the chief contemplator of the relationship between natural and human law.

Shakespeare clearly was aware of the emblem of Justice with sword and scale as he uses it in his imagery (*Winter's Tale* 3.2.122; *2 Henry VI* 2.1.214–15). In *1 Henry VI* and in *Titus Andronicus* he refers to Astraea with a clear sense of what her story is and how when Astraea leaves the earth, justice has gone from human society:

> TITUS: Come, Marcus, come; kinsmen, this is the way.
> Sir boy, let me see your archery.
> Look ye draw home enough, and 'tis there straight.
> *Terras Astraea reliquit.*
> Be you remembered, Marcus: she's gone, she's fled.
> Sirs, take you to your tools. You, cousins, shall
> Go sound the ocean, and cast your nets.
> Happily you may catch her in the sea;
> Yet there's as little justice as at land.
> No, Publius and Sempronius, you must do it.
> 'Tis you must dig with mattock and with spade
> And pierce the inmost centre of the earth.
> Then, when you come to Pluto's region,
> I pray you deliver him this petition.
> Tell him it is for justice and for aid,
> And that it comes from old Andronicus,
> Shaken with sorrows in ungrateful Rome. (*Titus* 4.3.1–17)

Escalus is technically Vienna's Astraea. He knows the pragmatics of "government," its institutions, "terms for common justice," (*MFM* 1.1.10–11), and the like. He knows the mechanics of positive law. Paired with him, Vincentio should be its Justitia, but fearful that he will appear too fierce after his long, permissive run, he turns aside from the task of discovering, announcing, or enforcing the law. He instead appears to leave the contemplative part of the administration of justice—the part of the administration of justice that requires that its bearer be illumined by the divine—to pious Angelo.

In contrast to the "functionary" Escalus, Angelo has a special sense of what is right; as Vincentio represents this, it is no daily bureaucratic habit. According to Vincentio, Angelo has been lit by heaven to show his "virtue" in the area of governing (*MFM* 1.1.33ff.). Vincentio believes Nature has given Angelo extraordinary gifts. Nature here means natural law, the law that first ordered the creation and the "common profit" of humankind, the law requiring human beings to respect their own species nature so that, for the common good, they give deference to conscience, rational discourse, property and marriage rights, and differentiated social roles. Angelo has these gifts so that he may use them in his role as Vincentio's substitute and the image of Justice in Vienna:[10]

> DUKE: There is a kind of character in thy life,
> That to th' observer doth thy history
> Fully unfold. Thyself and thy belongings
> Are not thine own so proper as to waste
> Thyself upon thy virtues, they on thee.
> Heaven doth with us as we with torches do,
> Not light them for themselves; for if our virtues
> Did not go forth of us, 'twere all alike
> As if we had them not. Spirits are not finely touched
> But to fine issues; nor nature never lends
> The smallest scruple of her excellence
> But, like a thrifty goddess, she determines
> Herself the glory of a creditor,

Both thanks and use. But I do bend my speech
To one that can my part in him advertise.
Hold therefore, Angelo.
In our remove be thou at full ourself.
Mortality and mercy in Vienna
Live in thy tongue and heart. Old Escalus,
Though first in question, is thy secondary.
Take thy commission. (1.1.28–47)

Shakespeare knew natural law theory as he has Exeter correctly cite the law of nature covering property rights, justifying Henry V's property right in the crown of France:

EXETER: He wills you, in the name of God Almighty,
That you divest yourself and lay apart
The borrowed glories that by gift of heaven,
By law of nature and of nations, 'longs
To him and to his heirs, namely the crown,
And all wide-stretched honours that pertain
By custom and the ordinance of times
Unto the crown of France. (*Henry V* 2.4.77–84)

As Vincentio has it, Nature has lent Angelo her excellence, which in a civic context would be the knowledge of natural law, and because of this loan, he putatively carries Justice's sword and the scales signifying Equity's equal and merciful treatment—"Mortality and mercy in Vienna" (*MFM* 1.1.44). As we later learn, the sword means much more than the scales to Angelo.

At the beginning Vincentio announces the dangerous fiction, given Renaissance political philosophy, that Angelo as his substitute can be Justice in Vienna. However, only the monarch can ultimately carry this responsibility.[11] While he can deputize assistants, he alone is the image of Christ under the corporate fiction. He continues to act when his deputy acts. If we are London people who know our country's constitution, we know that Justice left Vienna when Vincentio failed to use his sword as organized vice took over the city. He drives Justice out yet again by leaving an untried tyrant in his seat. Under Elizabethan natural law theory, he *cannot* leave his "absolute power and place here in Vienna." That power is his exclusively (*MFM* 1.3.13), and when in the last scene he confronts Angelo's failings, he confronts his own failure both to govern well in Vienna and to chose substitutes wisely; after all it was he who said, "In our remove be thou at full ourself" (1.1.43).

Almost everyone in *Measure for Measure* offers some piece of the picture of what divine and earthly justice should be. When the First Gentleman shows contempt for the Ten Commandments and refuses to pray for peace, he is telling us that Astraea—the observing of natural law, among the precepts of which are the Ten Commandments—is not his god. When Claudio first suffers Angelo's imprisonment, he thinks it ordered by divine justice. He knows, or thinks he knows, with St. Paul (Romans 9:15), that heavenly Justice is not the even-weighted scale of the emblem but only Absolute Will itself—what the will of the ruler imposes:

> CLAUDIO [to the PROVOST]: Fellow, why dost thou show me
> thus to th' world?
> Bear me to prison, where I am committed.
> PROVOST: I do it not in evil disposition,
> But from Lord Angelo by special charge.
> CLAUDIO: Thus can the demigod Authority
> Make us pay down for our offence, by weight,
> The bonds of heaven. On whom it will, it will;
> On whom it will not, so; yet still 'tis just. (1.2.96–103)

But it is not St. Paul who gives us the content of the last line as Claudio interprets his words. It is a warped version of Calvin's version of Paul.[12] Peter Lake has argued that Angelo as ruler becomes an image of the Calvinist God as Absolute Will, a figure that can be separated from the equal harmonies and penalties that make up justice.[13] If Will is everything, then Justice, enforcing divine or natural rules evenhandedly, has fled elsewhere. But even as a version of Calvin, this interpretation somewhat distorts Calvin since he would have asserted that justice could only appear to have fled elsewhere. He believed that what appears arbitrary and inscrutable to human beings in the actions of God is ultimately explicable from the divine perspective. Moreover, Calvin does not tolerate any human imitation of the absolute will of God or any fraud or injustice in civil government. Claudio's sarcasm points to Angelo's perversion of extreme Protestant doctrine.

If Angelo does not embody the rules, Elbow cannot embody their implementation. The constable who "leans" on Justice (*MFM* 2.1.46) cannot utter her terms correctly. He cannot help in the weighing of crimes when he does not even understand their very vocabulary. The religious Isabella—who comes to Angelo in his role as the ruler's vicar—does not pray for justice, as one should if the ruler is the embodiment of Astraea or Justitia. She does not even pray for equity—the sort of judgment that looks into circumstances, intentions, and commonsense notions as to whether equal crimes are being treated with equal responses.[14] She prays only for pure mercy, the mercy of God that led to the redemptive scheme (2.2.74–81). She cries out for the virtue that, ironically, it is preeminently her estate's role to administer. Nothing that Angelo has done can prevent mercy from acting to save Claudio's soul, and Angelo properly tells Isabella that his task is the application of the law and its penalties ("It is the law, not I, condemn your brother (2.2.83)."[15]

The other characters are no better. What they are in relation to justice all turns on Angelo. Angelo's initial fault in act 2, scene 2, is not that he does not obey the letter of the law (in the action of the play he does that until he endeavors to coerce Isabella into a sexual relation in act 2, scene 4). His initial and deepest fault is that he patterns out no sense of equity, no evenhandedness, no sense of circumstances, intentions, and rationality in his discovery of crime and exaction of penalties. Equity, as Thomas Aquinas argues, is to give to each person his due according to a consistent rule of application. As Matthew Winston points out, using William West's Elizabethan legal work, equity has to do with "mitigation or moderation of the law written," "a sound or upright will or judgment of an honest man," "a reasonable measure, containing in it selfe a fit proportion and rigor, a ruled kinde of Justice, allayed with the sweetness of mercy."[16] Mercy is part of equity, but that comes after the crime has been tried and the penalty set in the justice system's consistent application of like penalties for like crimes and an examination of mitigating circumstances. Equity does not offer us the absolute mercy of God as understood in some Christian conceptions. In Isabella's eyes, Angelo becomes the usurper of the powers of thundering Jove, the goddess Justice's ally (2.2.113ff). It is only in the last scene that considerations of equity enter into rule in Vienna—equity and ironically the penance that canon law should encourage.

Indeed, Angelo seems to carry within him no requirement that he be equitable. Claudio is to be executed, and Overdone lives. As Escalus observes in the introduction to the work's most profound meditation on the emblem of Justice:

> ESCALUS: You have paid the heavens your function, and the
>   prisoner the very debt of your calling. I have laboured for the
>   poor gentleman to the extremest shore of my modesty, but
>   my brother-justice have I found so severe that he hath forced
>   me to tell him he is indeed Justice.
> DUKE: If his own life answer the straitness of his proceeding, it
>   shall become him well; wherein if he chance to fail, he hath
> sentenced himself.
> ESCALUS: I am going to visit the prisoner. Fare you well.
> DUKE: Peace be with you! [*Exit* ESCALUS]
>   He who the sword of heaven will bear
>   Should be as holy as severe,
>   Pattern in himself to know,
>   Grace to stand, and virtue go,
>   More nor less to others paying
>   Than by self-offences weighing.
>   Shame to him whose cruel striking
>   Kills for faults of his own liking!

Twice treble shame on Angelo,
To weed my vice, and let his grow!
O, what may man within him hide,
Though angel on the outward side!
How may likeness made in crimes
Making practice on the times
To draw with idle spiders' strings
Most ponderous and substantial things?
Craft against vice I must apply.
With Angelo tonight shall lie
His old betrothed but despised.
So disguise shall, by th' disguised,
Pay with falsehood false exacting,
And perform an old contracting. (3.1.471–502)

Escalus sees Angelo's harshness and his denial of contingent consider-ations in Claudio's case. (For example, Claudio's precontract with Juliet would probably have been considered equivalent to marriage in most contexts in Shakespeare's England.) However, despite his reservations, the old lord speaks of Angelo as Brother Justice, the personification of enforcement's sword. But when he has left the stage, Vincentio clarifies his position on the basis of biblical precedent. He goes into a meditation denying that "Brother Justice" is Justice indeed.

He who the sword of heaven will bear
Should be as holy as severe,
Pattern in himself to know,
Grace to stand, and virtue go. (italics mine)

The figure of Justice that Vincentio means is a pattern, a myth—the same terminology as *Titus Andronicus* uses in the case of Philomela and Lavinia. If, says Vincentio, Angelo purports to be the allegory of Justice (as he should be) and wishes to bear the sword of heaven, as Justitia does, then he must be holy and disciplined himself, represent-ing—realizing in earthly time—the eternal pattern. To do this, he must stand firm in divine grace. Grace was thought to be required for the reading and application of natural law, and it was central in Calvinistic theology (as well as the theology of the Elizabethan and Jacobean church).

The ruler as Justice must realize grace as a virtue, not only applying the rule but applying it according to a fully developed sense of equity.[17] Vincentio is here drawing on definitions of justice that say it must operate both by rule (*ius*) and equity (*aequitas*)—the sword and the scales—and that whatever lapses are tolerated in a bishop after Augustine defeated Donatus, the ruler must be what he expects of others.[18]

Finally, in this speech, Vincentio considers how the heavenly pattern can be restored through *his* doing the practical things that he has asked Escalus to do. He must also do the things grounded in theory that Angelo has failed to do. At this stage in the degeneration of the state, the practical side of Justice, Astraea, requires that Vincentio develop a *poeta* strategy for undoing the tyrant's destruction of justice and his tarnishing of the sword of heaven.[19] The rest of the play appears to enact the Machiavellianism of the just prince's recreation of the pattern of justice. Vincentio becomes the righteous "Machiavell" through the bed trick and the substitution that saves Claudio's life by putting Rogazine's head in the place of Barnardine's and, ultimately, of Claudio's. Vincentio's righteous Machiavellianism culminates in the elaborately staged trial scene that confronts Angelo and Lucio and appears to mete out justice to all. This scene develops fully the logic of Justitia and Astraea, theoretical justice and equity and their practical outworking. When Isabella, Mariana, and the other witnesses tutored by Vincentio appear before him in the extended fifth act of the play, he presents himself as Justice in a final full and public manifestation.

At the beginning of act 5 Vincentio announces that he has made enquiry about Escalus and Angelo and has heard "such goodness of [their] justice that [his] soul cannot but yield [them] forth to public thanks" (*MFM* 5.1.6–8, brackets mine). He then walks before the citizens of his city holding by one hand the man to whom he has assigned the discovery of heavenly justice, Angelo, and by the other the man to whom he has assigned its practical application, Escalus, saying—as if they are heraldic emblems—that they are his supports (5.1.15). Seeing the tableau and prompted by Peter, Isabella, instead of begging for mercy as she has before, asks temporal authority for what it, Justitia and Astraea, can provide: "Justice, justice, justice, justice" (5.1.20–25). What comes from Vincentio, though, is not so much justice in Angelo's sense: justice as law condemning offenses robotically. Justice appears now to be punishment for the unrepentant; but for all the others who are repentant, justice is tempered with mercy and with a sense of the equity that Isabella should earlier have begged for her brother. Mercy and equitable treatment come to all but Lucio, and a species of mercy comes even to him in his escape from hanging.

EMBLEMS OF DECAY: POMPEY AND PYGMALION AS COUNTERMYTHS

If the myths of Justitia and Astraea undergird the plot-patterning given Vincentio, Escalus, and Angelo, the stories of Pompey the Great and Pygmalion/Galatea furnish the countermyths.[20] Remember that *Measure for Measure* takes place in the dynastic capital of the Holy Roman Empire. Of course, the Pompey after whom our pimp is named was a Roman general—not myth but history. But as used in this play, Pompey the Great becomes a mythic avaricious pimp, notable for his great bum and for his transformative powers as the Pygmalion of the sexual underworld. His and Mistress Overdone's armies or guilds are the whores who flood Vienna.

Two historical Pompeys appear in Shakespeare's plays: Pompey the Great, mentioned in *Julius Caesar*, and Sextus Pompeius, the younger son of Pompey the Great, who carouses in *Antony and Cleopatra*.[21] Since *Measure for Measure*'s Pompey is explicitly and comically named after Pompey the Great (*MFM* 2.1.193), we may assume that the reference runs to that Pompey, the figure who comes into *Julius Caesar* as Caesar's predecessor in the crowd's fickle favor:

FLAVIUS: But wherefore art not in thy shop today?
Why dost thou lead these men about the streets?

COBBLER: Truly, sir, to wear out their shoes to get myself into
more work. But indeed, sir, we make holiday, to see Caesar,
and to rejoice in his triumph.

MURELLUS: Wherefore rejoice? What conquest brings he
home?
What tributaries follow him to Rome
To grace in captive bonds his chariot wheels?
You blocks, you stones, you worse than senseless things!
O, you hard hearts, you cruel men of Rome,
Knew you not Pompey? Many a time and oft
Have you climbed up to walls and battlements,
To towers and windows, yea, to chimney-tops,
Your infants in your arms, and there have sat
The livelong day with patient expectation
To see great Pompey pass the streets of Rome . . . .
[Caesar] comes in triumph over Pompey's blood?
Be gone!
Run to your houses, fall upon your knees,
Pray to the gods to intermit the plague
That needs must light on this ingratitude.

FLAVIUS: Go, go, good countrymen, and for this fault
Assemble all the poor men of your sort;
Draw them to Tiber banks, and weep your tears
Into the channel, till the lowest stream
Do kiss the most exalted shores of all. (*JC* 1.1.26–41 and
50–59)

Pompey the Great was once the darling of the masses and sat at the
center of Roman power. Plutarch also presents him to us as a great
lover of the prostitute Flora.[22] In the New Rome, whether London
or Vienna, Pompey-the-Great-Pimp—master of many conquests,
commander of an army of women from his tapster post, "Pompey the
Great" for his great bum (*MFM* 2.1.193)—is a grotesque comedown
from pre-Imperial Rome's Pompey. Escalus wishes to play Caesar
to him and beat him to his tent (2.1.218–23). When Lucio is led

to prison, he says he is led in a triumph at the wheels of Caesar (3.1.298–99), a humiliation that the historical Pompey never endured because he was murdered by Septimus in the port of Alexandria after he fled Caesar and his Pharsalus loss. (To further the reunification of Roman sentiment, Caesar never even celebrated his conquest of Pompey with a triumph.) Though Pompey-the-Pimp is called a "wicked Hannibal" by Elbow, who ignorantly wishes to make him the external Carthaginian enemy of "Rome" rather than its internal one, he has Mistress Overdone as the co-commander of his internally corruptive army or guild (4.2.28ff), and he has a brigade of female professionals for his soldiers.

Lucio questions him about his "Pygmalion's images newly made woman" (*MFM* 3.1.299–300)—women "made real women" in the kingdom of Venus and easy riders to provide him bail and liberate him from Caesar's wheels. One of the Early Modern meanings of the Pygmalion story in Shakespeare's time is the ironic one that he is the faithful husband given a beautiful and modest wife for his adoration of her.[23] That is not Pompey/Pygmalion. This Pompey, with his conquering troops and his Pygmalion powers, leads the armies that drive the center of the Roman Empire, Vienna, into retreat and gives the Calvinist demigod Angelo his powers there. The crafty Caesar, Vincentio/Justice, meets the crafty Pompey/Pygmalion of sexual trafficking on Vienna's battlegrounds and battles with him over the soul of the empire and its civic order.

Scriptural Intertexts and Interpretations

Our third area of analysis—embedded scriptural principles and parables—furnishes moral armament in the battle between Caesar's and Pompey's forces. These intertexts appear first in the scriptural and theological applications that Angelo and Isabella make in their conversations, in those that Vincentio draws on in the judgment scene and its runup in act 5, and in the plot as a whole.[24] The state, in Renaissance political theory, is not under divine or scriptural law immediately. It enforces natural and positive law. But Angelo enforces rules concerning adultery and fornication that normally, in Shakespeare's time, would have belonged to the canon law courts. He does not often quote scripture, but when he does, he quotes it to rationalize what he knows to be sin. For example, his "We are all frail" (*MFM* 2.4.122) quotes Ecclesiastics 8:5. However, the passage, on its face, does not apply to known and deliberately willed evil. The passage in context refers to the need to show forbearance to those who have turned from evil because all people are frail in some ways.[25]

However, Vincentio is not exempt from similarly misusing biblical quotation. The title of *Measure for Measure* comes from the Sermon on the Mount, and Vincentio elicits its "measure for measure" passage to justify a punitive response to Angelo's punishment and would-be murder of Claudio.

> DUKE: For this new-married man approaching here,
>   Whose salt imagination yet hath wronged
>   Your well-defended honour, you must pardon
>   For Mariana's sake; but as he adjudged your brother—
>   Being criminal in double violation
>   Of sacred chastity and of promise-breach,
>   Thereon dependent, for your brother's life—
>   The very mercy of the law cries out
>   Most audible, even from his proper tongue,
>   'An Angelo for Claudio, death for death.'
>   Haste still pays haste, and leisure answers leisure;
>   Like doth quit like, and *measure* still *for measure.*
>   Then, Angelo, thy fault's thus manifested,
>   Which, though thou wouldst deny, denies thee vantage.
>   We do condemn thee to the very block
>   Where Claudio stooped to death, and with like haste.
>   Away with him. (5.1.392–408; emphasis mine)

Vincentio echoes Matthew 7:1–5 where Christ sets forth the principles underlying divine judgment, but he does so by giving the New Testament passage an Old Law meaning. As a temporal ruler, he misquotes divine law and does not bring in the natural law he has appointed Angelo to enforce. His phrasing of "measure for measure" contains an even more precise rhetorical balance, a more punitive tone, than does Matthew itself, even in the Geneva version:[26]

1. Ivdge[a] not, that ye be not iudged.

a. He commandeth, not to be curious or malicious to trye out, and condemne our neighbours fautes: for hypocrites hide their owne fautes, and seke not to amende them but are curious to reproue other mens.

2. For with what iudgement ye iudge, ye shal be iudged: and with what measure ye mette, it shal be measured to you againe.

3. And why seest thou the mote, that is in thy brothers eye, and perceiuest not the beame that is in thine owne eye?

4. Or how saiest thou to thy brother, Suffer me to cast out the mote out of thine eye; and behold a beame is in thine own eye?

5. Hypocrite, first cast out that beame out of thine own eye; and then shalt thou se clearely to cast out the mote out of thy brothers eye.

Conventional mainstream medieval and Early Modern understanding of Matthew 7:1–5 made it mean that God will judge mercifully those who are merciful in their private attitudes toward their neighbors and judge the unmerciful according to their logic in judging others.[27] It was not considered to apply to public judgments in most Early Modern thought. However, though conventional Protestant and Catholic theology said the passage applied only to private interactions, the Anabaptists disagreed and said the passage applied to all judgments, including those by magistrates. Christians, in their view, could not assume magisterial roles.[28]

When Vincentio uses this passage to apply to public judgments by Angelo, he affirms that Angelo—who sentenced Claudio to death for being guilty of breach of promise and for violating a virgin, but who is himself guilty of the same sins—should be similarly judged without regard to the contexts in which he acted or his expressed desire not to be made a ruler. Vincentio's Angelo has breached a promise to Mariana and violated her, though he thinks her Isabella ("in double violation / Of sacred chastity and of promise-breach" [5.1.396–97]). He must be similarly judged even if justice be tempered with mercy. But is Vincentio in any position to make this biblical judgment? Even in the most extreme versions of the claim of divine right, the monarch as head of the temporal government judges under the precepts of *natural law* and not under those of the divine. Vincentio's disguise as a priest may have given him a sense of priestly obligation, enlightenment, and responsibility to enforce divine law, but in judging his deputy, he is also implicitly judging himself and his perennial dereliction of duty in Vienna, and he does not repent of his own failures when he condemns Angelo's. He here claims to be ready to do divine judging in a civic context, but he does so without authority. His pronouncement can only be legitimate if he is putting on *a show of judgment*, in order to secure some greater good later.

Of course, some critics do not regard Vincentio's role as civic but as divine and allegorical. He is to them (Battenhouse and those who follow his line of argument) an allegory for Christ's divine judging and redeeming. Some aspects of the play do suggest that Vincentio is like Christ in some vague ways: he is there at the beginning of the play; he is for a time hidden from view; he returns when he is not expected to judge those who are surprised in their sins. But he can be understood in another way as well—a way that seems more nearly central to the play's meaning. Nothing in the play suggests that Vincentio is more than a temporal ruler who assumes the disguise of a cleric for a time. He is the administrator of the civil and canon law court systems (as the English monarch was in Shakespeare's time). He judges without formal reference to canon law in the canon law areas of adultery, fornication, and breach of promise, but that does not make him God or Christ save as the royal image of the divine. His confession of failure to enforce Vienna's law initially does not suggest a perfect God figure. His punishment of Lucio for *lèse-majesté* against him applies only to secular offenses against the dignity of the temporal monarch (see later discussion), and his knowledge of and interest in the technicalities of temporal law go with temporal responsibility.

It is not accidental that he draws back from his biblical divine law precepts when he faces Angelo and hears Isabella and Mariana's plea. He does not give to Angelo the retributive and harsh "measure" that Angelo has tried to give to Claudio and Mariana, because he is not a divine judge in charge of ultimate judgment. He can only do what the civil courts can do—punish people—or what church courts can do—penalize people to bring them to beg for mercy or to express repentance. He even seems to veer finally toward Anabaptist principles when, as a magistrate, he judges almost no one (Darryl Gless has argued that James also was wary of the use of the magistrate's sword).[29] However, Vincentio's punishment of Lucio keeps him from a full endorsement of Anabaptist quietism.

We can understand why Vincentio does not use "measure for measure" principles when he confronts and forgives Angelo. As a secular ruler he is in no position to claim *in toto* the principles of divine judgment as his own. His job as a civil ruler, save in Anabaptist ideology, is to invoke the penalties of secular law and to do so fairly and equitably on all citizens after due warning. Alternatively, if we regard him as a metaphor for the English ruler, as the head of the church he could theoretically use canon law. Since the secular law that Vincentio invokes to punish Angelo for sexual transgression is one that he presumably has failed to enforce when Vienna turned into a stew, it surely would be less than Christlike for him to come on now as if he were God in judgment.[30] Further, Angelo has been the ruler, Vincentio's image, and it is only in Anabaptist exegesis that the "measure for measure" and "judge not" passages would apply to Angelo's civic judgments. There it applies to say that the Christian should not judge at all.[31]

Conventional Protestant and Catholic exegetes argued that the mandate against judgment and the "measure for measure" principle did not refer to civil judgment but only to private judgments between fellow Christians.[32] The civil rule to which Vincentio ought to be appealing in judging Angelo is the precept that *the ruler is not above the law.* Vincentio ultimately uses his "eye for an eye" version of "measure for measure" as a hammer to produce a general petition for forgiveness for Angelo from Mariana and Isabella and for themselves from almost everyone else save Lucio.[33] Then, when Vincentio gets his petition for mercy, he goes back to what appear to be his old permissive ways from the beginning of the play. He does not enforce the law on Angelo or on several others who could be punished. But the difference separating the Vincentio of act 5 from the Vincentio of the beginning of the play—his real difference—is that his initially harsh stance in act 5 has produced confessions of fault and remorse from most of the characters in the play, whether to Vincentio as a monarch or to him as a friarlike religious authority.

Vincentio gradually learns that justice requires both the letter and the spirit of the law, procedure and penance, and he discovers that only as the *poeta* of his domain can he combine these two. He has learned through the play that neither his own earlier complete permissiveness in regard to the enforcement of the law nor his effort to use Angelo's apparent legal rectitude to do his job can make up an effective state. The conscience of the ruler and his ability to stage himself to create the spirit and the letter of good rule is everything. Vincentio is surprised that his initial deception, making Angelo his substitute, does not work. While his own permissiveness in the time before the play begins leads to organized corruption, the apparent rectitude of Angelo's employment of legal power does not support law. It only supports Angelo's private satisfaction, as the surprised Vincentio notes when he hears of his deputy's attempt at a legally coerced rape of Isabella: "but that frailty has examples for his falling, I should wonder at Angelo" (3.1.185–87). The heart of the government official is crucial to the exercise of legal judgment; at this point canon law and penance become active in the life of the state. Later when Vincentio thinks that Claudio's pardon is coming and his assignment of rule to Angelo has been vindicated (4.2.94), he hears instead the again surprising news that Claudio is to be executed (4.2.110–118). He again turns to his *poeta* role and improvises. Perhaps Barnardine will do for Claudio: "What is that Barnardine ..." (4.2. 119). Given that Vincentio in these earlier scenes gradually learns both the complexity of civil law enforcement and its dependence on conscience staging itself to govern, the byplay between the Friar Lodowick and the Duke

Vincentio in the artful execution of law in the final scene is predictable. What Vincentio-as-friar exacts from the various characters is something between private contrition and public penance, and this, in my opinion, accounts somewhat for his extraordinary forgiveness extended to such culprits as Angelo in the last act. Vincentio has not fully put aside the friar's persona.

Admittedly he treats Lucio differently from the others. He first condemns Lucio to marrying Kate Keepdown and later to whipping and hanging. He then forgives the whipping and hanging and commands him only to marry Kate. But Lucio is punished because he is a different kind of a culprit. In sentencing him, Vincentio *is* the civil ruler speaking. Lucio's crime of *lèse-majesté*—slandering the monarch—conventionally required hanging, drawing, and quartering. Consequently, even in Lucio's case, the duke substitutes a lesser and more comic punishment than the law would normally require.[34]

We may now answer why there is no "measure for measure" in the play, only a general amnesty, for Claudio, Barnardine, Angelo, and the provost (though he has committed no real fault).[35] Vincentio, as a friar *and* a monarch like the English monarch (who also headed the church), would have been seen as administering something like canon law's equity to the sexual transgressors in the last scene—applying the scales instead of the sword. Canon law was directed toward procuring repentance from the frail rather than punishment for the criminal. Though Vincentio is *a ruler over the second estate*—lords temporal—for a few acts he assumes the role of friar and dabbles in religious matters such as Claudio's penance. Under Catholic canon law he would not have been a legitimate friar without training or ordination, but it is hard to say how he would have been regarded in England. That the monarch in England was also the head of the church may have given Vincentio's friar disguise more credibility with an English audience.[36]

In any case, Vincentio does not model Christ in these scenes either. To the contrary, Christ is the model for the monarch—securing repentance, visiting those in prison, caring for the powerless.[37] Vincentio, as divine king, carries out in secular life a pattern of good works and imposes both secular and canon law judgments based on a carefully developed fiction of omniscience. As Darryl Gless has pointed out to me, he stages himself before his subjects' eyes, doing what he has earlier said he does not like to do, in order to be fully the moving image of an ideal monarch. He does so to be useful to the common profit of the state, particularly in his commanding of the convenient marriages at the end and his punishing Lucio for *lèse-majesté*. The state and its law, the church and its separate law, rather than Angelo's application of civil law punishments for canon law sins, are primary in the last scene. Lucio is the primary target of the civil law aspects of the scene. However, Vincentio also produces penitence as if, combining the roles of friar/church and king, as the English monarch did, he could act as the vehicle both of equity and of canon law's search for penitence when he deals with Angelo, Claudio, Barnardine, and the provost.

Measure for Measure is different from the other comedies in its last scene. Vincentio uses his *poeta* powers to produce a certain contrition and reform in those of his entourage's culprits who do not challenge the authority of the state.[38] The ruler's equity and forgiveness seem to substitute for the "marriage of true minds" that has characterized the earlier comedies' terminal declarations of social unity. Indeed, even the marriages in *Measure for Measure*, save possibly that of Claudio and Juliet, seem more like truces designed to serve the common weal than love that serves the participants. Though we are not to ask how many children Lady Macbeth had, we can hardly avoid, while watching act 5 of *Measure for Measure*, considering the prospects for the marriages of Kate Keepdown and Lucio, of Angelo and Mariana, and even perhaps of Vincentio and Isabella. The Duke's desired engagement to Isabella may be more than a truce. It may hint of love.

As the play progresses, the Duke gradually learns that he is not invulnerable to feminine attraction. In act 1, scene 3, he tells the Friar from whom he asks his friar's disguise that he has no assignation in mind in seeking the garb; no "dribbling dart of love / Can pierce [his] complete bosom" (1.3.1–3). Both in disguise and in his own person as a duke he initially appears invulnerable to love. However, he changes. Early on after meeting Isabella at Claudio's prison, the

Duke commends her virtue-embodying beauty: "The hand that hath made you fair hath made you good" and reassures her that her gracious virtue "shall keep the body of [her complexion] ever fair" (3.1.181–84). Later he greets her beauty and grace again: "Good morning to you, fair and gracious daughter" (4.3.104). Thus, his handfasting engagement proposal statement—suggesting that Isabella's beauty has partially guided his efforts on behalf of Claudio—though abrupt, is not without preparation:

> If he be like your brother, for his sake
> Is he pardoned; and, for your lovely sake
> Give me your hand, and say you will be mine.
> He is my brother too. (5.1.484–86)

Concomitantly, Isabella responds to "Friar Vincentio" at the prison with an air of innocent attraction to his "holiness" (see for example 4.3.105 ff.) that makes Vincentio's handfasting offer to her conceivable if not fully verisimilitudinous. He has, after all, sought what she has sought, surely an aspect of love.

Angelo, however, remains the Calvinistic literalist until the end. When he is found out, he is the legalist to himself in his last words in the play:

> I am sorry that such sorrow I procure,
> And so deep sticks it in my penitent heart
> That I crave death more willingly than mercy. (*MFM* 5.1.468–70)

But though Angelo asserts that he deserves death, Vincentio notes that his eye quickens when he sees that he is safe, that the penalty for his crimes has been remitted (5.1.489).

Alternative Intertexts

If the biblical precept of "measure for measure" does not entirely explain the logic of the play's judgments, then perhaps the biblical parables that have been said to furnish the operative intertext for the play do. Many critics have seen Angelo's carrying out his master's mandate inequitably, and his master's return to discover him misbehaving, as echoing a story familiar to Jacobean audiences. This is the tale of the unrighteous servant or steward. Versions of the story appear in the Bible and the *Gesta Romanorum*, among works that Shakespeare and his audience knew well. The unrighteous steward's story may give rise to some of the allegorical interpretations of *Measure for Measure*.[39] The story of the unrighteous steward appears as follows in Luke 12:37–47 in the 1560 Geneva Bible:[40]

37. Blessed *are* those seruants, whom the Lord when hee cometh shal finde waking: verely I say vnto you, hee wil gird himself about, and make them to sit down at table, and wil come forthe, & serue them.

38. And if hee come in the seconde watch, or come in the third watche, and shall finde them so, blessed are those seruants.

39. Now vnderstande this, that if the good man of the house had knowen at what houre the thefe wold haue come, he wolde haue watched, and wolde not haue suffered his house to be digged through.

40. Be ye also prepared therefore: for the Sonne of man wil come at an houre when yee thinke not.

41. Then Peter sayd vnto him, Master, tellest thou this parable vnto vs, or euen to all?

42. And the Lord said, Who is a faithful stewarde and wise, whome the master shall make ruler ouer his housholde, to giue them their portion of meat in season?

43. Blessed *is* that seruant, whome his master when he cometh, shal finde so doing.

44. Of a trueth I say vnto you, that he wil make him ruler ouer all that he hathe.

45. But if that seruant say in his heart, My master doeth deferre his comming, and shall beginne to smite the seruants, and maidens, and to eat, and drinke, and to be drunken,

46. The master of that seruant wil come in a day when he

thinketh not, & at an houre when he is not ware of, and will cut him off, and giue him his portion with the vnbeleuers.

47. And that seruant that knew his masters wil, and prepared not him self, nether did according to his wil, shal be beaten with manie *stripes*.

A parallel story is that in Mark 12:1–9 (1560 Geneva version) of the man who planted a vineyard, let it out to husbandmen, and went to another country, sending them two servants and his son in sequence to collect the fruit of the vineyard, only to have each of them be killed by the husbandmen. The parable, said in the Geneva gloss to be part of a genre that includes not only comparisons but "darke speeches and allegories," ends with the Lord of the vineyard returning, destroying the culprits, and giving the vineyard to others. The same parable is also told in Luke 20:9–17.

A narrative more closely resembling *Measure for Measure* is found in the *Gesta Romanorum*. The *Gesta* was a very popular book, and Shakespeare used it for the casket scene in *The Merchant of Venice*. In this parallel tale, a steward accepts the responsibility of caring for the emperor's daughter while he goes on a trip. Doing what Angelo can only design to do in his attack on Isabella, the steward ravishes the emperor's daughter, casts her out in the street to weep her shame, and makes her beg for her bread from door to door. Then the steward hears that the emperor is returning, and he decides to accuse himself to gain the emperor's grace. Coming before the emperor with three cords that signify the punishments he deserves, he asks for the emperor's forgiveness even before he confesses what his sins have been. The emperor grants the request for mercy. When the steward has confessed his sins, the emperor keeps his word about forgiveness *but commands that the steward marry the daughter he has raped*. The *moralitas* or moral that is attached to the story says that the emperor is Christ, the virgin daughter is humankind's soul, and the steward is every man to whom God has given a soul and who falls and destroys the soul's connection to heaven. The steward's ravishing the daughter is fallen reason's corruption of the soul. The return of the emperor is

Christ's return in judgment, the three cords are the parts of penance, and the marriage is the mercy of God.[41] Though the story reinforces Catholic sacramental theology, its meaning would have been accessible to Protestant readers.

In all three stories—the two gospel texts and the *Gesta*—the returning ruler is God or Christ in final judgment. The hints of these patterns in *Measure for Measure*, together with Vincentio's citing the "measure for measure" principle that is to govern final punishment and reward, may have tempted the critics to make the play concern final things and divine return.[42] But Vincentio pulls back from applying any eternal "measure for measure" principles to Angelo, Isabella, the provost, and others in the play who have offered unjust judgments of various other characters or of themselves (*MFM* 5.1.420–514). He utterly destroys no one. He offers a very lenient equity to the remorseful and administers only one temporal punishment, to Lucio, for a secular crime against a secular monarch. He does not do so according to any of the principles of final justice understood in Shakespeare's time. The deliberate or accidental patterning of the plot after stories of the End Time may be designed to remind the Jacobean audience that the divine king and his spies can, on a minor scale, catch a few people misbehaving in history and discover their wrongs to the multitudes as God can do for all people in End Time.

Act Five as Summation

To create the last scene, Vincentio has to have been a master *poeta* and playwright. He has to have arranged for the substitution of Barnardine for Claudio, then of Rogazine for Barnardine. He has to have rehearsed both Isabella and Mariana as to what the precise form of their accusations against Angelo are to be. He has to have rehearsed the provost as to what he is to say and to do. He has to have prepared for Claudio's entry. He has to be able to clothe himself instantly in the garb of a friar in midscene. He has to be able to forecast how Angelo, Escalus, and Lucio will react to his pronouncements and judgments. He has to know in what order each of the accusations is to be made. In short, as the *poeta*, he has to be the ruler/priest/playwright who, in enacting the play of justice and forgiveness, creates the possibility of the return of Astraea. But if he is at all Christlike, he is Christ-the-trickster envisaged in many medieval accounts of redemptive work. He may seem like one who works as a fishhook to catch the devil Angelo, but the leading analogy may more properly be Shakespeare's own Henry V, both as master of secular statecraft and as spy. That is, the craft of the comic playwright and the craft of empire are the same craft.

Angelo makes Vienna into a Geneva, a theocracy. This fictional Vienna/London has no canon law courts. In his new-minted world, Angelo feels compelled to punish all acts against God and the inner life as if they were crimes of violence, troubling the public order. Hence he commands that fornicators be put to death without any consideration of the meaning and context of their actions. Vincentio's apparent failure to provide for these courts in the first place may in part account for his remittal of Angelo's penalties at the end of the play. Chaucer, through his Friar in Fragment D, 1301–16 of *The Canterbury Tales*, describes the province of the traditional medieval canon law court run by an archdeacon:

> Whilom ther was dwellynge in my contree
> An erchedeken, a man of heigh degree,
> That boldely dide execucioun
> In punysshynge of fornicacioun,
> Of wicchecraft, and eek of bawderye,
> Of difamacioun, and avowtrye,
> Of chirche reves, and of testamentz,
> Of contractes and of lakke of sacramentz,
> Of usure, and of symonye also.
> But certes, lecchours dide he grettest wo;
> They sholde syngen if that they were hent;
> And smale tytheres weren foule yshent,
> If any persoun wolde upon hem pleyne.
> Ther myghte asterte hym no pecunyal peyne.
> For smale tithes and for smal offrynge
> He made the peple pitously to synge.

The canon law courts, having authority over the spiritual life of the individual, punished such crimes as disobedience to the church, witchcraft, slander, failure to abide by contracts, usury, simony, pimping, obscenity, adultery, and lechery. Though some modern scholarship has denigrated the role of the church courts after the Reformation, their significance is being recovered by recent work. Ingram finds them in the post-Reformation period doing almost exactly what Chaucer's Friar says they did in his time: that is, they punished disobedience to the church in all areas, including witchcraft, sorcery, defamation and slander, usury, drunkenness, failure to educate children in proper religion, and, most of all, sexual and matrimonial offenses.[43]

Though the common law and the church courts had some overlapping jurisdictions in the area of sexual offenses, one may use as a rule of thumb that the civil courts sought to control external order and extirpate external violence, whereas the canon law courts sought to order the individual internally while destroying all forms of false worship or worship failure. The typical exaction of the civil court was a prison term or execution. The typical exaction of a church court was a penitential imposition.[44] One is tempted to say that the common law courts and chancery administered justice according to English Early Modern understandings of the precepts of natural law—that is, of the rational self-interest of the species—and that the canon law courts appealed to those of natural *and* divine law—that is, equity under natural law supplemented by the revealed call to absolute charity and self-sacrifice.[45]

The canon law church courts were attacked by the Puritans as papist remnants and for being lenient with sexual sin. The common law court lawyers attacked them for violating the principles of common law in areas where jurisdictions overlapped. But recent studies of the church courts have found them flexible, efficient, and lacking in serious corruption in most of the diocesan areas examined.[46] For the Puritans the church courts were hammers with which to beat the bishops.

The same Puritans who wished to get rid of the canon law courts also called for much stiffer penalties for sexual transgression, whatever the courts that administered them. Some Puritans proposed the death penalty for adultery, though there appears to have been no rule of law

as rigorous as that in Vienna stipulating death to be the punishment
for fornication.[47] When Isabella hears that her brother has gotten
Juliet pregnant, she says, "O, let him marry her." To put the exclama-
tion in context:

LUCIO: Your brother and his lover have embraced.
   As those that feed grow full, as blossoming time
   That from the seedness the bare fallow brings
   To teeming foison, even so her plenteous womb
   Expresseth his full tilth and husbandry.
ISABELLA: Someone with child by him? My cousin Juliet?
LUCIO: Is she your cousin?
ISABELLA: Adoptedly; as schoolmaids change their names
   By vain though apt affection.
LUCIO: She it is.
ISABELLA: O, let him marry her!
LUCIO: This is the point.
   The Duke is very strangely gone from hence;
   Bore many gentlemen—myself being one—
   In hand and hope of action; but we do learn,
   By those that know the very nerves of state,
   His giving out were of an infinite distance
   From his true-meant design. Upon his place,
   And with full line of his authority,
   Governs Lord Angelo—a man whose blood
   Is very snow-broth; one who never feels
   The wanton stings and motions of the sense,
   But doth rebate and blunt his natural edge
   With profits of the mind, study, and fast.
   He, to give fear to use and liberty,
   Which have for long run by the hideous law
   As mice by lions, hath picked out an act
   Under whose heavy sense your brother's life
   Falls into forfeit. He arrests him on it,
   And follows close the rigour of the statute
   To make him an example ... (1.4.39–67)

Isabella, chaste and ascetic as she is, proposes as the solution to Claudio's problem exactly what the church courts of the day probably would have recommended—an immediate marriage for the couple. Perhaps, given that attitudes were becoming more rigorous in regard to premarital pregnancies even under the claim of a *de futuro* promise to marry, canon law equivalents would have required a mild private penance and a marriage.[48] What is wrong with Vienna that makes Vincentio not enforce its laws and Angelo enforce them so as to make them appear harsh, and what is wrong with Calvin's Geneva and the London that the Puritans sought, is the confusion of canon law offenses—sins—with offences against the state—crimes.[49] Angelo misunderstands the role of the state and the role of law in the control of sexual wrong, or he understands it as the Puritans did. Early in the play, Vincentio also did not understand these matters. He failed to establish canon law courts to reform Vienna and left it in the hands of an Angelo—gifted only with a sense of crime and punishment, not of sin and penance.[50]

The audience seeing the play would have recognized that England, unlike Vienna, had canon law courts for dealing with the penitential offenses. The burden of Shakespeare's play is that these should be used—not Geneva's theocracy, not that sought by the Puritans in London, not that potentially to be developed in Hungary under Bocskay, or the fictive one created for Vienna. Having confused the inner with the outer offense, Angelo can only create a "1984" where victimless wrong thoughts and wrong desires become capital crimes against the state. The end of the process is the corruption of all governance in the totalizing order of Angelo, an order in which his own ruling self declares itself exempt from both criminal and moral law.[51]

Though the Puritans wished to abolish the church courts, the courts remained, serving the function of mirroring sin and calling to repentance. The Vienna of the play, caught between the totalitarian state and moral anarchy, has only Vincentio acting in the friar's role: head of the church and head of the state. At the end he, friar and king, acts as a surrogate canon law court. He calls his people to self-recognition, remorse, and putting their wrongs right to the degree possible. He marries those who have wronged one another in a gesture to right their lapses, and Lucio alone resists such a marriage, though some of the other characters may be played as having silent reservations about their proposed marriages.

Ultimately *Measure for Measure* has to do with the role of law and inner decay in the lives of states and empires. Its themes apply to James I's state and empire and Rudolph's Vienna and Holy Roman Empire. Vienna cannot assist Hungary—neither its Catholics nor its Calvinists—until it has achieved more internal order. The play reflects on the old Catholic sexual order represented by Isabella and its "fugitive and cloistered" virtues, virtues sometimes naïve and sometimes harsh but still virtues. It displays the logic of the new order proposed by the Puritans wherein canon law would be abolished and the state would punish all evil with dispatch and rigor.[52] It contemplates the misappropriation of the biblical logic of sin and final judgment to purely civic matters, where natural law, crime, and punishment ought to be the primary frames. Penance, confrontation with and working out of inner evil, ought to be the first rule within the domain of the church courts.[53] Finally the plot reminds us of the dangers of hypocrisy, rigor, and polarization. Central Europe was to see these dangers in spades after 1618 and England after 1642. The play deals with the fates of empires as seriously as does *Antony and Cleopatra*, and far more relevantly, given the climate of Shakespeare's London.

And in Conclusion

We began with an examination of the lines in Ben Jonson's Folio tribute to Shakespeare praising his comedies as surpassing those of Plautus and Terence, on the one hand, and those of Aristophanes, on the other. Jonson preferred Shakespeare to the boy-meets-girl sitcoms of Terence and Plautus and to the satiric bludgeoning posing as comedy that Aristophanes created. He apparently saw Shakespeare as going beyond both New and Old Comedy (though he himself had a taste for Old Comedy and Aristophanes' work with the whole state of a society). I have argued in this book that what Jonson saw in Shakespeare is the high comic seriousness of comic genius—though not the high pomposity that led Matthew Arnold to dismiss Chaucer. "Serious" here means treating the whole of society as it faces its most significant crises. And if this is what Jonson meant, he was right in thinking that Shakespeare takes the relationship between human desire and whole commonwealths, the fates of empires, as his comic subject. Following the notion that poetry is a kind of philosophy or theology, he invests his comic myths with resonances from the most sacred and laughing, joyous scriptures of the Western world.

To create a comedy that would compete with the epic/tragic mode, the poet first restructured the form to make it cover more than private and domestic matters; indeed he made it touch the whole commonwealth—whether that commonwealth be Ephesus, the Forest of

Arden and its surroundings, Athens, Messina, Venice, Vienna, Illyria, the new world of trade and colonization, or any other constructed community. He does this by introducing a leader figure whose actions put whole communities and states at stake and then creating fusions of the masks or stock character types that he inherited from Roman New Comedy and commedia dell'arte. These fusions give us the sense that we are seeing significant whole communities struggle. In almost every comedy, we see most of Jaques's whole seven ages from the world stage of the Globe. We watch a scene various enough, conflicted enough, and inward enough to give us the sense that we are watching an important group at work and at play, seeking love and justice, struggling to find meaning in the wasteland of cruelty and lust that confronts them.

After *A Midsummer's Night's Dream* the comedies of Shakespeare's time generally included a morose or melancholy figure who must be defeated or transformed. Vouet's 1627 *Father Time Overcome by Love, Hope, and Beauty* captures the spirit of this theme. Time is overcome by love, procreation, and the renewal of communities. In Shakespeare, the morose or melancholy character is not always overcome. He may be transformed or rendered impotent. We may mock the cruelty and superficiality of Shylock's conversion, and Elizabethan audiences might have too, but he is apparently no longer a threat. We may laugh at Malvolio at the end of *Twelfth Night* when he says he will be revenged, but we do not fear his return as a righteous avenger. Shakespeare reserves a circle outside the ambience of heterosexual desire and courtship for the depressed, a circle where they can be converted, learn contemplation (Jaques), undergo an exorcism for love melancholy (Malvolio), be married (Angelo), reunite with supposedly dead wives (Leontes), or, most dangerously, be forgiven and partially returned to the commonwealth (the sour Neapolitans in *The Tempest*). Only Don John seems beyond help or hope.

In the comedies, the commonwealth faces—or has just faced—external political and military enemies, bad weather, and terrible disease. But its chief "problem" is not the defeat of those objective enemies. Its problem is rather the working out of internal conflicting passions—especially melancholy and malice. It has to come home to a solidarity that represents or simulates—on the surface at least—its general good, the common profit of society. The wisdom of the comedies is that while the leader must lead, no one person creates a decent society. The tragedies tell us, on the other hand, that one person can destroy a society.

To dampen the passions, the leader often begins with a judgment without mercy. He ends with merciful judgment or just plain mercy. To harmonize the conflicting passions of the group, the play often goes through a sequence where the barriers seem to be irremovable. Eventually trickery, wit, miracle and the frenzy of the artist or prophet combine to remove them. At the end of the play, a betrothal ceremony is performed, a marriage promised, of a kind that not only dampens the antisocial passions but also suggests a philosophic or religious alternative to endless internal chaos and hatred. The differing kinds of marriages proposed and the feasting and dancing at the end differ symbolically from play to play because the inscape of the central problem of the play is different in each. However, they all bring society home to an unwobbling pivot.

To endow his plots with a further dimension of high comic seriousness, Shakespeare invests his stories with resonances from the most sacred *and* joyous scriptures of the Western world: Ovid, Chaucer, the *Aeneid*, and the Bible. The myths he chooses are those that allow him to speak of the high subjects without which, as Faulkner says in stentorian voice, any story is ephemeral: "love and honor and pity and pride and compassion and sacrifice." When Shakespeare calls on the world of classical myth to help him articulate what he has to say of these themes, he calls on the myths that deal with innocence and fall (the golden age versus Frederick's England or France, Athens versus the forest), with the search for power through the achievement of desire (Falstaff, Theseus, Orsino, Angelo, and so forth), with gay (Ganymede) versus straight (Olivia) love, and with amorous desire for other human beings and for the divine (for example, the pairs of lovers at the end of *As You Like It*).

By giving the fairies and gods over to allegory and exemplum, Shakespeare can present us with those subtler interventions of the divine that Christians were to label providence—in history unknown to early Greek mythology but known to Ovid and Virgil—and can do so through plots so constructed that miracle seems conceivable, even plausible.

When Shakespeare calls on biblical stories, he calls on those that deal with the same subjects as do the myths. Again we have innocence and fall (Arden/Eden versus France, Athens blessed by Oberon versus the Wood, Ferdinand's Paradise and Trinculo's and the Neapolitans' fury-bound Hell). We have the search for power through the achievement of desire (Ephesian Solinus, Cainlike Duke Frederick, Puritan Malvolio, and false steward Angelo). To these themes the poet adds the primary "inspired" biblical and prophetic stories with ethical meanings having to do with our brotherhood and sisterhood: the Antipholuses in *Comedy of Errors*, Sebastian and Viola in *Twelfth Night*. Juxtaposed against such stories he places pictures of Cain-and-Abel-style fratricide and its avoidance in several plays and Hero-Hermione death and rebirth. In the very settings and imagery of the plays, he gives us cosmic struggles between darkness and light, such as those obvious in *A Midsummer Night's Dream* and *Twelfth Night* but present more subtly in many of the other comedies. As the poet's career develops, the comic conclusion is increasingly won out of acts of forgiveness and mercy that are almost wholly unpredictable before they occur but explicable and plausible after they have occurred. We may call this grace if we wish, or we may simply call it a nice way to roll up a play.

Though Shakespeare represents imperial life in his comedies—in Venice and the Illyrian provinces, in Spanish Habsburg Messina, in Habsburg Austrian Rome, and in Milan/England—he does not really love empire. He wrote when the dream of empire was coming alive in England as it had not for centuries, and his world was filled with some of the greatest land empires the world had ever known. But his comedies do not display much faith in empire, even if it be "civilizing" empire, such as Prospero's. Near the moment of his greatest triumph Prospero announces that what he has gained is only a dream, an insubstantial pageant that will leave nothing behind at the end. The earlier comedies lack this explicit eschatological vision, but they do contain a vision of renewal. Messina is not joyous because it has defeated the Turk and the end is coming. It is joyous because wit has created the resurrection of Hero, the exposure of Don John, and the savagely amorous contrapuntal runs of Beatrice and Benedict. Vienna is not happy because anyone has fallen on the King of Hungary or the hypocrite Angelo but because mercy has made the marriages possible. Belmont near Venice hears the harmonies of forgiveness, and Athens near the woods hears the call of "something of great constancy" (*MND* 5.1.26) that prepares for a nuptial celebration. The innocence of Sebastian's "This is the air, this is the blessed sun, this pearl she gave to me" pairs with the willed sacrifices of Viola to reveal the divine in Illyria. Before he comes to his final eschatological dismissal of empires, Shakespeare turns their fates not on their power or might in battle but on their internal condition—on the reconciled family, their capacity for forgiveness and mercy, and, to use a very old-fashioned concept, their confidence in "eternal providence."

Part of the art of Shakespeare's comedies is to begin his plots with dire situations so configured that because we have knowledge going beyond what the actors in the play know, we know from the beginning that whatever carries them along will in all likelihood carry them along to something happy.[1] The remainder of their art is to give us exactly this joy so that we carry its confidence beyond the Globe to the globe. When Gonzalo calls for rejoicing beyond a common joy, he is not calling for rejoicing only at the recognition of comic foibles on the part of others, comic foibles overcome. He not only points to a happy union between the chief young woman and young man but also calls for rejoicing at the recognition of self, the recognition of renewed social unity, the appearance of a kind of providence in how we encounter the wayward movement of history:

GONZALO: I have inly wept,
Or should have spoke ere this: look down you gods,
And on this couple drop a blessèd crown,

> For it is you, that have chalked forth the way
> Which brought us hither.
> ALONSO: I say amen, Gonzalo.
> GONZALO: Was Milan thrust from Milan, that his issue
> Should become kings of Naples? O rejoice
> Beyond a common joy! And set it down
> With gold on lasting pillars: in one voyage
> Did Claribel her husband find at Tunis,
> And Ferdinand her brother found a wife
> Where he himself was lost; Prospero his dukedom
> In a poor isle; and all of us ourselves,
> When no man was his own. (*Tempest* 5.1.202–16)

This is, taken a bit more generally than the specifics of *The Tempest* might allow, a definition of the essence of Shakespearean comedy as a celebration of self-knowledge. Gonzalo's speech begins with a series of disasters that end in happy outcomes, marriages between countries, and in Claribel's case between countries and civilizations. It finally rejoices that each of us can come to know ourselves despite the difficult divisions we find there, our common exile from our deepest selves. In so doing, Gonzalo implies, we may find one another in community. Gonzalo's "beyond a common joy," taken as a definition of the center of Shakespearean comedy, means that we rejoice at the end of his plays in the comic genre, particularly the later plays from about 1598 on, not just in a quotidian "and they lived happily ever after" and not in a Jonsonian retribution brought down on the knaves and fools. We rejoice in potential forgiveness, "marriage," social reconstruction. We discover some temporary or permanent lifting of the burden of the world. We do not laugh. We rejoice.

Shakespearean comedy valorizes the reconciliation—or at least the temporary harmonizing—of social units such as the families of the plays (Antonio and Sebastian are still around and potentially dangerous but under control). It praises the continuity of social groups and of the species in its admiration of coupling and marriage, but it also hearkens toward the continuation of significant reconciling dialogue between nations and civilizations: between Islamic Tunis and Spanish Naples, England-like Milan and Naples. The "beyond a common joy" arises out of the sense that somehow, miraculously, providentially—without our knowing where it comes from—renewal is possible at every social level.

Notes

Preface

1. Stephen Greenblatt, *Will in the World: How Shakespeare Became Shakespeare* (New York: W. W. Norton, 2004); James Shapiro, *A Year in the Life of William Shakespeare: 1599* (New York: HarperCollins, 2005).

1. On Historical Understandings of Shakespeare's Works

1. Wittgenstein, for example, struggles with the effort to find the essential meaning of the word *game* and finds that games do not have some single set of essential qualities but are characterized by a network of similarities and differences so that they bear *family resemblances* to each other: "I can think of no better expression to characterize these similarities than 'family resemblances'; for the various resemblances between members of a family: build, features, colour of eyes, gait, temperament, etc. etc. overlap and criss-cross in the same way. And I shall say: 'games' form a family." Ludwig Wittgenstein, *Philosophical Investigations*, trans. G. E. M. Anscombe (Oxford: Basil Blackwell, 1953), aphorism 67, 32e.

2. The most obvious example may be the removal of some profanity involving the use of the name of God from the quarto texts in the First Folio in the context of the 1606 parliamentary law against profanity in plays; see Gary Taylor, "'Swounds Revisited: Theatrical, Editorial, and Literary Expurgation," in *Shakespeare Reshaped: 1606–1623*, ed. Gary Taylor and John Jowett (Oxford: Clarendon Press, 1993), 51–106. For context and the changes in *King Lear*, see Gary Taylor, "Monopolies, Show Trials, Disaster, and Invasion: *King Lear* and Censorship," in *The Division of the Kingdoms: Shakespeare's Two Versions of "King Lear*,*"* ed. Gary Taylor and Michael Warren (Oxford: Clarendon Press, 1983), 75–119.

3. See the discussion of Renaissance comic theory in chapter 2.

4. Ernest Jones, *William Shakespeare: Hamlet with a Psychoanalytical Study* (London: Vision, 1947), 11.

5. Jones's study of *Hamlet* appeared in 1947, Olivier's *Hamlet* in 1948. Jones was a consultant to the film; see also Dale Silveria, *Laurence Olivier and the Art of Film Making* (London: Associated University Presses, 1985), 171.

6. In another context, Jones says that in *Hamlet* as Oedipal construction, Shakespeare shows that "the essence of man's Fate is inherent in his own soul." Ernest Jones, *Hamlet and Oedipus* (London: Victor Gollancz, 1949), 156–57.

7. Frank Cioffi, *Freud: Modern Judgements* (London: Macmillan, 1973), 76–86; Frank Cioffi, *Wittgenstein on Freud and Frazer* (Cambridge: Cambridge University Press, 1998). Some of the less philosophic objections to Freud's claims to have found human nature and to Freud's use of data are found in Frederick Crews, *The Memory Wars: Freud's Legacy in Dispute* (New York: New York Review of Books, 1995). Crews has written many other books and articles attacking psychoanalytical theory.

8. Wittgenstein, *Philosophical Investigations*, 194e.

9. E. K. Chambers, *William Shakespeare* (Oxford: Clarendon Press, 1966), 2:323–27.

10. Bacon, who prosecuted those involved in the Essex uprising, writes of Meyrick, who paid the Lord Chamberlain's Men for the performing of the play: "So ernest hee was to satisfie his eyes with the sight of that tragedie which hee thought soone after his lord should bring from the stage to the state, but that God turned it vpon their own heads." Chambers, *William Shakespeare*, 2:326. Bacon thus sees the play, performed in this context, as rehearsal for and legitimization of future political action. See also Samuel S. Schoenbaum, *William Shakespeare: A Compact Documentary Life* (Oxford: Clarendon Press, 1977), 218–19.

11. For a contrasting view, see Janet Clare, "Censorship and Negotiation," in *Literature and Censorship in Renaissance England*, ed. Andrew Hadfield (New York: Palgrave, 2001), 20–22.

12. Laura Bohannon, "Shakespeare in the Bush," in *Conformity and Conflict: Readings in Cultural Anthropology*, ed. James P. Spradley and David W. McCurdy (Boston: Little, Brown, 1987), 35–45. All later quotes are from these pages.

13. See Jacques Derrida, *Margins of Philosophy*, trans. Alan Bass (Chicago: University of Chicago Press, 1982).

14. For other discussions of *différance*, see the following works by Jacques Derrida: *Writing and Difference*, trans. Alan Bass (Chicago: University of Chicago Press, 1978); *Positions*, trans. Alan Bass (Chicago: University of Chicago Press, 1981); *Of Grammatology*, trans. Gayatri Spivak (Baltimore: Johns Hopkins University Press, 1976); and *Margins of Philosophy*.

15. In Derrida, language does not speak of what is but of what was. It is

constantly involved in giving us a deferred version of what was, supplementing and changing it as part of explication, and Derrida seems surprised by that. It is as if someone who talked about the Battle of Waterloo and mentioned that Napoleon lost the battle thought that by so saying he was placing Napoleon solidly on his horse on the battlefield—Swift's Grand Academician who tries to speak with things but now goes mad because even the things have changed from what they were. Since, in Derrida's view, the words are unstable in their meaning and do not refer to some present object, meaning is by definition unstable. The changing of the meaning of a sentence or its "reconfiguration" is what we are always doing, and therefore effacing, erasing, reconfiguring are part of the constant task of supplementing and explaining. Derrida seems to rely on a picture theory of meaning and to believe that language "works" only when it somehow "delivers" its referent to its speaker and hearer.

16. Irme Salusinzky, "An Interview with Harold Bloom," *Scripsi* 4 (1986): 69–88.

17. Harold Bloom, *Shakespeare: The Invention of the Human* (Riverhead: Putnam, 1998), 714, 731. The idea that Shakespeare invented "the human" confuses Freud's and/or other nineteenth- and twentieth-century understandings of "the human" personality with what is species-specific to *Homo sapiens*. Bloom says that Shakespeare invented "what has become the most accepted mode for representing character and personality in language" and thereby "invented the human as we know it." Is this the human as it is known to the Tiv, to the Arab world, to the Chinese before, during, and after Mao? Bloom's assertion confuses a set of cultural assumptions promoted in European and American intellectual circles in the last century with genetic characteristics that evolved long ago. Are we to say that Homer knows nothing of the human or that the Mosaic books or the Vedic hymns are ignorant of the human?

18. Erwin Panofsky, *Problems in Titian: Mostly Iconographic* (New York: New York University Press, 1969), 129–37. On *The Education of Cupid*, see http://www.wga.hu/frames-e.html?/html/t/tiziano/mytholo2/venuscup.html.

19. Panofsky, *Problems in Titian*, 135.

20. See Otto van Veen, *Amorum Emblemata*, with an introduction by Stephen Orgel (New York: Garland, 1979), 60. Fickle Fortune and blind Love are also associated in van Veen, *Amorum Emblemata*, 156. For a full account of blind Cupid as irrational love or lust, see Erwin Panofsky, *Studies in Iconology: Humanistic Themes in the Art of the Renaissance* (New York: Harper and Row, 1962), 9–128 and plates.

21. Panofsky, *Studies in Iconology*, 13.

22. John Searle, "Minds, Brains, and Programs," *Behavioral and Brain Sciences* 3 (1980): 417–24.

23. John Searle, "Is the Brain's Mind a Computer Program?" *Scientific American* 262 (1990): 26–31.

24. Derrida, *Of Grammatology*, 178.

25. Marvin Krims, "Romeo's Childhood Trauma?—'What Fray Was Here?'" *Psychart* (1999), http://www.clas.ufl.edu/ipsa/journal/articles/art_krims01 .shtml. Later sections of this book provide introductions to the methods of biblical and classical interpretation available in Shakespeare's time.

26. The quote from Tureck comes from the booklet in a two-CD package of her Bach work in the series *Great Pianists of the Twentieth Century*, by the Philips Music Group in CDs for Bach's partitas.

27. I owe the refinement of this point to suggestions from the philosopher Robert Herbert of the University of Oregon.

28. John Florio, *A Worlde of Wordes* (London: Arnold Hatfield, 1598), sig. [Nnn4ʳ].

29. Thomas Blount, *Glossographia* (London: printed by Thomas Newcomb, 1656), Rr4[ʳ].

30. Thomas Lodge, *A Reply to Stephen Gosson's Schoole of Abuse in Defence of Poetry Musick and Stage Plays* in *The Complete Works of Thomas Lodge*, ed. Edmund Gosse (New York: Russell and Russell, 1963), 1:36. For Lodge's relation to the group of university wits and playwrights with whom Shakespeare seems to have been marginally associated in his early days in London, see Greenblatt, *Will in the World*, 202–3, 200–304.

31. Of course, one of the popular uses of nasty characters in any period is to warn us against their nastiness. Thus we should not be too snobbish about the remark of Simon Forman, the Jacobean astrologer and charlatan, writing about Autocylus in *The Winter's Tale*: "Beward of trustinge feined beggars or fawning fellows." Stephen Greenblatt, ed., *The Norton Shakespeare: Comedies* (New York: W. W. Norton, 1997), 988.

2. Shakespeare and the Invention of Grand Comic Form

1. James D. Redwine Jr., ed., *Ben Jonson's Literary Criticism* (Lincoln: University of Nebraska Press, 1970), 166. For preliminary notes on Shakespeare's widening of the bounds of comedy, the subject of this chapter, see James Shapiro, *A Year in the Life of William Shakespeare: 1599* (New York: HarperCollins, 2005), 15.

2. Robert S. Miola, *Shakespeare and Classical Comedy: The Influence of Plautus and Terence* (Oxford: Clarendon Press, 1994). See George E. Duckworth, *The Nature of Roman Comedy: A Study of Popular Entertainment* (Princeton NJ: Princeton University Press, 1952). I am indebted to Duckworth throughout the present work. For Shakespeare's debt to Plautus at the end of his career, see James T. Svendsen, "The Fusion of Comedy and Romance: Plautus *Rudens* and Shakespeare's *The Tempest*," in Karelisa V. Hartigan, *From Pen*

to Performance: Drama as Conceived and Performed (Lanham MD: University Press of America, 1983), 121–30; Lester E. Barber, "*The Tempest* and New Comedy," *Shakespeare Quarterly* 21 (1970): 207–11; Bruce Louden, "*The Tempest*, Plautus, and the *Rudens*," *Comparative Drama* 33 (1999): 199–233; Joao Manuel Numes Torrao, "Reflexos da *Rudens* de Plauto em *The Tempest* de Shakespeare," *Arquipelago* 4 (1982): 195–224. For Shakespeare's indebtedness to Terence for the double plot in which one lover is serious and a bit of a dreamer and the other is practical (Shakespeare often adds several levels of doubling), see Catherine M. Shaw, "The Conscious Art of *The Comedy of Errors*," *New York Literary Forum* 5–6 (1980): 18. Several critics have also noted that Shakespeare adopts the New Comedy masks for the purposes of his tragedies also, and Shapiro (*Year in the Life*, 289) notes the parallelism between Hamlet and the comic lead. The tragedies are stories of persons of great estate caught in a domestic web; the comedies are also primarily stories of domestic conflicts among persons of great estate and their children, stories that play themselves out in the theater of the nation-state and empire.

3. Oscar Campbell, *Comicall Satyre and Shakespeare's Troilus and Cressida* (San Marino CA: Adcraft Press, 1938), 6, 13–14.

4. Redwine, *Ben Jonson's Literary Criticism*, 85.

5. Redwine, *Ben Jonson's Literary Criticism*, xxxix, xli, 36–37, 75–76, 108. See P. H. Davison, "*Volpone* and the Old Comedy," *Modern Language Quarterly* 24 (1963): 151–57, who argues that Jonson saw Old Comedy as carrying the gravity of tragedy. C. L. Barber argues that Shakespearean comedy more resembles the Aristophanic than any other in English because it leads to Saturnalian release; Barber, *Shakespeare's Festive Comedy: A Study of Shakespeare's Dramatic Form and its Relation to Social Custom* (Princeton NJ: Princeton University Press, 1972), 3–4. See Matthew Steggle, "Wars of the Theatres: The Poetics of Personation in the Age of Jonson," *English Literary Studies Monograph Series* 75 (1998): 25–26.

6. Redwine, *Ben Jonson's Literary Criticism*, 84–85.

7. Miola, in *Shakespeare and Classical Comedy*, tends to see the moral explanations of comedy current in Renaissance theory as rationalizations, but any explanation of a joke is likely to appear heavy-handed. We do not, I think, have much evidence that all of the Renaissance critics of comedy were mendacious or describing something that they did not understand.

8. A few critics have noted the appearance of the dux figure in Shakespeare, but his functions have not been fully described. For a suggestive comment, see John Arthos, "Shakespeare's Transformation of Plautus," *Comparative Drama* 1 (1967): 243.

9. Lewis Soens, ed., *Sir Philip Sidney's Defense of Poesy* (Lincoln: University of Nebraska Press, 1970), 28.

10. Stephen Orgel, "Shakespeare Imagines a Theatre," in *Shakespeare: Man of the Theater* (Newark: University of Delaware Press, 1983), 34.

11. Thomas Speght, ed., *The Works of our Antient and Lerned English Poet*, introduction by Sir Francis Beaumont (London, 1598), no. sig. Shakespeare may have seen the *Knight's Tale* as a comedy in that he used it as his main source for *Midsummer Night's Dream*. Aristotle in his *Poetics* (8.7–8) says that the *Odyssey* is a kind of tragedy that has a double-plot thread, provides differing endings for the good and the bad, and ends more like a comedy. For analysis, see Lane Cooper, *Aristotelian Theory of Comedy* (Oxford: Basil Blackwell, 1924), 61, 132, 201. Servius also points to tragic and comic elements in the *Aeneid*.

12. Jonson endeavors to treat the ruler and court in *Cynthia's Revels* and *The Poetaster*, but more in relation to cultural politics than the themes Shakespeare approaches that are analyzed in this volume. J. Dennis Huston, in *Shakespeare's Comedies of Play* (New York: Columbia University Press, 1981), 61, argues that Petruchio is a typical Old Comedy character because of his rough talk, but I think that *Shrew* comes closer to Old Comedy in the political critique of its final lines (see later discussion).

13. For discussions of what Shakespeare does to New Comedy in his early plays, see Robert S. Miola, "The Influence on New Comedy of *The Comedy of Errors* and *The Taming of the Shrew*," in *Shakespeare's Sweet Thunder*, ed. Michael J. Collins, 20–34 (Newark: University of Delaware Press, 1997); see also Miola, *Shakespeare and Classical Comedy*; Niall Rudd, "Shakespeare and Plautus: Two Twin Comedies," in *The Classical Tradition in Operation* (Toronto: University of Toronto Press, 1994), 32–60; Shaw, "The Conscious Art of *The Comedy of Errors*," 17–28.

14. Leah S. Marcus, *Puzzling Shakespeare: Local Reading and Its Discontents* (Berkeley: University of California Press, 1988), 187–88.

15. I assume that the duke in Shakespearean comedy is the dux in the Latin meaning of the word in the *Amphitruo*. The biblical Ephesus, which gives much of its imagery to the play, did not have a duke in the British sense. That city has a town clerk and proconsuls but no duke (Acts 19). Vienna (*Measure for Measure*) had no duke but an archduke. Shakespeare's dukes are not *under* royal authority. They *are* royal authority, from Solinus to Prospero. For an examination of the dux figure in Jacobean drama that associates it with Jacobean absolutism, see Leonard Tennenhouse, "Representing Power: *Measure for Measure* in its Time," *Genre* 15 (1982): 139–56. Anthony Gash notes the same three-stage movement in *Measure for Measure* in the duke's movement from Duke to Friar to Duke; see Anthony Gash, "Shakespeare, Carnival and the Sacred, *The Winter's Tale* and *Measure for Measure*," in *Shakespeare and Carnival, After Bakhtin*, ed. Ronald Knowles (New York: Macmillan, 1998), 205.

16. Standard Renaissance commentaries on classical poets do not ordinarily make classical poems into poems reenacting the biblical or soteriological narrative, and this is also true of Fairfax on Tasso or Harington on Ariosto. On the other hand, commentaries on the *Gesta Romanorum*, which Shakespeare uses, do contain such explanations, as do some comments on Ovid, such as Bersuire's and the *Ovide Moralisée*. We have no evidence that Shakespeare used works other than the *Gesta* in this mode.

17. In *The King's Two Bodies: A Study in Mediaeval Political Theology* (Princeton NJ: Princeton University Press, 1957), Ernst H. Kantorowicz demonstrates the origins of the idea of the king's two bodies in medieval legal traditions and legal theology. He also shows (pp. 24–41) how this concept operates in Shakespeare's *Richard II* as Richard explores his corporate and individual bodies and their relationship. A useful locus from Shakespeare's period that he cites is Plowden's *Reports*, where Plowden writes:

> For the King has in him two Bodies, *viz.*, a Body natural, and a Body politic. His Body natural (if it be considered in itself) is a Body mortal, subject to all Infirmities that come by Nature or Accident, to the Imbecility of Infancy or old Age, and to the like Defects that happen to the natural Bodies of other People. But his Body politic is a Body that cannot be seen or handled, consisting of Policy and Government, and constituted for the Direction of the People, and the Management of the public weal, and this Body is utterly void of Infancy, and old Age, [...] So that [the King] has a Body natural, adorned and invested with the Estate and Dignity royal; and he has not a Body natural distinct and divided by itself from the Office and Dignity royal, but a Body natural and a Body politic together indivisible.

Quotation from Edmund Plowden, *Commentaries or Reports* (London: printed by S. Brooke, 1816), 212a–20a. In Elizabethan and Jacobean political theology as well as its predecessors, the body natural of the king or dux is like the human body of Christ, mortal and limited; the body politic is like Christ-as-God, immortal and permanent. See Marcus, *Puzzling Shakespeare*, 53. This theology is also implicit in Chaucer; see Paul A. Olson, *The Canterbury Tales and the Good Society* (Princeton NJ: Princeton University Press, 1986), 68–69.

18. Kantorowicz, *King's Two Bodies*, passim; see also Olson, *Canterbury Tales and the Good Society*, 19–46.

19. Neil Rhodes, Jennifer Richards, and Joseph Marshall, eds., *King James VI and I: Selected Writings* (Aldershot, Hants.: Ashgate, 2003), 378.

20. Propaganda for the Elizabethan monarchy, at least during the early part of the reign, tended to emphasize the monarch's justice. For example, the 1558–59

public procession of the queen through London lists as two of the causes of a flourishing commonwealth "Vertue rewarded" and "Vice chastened." John Nichols, *The Progresses and Public Processions of Queen Elizabeth. Among which are Interspersed Other Solemnities, Public Expenditures, and Remarkable Events*, 3 vols. (London: printed by J. Nichols, 1823), 1:51; see Frances Yates, *Astraea: The Imperial Theme in the Sixteenth Century* (London: Routledge and Kegan Paul, 1975).

21. B. J. Sokol and Mary Sokol, *Shakespeare, Law, and Marriage* (Cambridge: Cambridge University Press, 2003), 30–41, and passim. There appears to have been some movement toward expecting freer choice in marriage matters and a movement away from pure family coercion in the actual practice of marriage in Shakespeare's time, and Shakespeare seems to endorse that movement. See Suzanne Gossett, "'I'll Look to Like': Arranged Marriages in Shakespeare's Plays," in *Sexuality and Politics in Renaissance Drama*, ed. Carole Levin and Karen Robertson (Lewiston NY: Mellen, 1991), 57–74. For another view, see Lawrence Stone, *The Family, Sex, and Marriage in England: 1500–1800* (New York: Harper and Row, 1979), 128. Clearly marriage practice often violated the laws providing for free choice in marriage; Frances Coke at fourteen was tied to the bedposts and whipped into consenting to her marriage. See Antonia Fraser, *The Weaker Vessel: Women in 17th Century England* (New York: Knopf, 1984), 12–16. To create the comic conclusion, Shakespeare generally, though not always, creates a compromise between societal need and individual love in constructing his betrothal or marriage conclusions.

22. I am told, although I have not read it, that Richard Strier has a fine paper about this move and sees Falstaff as a pivotal figure in Shakespeare's development of the rhetoric of mercy.

23. E. Gordon Rupp and Philip S. Watson, trans., *Luther and Erasmus: Free Will and Salvation* (London: SCM Press, 1969), 200ff. For Shakespeare's interest in the notion of the king as *deus absconditus* in the case of *Richard II*, see Kantorowicz, *King's Two Bodies*, 24–41.

24. England had, of course, long had a spy system abroad and a constabulary at home, but James also regarded himself as a "detective" of sorts, both in the case of the Guy Fawkes episode and in the cases of several other mysteries. See D. Harris Willson, *King James VI and I* (London: Jonathan Cape, 1956), 225–26, 309–11.

25. Michel Foucault, *Discipline and Punish: The Birth of the Prison*, trans. Alan Sheridan (New York: Vintage, 1995); Paul A. Olson, *The Kingdom of Science: Literary Utopianism and British Education, 1612–1870* (Lincoln: University of Nebraska Press, 2002).

26. Olson, *Kingdom of Science*, 17–40.

27. See Kantorowicz, *King's Two Bodies*, 38, for Shakespeare's use of the *deus absconditus* concept in relation to Richard II's kingship.

28. See Douglas Bruster, "Comedy and Control: Shakespeare and the Plautine Poeta," *Comparative Drama* 24 (1990): 217–31. I am indebted to Bruster throughout this book when I write of the *poeta*; he first introduced me to the concept when he was my student and set me thinking about it.

29. For play as creating and also reflecting the logic of authority systems, see Brian Sutton-Smith, *The Ambiguity of Play* (Cambridge MA: Harvard University Press, 1997), 52–110. Gash ("Shakespeare, Carnival, and the Sacred," 205) notes that it is difficult to tell in act 5 of *Measure for Measure* what speeches Vincentio has scripted. He apparently has scripted almost all of them by the accusers and their order also. Lovewit in *The Alchemist* acts in a role analogous to that of the dux in Shakespeare's comedies.

30. See chapter 4 for discussion of paintings by Fra Filippo Lippi and Benozzo Gozzoli.

31. Olson, *Canterbury Tales and the Good Society*, plates 1–3.

32. Wolfgang Riehle, *Shakespeare, Plautus, and the Humanist Tradition* (Cambridge: D. S. Brewer, 1990), 44–76.

33. Aelius Donatus, *Commentvm Terenti*, ed. Paul Wessner, 3 vols. (Leipzig: Teubner, 1902–1908); see Miola, *Shakespeare and Classical Comedy*. A partial English translation of Donatus on Terence is that by Michael J. Hilger, "The Rhetoric of Comedy: Comic Theory in the Terential Commentary of Aelius Donatus," PhD diss., University of Nebraska, 1970.

34. On the masks, see Duckworth, *Nature of Roman Comedy*, 88–94. See David Wiles, *The Masks of Menander: Signs and Meaning in Greek and Roman Performance* (Cambridge: Cambridge University Press, 1991).

35. Francis Meres, *Palladis Tamia: Wits Treasury* (London: P. Short, printer, 1598), sig. Oo2[ʳ].

36. Robert Parker Sorlien, ed., *The Diary of John Manningham of the Middle Temple, 1602–1603* (Hanover NH: University Press of New England, 1976), 48.

37. *Troilus and Cressida* "deserues such a labour, as well as the best Commedy in *Terence* or *Plautus*," according to a leaf in the second state of Q. Kenneth Palmer, ed., *Troilus and Cressida* (London: Methuen, 1982), 95.

38. These "types" do not appear to modern criticism to be as conventionalized as they are commonly represented to be in Renaissance criticism. See Duckworth, *Nature of Roman Comedy*, 236–71; Miola, *Shakespeare and Classical Comedy*.

39. For numerous Early Modern school versions of the six and seven ages of humankind, see T. W. Baldwin, *Shakespeare's Small Latine and Lesse Greeke* (Urbana: University of Illinois Press, 1944), 641–81. None of the other versions of the six or seven ages that I have seen arranges life as if it were a New Comedy or commedia dell'arte action.

40. The fact that the name and figure of Adam are the sources of Jaques's talk about the seven ages and the progress toward senescence is significant because Adam is, biblically, the beginning of death; yet in this play he is the source of continuing life for Orlando when he sacrifices his safety for Orlando's by warning him of the plots against him.

41. The figure of Lydus, who is a servant/tutor in Plautus's *Bacchides*, is called a *paedagogus* in the dramatis personae, but this kind of figure is much more prominent as the pedant in commedia dell'arte.

42. See Duckworth, *Nature of Roman Comedy*, 261.

43. Shakespeare knew the commedia dell'arte version of the pantaloon as he mentions in one list of roles for the play that *Taming of the Shrew*'s Gremio, its primary *senex* character, is a pantaloon (TS 1.1.45–50). He also knew of the zany and several other characters from the Italianate improvisational drama, but it is often difficult to determine whether his stock character titles come from New Comedy or commedia dell'arte.

44. Jaques has earlier in the same scene (*AYLI* 2.7) claimed for himself the privileges of satire in New Comedy terms—that is, that his impersonal invective harms no one unless the shoe fits. This defense of the satiric element in comedy is commonplace and appears in Lodge's *Reply to Stephen Gosson's Schoole of Abuse in Defence of Poetry Musick and Stage Plays*, which offers most of the clichés of comic theory from the period:

> Tully defines them thus. *Comedia* (sayth he) is *Imitatio vitæ, speculum consuetudinis, et imago veritatis*, and it is sayde to be termed of *Comai* (emongste the Greekes) whiche signifieth *Pagos*, & *Ode, Cantus* . . . whereupon *Eupolis* with *Cartinus*, & *Aristophanes*, began to write, and with ther eloquenter vaine and perfection of stil, dyd more seuerely speak agaynst the abuses then they: which *Horace* himselfe witnesseth. For sayth he ther was no abuse but these men reprehended it. a thefe was loth to be seene one there spectacle. a coward was neuer present at theyr assemblies. a backbiter abhord that company, and I myself could not haue blamed your (Gosson) for exempting yourselfe from this theater, of troth I should haue lykt your pollicy. These therefore, these wer they that kept men in awe, these restrayned the vnbridled cominaltie, whereupon *Horace* wisely sayeth,
>
> *Oderunt peccare boni, virtutis amore,*
> *Oderunt peccare mali, formidine penae.*
> The good did hate al sinne for vertues loue
> The bad for feare of shame did sin remoue. . . .
>
> But as these sharpe corrections were disanulde in Rome when they grewe to more licenciousnes: So I fear me if we shold practise it in

our dayes, the same intertainmente would followe. But in ill reformed Rome what comedies now? a poets wit can correct, yet not offend.

Arthur Freeman, ed., *The Schoole of Abuse by Stephen Gosson. A Reply to Gosson's Schoole of Abuse by Thomas Lodge* (New York: Garland, 1973), sig. [C2ᵛ]–[C3ᵛ]. Hamlet uses a similar justification for what he calls the comedy of *The Mouse-trap*. See chapter 4 of the present work for a discussion of Hamlet's aesthetic theory.

45. Miola, *Shakespeare and Classical Comedy*, 30.
46. For some comments on commedia dell'arte as having a close relationship to New Comedy, see Ninian Mellamphy, "Pantaloons and Zanies: Shakespeare's 'Apprenticeship' to Italian Professional Comedy Troupes," *New York Literary Forum* 5–6 (1980): 98–116. Mellamphy argues that the commedia tradition borrowed heavily from the erudite comedy of the age, which was rooted in New Comedy. For Shakespeare's indebtedness to the commedia dell'arte, see Andrew Grewar, "The Old Man's Spectacles and Other Traces of the Commedia dell'arte in Early Shakespearean Comedy," in *Scenery, Set and Staging in the Italian Renaissance: Studies in the Practice of Theatre* (Lewiston NY: Edwin Mellen, 1996), 289–317; Andrew Grewar, "Shakespeare and the Actors of the Commedia dell'arte," in *Studies in the Commedia Dell'Arte*, ed. Christopher Cairns, 13–47 (Cardiff: University of Wales Press, 1993). See also Wiles, *Masks of Menander*, 140–44. Several studies have seen the presence of the commedia dell'arte in such works as *The Tempest* and *Othello*, and it seems to me likely that Iago's improvisation of power, famously described by Stephen Greenblatt, using the stock narratives of the culture to destroy its leader, is at least partially derived from the improvisational impulse of the commedia dell'arte. See Stephen Greenblatt, *Renaissance Self-Fashioning* (Chicago: University of Chicago Press, 1980), 222–54.
47. Grewar, "Old Man's Spectacles," 307–8.
48. The prostitute of New Comedy becomes the wayward wife of the medieval comedies and her husband becomes jealous, an evolution of New Comedy styles in the Middle Ages that the commedia dell'arte retains. See Olson, *Canterbury Tales and the Good Society*, 71–72.
49. For a helpful catalogue of commedia dell'arte types see Andrew Grewar, "The Clowning Zanies: Shakespeare and the Actors of the Commedia dell'arte," *Shakespeare in South Africa* 3 (1989): 9–32, esp. 10–13.
50. Commedia dell'arte and *commedia erudita* influenced each other in complex ways, and Shakespeare gives us the fusion.
51. Shakespeare may have learned this technique from Terence; A. J. Brothers in his edition and translation of *The Eunuch of Terence* (Warminster: Aris & Phillips, 2000), 27–36. See Ann R. Raia, "Women's Roles in Plautine Comedy," a paper delivered at the Fourth Conference on Greek, Roman,

and Byzantine Studies (October 1, 1983), to be found on the Web at http://
www.vroma.org/~araia/plautinewomen.html. See D. Gilula, "The Concept
of the Bona Meretrix: A Study of Terence's Courtesans," *Rivista di Filologia
e di Istruzione Classica* 108 (1980), 142–65. For Van den Berg, see Jan Hen-
drik van den Berg, *The Changing Nature of Man: Introduction to a Historical
Psychology: Metabletica*, trans. H. F. Croes (New York: Norton, 1961).

52. The trick of pretending to be a eunuch for wooing purposes is present in
Terence's *Eunuch*; see John Sergeaunt, ed., *Terence* (London: William Heine-
man, 1959), 231–51. All citations and quotations are from this edition.

53. For the braggart soldier, see Duckworth, *Nature of Roman Comedy*, 264–65,
415–16; for the parasite, 265–67 and 416.

54. The same sort of inversion of the expectations attached to the stock characters appears regularly in Plautine comedy. See Wiles, *Masks of Menander*,
136–37.

55. Plautus citations from Titus Maccius Plautus, *Works*, ed. Paul Nixon, 5 vols.
(London: William Heinemann, 1916–38); Terence quotations are from the
Sergeaunt edition already cited in note 51. For medieval masks in drama
and late medieval–Early Modern understandings of classical drama and its
relationship to the masked aspects of medieval and early Tudor drama, see
Meg Twycross and Sarah Carpenter, *Masks and Masking in Medieval and
Early Tudor England* (Aldershot, Hants.: Ashgate, 2002), 280–310.

56. Franciscus Robertellus, "On Comedy," in *Comic Theory in the Sixteenth Century*, trans. and ed. Marvin T. Herrick, 238 (Urbana: University of Illinois
Press, 1964).

57. See several important articles on the character of the prostitute in New
Comedy, all of which provide important points for consideration, specifically:
E. Fantham, "Sex, Status, and Survival in Hellenistic Athens: A Study of
Women in New Comedy," *Phoenix* 29 (1975): 44–74; D. Wiles, "Marriage
and Prostitution in Classical New Comedy," *Themes in Drama* 11 (1989):
31–48; and P. G. McC. Brown, "Plots and Prostitutes in Greek New Comedy," *Papers of the Leeds International Latin Seminar* 6 (1990): 241–66.

58. Duckworth, *Nature of Roman Comedy*, 253–54.

59. Duckworth, *Nature of Roman Comedy*, 258–61.

60. Shapiro, *Year in the Life*, 204–11.

61. I derive the basis for this point from the late Gerald Eades Bentley. For
Bentley on the boy actors, see Gerald Eades Bentley, *Shakespeare and His
Theatre* (Lincoln: University of Nebraska Press, 1964), 37–39.

62. Northrop Frye, *The Anatomy of Criticism: Four Essays* (Princeton NJ: Princeton
University Press, 1957), 163–86. In classical and Early Modern theory, a
comedy had to end with a discovery. Marvin T. Herrick, ed., *Comic Theory in
the Sixteenth Century* (Urbana: University of Illinois Press, 1964), 123–25.

63. William S. Anderson, *Barbarian Play: Plautus' Roman Comedy* (Toronto: University of Toronto Press, 1993), 65–87.

64. I do not agree with Greenblatt that Shakespeare's presentation of the marriage prospect is endlessly forlorn; Greenblatt often tends, in my view, to view premarital *remedia amoris* flirtatious banter as somehow seriously predictive of what the marriage will be like. See Stephen Greenblatt, *Will in the World: How Shakespeare Became Shakespeare* (New York: W. W. Norton, 2004), 118–49.

65. Philippe Ariès, *Centuries of Childhood* (Harmondsworth, UK: Penguin, 1979); Roger Chartier, ed., *A History of Private Life: Passions of the Renaissance* (Harvard: Belknap Press, 1993), 3:397–607; Stone, *Family, Sex, and Marriage in England*, 102–5, 180–81, and passim. Stone tends to emphasize the exceptional nature of Shakespearean love and marriage more than seems suitable. Protestant exegetes regarded the Song of Songs as recording a married love. See Sokol and Sokol, *Shakespeare, Law, and Marriage.*

66. For some of the various kinds of aristocratic families in late medieval England, see Richard Eales, ed., *Family and Dynasty in Late Medieval England, Harlaxton Medieval Studies* 9 (1997). Dynastic marriage was obviously a major foreign policy tool of both the Tudors and Stuarts.

67. Robert Burton, *The Anatomy of Melancholy*, ed. Floyd Dell and Paul Jordan-Smith (New York: Tudor, 1927), 798ff.

68. See John Witte Jr., "The Perils of Celibacy: Clerical Marriage and the Protestant Reformation," Kessler Reformation Lecture, Candler School of Theology, Emory University, October 22, 2002, reproduced at http://www.law .emory.edu/cisr/documents/jwitte02.pdf.

69. Saturn, as the planet of melancholy, "symbolized the 'Mind' of the world where Jupiter merely symbolized its 'Soul'; he had thought out what Jupiter had merely 'learned' in order to govern; he stood, in short, for profound contemplation as opposed to mere practical action." Erwin Panofsky, *The Life and Art of Albrecht Dürer* (Princeton NJ: Princeton University Press, 1955), 16ff. esp. 167. See Olson, *Canterbury Tales and the Good Society*, 83–84. For Saturn's symbolism, see Alan Gaylord, "The Role of Saturn in the Knight's Tale," *Chaucer Review* 8 (1973–74): 171–90.

70. D. J. Gordon, in *"Hymenaei*: Ben Jonson's Masque of Union," *Journal of the Warburg and Courtauld Institute* 8 (1945): 107–45, gives a rich sample of meanings; see Enid Welsford, *The Court Masque* (New York: Russell and Russell, 1962), 70–71, 106–8, 178–80, 195, for other samples.

71. Kantorowicz, *King's Two Bodies*, 212. See Queen Elizabeth's remark in note 77 to this chapter.

72. On bishops, see Kantorowicz, *King's Two Bodies*, 212.

73. *The 1599 Geneva Bible*, [Ee7ᵛ].

74. Sears Jayne, "Marsilio Ficino's Commentary on Plato's Symposium," *University of Missouri Studies* 19 (1944): 121–247, esp. 141ff., 144, 178ff., 181, 187, 191, 193, 195, 226.

75. *Ludovico Ariosto's Orlando Furioso*, trans. Sir John Harington (Oxford: Clarendon Press, 1972), 564, makes four women stand for four kinds of love: Angelica for proud love, Doralyce for lightness of manners and behavior, Olympia for chaste love hardly requited, and Bradamante for the "perfect patterne of true honourable love," respectful of the beloved, constant, without avarice, and fulfilling a prophesied pattern. These levels somewhat resemble those in *As You Like It*.

76. Olson, *Canterbury Tales and the Good Society*, 258–60.

77. For a comparison of the letter of the two narratives, see Carolyn E. Brown, "Katherine of *The Taming of the Shrew*: 'A Second Grissel,'" *Texas Studies in Literature and Language* 37 (1995): 285ff. Two essays suggesting that Petruchio acts more as ruler and educator than as tyrant are Dennis S. Brooks, "'To show scorn her own image': The Varieties of Education in the *Taming of the Shrew*," *Rocky Mountain Review* 48 (1994): 7–32; and Dale G. Priest, "Katherina's Conversion in *The Taming of the Shrew*: A Theological Heuristic," *Renascence* 47 (1994), 31–40. For a reversal, Elizabeth's use of the metaphor that made her as one married to her realm, and her use of the figure of wifely submission for herself, see Leah Marcus, *Puzzling Shakespeare: Local Reading and Its Discontents* (Berkeley: University of California Press, 1988), 59. Einer J. Jensen has argued vigorously against the privileging of the conclusion and closure in Shakespearean comedy in recent criticism, and generally he makes a good point, but often the marriage/betrothal conclusions explicate a symbolism latent in the earlier parts of the plot but not fully apprehensible until stipulated. See Einer J. Jensen, *Shakespeare and the Ends of Comedy* (Bloomington: Indiana University Press, 1991).

78. For the whole ring ceremony, see *The Boke of Common Praier, and [Ad]ministracion of the Sacramentes . . .* (London: Richard Grafton, printer, 1552), sig. [Qvii^v]–[Qviii^r].

79. Shapiro, *Year in the Life*, 224–26.

80. For the magician and presenter, see John G. Demaray, *Shakespeare and the Spectacles of Strangeness: The Tempest and the Transformation of Renaissance Theatrical Forms* (Pittsburgh: Duquesne University Press, 1998). Rosalind anticipates Prospero as magician/presenter.

81. See the "Resources for Placing the Comedies in an Early Modern Frame" at the end of this volume for complete publication details for the works mentioned in each chapter's resources section.

82. Thomas Heywood, *An Apology for Actors* (1612), introduction and annotation by Richard Perkinson (New York: Scholars' Facsimiles, 1941).

83. Louis B. Wright, "Will Kemp and Commedia dell'Arte," *MLN* 41 (1926): 516–20.
84. Giacomo Oreglia, *The Commedia dell'Arte* (New York: Hill and Wang, 1968).
85. Pierre Louis Duchartre, *The Italian Comedy*, trans. Randolph T. Weaver (New York: Dover, 1966).
86. K. M. Lea, *Italian Popular Comedy*, 2 vols. (Oxford: Clarendon Press, 1934). See especially the section on Italian comedy in England, 2:339–455.
87. Leo Salingar, *Shakespeare and the Tradition of Comedy* (Cambridge: Cambridge University Press, 1974); Louise George Clubb, *Italian Drama in Shakespeare's Time* (New Haven: Yale University Press, 1989), see especially 49–64 and 249–80.

3. Shakespearean Comedic Myths

1. James Shapiro, *A Year in the Life of William Shakespeare: 1599* (New York: HarperCollins, 2005), 62.
2. The myths in the comedies become, as Early Modern followers of Plato would have them be, the repositories of the paradigms of truth. They pattern out societal destruction and reconstruction. The building of myth into comedy is not unknown in ancient writing, for Aristophanes inverts the mythic journey into Hades for his *Frogs*, and Plautus tells of Jupiter's bed trick with Alcmena that leads to the birth of Hercules in his *Amphitruo*, the only mythological New Comedy that remains. In early Roman literature—that is, New Comedy—the mode comes without the effects of the massive turning of myth into apparent symbol and allegory that begins with the later Platonists. When they defend Homer against Plato's charge that he was a liar, they make him an allegorist and so begin the project of coming to a figurative understanding of myth. This work continues with the allegorical and ethical ordering of the Roman myths in the fourth-century work of Servius and in the later Christian mythographers. See Robert Lamberton, *Homer as Theologian: Neoplatonist Allegorical Reading and the Growth of Epic Tradition* (Berkeley: University of California Press, 1990); Paul A. Olson, *The Journey to Wisdom: Self-Education in Patristic and Medieval Literature* (Lincoln: University of Nebraska Press, 1995). For *Amphitruo* as the only extant Roman comedy to retell a myth, see George E. Duckworth, *The Nature of Roman Comedy* (Princeton NJ: Princeton University Press, 1952), 24, including the play's possible relation to Middle Comedy.
3. C. L. Barber, *Shakespeare's Festive Comedy* (Princeton NJ: Princeton University Press, 1959), 122.
4. This means that we ought to approach his use of myth looking for philosophical fables and moral and natural allegories and that the solvents of myth

include the genealogy of the mythic being, the etymology of his or her name as understood in the false etymologies of Shakespeare's times, the analogies to other myths and their explanations, and the like. Learning to read myth as Renaissance writers and painters learned to read it is like learning a language. The indebtedness of this chapter to the work of Jean Seznec, Erwin Panofsky, Edgar Wind, Rosamund Tuve, and my former student David Brumble should be obvious at every turn. In addition to the English versions of Ovid and the Renaissance Latin editions of Ovid that contained allegorical commentaries, see also the allegorical commentaries written by Johannes Spreng, which much influenced Renaissance art, at http://etext.lib.virginia.edu/latin/ovid/ovid1563.html, where Spreng's Latin allegorizations are reproduced in both English and Latin. The most common sources of mythic understanding are the Latin mythographies by Natalis Conti, Cinthio Giraldi, and Vincenzo Cartari. See Natalis Conti, *Mythologiae: Sive explicationis fabularum libri decem* (Geneva: Gabriel Carteri, printer, 1596); Vincenzo Cartari, *Seconda novissima editione delle imagini de gli dei delli antichi* (Padua: Pietro Paolo Tozzi, printer, 1626); Lilio Gregorio Giraldi, *De deis gentilium libri: Sive syntagmata XVII* (Lyon: Jacobi Junctae, printer OKPAO, 1565). The most useful English mythography written in Shakespeare's time is Abraham Fraunce, *The Countesse of Pembrokes Yvychurch* (London: Thomas Orwyn, printer, 1591); a useful mythography written slightly after Shakespeare but reflecting Latin traditions is Alexander Ross, *Mystagogus Poeticus, or The Muses Interpreter* (New York: Garland, 1976). Many of the emblem books such as by Alciati and Ripa are also figurative treatments of the stories of the classical gods.

5. Lewis Soens, ed., *Sir Philip Sidney's Defense of Poesy* (Lincoln: University of Nebraska Press, 1970), 14ff.

6. For Golding, see *Shakespeare's Ovid: Being Arthur Golding's Translation of the Metamorphoses*, ed. W. H. D. Rouse (London: Centaur Press, 1961), 3–4.

7. The idea of pattern or architectonic is central in Sidney; see Soens, *Sir Philip Sidney's Defense of Poesy*, 14–24.

8. Erwin Panofsky, *Studies in Iconology: Humanistic Themes in the Art of the Renaissance* (New York: Harper and Row, 1962), 95–128.

9. Shapiro, *Year in the Life*, 28–29, argues that an *impresa* is highly personal in its significance, unlike an emblem, which carries a general moral meaning. However, when a character in a play carries an impresa, it is bound up with the action and explicates and is explicated by it, as is an emblem. An impresa in a play, however, is also attached to a particular fictional person.

10. The families of meanings of the word *device* may be studied in the *Oxford English Dictionary*, second edition; particularly examine the overlapping meanings of usage 6 and usage 9 in this edition in relation to Renaissance theory of emblems.

11. Medea's Hecate is related to Titania; see note 13 to this chapter.

12. Fable was generally regarded as neither true seeming nor true on the surface but a vehicle communicating a truth; for example, Sandys writes concerning what he is doing with Ovid's fables:

> Since it should be the principall end in publishing of Bookes, to in-forme the vnderstanding, direct the will, and temper the affections; in this second Edition of my Translation, I haue attempted (with what successe I submit to the Reader) to collect out of sundrie Authors the Philosophicall sense of these fables of *Ouid*, if I may call them his, when most of them are more antient then any extant Author, or perhaps then Letters themselues; before which, as they expressed their Conceptions in Hieroglyphickes, so did they their Philosophic and Diuinitie vnder Fables and Parables: a way not vn-trod by the sacred Pen-men.

George Sandys, trans., *Ovid's Metamorphosis: Englished, Mythologized, and Represented in Figures*, ed. Karl K. Hulley and Stanley T. Vandersall (Lincoln: University of Nebraska Press, 1970), 8.

13. G[eorge] S[andys], *Ovid's Metamorphoses* (London: J. L., printer, 1640), sig. B [1]ʳ.

14. Minor White Latham, *The Elizabethan Fairies* (New York: Columbia University Press, 1930), 44–49. T. P. Roche and Isabel Rathborne have characterized Spenser's fairyland as a land of classical heroes and gods who are allegories and types.

15. See my article, "*A Midsummer Night's Dream* and the Meaning of Court Marriage," *English Literary History* 24 (1957): 97–98.

16. Soens, *Sir Philip Sidney's Defense of Poesy*, 10. Sidney speaks of "such a Cyrus as will make many Cyruses." The idea of the Shakespearean stage as the interior theater of imagination invites us to see the concrete image as convey-ing the pattern of an abstraction if we think of imagination in Renaissance terms. See A. B. Kernan, "This Goodly Frame, the Stage: The Interior Theater of Imagination in English Renaissance Drama," *Shakespeare Quarterly* 25 (1974): 1–5. The possibility that the players made emblems of themselves and their costumes as they acted, as Fluellen does comically when he describes the emblem of Fortune, should not be dismissed. John Dixon Hunt, "*Pictura, Scriptura*, and *Theatrum*: Shakespeare and the Emblem," *Poetics Today* 10 (1989): 155–71, usefully explores the tensions between the visual emblem and the text in Shakespeare, but his notion of the emblem as static is overly simple in that the emblems are frequently classical stories, and their texts frequently retell these.

17. The paradox of a licentious goddess of chastity may be solved if we look at

the Diana in one of Shakespeare's main intertexts, *The Knight's Tale*. There Emelye's prayer addresses her as goddess of heaven and earth, and "Queene of the regne of Pluto derk and lowe" (A, 2299) or Proserpina/Lucina/Hecate. In the Renaissance, as in the fourteenth century, Diana presented three aspects: "in heaven she is called Luna, in the woods Diana, under the earth Hecate, or Proserpina." Emelye's prayer emphasizes the Proserpina aspects of the goddess, and in Shakespeare's time, Thynne described her sacrifice as addressed to Diana/Hecate. Shakespeare, using his Chaucerian sources freely, developed his woodland goddess from such a figure. For an Early Modern mythographic recreation of Diana/Proserpina/Hecate's meaning, see Ross, *Mystagogus Poeticus*, 97–98.

18. Titania's attendants, Peaseblossom and Mustardseed, come as earthy plants to wait upon her court, and like Lyly's Tellus, she surrounds herself with floral images. Her title of queen in the fairy world is taken over in *Romeo and Juliet* by Mercutio's Mab, whose aphrodisiac powers are well known; and near her bower, Philomela sings her melody of love gone wrong, as if transported from *Titus Andronicus*. Here the wise owl hoots at "quaint" spirits (*MND* 2.2.1–26) as Titania apparently plays with the changeling boy and later with Bottom.

In the play, the moon appears in its last phase through most of the action, and so it is appropriate that Diana/Hecate should rule that action. Lyly creates a Luna in *The Woman in the Moone* who is both queen of the woods and wife of Pluto (5, 1, Q81–84); and Campion has an air, "Harke, al you ladies that do sleep," sometimes cited as a source or analogue of *A Midsummer Night's Dream*, that sings of a "fayry queen," Proserpina, who, like Titania, dwells in an arbor, leads dancing by moonlight, and sends abroad her servants to satisfy her capricious desires. Campion's song notes that "The Fairie Queene Proserpina / Bids you encrease that loving humour more" (11.30–31). Similarly, Drayton's *Nimphidia* tells us that Oberon's wife is a Queen Mab aided by her ally and ancient friend (1.574), Proserpina. A Renaissance audience who knew their classics would have caught this idea when they saw Titania appearing among the flowers or altering the seasonal cycle. Puck's assertion that the fairies run "By the triple *Hecate*'s team" (*MND* 5.2.14) and the fact that the snake leaves his "enamelled skin" (*MND* 2.1.255) near her bower may have further signaled her relationship with the Roman goddess. Since the latter had power over the coming and going of the seasons, she represented the potency both of seeds and of the lower passions. Chaucer's *Merchant's Tale* gives this figure the wit to defend the young woman, May, while the latter engages in a very comic cuckolding of an old man (E, 2316ff.).

19. Sandys, *Ovid's Metamorphosis*, 653–54. I remove the heavy use of italics from Sandys's text to improve readability. Sir John Harington in his interpretation

of Ariosto's *Orlando Furioso* says, "men given over to sensualitie, leese . . .
the verie forme of man (which is reason) and so become beastes"; *Orlando
Furioso in English Heroical Verse*, trans. John Harington (London: Richard
Field, printer, 1591), 47; hereafter cited as Harington. Bottom becomes a
literal beast before he becomes a metaphoric one. His ass's ears have been
related to his sensual relation with Titania, but they probably also refer to his
ignorance and insensitivity. Harington speaks of his (or Ariosto's) monster
of covetousness as having ass ears because he represents ignorance and indifference to others' opinions. For a more moralistic version of the same motif,
see Acracia's Bower of Bliss in book 2 of *The Faerie Queene*, stanzas 50–87,
in Edmund Spenser, *The Faerie Queene*, ed. Thomas P. Roche (New Haven:
Yale University Press, 1978).

20. For a good discussion of the complexity of the ass motif, see Deborah Baker
Wyrick, "The Ass Motif in *The Comedy of Errors* and *A Midsummer Night's
Dream*," *Shakespeare Quarterly* 33 (1982): 443–48.

21. Sandys, *Ovid's Metamorphosis*, 653–54.

22. *Henry VI*, part 1 (5.4.5–6), includes a reference to Joan of Arc as if she were
a transformative witch. See Judith Yarnall, *Transformations of Circe: The History of an Enchantress* (Urbana: University of Illinois Press, 1994), especially
chapters 3–7. Harington's Alcina turns her lovers into trees and she is said
to be the witch of sensuality whose enchantments are dissolved by reason.
Harington, *Orlando Furioso in English Heroical Verse*, 55.

23. See Michelangelo's temptation painting at http://artchive.com/artchive/m/
michelangelo/tempt.jpg.html.

24. Puck as Cupid resembles Atlas-as-Cupid (or Atlanta) as Harington sees
him (i.e., that "fond fancie we call love"). Harington compares Atlas's place
of dwelling to Dante's or Petrarch's dark woods, perhaps suggesting why
Puck reigns in these labyrinthine woods. See Harington, *Orlando Furioso in
English Heroical Verse*, 30.

25. All Chaucer quotations and citations are from Larry D. Benson, ed., *The
Riverside Chaucer* (Boston: Houghton Mifflin, 1987).

26. In *Orlando Furioso*, Astolfo dissolves Atlas's enchantments with his book, or
wisdom in Harington's view, and his horn or eloquence. Harington, *Orlando
Furioso in English Heroical Verse*, 174–75; compare pages 30 and 406. In my
"*A Midsummer Night's Dream* and the Meaning of Court Marriage," I argued
that the woods in *A Midsummer Night's Dream* resemble Spenser's Wood
of Error, Dante's dark woods, and so forth; this was largely overwhelmed
later in Frye's theory of Shakespeare's comic green world. For a reinstate-
ment of the Wood of Error interpretations, see Jeanne Addison Roberts,
Shakespeare's English Comedy (Lincoln: University of Nebraska Press, 1979),
121. Darryl Gless has argued that Spenser's Wood of Error is simply the

"world's manifold activities" which make "living engrossing . . . valuable and beautiful" but which can also make it "spiritually dangerous." The woods in *Midsummer Night's Dream* have some of this character in that they make solipsistic loving that is not included in larger loves "spiritually dangerous." Darryl J. Gless, *Interpretation and Theology in Spenser* (Cambridge: Cambridge University Press, 1994), 61. For Harington's role in Shakespeare's London and Elizabeth's court, see Shapiro, *Year in the Life*, 69–79 and passim.

27. Xenophon, *Memorabilia and Oeconomicus*, trans. E. C. Marchant (London: William Heinemann, 1923), 95–103.

28. Barber, *Shakespeare's Festive Comedy*, 93.

29. Jonson's masque of *Pleasure Reconcild to Vertue* presents Hercules defeating Comus and the pygmies and being crowned by Mercury for his battles for Virtue and against Comus, whereupon Atlas orders a cessation of conflict between Pleasure and Virtue, and Daedalus leads a dance that mingles Virtue and Pleasure. See C. H. Herford, Percy Simpson, and E. M. Simpson, eds., *Ben Jonson*, 11 vols. (Oxford: Clarendon Press, 1925–52), 7:479–91.

30. Otto Vaenius, *Amorum Emblemata* (Burlington VT: Ashgate, 1996), 32–33. See figure 11 in chapter 3. Vaenius's quotations that go with the emblem stress that love is the cause of heroic virtue and that the deeds of Hercules began with the arrow of love.

31. Golding, *Shakespeare's Ovid*, 3.

32. See Michael John Petry, *Herne the Hunter: A Berkshire Legend* (Reading: William Smith, 1972). For Falstaff as Actaeon, see John M. Steadman, "Falstaff as Actaeon: A Dramatic Emblem," *Shakespeare Quarterly* 14 (1963): 231–44. See also Roberts, *Shakespeare's English Comedy*, 127ff. For the possible relationship of Falstaff to Robert Greene, see Stephen Greenblatt, *Will in the World: How Shakespeare Became Shakespeare* (New York: W. W. Norton, 2004), 203–211; however, any possible Falstaffian *reference* to Greene does not, in my view, have much to do with Falstaff's *meaning* now or for audiences in Shakespeare's time

33. Sandys, *Ovid's Metamorphosis*, 150–51.

34. Sandys, *Ovid's Metamorphosis*, 58–59. Christopher St. Germane, in *A dialog in Englysshe, betwyxt a doctoure of dyunyte and student in the lawes of Englonde* (n.p.: R. Wyer, printer, 1531), fol. iiii ff., argues that community of goods is natural law only when people are placed in situations of extreme necessity. This may explain why the duke's company seems to live partially as the golden age people did.

35. The Renaissance assumption, reflected in Milton, is that not only did God speak to humankind in Eden but also the garden itself spoke emblematically of Nature, the divine, and human potential for love and virtue; see, for example, the notes for book 4, lines 689–725, in *Paradise Lost* and annotations

in *The Poems of John Milton*, ed. John Carey and Alastair Fowler (London: Longmans, 1968), 653–56. Michael Taylor, in "'As You Like It': The Penalty of Adam," *Critical Quarterly* 15 (1973): 76–80, suggests that Duke Senior windbags in this scene. However, the duke's speech clearly admits that the group at one level feels some of the penalty of Adam in that they know the seasonal differences (not all exegetes believe that they began after the Fall). They do not feel the penalty as court flattery, Cain-like fratricidal conspiracy (see chapter 4) or a meaningless life. Adversity teaches the duke as it does the central figure in Queen Elizabeth's translation of Boethius's *Consolation of Philosophy*. See the history of interpretation of these lines in *A New Variorum Edition of Shakespeare: "As You Like It*," ed. Richard Knowles (New York: Modern Language Association, 1977), 66–71. In the forest, not everyone sees the woods as banishment, perhaps because, as Rawdon Wilson remarks, Arden "leads away from property and *its* appropriate concerns to a new experience of the value of feeling"; actually *feeling* is *love* in all its forms. See Rawdon Wilson, "The Way to Arden: Attitudes toward Time in *As You Like It*," *Shakespeare Quarterly* 26 (1975): 16–24. The forest seems, in Bakhtin's terms, a carnival rest from hierarchical living and creates initially a social arena where, in something like Bakhtin's conception of the Gospels, "rulers, rich men, thieves, beggars, hetaera, etc. come together on equal terms," though hierarchy becomes obvious as the play progresses. See Anthony Gash, "Shakespeare, Carnival and the Sacred: *The Winter's Tale* and *Measure for Measure*" in *Shakespeare and Carnival: After Bakhtin*, ed. Ronald Knowles, 178 (New York: Macmillan, 1998).

36. Much of the land in the historical Forest of Arden in England (as opposed to the Ardenne in France) had been enclosed with an increasing concentration of wealth, a transfer of land from the smaller holders to the larger ones, and a great increase of landless poor or cotters. As dwellers in a "coate" or the simplest of cottages, Corin and Silvius do not own even the dwelling place and fear to have it and the sheep they take care of for their landlord sold out from under them. See Victor Skipp, "Economic and Social Change in the Forest of Arden, 1530–1649," in *Land, Church, and People*, ed. Joan Thirsk, 84–111 (Reading, UK: Museum of English Rural Life, 1970); Victor Skipp, *Crisis and Development: An Ecological Case Study of the Forest of Arden, 1570–1674* (Cambridge: Cambridge University Press, 1978). For additional information on agricultural rights and the situation in the midlands in Shakespeare's time, see Edward Berry, *Shakespeare and the Hunt* (Cambridge: Cambridge University Press, 2001), 168–70.

37. Shapiro, *Year in the Life*, 242.

38. Erwin Panofsky, *The Life and Art of Albrecht Dürer* (Princeton NJ: Princeton University Press, 1955), 156–71. Jaques as a Saturnine character represents

the kind of figure that knows time's successions (Saturn was an allegory for time) but also one that can rise above time to the One. His consciousness of time as decay contrasts with Orlando's lack of time-sense early in his stay in Arden and Rosalind's sense of time-to-the-thousandth-part-of-a-minute lover's sense. While Jaques, as a Saturnine figure, senses time but not occasion, the lovers have the sense of occasion, sometimes comically so. For a fuller account, see "'Try in Time in Despite of a Fall': Time and Occasion in *As You Like It*," *Texas Studies in Literature and Language* 24 (1982): 121–36. That Jaques's melancholy and satiric tendencies are caused by syphilis is argued by Duke Senior and by many contemporary and nineteenth-century critics. See Sander L. Gilman, *Love + Marriage = Death* (Stanford: Stanford University Press, 1998), 28–30. As far as I know, the medical literature does not preclude the syphilitic from being the contemplative. Jaques also associates the fool with the contemplative state (*AYLI* 2.7.31, 49), a comparison that may suggest Jaques is, in many ways, a double of Touchstone; see Erika Hamilton, "Two Fools in the Forest in *As You Like It*," unpublished paper in possession of the author.

39. For Jaques as satirist and the development of stage comical satire, see Shapiro, *Year in the Life*, 219–21.

40. The confrontation in the Arden forest between Orlando and the snake and the lioness, which in turn seek to destroy Oliver, is the turning point in the political action of the poem. The lion and the serpent or dragon are both present as rival carriers of the church and its enemies in Arthurian romance and in the first book of *The Faerie Queene*, but Psalms 91:13 may carry a better explanation. The Geneva version of this passage, with comment, reads:

> 91:13 Thou shalt walke vpon the lyon and aspe: the[h] yong lyon, and the dragon shalt thou tread vnder feet.
>
> h. Thou shalt not onely be preserued from all euill, but ouercome it whether it be secret or open.

John K. Hale, "Snake and Lioness in *As You Like It*, IV, iii," *Notes and Queries* 245 (2000): 79, interprets the passage as emblemizing the fight against secret fraud (the serpent) and open force (the lion) and makes the snake represent Orlando's struggle with Oliver's earlier duplicities and the lion his struggle with his own anger. Orlando has some Hercules/Cupid touches also in his extraordinary wrestling ability, resembling that of Hercules in his encounters with Antaeus, the serpent-hydra, and the lion. Rosalind greets his wrestling with "Hercules be thy speed" (*AYLI* 1.2.175), and then turns his Herculean wrestling into Cupid's wrestling conquest over her (1.2.221; see also 1.3.18–23). See Einer J. Jensen, *Shakespeare and the Ends of Comedy* (Bloomington: Indiana University Press, 1991), 75.

41. Sandys, *Ovid's Metamorphosis*, 27–28, 58–59.
42. The doctrine of the Fortunate Fall included the idea that redemption meant the birth of Christ, the salvation scheme, and some sort of ultimate unity or sacred marriage with the One that Eden did not allow. For various versions of the *felix culpa*, including Langland's interest in unity, see Hugh White, "Langland, Milton, and the *Felix Culpa*," *Review of English Studies* 45 (1994): 336–57. Anne Davidson Ferry argues that the Fortunate Fall in Milton replaces the world of pastoral innocence with the harsher but brighter world of illumination, approximately what happens in *As You Like It*. See J. A. Mazzeo, ed., "The Bird, the Blind Bard, and the Fortunate Fall," *Reason and the Imagination: Studies in the History of Ideas* (London: Routledge and Kegan Paul, 1962), 183–200.
43. Dom Peretz, *Dictionnaire Mytho-Hermetique* (Paris: E. P. Denoël, 1972), 147.
44. Ross, *Mystagogus Poeticus*, 130, remarks that the "quick-sighted Eagle, is Divine contemplation or meditation, by *Ganimedes*, the soul, is caught up to Heaven." This usage appears in Dante's *Purgatorio*, Chaucer's *House of Fame*, and many Renaissance works. Italian artists such as Michelangelo used Ganymede to represent both the contemplative flight and the gay life. See Gerda Kempter, *Ganymedi Studien zur Typologie, Iconographie, and Iconologie* (Cologne: Böhlau, 1980); Jim Saslow, *Ganymede in the Renaissance: Homosexuality in Art and Society* (New Haven: Yale University Press, 1986). Richard Barnfield's Ganymede poems appear to be homoerotic in central content. That androgynous figures may often be important in the movement toward mystical union is suggested in the gnostic literature, in medieval mystics like John Scotus Erigena, and in the literature of alchemy and magic; for this feature of Elizabeth's self-representation, see Leah Marcus, *Puzzling Shakespeare: Local Reading and Its Discontents* (Berkeley: University of California Press, 1988), 61.
45. Hymen descends from the celestial Venus or celestial love. See, for example, Ross, *Mystagogus Poeticus*, 186–88.
46 Shapiro, *Year in the Life*, 226.
47. D. J. Gordon, "Ben Jonson's *Hymenaei*: Ben Jonson's 'Masque of Union,'" *Journal of the Warburg and Courtauld Institutes* 8 (1945), 107–45. For the issue of whether Hymen is a product of magic and an emblem, see Jensen, *Shakespeare and the Ends of Comedy*, 78.

4. Biblical Story and Festival Enter Shakespearean Comedy

1. Some of these are: *Shrew*'s references to the Ten Commandments and the symbolic marriage, *Midsummer*'s inversion of St. Paul's vision, *Merchant of Venice*'s mistaken representation of Jewish exegesis of Genesis and of the

Rachel-Leah story, *Much Ado*'s fake resurrection, *As You Like It*'s Eden (already discussed), *Twelfth Night*'s journey into Magi country, and *Measure for Measure*'s inversions of the Sermon on the Mount. If one counts holy day references, one has the reminder of the significance of the feast of St. John in *Midsummer Night's Dream* and of the Epiphany in *Twelfth Night*.

2. Naseeb Shaheen, *Biblical References in Shakespeare's Comedies* (Newark: University of Delaware Press, 1993); Roland Mushat Frye, *Shakespeare and Christian Doctrine* (London: Oxford University Press, 1963). See Maurice Charney, "Shakespeare's *Hamlet* in the Context of the Hebrew Bible," *Journal of Theatre and Drama* 2 (1996): 93–100 for a powerful argument that we ought to pay as much attention to biblical as to classical intertexts. For a useful examination of the use of one biblical intertext and its metaphorical implications in a number of Shakespearean plays, see Darryl Tippens, "Shakespeare and the Prodigal Son Tradition," *Explorations in Renaissance Culture* 14 (1988): 57–77. Tippens does not examine Orlando as a prodigal, forced to eat the husks at home, and feasted in the woods in a far country, finally returning to his country and love (*AYLI* 1.1.31ff.).

3. For Colet, see Ernest William Hunt, *Dean Colet and His Theology* (London: SPCK for the Church Historical Society, 1956), 88–102. For Erasmus's exegetical principles, see J. B. Payne, "Toward the Hermeneutics of Erasmus," vol. 2 of *Melanges, Scrinium Erasmianum*, ed. J. Coppens, cited in John B. Payne, *Erasmus: His Theology* (Richmond VA: John Knox Press, 1970), 45, 46, 252. See also David S. Dockery, "The Foundation of Reformation Hermeneutics: A Fresh Look at Erasmus," *Premise* 2, no. 9 (1995): 6 at http://web.archive.org/web/19980117040251/capo.org/premise/95/octp95 0906.html.

4. Luther on the Psalter cites eight directions of scriptural interpretation: the four conventional levels—letter, tropology, allegory, and anagogy—first understood somewhat historically and in Old Testament terms and then the same levels understood prophetically as anticipating aspects of the New Covenant. See Alistair E. McGrath, *Reformation Thought* (Oxford: Blackwell, 2000), 149. After Psalm 30, Luther emphasizes the tropological, and Erasmus, Bucer, and Zwingli all do the same things in their exegesis (McGrath, *Reformation Thought*, 149). For Luther's exegetical practice, see Jaroslav Pelikan, *Luther the Expositer* (St. Louis: Concordia, 1959), 126–28. Luther's commentaries on the Psalms are full of allegorical, anagogical, and tropological materials: see his interpretation of Zion in *Selected Psalms III*, in *Luther's Works*, ed. Jaroslav Pelikan, 54 vols. (St. Louis: Concordia, 1956–86), 14:324–28. See David C. Steinmetz, *Luther in Context* (Bloomington: Indiana University Press, 1986), 97–111.

5. For Donne's indebtedness to Nicholas de Lyra and other medieval commentaries and to Luther, see Evelyn M. Simpson and George R. Potter, eds., *The Sermons of John Donne* (Berkeley: University of California Press, 1953–62), 10:364ff. For the use of this kind of approach in a conventional sermon, including a citation of Augustine's *On Christian Doctrine* and Ticonius as justifications for the method, see Thomas Holland, *A Sermon Preached in Pauls Church at London the 17 of November 1599 . . .* (Oxford: J. Barnes, printer, 1600), sig. [B2]^v, D[1]^r, E3^r. William Whitaker says that the Jesuits make two senses of scripture, the historical or literal and the mystical or spiritual, and in the latter, they place the three spiritual levels—the allegorical, the anagogical, and the tropological. However, he argues that these three are not senses but applications: "Etsi enim verbi varie accommodari & applicari possunt," but the sense is one. This seems to make little difference in practical exegesis. See William Whitaker, *Disputatio de Sacra Scriptura* (Cambridge: T. Thomas, printer, 1588), sig. [Vvi^r]–[Vvii^r]. For Spenser and later writers, including Shakespeare, in relation to this tradition, see Walter Davis, "Spenser and the History of Allegory," *English Literary Renaissance* 32 (2002): 152ff. For a history of Renaissance Protestant exegesis that somewhat underestimates the continued force of figurative readings, see *The Cambridge History of the Bible* (Cambridge: Cambridge University Press, 1978), 1–74.

6. Andrewes's hermeneutic, even at its broadest level, vigorously affirms the medieval metaphor of an outer shell disguising a meaty nut. Fourfold allegorical methods of exegesis often inform the sermons:

> Closely related to Andrewes' preference for the signified over the sign is his call to go straight to the moral and allegorical sense of Scripture, and to "leave the letter." He urges, "Go we then to the kernel!, and let the huske lie: let go the dead letter, and take we to us the spiritual! meaning that hath some life in it" (568). Such a dismissal of the literal does not constitute a total revocation of all things external. Andrewes would be the first to argue that the husk—whether it takes the form of the literal sense of Scripture, the "sign" of a word, or rhetoric itself—figures the very attributes of the kernel within. The two, although distinct, form an organic whole. "Signum" cannot be severed from "signatum." To speak of "levels" of allegory destroys the compact cohesion of the myriad senses that makes allegory artful in the first place, thus killing by dissection. The critical separation of Andrewes's style from the theology that informs it constitutes a similar crime.

The quotation is from Peter E. McCullough, "Lancelot Andrewes and Language," section 5, in www.geocities.com/magdamun/andrewesmccullough .html.

The reader should understand that this chapter is not an examination of Shakespeare's private knowledge of how to read scripture—it is irrecoverable and irrelevant to the public meaning of his plays. Rather, as in the case of the treatment of classical myth, it looks at what an Elizabethan or Jacobean audience of fairly well-educated people might make of a series of significant intertexts. For the origins of Shakespeare's personal knowledge of the Bible in private reading, see Naseeb Shaheen, "Shakespeare's Knowledge of the Bible—How Acquired," *Shakespeare Studies* 20 (1988): 201–14.

7. See the *Oxford English Dictionary* entry under *tropological*. The best evidence that *tropical* means *tropological* in Hamlet's speech is that *The Mousetrap* is used to convict Claudius of ethical fault and catch his conscience initially. See Thomas Blount, *Glossographia* (London: printed by Thomas Newcomb, 1656), sig. [Rr7ʳ], where *tropological* and *tropical* are equated.

8. Hamlet's justification for his "comedy" as dissuading from vice and evil parallels that of the comic theorists, and *The Mousetrap* shows how the theory works in practice.

9. After *The Mousetrap* Hamlet also chooses to ignore the time when he could have killed the tyrant (*Hamlet* 3.4.73ff.). John of Salisbury and some political theorists of Shakespeare's time would have a just man do the killing after conviction. At that point in the play, Hamlet ignores the biblical precepts about vengeance and chooses to seek a murder of Claudius that will damn him. The duel permits him a just execution for known crimes. Numerous articles testify to Shakespeare's echoing not only of the Geneva text but also of the Geneva commentary. See, for example, R. A. L. Burney, "Shakespeare and the Marginalia of the Geneva Bible," *Notes and Queries* 26 (April 1979): 113–14. The Geneva version of Genesis 4:9–12 with gloss goes as follows:

> 4:9 Then the LORD sayd unto Kain, Where is Habel thy brother? Who answered, I cannot tell[h] Am I my brothers keeper?
>
> h. This is the nature of the reprobate when they are reproued of their hypocrisie, euen to neglect God and despight him.
>
> 4:10 Again he said, What hast thou done? the[i] voyce of thy brothers blood crieth vnto mee from the earth.
>
> i. God reuengeth the wrongs of his Saints, though noon complaine: for the iniquitie it selfe crieth for vengeance.
>
> 4:11 Now therefore thou art cursed[k] from the earth, which hath opened her mouth to receiue thy brothers blood from thine hand.
>
> k. The earth shall be a witnesse against thee, which mercifully receiued that blood which thou most cruelly sheddest.
>
> 4:12 When thou shalt till the ground, it shall not hencefoorth yeeld

vnto thee her strength: a¹ vagabonde and a runnagate shalt thou be in the earth.

l. Thou shalt neuer have rest: for thine heart shall be in continuall fear and care.

All quotations and citations from the Geneva Bible are from *The 1599 Geneva Bible*, ed. Michael H. Brown (Pleasant Hope MO: L. L. Brown, 1990). Citations are given by chapter and verse unless commentary alone is cited, and then by signature.

10. See Augustine's *On Christian Doctrine*, trans. and introduction by D. W. Robertson (New York: Liberal Arts Press, 1958), passim.

11. See notes 2–5 to this chapter.

12. My colleague Ruth Nisse has examined Hebrew commentary concerning the Laban story from the period, and as far as she can determine, none of it justifies usury. Shakespeare is inventing an exegetical point to show that the devil can quote scripture.

13. Obviously the Shylock figure taps into the Elizabethan period's deepest fears and prejudices about Jews, but it does not offer much of a critique of them save for the propagation of pure hatred. The Jews existed as *conversos* historically in England since they could not publicly exist as Jews-in-religion, Shylock's situation at the end of *Merchant*. See James Shapiro's brilliant study *Shakespeare and the Jews* (New York: Columbia University Press, 1996). For a classic argument that Shylock is a figure for the Puritans, differing somewhat from mine, see Paul N. Siegel, "Shylock the Puritan," *Columbia University Forum* 5 (1962): 14–20.

14. R. S. White, in *Natural Law in English Renaissance Literature* (Cambridge: Cambridge University Press, 1996), 159–69, has argued, correctly in my view, that the two contradictory laws—the pound of flesh required by contract law and the Venetian law against the shedding of Christian blood—point to the limitations of literal readings of positive law and give focus to the need for appeals to equity, charity, and natural law.

15. The paranoid law against the shedding of Christian blood reflects common medieval and Renaissance anti-Semitic rules designed to prevent Jews from martyring Christians, especially Christian children, through blood sacrifices that would somehow repeat the Crucifixion (as in the Hugh of Lincoln story or Chaucer's bigoted Prioress's tale). Obviously Antonio is no innocent. He accepts the bargain in full confidence that he will never have to fulfill it.

16. Shakespeare's audience could have been somewhat aware of the extent to which Venice exploited its Jewish moneylenders. William Thomas in his sixteenth-century Italian history says, in discussing the revenues of the Ve-netian state: "It is almost incredible what gain the Venetians received by the usury of the Jews, both privately and in common." William Thomas, *The*

History of Italy (1549), ed. George B. Parks (Ithaca: Cornell University Press, 1963), 69.

17. Geneva says of Laban, "He was an Idolater, and therefore would not acknowledge the God of Jaakob for his God." *Geneva Bible*, sig. [B4ᵛ]. For a useful exploration of the irony and comedy at the expense of the Christian merchants and Venice in *Merchant of Venice*, see Horst Meller, "A Pound of Flesh and the Economics of Christian Grace: Shakespeare's *Merchant of Venice*," in T. R. Sharma, ed., *Essays on Shakespeare in Honour of A. A. Ansari* (Meerut, India: Shalabh Book House, 1986), 150–74. Barbara Lewalski and others have argued that the play dramatizes Old Law–New Law dichotomies; see "Biblical Allusion and Allegory in *The Merchant of Venice*," *Shakespeare Quarterly* 13 (1962): 327–43. But the play rather centers on the nature of contract and hermeneutics. It presents emblems such as the caskets or the play with Old Law–New Law differences to give us a sense of the comic inadequacy of the Venetians (Londoners) in living up to their New Law professions while administering Old Law justice to Jews, a kind of administration that Vincentio avoids ultimately in *Measure for Measure*. The interplay of biblical abstractions in the *hinein* of the play is complex; see Judith Rosenheim, "Allegorical Commentary in *The Merchant of Venice*," *Shakespeare Studies* 1996 (24): 156–210, for an excellent analysis of one facet of this interplay, the Lancelot–Old Gobbo relationship. *Measure for Measure* seems to associate the encouragement of usury with the Puritan era in saying that the new administration has put down the better usury of copulation and "the worser [i.e., usury in the common sense] allow'd by order of law" (3.2.5–7). See Stephen A. Cohen, "'The Quality of Mercy': Law, Equity, and Ideology in *The Merchant of Venice*," *Mosaic* 4 (1994): 35–54.

18. One should understand that the secondary meanings are often latent even though they may seem to be utterly irresponsible readings, given contemporary reading assumptions. For example, the Song of Songs was often seen as representing the erotic love of Solomon for one of his wives or mistresses but also the love of God for the soul. The 1620 appropriation of *Romeo and Juliet* that Nicholas Richardson quotes from a clergyman's sermon (in all probability) is justified given Renaissance iconology and hermeneutics. Juliet's speech to Romeo says that she "would have [him] gone" but no further than a silk-thread-bound bird that can be pulled back again. The clergyman apparently compared Juliet's contemplated action to God's pulling back the soul hurt with sin or adversity, thereby anticipating George Herbert's "The Pulley." See Stephen Greenblatt, ed., *The Norton Shakespeare: Comedies* (New York: W. W. Norton, 1997), 3345.

19. Donna B. Hamilton, *Virgil and "The Tempest"* (Columbus: Ohio State University Press, 1990).

20. Ann Pasternak Slater, "Variations within a Source: From Isaiah XXIX to 'The Tempest,'" *Shakespeare Survey* 25 (1972): 125–35. Isaiah was a prominent text during the Christmas season when *The Tempest* was performed in 1612/13. Isaianic prophecies from the *Book of Common Prayer* were read in the Christmas season when the 1612/13 *Tempest* was performed—prophecies in essence repeated in the later Isaianic apocalypses of Isaiah 24:1–27:13, where world-judgment, the salvation of Israel, and a resurrection of God's chosen are adumbrated; and in those of Isaiah 28:1–33:24, where the pattern is repeated in an account of the sin of Zion and its overthrow, captivity, and deliverance under a messianic king. The Sibylline oracles had also become apocalyptic works in Renaissance readings. The sibyl's revelations to Aeneas in book 6 of the *Aeneid*, complemented by apocalyptic elements in the *Aeneid* as a whole, acquired a spiritual authority parallel to that of the Bible. The fall of Troy, the struggles of Aeneas to keep alive a remnant, the revelation that the translated empire had been selected by the gods for a divine destiny, and the reestablishment of the empire to ensure a thousand years of peace fulfill the pattern.

21. Lancelot Andrewes, *Seventeen Sermons on the Nativity* (London: Griffith, Farran, Okeden and Welsh, 1898), 251. For Andrewes at court in 1599, see James Shapiro, *A Year in the Life of William Shakespeare: 1599* (New York: HarperCollins, 2005), 77–84.

22. Andrewes, *Seventeen Sermons*, 250–51, 251–59. The fourth eclogue was still being referred to Christ. Andrewes's point is that Virgil did not heed his own prophecy but misinterpreted it. See Lodovic Vives on the fourth eclogue in Virgil, *Opera*, ed. Fabricius (Basil, 1586), col. 52.

23. Geneva says that Ariel signifies the Zion altar for David's city that devoured the sacrifices: *Geneva Bible*, sig. Cccii ʳ. Ariel's role in the play as a devouring fury is obvious.

24. When Ariel sings a song to protect the king (2.1.295–300; 2.1.302–03), Sebastian and Antonio unwittingly cast themselves as the roaring lions and Bashan bulls of Psalm 22:12–13 (2.1.306–07) that in Renaissance glossed Bibles represented the forces surrounding Christ to crucify him. The lions and bulls thus make even the culpable Alonso into the "Rex-Christus" of medieval monarchic myth.

25. *Geneva Bible*, sig. Cciiʳ. Cf. Agrippa, *Three Books of Occult Philosophy*, sig. [V2ᵛ], sig. Ff2ʳ–[Ff2ᵛ].

26. See also *Geneva Bible*, sig. Ccciiʳ.

27. The *Geneva Bible* (sig. Ccciiʳ) says: "thundre . . . shaking. . . a great noyse, a whirlwinde, a tempest, . . .a flame of a devouring fyre."

28. Geneva associates this speaking from the ground with the idea that the humiliated Zion will speak like a charmer, certainly Ariel's function. *Geneva Bible*, sig. Ccciiʳ.

29. The magician's Ariel, too, is the patron of kingship—in Agrippa's book, a familiar spirit or daemon belonging to the sign of Aries in which signs are placed on those who are "acceptable, eloquent, ingenious and honorable," those who govern through righteous wrath—precisely what Prospero does. Agrippa, *Three Books of Occult Philosophy* (London: R. W., 1650), sig. [V2^v]–[V3^v].

30. See Paul A. Olson, *The Kingdom of Science: Literary Utopianism and British Education, 1612–1870* (Lincoln: University of Nebraska Press, 2002), 35.

31. Before Alonso decides to "stand to, and feed" (3.3.49), Sebastian and Antonio remark that the banquet persuades them of the possibility of unicorns and a phoenix (3.3.22–27), two standard images of Christ. They do not seek the equivalent of phoenix and unicorn, only the Harpy's ephemeral food. The only messiah who appears to them is the Fury demanding their repentance.

32. The Geneva Bible makes what appears in the dream as food or nourishing support into the false friends of Zion who ultimately appear as its real enemies. Shakespeare reverses the roles in that those who dream they are fed are not Ariel's false friends but his obvious enemies. Ariel's denial of food reveals the real opposition between the Neapolitan forces and Ariel.

33. Virgil, *Opera Omnia*, col. 1081–82.

34. William Shakespeare, *The Tempest*, ed. Frank Kermode (Cambridge MA: Harvard University Press, 1954), xxxiv–xxxvi, 67; *Aeneid* 3, 568–718.

35. Interpretation based on glosses in *Geneva Bible*, sig. Ccci ^{v}, and on Shakespeare's text. The Geneva Bible commentary says the "drunkards of Ephraim" were "dronken with worldly prosperitie," what the grotesques of the play in their inebriation imagine to be just around the corner: *Geneva Bible*, sig. [Ccci^v]. The drunkards of the play are thrown down by a tempest, which Ferdinand attributes to hell and the devils; the Isaiah passage says that the Isaiah tempest is God's punishment on the wicked, an interpretation Ariel assigns to his tempest (3.3.53–61). Geneva Bible commentary makes the tempest a metaphor for Israel's enemies, standing for the Assyrians; the enemies conceptualized in the *Tempest* represent a conspiracy of internal and external forces, such as the establishment feared both from Catholic forces and from extreme Puritan ones. I use the King James Version for quotations in this section as it was newly minted in 1612; I also use the Geneva Bible's glosses.

36. For additional material on the betrothal masque, see Hamilton, *Virgil and "The Tempest,"* 78–85.

37. John Calvin, *Calvin's Commentaries: The Acts of the Apostles 14–28*, trans. John W. Fraser, ed. David W. Torrance and Thomas F. Torrance (London: Oliver and Boyd, 1966); Peter Stephens, "The Church in Bucer's Commentaries on the Epistle to the Ephesians," in *Martin Bucer: Reforming Church and*

Community, ed. D. F. Wright (Cambridge: Cambridge University Press, 2002).

38. See Helen Shall, "Divining Paul in Shakespeare's Comedies," *Journal of Poetry and the Humanities* 7 (1996): 29–37. For an account of biblical echoes demanding more complex associations than playgoers could gather from performance, see Patricia Parker, "Shakespeare and the Bible: *The Comedy of Errors*," *Semiotic Inquiry* 13 (1993): 47–72. Catherine Shaw has argued for the relationship of the play to Innocents Day in December 1594, and this seems possible though not necessary to the semiology of the play. Catherine M. Shaw, "The Conscious Art of *The Comedy of Errors*," *New York Literary Forum* 5–6 (1980): 17–28. For a discussion of Plautus and Acts, see Niall Rudd, *The Classical Tradition in Operation* (Toronto: University of Toronto Press, 1994), 40ff.

39. *Geneva Bible*, sig. Hhh^r. *The Commentaries of M. John Calvin upon the Actes of the Apostles*, 19, do condemn those that claim to have spiritual gifts that they do not have, certainly part of Pinch's comedy.

40. D. P. Walker, *Unclean Spirits: Possession and Exorcism in France and England in the Late Sixteenth and Early Seventeenth Centuries* (Philadelphia: University of Pennsylvania Press, 1981), 43–73.

41. Thomas P. Hennings, "The Anglican Doctrine of the Affectionate Marriage in *The Comedy of Errors*," *Modern Language Quarterly* 47 (1986): 91–107.

42. Erasmus, *Second Tome of Paraphrase*, sig. AA1^r–AA1^v. For other essays on the Bible and *Comedy of Errors*, see Glyn Austin, "Ephesus Restored: Sacramentalism and Redemption in *The Comedy of Errors*," *Literature and Theology* 1 (1987): 54–69. Austin emphasizes that the reconciliation in the last act is grace-driven. See Brian Gibbons, "Erring and Straying Like Lost Sheep: *The Winter's Tale* and *The Comedy of Errors*," *Shakespeare Survey* 50 (1997): 111–23.

43. John Styles, "The Goldsmiths and the London Luxury Trades, 1550–1750," *Goldsmiths, Silversmiths, and Bankers: Innovation and the Transfer of Skill, 1550–1750*, Centre for Metropolitan History Working Papers, Series 2 (London: Alan Sutton, 1995), 112–20; see also George Unwin, *The Gilds and Companies of London* (London: Methuen, 1908).

44. Barbara Freedman describes the lack of recognition of the obvious in the play as an "infiltration of unconscious representation" that "interrupts it." However, my reading of the play suggests that recognition is *normative* and its absence creates much of the comedic in the play; see Barbara Freedman, *Staging the Gaze: Postmodernism, Psychoanalysis, and Shakespearean Comedy* (Ithaca: Cornell University Press, 1991), 78–113.

45. See Richard Henze, "*The Comedy of Errors*: A Freely Binding Chain," *Shakespeare Quarterly* 22 (1971): 35–41. As Henze observes, "The chain is already

an emblem of the marriage bond, and as the chain gets misplaced, so the bond weakens. But as the chain, a symbol of other social bonds as well, fulfills its function even as it wanders, so the bonds, even as they apparently weaken, continue to do their job" (39). *The Commentaries of M. John Calvin upon the Actes of the Apostles,* 466, sees Demetrius as like the bishops, monks who defend superstition when profit accrues.

46. Geneva interprets Ephesians 4:17 to make it describe the fruits of Christian teaching that touch those whose minds are not corrupted, who seek to become the New Man as opposed to the Old. New Man–Old Man or Old Adam–New Adam imagery is found in *Comedy of Errors* 4.3.12–31. See Jonathan Crewe, "God or the Good Physician: The Rational Playwright in *The Comedy of Errors,*" *Genre: Forms of Discourse and Culture* 15 (1982): 203–33.

47. *Geneva Bible,* sig. Lll5^r.

48. The glosses on Paul's assertion that husbands are to love their wives as Christ loved the church are quite various, ranging from paternalistic assertions of the husband's authority over the childlike wife to assertions that imply real sacrifice on the husband's part and genuine mutuality in the marriage. See *The Sermons of M. John Calvin upon the Epistle of S. Paule too the Ephesians* (London: George Bishop, 1577), sig. [Ppiiii^r]ff.; Nicholas Hemminges, *The Epistle of the Blessed Apostle Saint Paule . . . . to the Ephesians* (London: Thomas East, printer, 1580), sig. Cc[I^r]ff.; *The Second Tome of Volume of the Paraphrase of Erasmus upon the Newe Testament* (London: Edward Whitechurche, 1549), fol. xii ff. In explaining this passage, *Chrysostome upon the Ephesians* (n.p.: H. Binneman printer, 1582), sig. Kkiii^r, emphasizes Christ's tender love of the Church and his unwillingness to resort to fear as a tactic as a model for husbands. For a somewhat similar Renaissance Protestant position, see William Perkins, *Christian Oeconomie . . .* (n.p.: F. Kynaston, printer, 1609), 127ff.

49. That this may be a serious critique of Elizabethan mistreatment of indentured servants is suggested by Maurice Hunt, "Slavery, English Servitude, and *The Comedy of Errors,*" *English Literary Renaissance* 27 (1997): 31–56. However, unlike the Roman New Comedy writers, Shakespeare never liberates his human servant characters, only Ariel.

50. For more analysis of the Old Adam imagery, see Patricia Parker, "Shakespeare and the Bible: *The Comedy of Errors,*" *Semiotic Inquiry* 13 (1993): 61–62.

51. J. Dennis Huston, *Shakespeare's Comedies of Play* (New York: Columbia University Press, 1981), 28, argues that the revelation that Emilia is Egeon's wife reminds us that the godlike perspective on the play the audience has assumed itself to have is after all a very limited one. This revelation may have opened up the play for the Renaissance audience for reflections like Gonzalo's in *The Tempest* (5.1.203–16) on the providence of the action.

52. *Certain Sermons or Homilies Appointed to be read in churches in the time of Queen Elizabeth* (London: SPCK, 1864), 468. Also to be found at http://www.angli canlibrary.org/homilies/bk2hom14.htm.

53. See Einer J. Jensen, *Shakespeare and the Ends of Comedy* (Bloomington: Indiana University Press, 1991), 58ff.

54. For a discussion of *Comedy of Errors* and the Feast of the Holy Innocents, see Arthur F. Kinney, "Shakespeare's *Comedy of Errors* and the Nature of Kinds," in *The Comedy of Errors: Critical Essays*, ed. Robert S. Miola (New York: Garland, 1997), 155–82.

55. See C. L. Barber, *Shakespeare's Festive Comedy: A Study of Dramatic Form and Its Relation to Social Custom* (Princeton NJ: Princeton University Press, 1959), 123.

56. For more on Midsummer's Night or the Vigil of John the Baptist, see H. Carew Hazlitt, *Faiths and Folklore of the British Isles* (New York: Benjamin Blom, 1965), 2:346–50; for *Midsummer Night's Dream*'s emphasis on Titania's banks of flowers, see 2:410. See James Gordon Frazier, *The Golden Bough: A Study in Magic and Religion* (New York: Macmillan, 1956), 724ff., which establishes that witches and evil spirits are at large on Midsummer's Eve, these perhaps referenced lightly in *MND* in Titania in her Hecate-Circe aspect and in Puck as a minor demon. For more, see Phillip Stubbes, *The Anatomie of Abuses*, preface by Arthur Freeman (New York: Garland, 1973), sig. [M1ᵛ]–M4ʳ.

57. St. Jerome says of the people demonically possessed who were around John the Baptist's tomb that the men went howling like wolves, barking like dogs, roaring like lions, hissing like serpents, and bellowing like bulls. People twisted their necks and bent backward until they touched the ground; the women hung themselves upside down and their clothes did not fall down. St. Jerome, "Ad Eustochium Virginum," *Patrologia Latina* 22:490–91 (Epistola CVIII, section 13).

58. Jacobus da Voragine, *The Golden Legende* (n.p.: W. de Worde, printer, 1512), sig. [tiiiᵛ]. *The Golden Legende* may not have circulated much in late sixteenth- and early seventeenth-century England.

59. Da Voragine, *Golden Legende*, sig. [tiiiᵛ].

60. For example see *Certain Sermons or Homilies*, 431; Simpson and Potter, *Sermons of John Donne*, 3:348ff., 4:145ff (preached on Midsummer's Day), and 4:210.

61. Renaissance England, like Scandinavia until fairly recently, was on St. John's night covered with bonfires lighted to ward off witches and evil spirits and visited by parades of grotesque animal-people. Its youth stayed up all night, performing rituals of jumping through the fires and marching around as garlanded revelers. Players took the parts of the unicorn, the dragon, and the riders of hobbyhorses. Others sought poetic inspiration.

62. Stubbes, *The Anatomie of Abuses*, sig. [M1ᵛ]–M4ʳ and passim.
63. See Thomas B. Stroup, "Bottom's Name and His Epiphany," *Shakespeare Quarterly* 19 (1978): 79–82. Contrast John S. Mebane, "Source, Structure, and Meaning in *A Midsummer Night's Dream*," *Texas Studies in Literature and Language* 24 (1982): 265–66.
64. See Wilfred R. Prest, *The Inns of Court under Elizabeth I and the Early Stuarts: 1590–1640* (London: Longmans, 1972), 21–46.
65. Leslie Hotson, *The First Night of "Twelfth Night"* (New York: Hart-Davis, 1954), passim.
66. Barber, *Shakespeare's Festive Comedy*, 240–61; for the Lord of Misrule, see 24–50. John Stow tells us in his *Survey of London*:

> Now for sportes and pastimes yearely vsed, first in the feaste of Christmas, there was in the kinges house, whersoever hee was lodged, a Lord of Misrule, or Maister of merry disports, and the like had yee in the house of every noble man, of honor, or good worshippe, were he spirituall or temporall. Amongst the which the Mayor of London, and eyther of the shiriffes had their seuerall Lordes of Misrule, euer contending without quarrell or offence, who should make the rarest pastimes to delight the Beholders. These Lordes beginning their rule on Alhollon Eue, continued the same till the morrow after the Feast of the Purification, commonlie called Candlemas day.

John Stow, *A suruay of London Conteyning the originall, antiquity, increase, Modern estate and description of that city* (London: Iohn Windet, printer, 1603), sig. H[1ᵛ]. For Misrule as a blasphemous figure, see Stubbes, *Anatomie of Abuses*, sig. [M1ᵛ]–M4ʳ. Stubbes talks of May games but Shakespeare also speaks of maying in *MND*. See also other key works demonstrating Shakespeare's use of the calendar and festive tradition such as Françoise Laroque's *Shakespeare's Festive World: Elizabethan Seasonal Entertainment and the Professional Stage* (Cambridge: Cambridge University Press, 1991); Barber's *Shakespeare's Festive Comedy*; David Wiles's *Shakespeare's Almanac: "A Midsummer Night's Dream," Marriage, and the Elizabethan Calendar* (Cambridge: D. S. Brewer, 1993); and R. Chris Hassel Jr.'s *Renaissance Drama and the English Church Year* (Lincoln: University of Nebraska Press, 1979).

67. The argument, in Michael D. Bristol, *Carnival and Theater: Plebeian Culture and the Structure of Authority in Renaissance England* (Methuen: New York, 1985), 202ff., that Toby and Andrew's drinking bout represents the serious "Carnival" of bodily satisfaction and that Malvolio represents "Lenten" severity is surely mistaken; Andrew and Toby are tired and engaged in a form of desperate fooling. They only attempt to cheer themselves up in the drinking bout. What Malvolio represents may be the mask of Lent, but his erotic

and autoerotic fantasies in the letter-dropping scene hardly suggest Lent. In general, Bahktin's view of Carnival as necessarily a revolutionary type of activity does not lend itself well to the analysis of conflicts between partying and repression as these take place in such varying contexts and involve such varied classes as not to carry an "objective" political meaning. Edward Muir, *Civic Ritual in Venice* (Princeton NJ: Princeton University Press, 1981), 156ff., argues that Carnival from Christmas to Lent in Venice in the period was a time "to be seriously playful and gaily disrespectful" and that both rulers and plebes played games with authority in the period. Sir Andrew and Sir Toby are knights after all; they *are* the authority structure; there is nothing plebian about them save their clumsiness at executing all "aristocratic" moves, whether dancing or singing or swordplay or wooing.

68. The Council of Tours in 567 CE proclaimed the twelve days from Christmas to Epiphany to be a time for holy celebration and set the Advent fast as preparation. See Clement A. Miles, *Christmas in Ritual and Tradition: Christian and Pagan* (London: T. Fisher Unwin, 1913), 20–25.

69. Da Voragine, *Golden Legende*, sig. bii [r]–[biiiiᵛ]. *The Golden Legend*'s account of Epiphany calls it a theophany that includes these four events and indicates that the star is more than a material star. It is the heart or faith that permits the Magi to see what the star means and its material and spiritual implications. The Book of Common Prayer for the Epiphany season emphasizes the idea of the new star, Jesus in the temple, the wedding at Cana, and so forth. See *The Boke of Common Prayer* (London: Whitchurche, printer, 1552), sig. [cvʳ]–[cviʳ] and following.

70. Donne writes that, though the church calls the twelfth day Epiphany, because of the manifestation to the Wise Men, the ancient church called the day of Christ's birth Epiphany because then Christ was made manifest to the world and "[e]very manifestation of Christ to the world, to the Church, to a particular soule, is an Epiphany." Simpson and Potter, *Sermons of John Donne*, 7:279. Since Joyce's reconfiguration of the meaning of Epiphany, epiphanies appear everywhere in Shakespeare criticism. See Robert L. Reid, "Epiphanal Encounters in Shakespearean Dramaturgy," *Comparative Drama* 32 (1998–99): 518–40; Cynthia Lewis, "Viola, Antonio, and Epiphany in *Twelfth Night*," *Essays in Literature* 13 (1986): 187–99. See Richard Henze, "*Twelfth Night*: Disposition on the Sea of Love," *Sewanee Review* 83 (1975): 267–83. Ben Jonson's Epiphany masques celebrate the coming of light, the tension between flesh and spirit, their harmonization in the birth of Christ, and the replacement of false with true love, the lower Venus with the celestial. These are all significant in *Twelfth Night*. For a summary, see Hassel, *Renaissance Drama and the English Church Year*, 54–76.

71. For some of this, see for example Hugh Latimer, "A Sermon Preached

... On Twelfth Day, ... Anno 1553," *Sermons and Remains of Hugh Latimer* (Cambridge: Cambridge University Press, 1845), 130ff.

72. For example, *Festa Anglo-Romana: or, The Feasts of the English and Roman church* (London: William Jacob, printer, 1678), 7, calls Melchior "an aged Man, with a long Beard, who offered Gold to our Saviour, as to a King, in testimony of his Regality"; he calls Jasper "a Beardless Youth, who offered Frankincense, as unto God, in acknowledgment of his Divinity" and says that Balthasar is a "Black, or Moor with a large spreading Beard who offered Myrrh, as to a Man, that was ready or fit for his Sepulchre, thereby signifying his Humanity." These equivalences or permutations of them are present in a vast number of sixteenth- and early-seventeenth-century paintings.

73. See for example Hugh Latimer, "A Sermon Preached ... On Twelfth Day," 132. See Roger Hutchinson, *The Works of Roger Hutchinson* (Cambridge: Cambridge University Press, 1842), 255. See also *The Crib of Joy* (London: R. Field, printer, 1611), F4^v; Joannes of Hildesheim, *Liber de Gestis et translatione trium regum* (Westminster: Wynkyn de Worde, printer, 1496?).

74. Barbara Haegar, "Rubens' *Adoration of the Magi* and the Program for the High Altar of St Michael's Abbey in Antwerp," *Similolus: Netherlands Quarterly for the History of Art* 25 (1997): 45–71.

75. *Geneva Bible*, sig. [Aaa5^r]; see sig. [Aaa8^r].

76. Richard C. Trexler, *The Journey of the Magi: Meanings in History of a Christian Story* (Princeton NJ: Princeton University Press, 1997), 169–85. Trexler also shows that two Magi were often posited and that one Magus was frequently feminine or effeminate in appearance, as Viola is when she plays at being a eunuch or appears in women's clothes (see Trexler, *Journey of the Magi*, 107–18).

77. The best explanation of Malvolio's exegesis comes from J. L. Simmons, who argues that Malvolio's literal following of the epistle's commands concerning his clothing and persona suggests Puritan literal-minded understandings of the Bible. His application of the epistle to himself through twirling the "M.O.A.I." reflects the common charge that the Puritans pursued self-love so assiduously that it led to "[c]ontempt of authority, ambition, and covetousness." Simmons also argues that the M.O.A.I. has no point save when Malvolio gets the point that he is M.O.A.I. Simultaneously, in matters that do not promise advancement to him, he "cleaveth to the bare letter and leaveth the meaning and the inward grace." See J. L. Simmons, "A Source for Shakespeare's Malvolio: The Elizabethan Controversy with the Puritans," *Huntington Library Quarterly* 36 (1973): 181–201; see also James F. Forrest, "Malvolio and Puritan 'Singularity,'" *English Language Notes* 11 (1974): 259–62.

78. For discussions of the light, see Stephen M. Buhler, "Marsilio Ficino's *De*

stella magorum and Renaissance Views of the Magi," *Renaissance Quarterly* 43 (1990): 348–71, giving Ficino's discussion of the astronomy and astrology of the Magi. For an exploration of the star as a symbol of the light of faith that brings one out of darkness to the sun of Christ, see Lancelot Andrewes, "Sermon XV . . . on Wednesday, the Twenty-fifth of December, AD 1622," *Seventeen Sermons on the Nativity* (London: Griffith, Farran, Okeden, and Welsh, 1887), 245–59. The light without, of the star, is contrasted with the light within "that must come from Him and the enlighting of his Spirit" (p. 5). Roger Hutchinson says that the star "was ordained to preach Christ"; Hutchinson, *Works*, 6. For an elaborate account of Epiphany light imagery see *Crib of Joy*, sig. F3^r–[F3^v]. Calvin argues that the star that led the Magi was not a natural star and that astrology alone could not have led the Magi to Christ. See John Calvin, "Harmonia Evangelica," *Opera* (New York: Johnson Reprint Company, 1964), 45: cols. 80–81. It is ironic that commentary on the play has argued either that it suggests a morality favoring indulgence or a middle way, since the ascetic of the play, Malvolio, is a fake ascetic, as is Olivia in her posturing as if in mourning. The hedonists get no joy. The play comes home to an Epiphanic, not an Aristotelian middle-way morality. For a list of articles discussing this matter, see Elliot Krieger, *A Marxist Study of Shakespeare's Comedies* (London: Macmillan, 1979), 97–130. Antonius Corvinus, *A postill or collection of moste godly doctrine* . . . (London: Reynold Wolfe inter, 1550), sig. eır, argues that the Jews were dominated by the flesh and did not see the promised Messiah. Calvin also emphasizes that the star is designed to inform the Magi and the world that the new kingdom is spiritual.

79. *The Sermons of Martin Luther*, ed. and trans. Eugene F. A. Klug (Grand Rapids MI: Baker Book House, 1996), 1:324–67.

80. Klug, *Sermons of Martin Luther*, 1:324–67.

81. Paul N. Siegel, "Malvolio: Comic Puritan Automaton," *New York Literary Forum* 5–6 (1980): 217–29, correctly calls attention to the class division between Toby and Malvolio and their relation to Puritan upward mobility. Inge Leimberg, "Maria's Theology and Other Questions (An Answer to John Russell Brown)," *Connotations* 12 (1991): 191–96, argues, somewhat plausibly, that M.O.A.I. suggests Malvolio's sense that he is God, Alpha and Omega. Gash, following Erasmus's analysis of defective medieval clerics, says that Malvolio is a fake Puritan who has disowned his common human nature, privileged literalism over spiritual reading, and is a "proud man / dressed in a little brief authority," who is the opposite of the Erasmian Christian; see Anthony Gash, "Shakespeare, Carnival, and the Sacred, *The Winter's Tale* and *Measure for Measure*," in *Shakespeare and Carnival, After Bakhtin*, ed. Ronald Knowles (New York: Macmillan, 1998), 200.

82. The Lord of Misrule events sometimes included rehearsals of the overthrow

of authority and parodies of the essential structures of cultural rules, but as Barber points out in his analysis of the Talboys Dymoke trial, the Earl of Lincoln and his associates, who were the butt of most of Talboys Dymoke's defiance, were the subjects of repeated accusations before the Privy Council for their inhumanity and avarice (Barber, *Shakespeare's Festive Comedy*, 36–51, esp. 38). At times in such festivities, the spirit of excessive abandon and repression both seem to be mocked. Indeed, anyone who has participated in school games mocking authority knows how quickly the mockery turns into chaos and satire or mocking of the chaotic.

83. The twins bear to Illyria the message of two loves: human love that includes innocent wonder and full sacrifice and the cosmic love celebrated in Elizabeth's translation of Boethius's *Consolation of Philosophy* and everywhere in post-Ficinian Platonic writing. The praise of cosmic love as holding the universe together appears nicely in Queen Elizabeth's translation of Boethius's *Consolation*, book 2, meter 8, in *Queen Elizabeth's Englishings* (London: Kegan Paul, 1899), 41–42.

84. Roberto Bellarmino, "Disputationes de controversiis Christianae Fidei ..." Sections I, I, 33 in *Opera Omnia* (Naples: Joseph Giulano, 1856–62), vols. 1–4.

85. St. Augustine, *On Christian Doctrine* (New York: Liberal Arts Press, 1958); Erasmus *Enchiridion Militis Christiani*, ed. Anne M. O'Donnell (Oxford: Oxford University Press, 1981); John Colet, *Two Treatises on the Hierarchics of Dionysius*, ed. J. H. Lupton (London: Bell and Paldy, 1869). See Ernest William Hunt, *Dean Colet and His Theology* (London: SPCK for the Church Historical Society, 1956), 88–102, for a good account.

86. *Luther's Works*, ed. Jaroslav Pelikan, 54 vols. (St. Louis: Concordia, 1955–86), 10:6–7; see A. Skevington Wood, *Luther's Principles of Biblical Interpretation* (London: Tyndale Press, 1946). See William Whitaker, *Disputatio de Sacra Scriptura* (Cambridge: T. Thomas, printer, 1588).

87. Emile Mâle, *The Gothic Image: Religious Art in France of the Thirteenth Century*, trans. Dora Nussey (New York: Harper, 1958).

88. See Erwin Panofsky, *The Life and Art of Albrecht Dürer* (Princeton NJ: Princeton University Press, 1955), 78–79 and fig. 101.

89. Francis Quarles, *Emblems* (1635), intro. A. D. Cousins (Delmar NY: Scholars' Facsimile & Reprints, 1991).

90. See James I of England, reissued by Charles I, *The King's Maiesties Declaration to His Subjects, Concerning Lawful Sports to Be Used* (London: Robert Barker, printer, 1633). For Hooker's theology of festival, see Richard Hooker, *Of the Lawes of Ecclesiasticall Politie: Books I–V* (Menston, UK: Scolar Press, 1969), 190–204.

91. Simpson and Potter, *Sermons of John Donne*, 4: 145–63.

5. Empire and Conquest in the Comedies

1. The best account of the Russians from the late Elizabethan period is Giles Fletcher the Elder's "The Russe Commonwealth," in *The English Works of Giles Fletcher the Elder* (Madison: University of Wisconsin Press, 1964), 135–309. Fletcher calls the leader of the Russians the "emperor."

2. Sir Walter Raleigh, *The History of the World*, ed. C. A. Patrides (London: MacMillan, 1971), 395.

3. For Shakespeare's Roman Empire, see J. Leeds Barroll, "Shakespeare and Roman History," *Modern Language Review* 53 (1958): 327–43; and Clifford J. Ronan, *"Antike Roman": Power Symbology and the Roman Play in Early Modern England, 1585–1635* (Athens: University of Georgia Press, 1995). This chapter assumes that Shakespeare, while living in the port city of London and as a servant of the court, had a fairly good knowledge of the events in Europe and the Mediterranean and that he had a fairly good knowledge of the geography of his continent and areas proximate to it; it assumes that the more sophisticated portion of his audience had a similar knowledge. See Joan Gillies and Virginia Mason Vaughn, eds., *Playing the Globe: Genre and Geography in English Renaissance Drama* (Madison: Farleigh Dickinson University Press, 1998).

4. Leah Marcus, *Puzzling Shakespeare: Local Reading and Its Discontents* (Berkeley: University of California Press, 1988), 106–48.

5. Neil Rhodes, Jennifer Richards, and Joseph Marshall, eds., *King James VI and I: Selected Writings* (Aldershot, Hants.: Ashgate, 2003), 364–66.

6. For more details see Sir John Seeley, *The Growth of British Policy* (Cambridge: Cambridge University Press, 1895).

7. Venice saw itself as the successor to ancient Rome and to the Byzantine Roman Empire. See Debra Pincus, "Venice and the Two Romes: Byzantium and Rome as a Double Heritage in Venetian Cultural Politics," *Artibus et Historiae* 13 (1992): 101–14. The newly united Protestant Netherlands was beginning in the direction of an imperialist quest.

8. Fernand Braudel, *The Mediterranean and the Mediterranean World in the Age of Philip II*, trans. Sian Reynolds, 2 vols. (London: HarperCollins, 1972), passim, esp. 2:1238–44. Braudel (1187ff.) also shows that there was a renewal of imperial struggle in the Mediterranean in the 1590s, though not on the scale of the period 1550–89.

9. Christopher Hodgkins, *Reforming Empire: Protestant Colonialism and Conscience in British Literature* (Columbia: University of Missouri Press, 2002). Leah Marcus (*Puzzling Shakespeare*, 162) makes a similar point in her picture of London and Vienna as partial mirrors of each other in *Measure for Measure*.

10. Walter R. Chalmers, "Plautus and His Audience," in *Roman Drama*, ed. T. A. Dorsey and Donald R. Dudley (New York: Basic Books, 1965), 23–25.
11. However, not all of the great empires are under Shakespeare's lens. Russian history appears hardly at all, and the further empires of China or Cathay, Persia, and those of the New World are outside his purview, save perhaps the New World in *The Tempest*.
12. The tale may only be about the union of England and Scotland in its political reference, as has been suggested by Donna B. Hamilton, "*The Winter's Tale* and the Language of Union, 1604–1610," *Shakespeare Studies* 21 (1993): 228–50. I am unable to see any particular reason why in 1610 Shakespeare should be playing with divisions between the Austrian/Holy Roman Empire part of the Habsburg domain (Bohemia) and the Spanish part (Sicily), though there were some such differences. My best guess is that the domain is purely a metaphor for British topics.
13. Marcus, *Puzzling Shakespeare*, 134.
14. See Susan Skilliter, "William Harborne, the First English Ambassador 1583–88," in *Four Centuries of Turco-British Relations: Studies in Diplomatic, Economic, and Cultural Affairs*, ed. William M. Hale and Ali Ihsan Bagis, 10–25 (Beverly, North Humberside, England: Eothen Press, 1984); John Carswell, "The Queen, the Sultan, and the Organ," *Asian Affairs* 25 (1994): 13–23.
15. Susan Skilliter, *William Harborne and the Trade with Turkey* (Oxford: Oxford University Press for the British Academy, 1977), 150–75. Harborne, British ambassador to the court of the sultan, was much vexed in 1581 that the British *Bark Roe*, sailing the Mediterranean under French protection, acted as a pirate ship and attacked two Greek boats sailing to Venice. The vessels were owned and sailed by subjects of the Sultan. The *Bark Roe* with the two Greek boats in tow then sailed to Malta, where the British sailors were to be tried; Venice also intervened against the British in this episode in order to protect certain of its Mediterranean monopolies. The incident must have occurred close to Venice's Illyrian possessions on the Adriatic.
16. For commentary on Italy and Venice as distant and sometimes distorted mirrors of England in Early Modern plays, see G. K. Hunter, "English Folly and Italian Vice: The Moral Landscape of John Marston," in his *Dramatic Identities and Cultural Tradition: Studies in Shakespeare and His Contemporaries*, Liverpool English Texts and Studies (Liverpool: Liverpool University Press, 1978), 103–21; Murray J. Levith, *Shakespeare's Italian Settings and Plays* (Basingstoke: MacMillan, 1989); and David C. McPherson, *Shakespeare, Jonson, and the Myth of Venice* (Newark: University of Delaware Press, 1990); *Shakespeare's Italy: Functions of Italian Locations in Renaissance Drama*, ed. Michele Marrapodi, A. J. Hoenselaars, Marcello Capuzzi, and L. Falzon Santucci (Manchester: Manchester University Press, 1993).

17. For a useful summary see Lord Kinross, *The Ottoman Centuries: The Rise and Fall of the Turkish Empire* (New York: William Morrow, 1977), passim, esp. 217–95.

18. Halil Inalcik, *The Ottoman Empire: The Classical Age, 1300–1600*, trans. Norman Itzkowitz and Colin Imber (London: Weidenfeld and Nicolson, 1973), 37. The Ottomans forced the Holy Roman Empire to give concessions to the Protestants and also protected the Calvinists in Hungary. See A. C. Hess, "The Moriscos: An Ottoman Fifth Column in Sixteenth-Century Spain," *American Historical Review* 54 (1968): 14–21, for Ottoman support of the Protestants.

19. Palmira Brummett, *Ottoman Seapower and Levantine Diplomacy in the Age of Discovery* (Albany: State University of New York Press, 1994), 27–50, 175–82.

20. For Venetian tolerance of Protestants and papal opposition to this, see John Julius Norwich, *A History of Venice* (New York: Vintage Books, 1989), 508–9.

21. Skilliter, *William Harborne and the Trade with Turkey*, 22.

22. Brummett, *Ottoman Seapower and Levantine Diplomacy*, 27–50.

23. See Wallace T. MacCaffrey, *Elizabeth I: War and Politics, 1588–1603* (Princeton NJ: Princeton University Press, 1992), 73–106.

24. Elizabeth sponsored English privateering and piracy at sea, and while James did not condone this form of military action, he did little to suppress it, though the Levant Company and the Ottoman government complained. The English furnished tin, gunpowder, and cloth to the Ottomans. See Lee W. Eysturlid, "'Where Everything Is Weighed in the Scales of Material Interest': Anglo-Turkish Trade, Piracy, and Diplomacy in the Mediterranean during the Jacobean Period," *Journal of European Economic History* 22 (1993): 613–26.

25. Esther Benbassa and Aron Rodrigue, *Sephardic Jewry: A History of the Judeo-Spanish Community, 14th to 20th Centuries* (Berkeley: University of California Press, 2000), xxxv–liv, 36–60. For more on the relationship between Morocco and Venice, and also on the rise of anti-Semitism in Venice connected to the threat of the Turk, see Benjamin Ardel, *Trading Nations* (New York: Brill, 1995), 185–89.

26. Brummett, *Ottoman Seapower and Levantine Diplomacy*, passim. Turkey's Persian war came to a temporary end in 1590.

27. A parallel to the idea of deniability is Barnaby and Wry's idea that Shakespeare used Vienna as a metaphor for London to provide a "conceptual buffer": Andrew Barnaby and Joan Wry, "Authorized Versions: *Measure for Measure* and the Politics of Biblical Translation," *Renaissance Quarterly* 51 (1998): 1250.

28. Moroccan gold dinars made from sub-Saharan African gold were the most plentiful currency in the Mediterranean world; see Pekka Masonen, "Trans-Saharan Trade and the West African Discovery of the Mediterranean World," in *Ethnic Encounter and Culture Change*, ed. M'hammed Sabour and Knut S. Vik (London: C. Hurst and Company, 1997), 116–42.

29. The discovery of the Potosi mine and other veins in the New World made silver the primary Spanish precious metal after 1550.

30. For example, Proverbs 26, 4ff.; Proverbs 12, 15.

31. McPherson, *Shakespeare, Jonson, and the Myth of Venice*, 14, 48–51, 122. The argument as to whether Venice is Venice or London seems to me to be gratuitous since Venice is sometimes Venice, sometimes London, and often both, as the play as mirror of history is turned to various angles.

32. The iconology is a variant of that in the popular *Gesta Romanorum* story, where the King of Ampluy's daughter, Portia's equivalent, is said to be the human soul seeking to marry Christ. She chooses among (1) the gold vessel that carries the motto, "Who chooses me shall find that he deserveth," and finds within dead men's bones, an allegory for worldliness; (2) the silver vessel that carries the motto, "Who chooses me shall find that he desireth," and finds worms and earth, an allegory for the lust of the flesh; and (3) the lead vessel that carries the motto, "Who chooses me shall find that God hath disposed for him," and finds within gold and precious stones, an allegory for the riches within found through obedience to God, simplicity, and poverty. Portia's father's test changes the gold from worldly avarice to vainglory (popularity), changes the silver vessel from an allegory for lust and its decay to one suggesting vainglory in the sense of excessive self-assurance, and alters the third test to make it a test of married love (or lust) and the faith that is to go with it, as opposed to direct obedience to God. The tests are, in short, tests of marriage and love as opposed to tests of union with God. See *A Record of Auncient Histories, intituled in Latin Gesta Romanorum* (London: Tomas Este, printer, 1602), [Nviii^r]–[Oviii^r].

33. Luther, in writing of the good works that flow spontaneously from the hazarding implicit in faith, says, "A man is to live, speak, act, hear, suffer, and die for the good of his wife and child, the wife for the husband, the children for the parents, the servants for their masters, the masters for their servants, the government for its subjects, the subjects for the government, each one for his fellow man, even for his enemies, so that one is the other's hand, mouth, eye, foot, even heart and mind." *Sermons of Martin Luther: The House Postils*, ed. and trans. Eugene F. A. Klug (Grand Rapids MI: Baker Book House, 1996), 1:37. The Church of England's doctrine on faith and works in the 1571 "Thirty-Nine Articles" essentially says that salvation is through faith alone and that good works are natural and "spring necessarily of a true

and liuely faith," a doctrine similar to Luther's. See Martin Luther, *Werke: kritische Gesammtausgabe* (Weimar ed., 1964), XIX, 212–13. For Luther on faith as a gamble, see Elisabeth Sommer, "Gambling with God: The Use of the Lot by the Moravian Brethren in the Eighteenth Century," *Journal of the History of Ideas* 59 (1998): 267–86. For the 1571 Articles that prevailed in Shakespeare's time and comparisons with the 1553 and 1563 versions, see C. Hardwick, *A History of the Articles of Religion* (London: George Bell and Sons, 1881), 305.

34. For these fictions, see Paul A. Olson, "The Merchant's Lombard Knight," *Texas Studies in Literature and Language* 3 (1961): 259–63. For traditional Venetian banking, often based in Florence, in the Renaissance and its charging of interest, see Reinhold C. Mueller, *Money and Banking in Medieval and Renaissance Venice*, vol. 2, *The Venetian Money Market: Banks, Panics, and the Public Debt, 1200–1500* (Baltimore: Johns Hopkins University Press, 1997), passim; by 1584 the last private bank in Venice closed its doors, and public banking, also charging and paying interest, followed. I cannot discover how much was known of Venetian banking and moneylending practice in the port city of London, though how Venice was run should have been fairly well known. Thomas Wilson's *A Discourse upon Usury by Way of Dialogue and Orations*, ed. R. H. Tawney (London: G. Bell, 1925), takes a fairly medieval view of usury as including all interest; English law after 1543, renewed in 1571, permitted an interest charge of up to 10 percent on loans.

35. For an analysis of international monetary practice and the language of *The Merchant*, see Mark Netzloff, *England's Internal Colonies: Class, Capital, and the Literature of Early Modern English Colonialism* (London: Palgrave Macmillan, 2003), 17–51.

36. James Shapiro's *Shakespeare and the Jews* (New York: Columbia University Press, 1996) demonstrates the depths of Shakespeare's understanding of Jewish-Gentile issues in Early Modern Europe; I do not wish to say that Shylock is not about Jewish issues because England had few Jews in Shakespeare's day. Like many other figures in Shakespeare, he is a many-faceted mirror. For the Puritans' conception of Christians as bound by significant portions of Old Testament law, see Leonard Trinterud, *Elizabethan Puritanism* (New York: Oxford University Press, 1971), 312, 302–73, and passim. For a more extensive analysis of Puritanism in relation to Talmudic Judaism, see Max Weber, *The Protestant Ethic and the Spirit of Capitalism* (London: Unwin, 1965), 165–80.

I do not agree with Horst Meller's point ("A Pound of Flesh and the Economics of Christian Grace: Shakespeare's *Merchant of Venice*," in *Essays on Shakespeare in Honour of A. A. Ansari Meerut* [India: Shalabh Book House, 1986], 150–74) that Shylock represents the "old" medieval economy while

Antonio represents a new low-interest, capitalistic economy. "Mercantile capitalism" with interest had long flourished in both Italy and England; Shylock, if he stands for any "economy," probably stands for the defense of interest rates, even high interest rates, by Calvinistic theorists who also cast themselves as a Covenant people in sixteenth-century London. Einer J. Jensen argues that the play as a whole celebrates "giving, good judgment, life, and love," and this may be plausible if one ignores the difference between what the Christians say they are and what they actually must be in sixteenth-century Venice or London. See Jensen's *Shakespeare and the Ends of Comedy* (Bloomington: Indiana University Press, 1991), 42.

37. Among the Protestant theorists who might be considered important by one or another member of the Puritan party, Calvin, Du Moulin, Francois Hottman, and Bucer allowed that charging usury, interpreted as *some* interest, was acceptable if (1) the interest was not exacted from paupers or calamity sufferers, (2) did not exact more than the cost of the loan, and (3) served the common weal and natural equity. In England the usury debate changed so that usury became no longer charging interest but one's intention in charging interest, an unknowable matter not subject to the control of civil law. See Norman Jones, *God and the Money Lenders* (Oxford: Blackwell, 1989), 145–74, 15–22. The identification of usurers in the Puritan camp or any other camp with Jews is suggested by the 1605 Lord Chancellor's remark that all lending at interest is "judaisme" and all usurers are "mercatores Judaizantes." See John Howard, *Les Reportes del Cases in Camera Stellata: 1593 to 1609*, ed. W. P. Baildon (London: privately printed, 1894), 236–37.

38. Abraham Ortelius, *His Epitome of the Theater of the Worlde* (London: Jeames Shawe, printer, 1603), sig. [M1ᵛ], describes Illyria and its chief city, Ragusa (or Dubrovnik), as located in an area formerly given to robbery but now civil and very rich. The modern assumption that Shakespeare was creating a fairyland Illyria might not have been shared by his audience.

39. See Catherine Wendy Bracewell, *The Uskoks of Senj: Piracy, Banditry, and Holy War in the Sixteenth-Century Adriatic* (Ithaca: Cornell University Press, 1992). Fynes Moryson traveled from Constantinople to Venice in 1597, and his account notes the persistent presence of pirates in the area, most of them in his opinion of Turkish origin. See *Fynes Moryson, An Itinerary*, 4 vols. (Glasgow: James Maclehose, 1907), 2:102–13.

40. See note 15 to this chapter and Skilliter, *William Harborne and the Trade with Turkey*, 150–75.

41. Hegemonic stability theory suggests that the hegemon must induce or coerce client states to support its system through providing what appear as the costs, helps, or services that create the infrastructure of its hegemonic power.

42. For Italy in this period, see Eric Cochran, *Italy: 1530–1630*, ed. Julius

Kirshner (Longman: New York, 1988). The general amity among the *Much Ado* visitors to Messina (save for Don John's attitude) contrasts strongly with the disunity that characterized the attitudes of the Holy League fighters toward each other as they waited at Messina prior to Lepanto. See Robert F. Marx, *The Battle of Lepanto: 1571* (Cleveland: World, 1966), 77–83. James I says almost nothing about Messina in his poem save that the Christian forces assembled there; see James I, *His Maiesties Lepanto or Heroicall Song* (London: Stafford and Hooke, printers, 1603), [B2ᵛ]. For additional comments on Messina and Lepanto in relation to *Much Ado*, see Levith, *Shakespeare's Italian Settings*, 76–82. Levith noticed the connection to Lepanto before I did (1989) but interprets it differently. He cites works aside from James's that deal with Lepanto, especially George Gascoigne's 1572 wedding masque in honor of the "English Montague's weddings" and Abraham Holland's *Naumachia* (London: T[homas] P[urfoot], printer, 1622). Levith explains Shakespeare's antipathy to the Don John of the play as reflecting Elizabeth's indignation that Lepanto's Don John refused to woo her. The reference to the refusal to woo seems to me unlikely since the effort to create a marriage match between Don John and Elizabeth was not widely publicized. Whereas Levith sees a precise topical allegory in the Messina–Don John nexus, I am inclined to see a commentary on the transient nature of imperial conquest and the more significant need for unity, internal order, and "marriage" if there is to be strength in European culture. Attitudes toward Don John may also vary in relation to attitudes toward the Habsburgs and the Holy Roman Empire; Richard Knolles's *The Generall Historie of the Turkes: From the First Beginning* ([London]: Adam Islip, printer, 1610) treats the empire generally favorably, especially in its fights with the Ottomans, and speaks of Don John as "a man then about 24 yeares old, in whom wanted no honourable parts, his mother blemish only excepted" (see sig. [Eeeeiiiᵛ]). Knolles's later accounts of Don John's role in Lepanto itself are wholly positive.

43. The action may be fictively set before Lepanto, but then it is difficult to imagine what the common war might be that would bring these allies together.

44. At the same time, Philip was not always successful. He lost the Spanish Armada to Elizabeth's forces in 1588, and thereafter his power remained less a danger on the horizon of Shakespeare's England, though it was still a danger. After Philip II's death, England's relations with Spain were less strained. For example, in 1604, James I and Spain's monarch, Philip III, made peace and thereafter were at various times said to be forging a dynastic marriage.

45. Iain Fenlon, "Lepanto and the Arts of Celebration," *History Today* 45 (September 1995): 24–30, and, by the same author, "Lepanto and the Arts of Celebration in Renaissance Venice," *Proceedings of the British Academy* 73 (1987): 201–35.

46. Marx, *The Battle of Lepanto: 1571*, 81–82.
47. The Turkish fleet was rebuilt in six months, however, and Lepanto did not stop the Turkish conquest of Cyprus.
48. "I know the special thing misliked in it, is, that I should seeme far contrary to my degree & Religion, like a mercenarie Poet, to pen a worke, *ex professo*, in praise of a forraine Papist bastard." James I, *His Maiesties Lepanto*, sig. A2^r. James goes on to explain his structure as a preface that does not praise Don John, an invocation to God and not to the saints, a historic comparison (i.e., Turks are to Catholics as Catholics are to Protestants), the song of the angels that again makes the application, and finally an explanation of the comparison. In the end, James again repeats that he does not intend to treat Don John as the cause of the Lepanto victory.
49. *His Maiesties Lepanto*, sig. B[1]^v.
50. See R. N. Watson, "*Othello* as Protestant propaganda," in *Religion and Culture in Renaissance England*, ed. C. McEachern and D. Shuger (Cambridge: Cambridge University Press, 1997), 234–57. I do not accept Watson's argument beyond his representation of Iago as practicing what Protestants would have seen as a Jesuitical casuistry.
51. For this complex history, see Miklos Molnar, *A Concise History of Hungary*, trans. Anna Magyar (Cambridge: Cambridge University Press, 2001), 87–138; see István Lázár, "In the Wan Light of the Crescent," *Hungary: A Brief History*, chapter 7 in the Historical Text Archive edition, ed. Donald Mabry, 1999–2003 (http://historicaltextarchive.com/books.php?op=view book&bookid=6). See Braudel, *Mediterranean World in the Age of Philip II*, 2:1188–1204.
52. Marcus argues that the King of Hungary in act 1, scene 2, line 2 is actually the Emperor Rudolph II, but the more likely reference is to the free area of Hungary, headed by István Bocskay, who in 1604 had liberated much of Transylvania from Turkish and Habsburg control and acted as the leader or "king" until such time as he was formally declared the prince or king of Hungary by the Diet in 1605. He was killed in mysterious circumstances in 1606.
53. See Knolles's *The Generall Historie of the Turke*, sig. [Ooooo^v]–sig. [Ooooviii^v].
54. Marcus suggests that these would be the Habsburg dukes who might "fall upon" Rudolph II, but that construction seems improbable. The Catholic princes of the empire in general are surely suggested by the phrase "the dukes." See Marcus, *Puzzling Shakespeare*, 187. In Marcus's interpretation, the duke with the other dukes would mean that Rudolph, as leader of the empire, would fall upon himself. It is not clear that England knew much about the Habsburg dukes' discontent with Rudolph in 1604, since that did not come fully to a head until 1606; and it is a touch odd to call him the

King of Hungary, particularly in view of the fact that Marcus argues that Vincentio is also in some measure Rudolph. The duke as Vincentio would in this view "come to composition" with himself as the King of Hungary. In my view the "King of Hungary's peace" that the First Gentleman prays against is the peace that István Bocskay might impose were he to continue to be successful.

55. See R. J. W. Evans, *Rudolph II and His World: A Study in Intellectual History* (Oxford: Clarendon Press, 1973), 80–82, for similarities between James and Rudolph. For an example of James's view of himself as a master of spying out mischief in the realm, see his November 9, 1605, speech to Parliament, given shortly after the Gunpowder Plot events, where James claims that although he had not ordinarily been given to suspicion, when he read an obscure letter concerning the plot he "did vpon the instant interpret and apprehend some darke phrases therein, contrary to the ordinary Grammar construction of them, (and in an other sort then I am sure any Diuine, or Lawyer in any Vniuersitie would have taken them) to be meant by this horrible forme of blowing vs vp by Powder; And thereupon ordered that search to be made, whereby the matter was discouered, and the man apprehended." King James VI and I, *Political Writings*, ed. Johann P. Sommerville (Cambridge: Cambridge University Press, 1994), 150.

56. See Darryl J. Gless, *"Measure for Measure," the Law, and the Convent* (Princeton NJ: Princeton University Press, 1979). The suggestion that the monarch can play the role of mediator and peacemaker in the Calvinistic-Catholic struggle would have pleased James, who regarded himself as Europe's great peacemaker; see W. B. Patterson, *King James VI and I and the Reunion of Christendom* (Cambridge: Cambridge University Press, 1997), especially index items under "James VI and I as peacemaker."

57. For a fuller discussion of these matters, see Paul A. Olson, *The Kingdom of Science: Literary Utopianism and British Education, 1612–1870* (Lincoln: University of Nebraska Press, 2002), 17–40.

58. Shakespeare may be playing with Francesco Sforza's (Francesco II) having been driven out of Milan in the 1530s by the French king; his reconciliation with the emperor; his being required to marry the emperor's niece, the daughter of the king of Denmark; and his being forced to pay the emperor nine hundred thousand ducats and to leave Milan to the emperor should he die without heir. Francesco died shortly after, and Milan fell into the emperor's hands. Later when Emperor Charles V divided his lands into German and Spanish territories, Milan became a Spanish dependency. Naples, as a Spanish Habsburg dependency, is substituted for the empire in *The Tempest*, but Milan's dependency in the play is similar to its historical dependency, and the significance of having a royal marriage like Ferdinand and Miranda's

and an heir to the throne is driven home by the Sforza/Milan case. For a contemporary account, see William Thomas, *The History of Italy (1549)*, ed. George B. Parks (Ithaca: Cornell University Press, 1963), 116–17.

59. See J. B. Black, *The Reign of Elizabeth: 1558–1603* (Oxford: Clarendon Press, 1959), 37–38.

60. See Olson, *Kingdom of Science*, 17–40.

61. From the Neapolitan side, we also have Claribel's marrying a man who must have been visualized as an Islamic prince at Tunis—ancient Carthage—in what would have been Ottoman territory from 1574 on, and without any of the sense of marrying Otherness that accompanies Othello's marriage to Desdemona. Finally, Caliban's mother comes from Argiers or Algiers, also Ottoman territory from the late sixteenth century on.

62. Levith (*Shakespeare's Italian Settings*, 82–86) makes some interesting suggestions as to where Shakespeare got his names for *The Tempest*. However, these have to do with sources and not with audience understanding, in my view.

63. For Spain, see Benjamin Keen, "The Legacy of Bartolomé de las Casas," *Ibero-Americana Pragensia* 11 (1977): 57–67, based on a talk given at the University of Nebraska, April 25, 1974; for England, see Netzloff, *England's Internal Colonies*, 192–97.

64. Otto J. Scott, *James I* (New York: Mason-Charter, 1976), 325.

65. Godfrey Davies, *The Early Stuarts: 1603–1660* (Oxford: Clarendon Press, 1959), 54–59.

66. *The Essays of Montaigne*, trans. John Florio (London: David Nutt, 1892), 1:222.

67. Though France was deeply involved in the Catholic-Protestant wars and the ultimate development of its own imperial project, I do not discuss Shakespeare's two French comedies, *Love's Labour's Lost* and *All's Well that Ends Well*, because they do different things from the other comedies. For some speculations about *Love's Labour's Lost* and history, see Frances Yates, *A Study of "Love's Labour's Lost"* (Cambridge: Cambridge University Press, 1936). *All's Well* is a puzzle as it is set in medieval Tuscany and literally reflects history having to do with the rivalry between Florence and Siena that would not have meant much to Shakespeare's audience.

68. See Felicia Hardison Londré, "Elizabethan Views of the 'Other': French, Spanish, and Russians in *Love's Labour's Lost*," in *"Loves Labour's Lost": Critical Essays*, ed. Felicia Hardison Londré (New York: Garland, 1997), 328–31. I obviously reject the author's Oxfordian perspective.

69. For a modern edition, see Servius, *In Vergilii Carmina Commentarii* (Lancaster PA: American Philological Society, 1946–), vols. 2–3. Many Renaissance editions of Virgil in Shakespeare's time contained the Servius commentary.

70. *The Works of Francis Bacon*, ed. J. Spedding, R. L. Ellis, D. D. Heath, 14 vols. (London: Longman, 1857–74), 6:457–59.

71. However, for some English people, especially for the Puritans and the "left" of British religious thought, Rome meant the papacy as the successor to the empire, the seven-headed beast, and the whore of Babylon. One should not assume a univocal understanding of Rome in Shakespeare's audience.

6. *Measure for Measure* as Form, Myth, and Scripture

1. Oscar James Campbell, *Shakespeare's Satire* (London: Oxford University Press, 1943), 121–41. I am indebted throughout this chapter to Darryl Gless for his critique of its argument.

2. The analysis by Barbara J. Baines, "Assaying the Power of Chastity in *Measure for Measure*," *Studies in English Literature, 1500–1900* 30 (1990): 283–301, in my view approximates that of Darryl F. Gless, *"Measure for Measure," the Law, and the Convent* (Princeton NJ: Princeton University Press, 1970).

3. J. Leeds Barroll, *Politics, Plague, and Shakespeare's Theater: The Stuart Years* (Ithaca: Cornell University Press, 1991), 119–29. Barroll's later date for the first royal performance of *Measure for Measure* (1605) enhances the likelihood that the Hungarian references apply to the Protestant king of Hungary and his revolt since 1605 would mean that Bocskay has claimed to be prince of Hungary for well over a year. For a different argument as to historical references bringing together London and Vienna, England and Empire, see Leah S. Marcus, *Puzzling Shakespeare: Local Reading and Its Discontents* (Berkeley: University of California Press, 1988), 160–202.

4. George E. Duckworth, *The Nature of Roman Comedy* (Princeton NJ: Princeton University Press, 1971), 261.

5. Barnaby and Wry claim Vincentio's entire "enterprise depends on strategies of manipulation that derive from theatrical practice: the use of the disguise, the staging of scenes for public viewing, the arts of story-telling. By this analogy, authority comes to look very much like a form of role playing." This is a precise definition of what the Shakespearean *poeta* does after the early plays. Andrew Barnaby and Joan Wry, "Authorized Versions: *Measure for Measure* and the Politics of Biblical Translation," *Renaissance Quarterly* 51 (1998): 1225–54.

6. Roy Battenhouse, *"Measure for Measure* and the Christian Doctrine of Atonement," *PMLA* 61 (1946): 1029–59. Darryl Gless, in *"Measure for Measure," the Law, and the Convent*, 214–55, correctly, I believe, interprets Vincentio as often acting as the representative of God, as a king was to do, and creating a kind of temporal simulacrum of final judgment in the last act of the play.

7. Godfrey Davies, *The Early Stuarts: 1603–1660* (Oxford: Clarendon Press, 1959), 32. James was infamous for the amount of time that he spent away from court and hunting, and he was quite competent as a sleuth, particularly of imposters in the area of witchcraft.

8. This analysis does not deal extensively with marriage law in the work. Suffice it to say that under Elizabethan law Claudio and Juliet would have a *de praesenti* marriage. Angelo and Mariana's contract is a *de futuro* contract conditioned on the dowry, if Angelo wishes to hold to the provision, and it becomes a kind of marriage-in-the-bed trick. For the complexities of marriage law, see Margaret Loftus Ranald, "'As Marriage Binds and Blood Breaks': English Marriage and Shakespeare," *Shakespeare Quarterly* 30 (1979): 77–79; B. J. Sokol and Mary Sokol, *Shakespeare, Law, and Marriage* (Cambridge: Cambridge University Press, 2003).

9. Geoffrey Whitney, *A Choice of Emblemes*, ed. Henry Green (New York: Benjamin Blom, 1967), 123.

10. See Paul A. Olson, "*The Parlement of Foules*: Aristotle's Politics and the Foundations of Human Society," *Studies in the Age of Chaucer*, 2 (1980): 59 and 53–69 passim. See also note 14 to this chapter.

11. Ernst Kantorowicz, *The King's Two Bodies: A Study in Mediaeval Political Theology* (Princeton NJ: Princeton University Press, 1957), 366–450, discusses the inalienability of crown prerogative and property even when the king is a minor. All decisions made for him must be reconfirmed when he comes of age. Vincentio at the beginning of the play tells Angelo, "In our remove be thou at full ourself" (1.1.43). This means that Angelo as Vincentio's deputy is actually acting for Vincentio in the fiction of the eternity of the crown; Vincentio is responsible for Angelo's crimes in this fiction. Vincentio can only separate his rule from the public body of Angelo's rulership in his name by recognizing his rule as performed by Angelo as a tyranny, a recognition that he is spared by Marianna's and Isabella's pleas in act 5. Most Elizabethan-Jacobean political theory denied the right of tyrannicide, though Shakespeare is ambiguous on the point; in any case, Vincentio would rightly have to execute himself were he to execute Angelo for his crimes. For Richard II on these matters, see Kantorowicz, *King's Two Bodies*, 24–41.

12. See Howard C. Cole, "The 'Christian' Context of *Measure for Measure*," *Journal of English and Germanic Philology* 64 (1965): 447.

13. Peter Lake, "Ministers, Magistrates, and the Production of 'Order' in *Measure for Measure*," *Shakespeare Survey* 54 (2001): 179 and 165–82 passim; Anthony Gash, in "Shakespeare, Carnival, and the Sacred, *The Winter's Tale* and *Measure for Measure*," in *Shakespeare and Carnival, After Bakhtin*, ed. Ronald Knowles (New York: Macmillan, 1998), 200. See also Gash's characterization of Malvolio, in chapter 4.

14. For a good discussion of natural law conceptions of equity, such as those in Aquinas or Fortescue that are imbedded in Christopher St. Germane's 1523–30 *Doctor and Student*, see R. S. White, *Natural Law in English Renaissance Literature* (Cambridge: Cambridge University Press, 1996), 50–53. For

the medieval tradition of natural law teaching, see Olson, "*The Parlement of Foules*: Aristotle's Politics," 53–69. Consider also Christopher St. Germane's understanding of natural law as that law by which reason orders us to felicity in this life (i.e., pursuing the good, shunning evil, following the golden rule, living peacefully, doing justice, punishing trespassers, loving benefactors, resisting force with force, and so on). See Christopher St. Germane, *A Dialog in Englysshe, betwyxt a Doctoure of Dyunyte and Student in the Lawes of Englonde* (n.p.: R. Wyer, printer, 1531), fol. iiii ff. Richard Hooker also gives excellent explanations of natural law in his *Of the Laws of Ecclesiastical Polity*, in *Hooker's Works*, ed. John Keble (Oxford: Clarendon Press, 1888).

15. Later in the scene (*MFM* 2.2.133–45), Isabella, in a set of profoundly ironic speeches, does appeal to conceptions of equity that ask Angelo to consider his inner self and its semblance to Claudio's as he has revealed it in outer action.

16. Matthew Winston, "'Craft against Vice': Morality Play Elements in *Measure for Measure*," *Shakespeare Studies* 14 (1981): 241–43.

17. Ronald R. MacDonald calls attention to the fact that the characters in *Measure for Measure* "ceaselessly attempt to allegorize themselves and those with whom they have to deal." That this is the case should not preclude the characters' seeking "pattern in themselves to know"—that is, the effort to realize in themselves the paradigm to which they are committed by role, vocation, or ethical demand. It would not preclude an Early Modern audience's seeking to see when the characters have or have not done this. Ronald R. MacDonald, "Measure for Measure: The Flesh Made Word," *Studies in English Literature, 1500–1900* 30 (1990): 275. Gash calls attention to the fact that the Puritans proposed to make adultery a capital crime and, as magistrates, administered extreme punishment to fornicators after the 1570s. See Gash, "Shakespeare, Carnival and the Sacred," 201.

18. For an account of the evolution of the image of justice and of the meanings attached to the sword and scales, see Dennis E. Curtis, "Images of Justice," *Yale Law Journal* 96 (1986–87): 1727–72.

19. Winston, "'Craft against Vice': Morality Play Elements in *Measure for Measure*," 243, compares Vincentio's craftiness with the techniques of the Vice in the morality plays, making him a kind of Counter-Vice.

20. Gash, "Shakespeare, Carnival, and the Sacred," 204, argues that Pompey is a lord of misrule who makes fun of the body politic. My point is similar.

21. Though Sextus Pompeius appears as an Epicurean in the Renaissance sense in *Antony and Cleopatra* and was commonly compared with Pompey the Great, the Pompey in *Measure for Measure* appears much more to be cast in the semblance of Sextus's greater relative. The *Measure for Measure* pimp is called "Pompey the Great"—that is, Pompey of the Great Bum (Act 2.1).

While Sextus Pompeius receives accolades as another Pompey the Great in *Antony and Cleopatra* 1.3.49–54 and sponsors the Bacchanalian party that separates out the values of Antony from those of Octavius, he is never labeled anything like Pompey the Great, as *Measure for Measure*'s pimp is.

22. For Pompey the Great as a great lover in the eyes of Flora, a prostitute, see Plutarch's account in *The Lives of the Noble Grecians and Romanes*, trans. Thomas North (London: Richard Field, printer, 1595), sig. [Llli^v]. Plutarch says: "It is reported also, that when Flora the curtisan waxed old, she much delighted to talke of the familiaritie which she had with Pompey being a young man," and he then continues to describe the delights of Pompey's relationship with Flora, as experienced by Flora.

23. Sandys explains the tale as follows:

> Pygmalion . . . fell in loue with his owne workmanship. . . . But taken historically, this statue may be some Virgin on whom Pygmalion was enamoured, who long as obdurat as the matter whereof she was made, was mollified at length by his obsequiousnesse: the Ivory expressing the beauty of her body, and her blushes the modesty of her mind.

> His lips to hers he ioynes, which seeme to melt.
> The blushing Virgin now his kisses felt:
> And fearefully erecting her faire eyes,
> Together with the light her lover spies.

> Blushing is a resort of the blood to the face; which, in the passion of shame, labours most in that part, and is seene in the brest as it ascendeth: but most apparent in those that are young; in regard of their greater heat, and tender complexions. Which proceeds not from an infirmity of the mind, but the nouelty of the thing; nor can bee either put on or restrained. The ensigne of natiue Modesty, & the colour of virtue. A beautifull and modest wife is therefore here said to be giuen him by the Goddesse, in reward of his deuotion, as the greatest temporall happinesse.

> See George Sandys, trans., *Ovid's Metamorphosis: Englished, Mythologized, and Represented in Figures*, ed. Karl K. Hulley and Stanley T. Vandersall (Lincoln: University of Nebraska Press, 1970), 484–85.

24. That *Measure for Measure* was apparently first performed on St. Stephen's Day, the day after Christmas and a day on which the matins and evensong texts celebrate the strengths of good rule, and the need for liberation from ignorant and oppressive rule, may be relevant to the meaning of the play, especially in view of its interest in asceticism, martyrdom, and rule. C. Margaret Hotine, "Two Plays for St. Stephens Day," *Notes and Queries* 227 (1982): 119–21.

See also John Wasson, "*Measure for Measure*: A Text for Court Performance,"
Shakespeare Quarterly 21 (1970): 17–24. Earlier work by Josephine Waters
Bennett and Ernest Schanzer is also relevant to this argument. For a useful
cautionary answer see Richard Levin, "The King James Version of Measure
for Measure," *Clio* 3 (1974): 129–63. Though the play may have had a rather
explicit application to James in 1605, it obviously was later to be played
outside the court and there works at the definition of the constitutional place
of the monarch—any monarch. For the view that, played in public theater
contexts, the play "represents a sovereign's attempt to reinforce his power
but enacts a loss of authority," see William Dodd, "Power and Performance:
Measure for Measure in the Public Theater of 1604–05," *Shakespeare Studies*
24 (1996): 211–40.

25. Most of the scriptural quotations in *Measure for Measure* are assigned to
Isabella or Vincentio; see Naseeb Shaheen, *Biblical References in Shakespeare's
Comedies* (Newark: University of Delaware Press, 1993), 185–202.

26. Andrew Barnaby and Joan Wry, "Authorized Versions: *Measure for Measure*
and the Politics of Biblical Translation," 1244, observe that the phrasing
suggests the essential equitableness of the proceedings, and the logic and
impersonality of the judge as if he were but serving a higher law, but that this
rhetorical appearance is deceptive. The passage quoted from the Geneva Bible
is from the 1560 edition, and it includes only the relevant Geneva glosses.

27. Luther's sermons on Matthew 5–7 are found in Dr. Martin Luther's "Das
V. VI. und VII. Capitel G. Matthei," *Sämmtliche Werke*, ed. J. K. Irmscher
(Erlangen: C. Hayden, 1826–57), 43: 260–77. For a translation, see Martin
Luther, *The Sermon on the Mount and the Magnificat* in *Luther's Works*, ed.
Jaroslav Pelikan, 54 vols. (Saint Louis: Concordia , 1956–86), 21:210–11
and 3–294. Tyndale argues that Matthew 7 does not apply to temporal judgment and applies the measure-for-measure passage to Catholic legalism in
following ceremonial laws without attending to the deeper intention of the
gospels. See William Tyndale, *Expositions and Notes on Sundry Portions of
the Holy Scriptures*, ed. Henry Walter (Cambridge: Cambridge University
Press, 1849), 112–14. For a detailed analysis of the Sermon on the Mount
and *Measure for Measure*, see Gless, "*Measure for Measure*," the Law, and the
Convent, 15–60 and passim; also Stacy Magedanz, "Public Justice and Private
Mercy in *Measure for Measure*," *Studies in English Literature 1500–1900* 44
(2004): 317–32. Magedanz developed this argument years ago as a student in
one of my classes, and her work has influenced mine a great deal. Magedanz's
emphasis on the importance of equity to the logic of Vincentio's judgments
in act 5 goes with my sense that most of the judgments reflect the canon
law courts' search for contrition, not the civil courts' more punitive regimen.
For the medieval roots of the mainstream Renaissance understanding of the

beginning verses of Matthew 7, see Paul A. Olson, "The Reeve's Tale: Chaucer's Measure for Measure," *Studies in Philology* 50 (1962): 1–17. Aquinas's *Catena Aurea* quotations on Matthew 7:1–5 support judging as related to the role of bishop or ruler but forbid malicious private judgment.

28. For Anabaptist interpretations of the obligations of the magistrate and Christian duty not to judge, see http://www.goshen.edu/mqr/pastissues/july02roth .html. The Schleitheim Confession, section 6, created by the Swiss Brethren, forbade the magistracy to Anabaptists. Article 36 of the Church of England's Forty-Two Articles of 1553 is an orthodox effort to combat Anabaptist antistatist sentiments. English Anabaptism and its successors continued to deny the magistracy to Christians and argued that Christians could not judge other Christians; see George H. Williams, *The Radical Reformation* (Philadelphia: Westminster Press, 1962), 778–90. For a seventeenth-century Hutterite sermon that sets forth standard doctrine concerning "Judge not" as forbidding the magistracy to Christians, see www.anabaptistchurch.org/sermon1.htm. See also Michael Sattler's testimony in 1527 that the Word of God does not allow Count Joachim of Zollern to judge (see www.anabaptistnetwork.com/ book/view/161). For a contrasting view on the religious left in the period, namely that the use of the sword is legitimate, see Balthasar Hubmaier, "On the Sword (June, 1527) in Anabaptist Beginnings (1523–1533): A Source Book," in *Bibliotheca Humanistica & Reformatorica*, ed. William R. Estep Jr. (Nieuwkoop: B. de Graaf, 1976), 16:107–26. See www.bibleviews.com/ Nonresistance-Horsch.html.

29. Gless, *"Measure for Measure," the Law, and the Convent*, 252–53.

30. Gash, "Shakespeare, Carnival, and the Sacred," 205, says that Vincentio is neither adequately Providence nor James because he is subject to the test of laughter. However, laughter is a proper test only if the laughter is not scorn directed against the dignity of the state but directed against the monarch's private body; hence only Lucio is punished for his slander of the monarch. Gash, "Shakespeare, Carnival, and the Sacred," 204.

31. For sources, see http://www.bibleviews.com/Nonresistance-Horsch.html.

32. For examples see note 27 to this chapter.

33. Winston makes Lucio a morality-play vice character; while he may have some of the characteristics of the Vice, he is punished for "slandring a prince"; see Winston, "'Craft against Vice': Morality Play Elements in *Measure for Measure*," 229–44.

34. Clifford Leech puzzled at the severity of Lucio's punishment, but the duke punishes Lucio not for wronging Kate Keepdown or for his gossip about little faults, which he attributes to the duke; Lucio's accusations against the duke of violating the laws against prostitution and drunkenness, his assertion of the duke's ignorance and lack of deliberation, strike at Vincentio's very

capacity to rule (see *MFM* 3.1.336–900); further, his frequent interruptions of the court scene show a lack of respect for the process of court itself. Together these two actions by Lucio strike at the heart of Vincentio's action as a ruler and are a form of public treason (*lèse-majesté*), destroying the dignity of the monarch as the head of the corporate state. The modern equivalent crime is contempt of court. The standard punishment for *lèse-majesté* was hanging, drawing, and quartering, a punishment similar to that imposed on Lucio before he receives leniency. See Clifford Leech, "The 'Meaning' of *Measure for Measure*," in *Shakespeare: The Comedies: A Collection of Critical Essays*, ed. Kenneth Muir, Twentieth Century Views (Englewood Cliffs NJ: Prentice Hall, 1965), 114. See Barnaby and Wry, "Authorized Versions: Measure for Measure and the Politics of Biblical Translation," 1246, for a parallel assertion that Lucio is punished for treason, though the term *lèse-majesté* is not invoked.

35. For an analysis of the peculiar character of Vincentio's judgment, see Patricia Howe, "'Mortality and Mercy in Vienna': Moral Relativism in Shakespeare's *Measure for Measure* and Schnizler's *Das weite Land*," in *Patterns of Change: German Drama and the European Tradition*, ed. Dorothy James and Silvia Ranawake (New York: Peter Lang, 1990), 215–27.

36. One suspects that even English audiences with their somewhat Erastian religious system would have wondered at the efficacy of Vincentio's religious actions when he is in the disguise of a friar. The most ardent of the period's theologians supporting the royal prerogative, Richard Hooker, in his *Of the Laws of Ecclesiastical Polity* (3:431ff.), says his opponents have argued that he says a king may sit with bishops in consistory, decide matters of faith, excommunicate, and act as a full ecclesiastical judge. However, Hooker says the king, as the head of the church, has no such particular office but has general authority to see that consistory, church courts, debates about faith and morals, and so forth are carried out according to due process and in conformity to ecclesiastical tradition.

37. Julia Brett argues that "Renaissance political language was spiritual language" and that the central political issue in 1603–4 did not involve whether the papacy would dominate James but whether James would dominate the English church and rule with a proper sense of the conflation of divine and human authority in his role. Julia Brett, "'Grace Is Grace, Despite of all the Controversy': *Measure for Measure*, Christian Allegory, and the Sacerdotal Duke," *Ben Jonson Journal* 6 (1999): 201–2.

38. For the character of the contrition produced by Vincentio and its varieties, see Douglas L. Peterson, "'Measure for Measure' and the Anglican Doctrine of Contrition," *Notes and Queries* 119 (1964): 135–37; Eric D. Turley, "'Cucullus Non Facit Monachum': Friar Penance and Contritionist Theology

from Chaucer to Shakespeare," master's thesis, University of Nebraska, 2003, passim.

39. For a sensible discussion of the issues in the allegorical/antiallegorical controversy with respect to *Measure for Measure*, see Brett, "Grace Is Grace," 189–207. Brett sees Vincentio as "transformed and recreated at the end of the play," as "standing for the ideal Christian ruler and the successful marriage of religion and politics." One might better say that Vincentio is moving toward knowing such a pattern in himself by the end of the play. Brett, "Grace Is Grace," 205.

40. For a general argument that the play enacts the parable of the unmerciful servant, see Arthur C. Kirsch, "The Integrity of *Measure for Measure*," *Shakespeare Survey* 28 (1975): 89–105. Originally the idea that *Measure for Measure* should be read as a parable was developed by G. Wilson Knight, "*Measure for Measure* and the Gospels," in *The Wheel of Fire*, 4th ed. (London: Methuen, 1949), 73–96. For a graceful summary of the soteriological, allegorical versions with which this chapter disagrees, see Steven Marx, *Shakespeare and the Bible* (Oxford: Oxford University Press, 2000), 79–103.

41. See *A Record of Auncient Histories, intituled in Latin Gesta Romanorum* (London: Tomas Este, printer, 1602), sig. Hii^v–[Hviii^r].

42. See Gash, "Shakespeare, Carnival, and the Sacred," 206, for the argument that Vincentio is the God/fool in this scene and that the center of the sacred in the scene comes when Isabella kneels and asks forgiveness for Angelo. This invasion of the sacred into the logic of secular justice demonstrates why the marriage of the sacred and the temporal administration is requisite.

43. Martin Ingram, *Church Courts, Sex, and Marriage in England, 1570–1640* (Cambridge: Cambridge University Press, 1987), 3, 17.

44. Ingram, *Church Courts, Sex, and Marriage*, 3. Since sin and not crime were in question, penance, confession, and participation in Anglican worship were the central acts that the church courts required in Shakespeare's time when allowing accused recusants to be reconciled to the Anglican Church. The sincerity of the penance might be monitored for some time; see Michael C. Questier, *Conversion, Politics and Religion in England, 1580–1625* (Cambridge: Cambridge University Press, 1996), 98–105. See also Paul A. Olson, *The Canterbury Tales and the Good Society* (Princeton NJ: Princeton University Press, 1986), 183–213.

45. Olson, "*The Parlement of Foules*: Aristotle's Politics," 53–69.

46. Ingram, *Church Courts, Sex, and Marriage*, 4–17.

47. See Keith Thomas, "The Puritans and Adultery: The Act of 1650 Reconsidered," in *Puritans and Revolutionaries: Essays in Seventeenth-Century History Presented to Christopher Hill*, ed. Donald Pennington and Keith Thomas (Oxford: Clarendon Press, 1978), 257–82.

48. For a brilliant discussion, see Ingram, *Church Courts, Sex, and Marriage*, 219–37.

49. For Puritan efforts to impose draconian measures punishing sexual sin, see Thomas, "The Puritans and Adultery," 257–82. Ingram, *Church Courts, Sex, and Marriage*, 3, argues that the period did not have a very secure sense of the distinction between crimes and sins. Harriet Hawkins argues that Shakespeare takes a relativistic and permissive view of sexual conduct in *Measure for Measure*; in this she appears to me to confuse the granting of mercy with ambiguity about evil and to suggest that people in the audience who have lapsed will condone lapses in the play's characters. I am not sure that this is true; those who have lapsed, especially the reformed lapsed, are often the most censorious about others: Harriet Hawkins, "The Devil's Party: Virtues and Vices in *Measure for Measure*," *Shakespeare Survey* 31 (1978): 105–13.

50. Leah Marcus, in *Puzzling Shakespeare*, 165, argues that Angelo's justice is like that which the civil courts were beginning to impose in England based on a statute of 18 Elizabeth, but that statute was to determine bastardy, a civil law situation having to do with property rights. The canon law courts were to determine issues of fornication and adultery. Marcus also argues that Escalus and Angelo act as civil law interrogators and that Vincentio, in his role as a friar, acts as the canon law interrogators did—secretly and generally more moderately—though the new canons of 1604 did make the issue of whether clandestine marriage between parties who promised themselves to each other, and had sexual relations thereafter, was a marriage. In fact, Vincentio acts as Justice Personified and, though in the disguise of a friar as he looks around Vienna, remains a lord temporal and tries the culprits in act 5 as the chief civil and canon law official of the realm. A royal tribunal from the late sixteenth century onward heard appeals from the principal canon law courts, and in act 5 Vincentio seems to personify that tribunal's sort of power. See Ingram, *Church Courts, Sex, and Marriage*, 37. Though James I never acted as the canon law court official of final appeal, he did, as monarch and head of the church, endeavor to uphold the authority of the canon law courts. A play obviously requires a simplification of the tedium of court processes. The mercy that Vincentio shows in act 5 somewhat characterizes what was traditional to canon law courts when the accused was penitent. Vincentio "returns" to Vienna to impose the rule of mercy in matters subject to controversy between the civil and canon law courts (but considered matters for the latter courts by tradition): adultery, fornication, oath breaking, and the like. That he must do so to preserve justice suggests the dangers of Angelo-style totalization of religious power in the state. This totalization existed in Calvin's Geneva. The play may also critique the concentration of power in an apparent pluralistic system, as in the Vienna of Shakespeare's time, for

Vienna's system left ultimate canon law punishments in the hands of the state under its Inquisition. See Marcus, *Puzzling Shakespeare*, 165–84.

51. Gash cites Louis Dumont's argument that Calvinism's attempt to unify civil government and religion created the conditions for a new individual in whom there appeared a decline of acceptance of alterity and provisionality and who thinks of himself as "an instrument of God's will in purifying." Gash, "Shakespeare, Carnival, and the Sacred," 201.

52. Gless, in *"Measure for Measure," the Law, and the Convent*, 61–141, argues that Isabella's portrait reflects a great deal of the antifraternal satire of the later Middle Ages and the Renaissance—the accusations of righteousness based on good works rather than grace, the substitution of the rule of the order for the call to divine charity, the replacement of love with self-righteousness and pride.

53. R. S. White, in *Natural Law in English Renaissance Literature*, 171–74, cites natural law arguments from the period for a permissive attitude toward sexual matters by the civil courts. These arguments were largely made after Shakespeare's time, but by acting as both prince and leader of the church courts overseeing penance, Vincentio is able to provide for leniency and the self's confrontation with responsibility.

And in Conclusion

1. For an explanation of how comic plots do this, see R. S. Crane, "The Concept of Plot and the Plot of *Tom Jones*," in *Critics and Criticism, Ancient and Modern*, ed. R. S. Crane (Chicago: University of Chicago Press, 1952), 616–47.

Resources for Placing the Comedies
in an Early Modern Frame

Aristotle. *On the Art of Poetry* [Aristotle's *Poetics*]. Translated by S. H. Butcher and Milton Nahm. New York: Liberal Arts Press, 1948.

Bacon, Sir Francis. *De Sapientia Veterum, 1609 and the Wisdom of the Ancients.* Translated by Arthur Gorges. London: 1619; facsimile, New York: Garland, 1976.

Berchorius, Petrus [Pierre Bersuire]. *De Formis Figurisque Deorum: Ovidius Moralizatus.* Lyon: n.p., 1509. [Bersuire's commentary on Ovid has been republished in a facsimile edition by Garland.]

Black, J. B. *The Reign of Elizabeth: 1558–1603.* Oxford: Clarendon Press, 1959.

Boccaccio, Giovanni. *Boccaccio on Poetry: Being the Preface and Fourteenth and Fifteenth Books of Boccaccio's* Genealogia deorum gentilium libri. Edited by Charles G. Osgood. Princeton NJ: Princeton University Press, 1930; rpt. New York: Liberal Arts Press, 1956.

Braudel, Fernand. *The Mediterranean and the Mediterranean World in the Age of Philip II.* Translated by Sian Reynolds. 2 vols. London: Harper Collins, 1972.

Brumble, H. David. *Classical Myths and Legends in the Middle Ages and Renaissance: A Dictionary of Allegorical Meanings.* Westport CT: Greenwood, 1998.

Cartari, Vincenzo. *Le imagini degli Dei degli antichi.* New York: Garland, 1979.

Clubb, Louise George. *Italian Drama in Shakespeare's Time.* New Haven: Yale University Press, 1989.

Colet, John. *Two Treatises On The Hierarchies Of Dionysus,* in *A Treatise on the Sacraments of the Church,* with an introduction by J. H. Lupton. Farnborough, UK: Gregg Press, 1968.

Conti, Natalis. *Mythologiae: Sive explicationis fabularum libri decem.* Geneva: Gabriel Carteri, printer, 1596.

Daley, Peter M., ed. *The English Emblem and the Continental Tradition.* New York: AMS, 1988.

Davies, Godfrey. *The Early Stuarts: 1603–1660.* Oxford: Clarendon Press, 1959.

de Montenay, Georgette. *Emblemes, ou, Deuises chrestiennes.* Lyon: Jean Marcorelle, 1571.

Duchartre, Pierre Louis. *The Italian Comedy.* Translated by Randolph T. Weaver. New York: Dover, 1966.

Durandus, William. *Rationale Divinorum Officiorum.* Lyons: Sacon, 1510; Antwerp: Belleri, 1614.

Erasmus. *Enchiridion Militis Christiani.* Edited by Anne M. O'Donnell. Oxford: Oxford University Press, 1981.

Fehl, Philipp. *Decorum and Wit: The Poetry of Venetian Painting.* Vienna: IRSA, 1992.

———. "The Rocks in the Parthenon Frieze." *Journal of the Warburg and Courtauld Institutes* 24 (1961): 1–44.

Fraunce, Abraham. *The Countesse of Pembrokes Yvychurch.* London: Thomas Orwyn, printer, 1591.

Giraldi, Lilio Gregorio. *De deis gentilium libri: Sive syntagmata XVII.* Lyon: Jacobi Junctae, printer OKPAO, 1565.

Golding, Arthur. *Shakespeare's Ovid: Being Arthur Golding's Translation of the Metamorphoses,* edited by W. H. D. Rouse. London: Centaur Press, 1961.

Harington, Sir John, trans. *Orlando Furioso in English Heroical Verse.* London: Richard Field, 1591.

Herford, C. H., Percy Simpson, and E. M. Simpson, eds. *Ben Jonson.* 11 vols. Oxford: Clarendon Press, 1925–52.

Herrick, Marvin T., ed. *Comic Theory in the Sixteenth Century.* Urbana: University of Illinois Press, 1964.

Heywood, Thomas. *An Apology for Actors* [1612]. Introduction and annotation by Richard Perkinson. New York: Scholars' Facsimiles, 1941.

Hilger, Michael J. "The Rhetoric of Comedy: Comic Theory in the Terential Commentary of Aelius Donatus." PhD diss., University of Nebraska, 1970.

Holland, Abraham. *Naumachia, or Hollands Sea-Fight.* London: T[homas] P[urfoot], printer, 1622.

James I of England, *His Maiesties Lepanto or Heroicall Song.* London: Stafford and Hooke, printers, 1603.

———. *The King's Maiesties Declaration to His Subjects, Concerning Lawful Sports to Be Used.* London: Robert Barker, printer, 1633.

Knolles, Richard. *The Generall Historie of the Turkes: From the First Beginning.* London: Adam Islip, printer, 1610.

Lamberton, Robert. *Homer as Theologian: Neoplatonist Allegorical Reading and the Growth of Epic Tradition.* Berkeley: University of California Press, 1990.

Lea, K. M. *Italian Popular Comedy.* 2 vols. Oxford: Clarendon Press, 1934.

Levy, F. J. *Tudor Historical Thought.* San Marino CA: Huntington Library, 1967.

Lodge, Thomas. *A Reply to Stephen Gosson's Schoole of Abuse in Defence of Poetry Musick and Stage Plays in The Complete Works of Thomas Lodge.* Edited by Edmund Gosse. New York: Russell and Russell, 1963.

Mâle, Emile. *The Gothic Image: Religious Art in France of the Thirteenth Century.* Translated by Dora Nussey. New York: Harper, 1958.

Marshall, Tristan. *Theatre and Empire: Great Britain on the London Stages under James VI and I.* Manchester: Manchester University Press, 2000.

Moryson, Fynes. *An Itinerary.* 4 vols. Glasgow: James Maclehose, 1907.

Nichols, John. *The Progresses and Public Processions of Queen Elizabeth. Among which are Interspersed Other Solemnities, Public Expenditures, and Remarkable Events.* 3 vols. London: J. Nichols, 1823.

———. *The Progresses, Processions, and Magnificent Festivities, of King James the First, His Royal Consort, Family, and Court.* 4 vols. London: J. Nichols, 1828.

Olson, Paul A. *The Journey to Wisdom: Self-Education in Patristic and Medieval Literature.* Lincoln: University of Nebraska Press, 1995.

Oreglia, Giacomo. *The Commedia dell'Arte.* New York: Hill and Wang, 1968.

Panofsky, Erwin. *Meaning in the Visual Arts.* Chicago: University of Chicago Press, 1983.

———. *Studies in Iconology: Humanistic Themes in the Art of the Renaissance.* New York: Harper and Row, 1962.

Patterson, Annabel. *Reading Holinshed's Chronicles.* Chicago: University of Chicago Press, 1994.

———. "Rethinking Tudor Historiography." *South Atlantic Quarterly* 92 (1993): 185–208.

Quarles, Francis. *Emblems* [1635]. Introduction by A. D. Cousins. Delmar NY: Scholars' Facsimile & Reprints, 1991.

Redwine, James D., Jr., ed. *Ben Jonson's Literary Criticism.* Lincoln: University of Nebraska Press, 1970.

Reeves, Marjorie. *Elizabethan Explorers: Illustrated from Contemporary Sources.* Harlow, UK: Longman, 1990.

Robertellus, Franciscus. "On Comedy." In *Comic Theory in the Sixteenth Century,* translated and edited by Marvin T. Herrick. Urbana: University of Illinois Press, 1964.

Ross, Alexander. *Mystagogus Poeticus, or The Muses Interpreter.* New York: Garland, 1976.

Salingar, Leo. *Shakespeare and the Tradition of Comedy.* Cambridge: Cambridge University Press, 1974.

Sandys, George, trans. *Ovid's Metamorphosis: Englished, Mythologized, and Represented in Figures.* Edited by Karl K. Hulley and Stanley T. Vandersall. Lincoln: University of Nebraska Press, 1970.

Seznec, Jean. *The Survival of the Pagan Gods.* Translated by B. F. Sessions. New York: HarperTorch Bollingen, 1961.

Soens, Lewis, ed. *Sir Philip Sidney's Defense of Poesy*. Lincoln: University of Nebraska Press, 1970.

Speght, Thomas, ed. *The Works of our Antient and Lerned English Poet*. Introduction by Sir Francis Beaumont. London, 1598.

Spenser, Edmund. *The Faerie Queene*. Edited by Thomas P. Roche. New Haven CT: Yale University Press, 1987.

St. Augustine. *On Christian Doctrine*. Translated and introduced by D. W. Robertson. New York: Liberal Arts Press, 1958.

Thomas, William. *The History of Italy* [1549]. Edited by George B. Parks. Ithaca: Cornell University Press, 1963.

Thynne, Francis. *Animaduersions vppon the annotacions and corrections of some imperfections of impressiones of Chaucers works*. London: EETS, 1865.

Veltz, John W. "Shakespeare's Ovid in the Twentieth Century: A Critical Survey." In *Shakespeare's Ovid*, edited by A. B. Taylor. 181–97. Cambridge: Cambridge University Press, 2000.

Watt, Robert. *Bibliotheca Britannica*. Edinburgh: A. Constable and Company, printer, 1824.

Whitaker, William. *Disputatio de Sacra Scriptura*. Cambridge: T. Thomas, printer, 1588.

Whitney, Geoffrey. *A Choice of Emblemes* [1586]. Edited by Henry Green. New York: Benjamin Blom, 1967.

Willet, Andrew. *Sacrorum Emblematum Centuria Una*. Cambridge: John Legate, printer, 1592.

Index

www.ingramcontent.com/pod-product-compliance
Lightning Source LLC
Chambersburg PA
CBHW030422100426
42812CB00028B/3058/J